THE CRAFT OF THE ESSAY

EDITED BY

Halsey P. Taylor
California State Polytechnic University, Pomona

Victor N. Okada
California State Polytechnic University, Pomona

HARCOURT BRACE JOVANOVICH, INC.
New York   Chicago   San Francisco   Atlanta

Cover photograph: © 1976 Geoffrey Gove

© 1977 by Harcourt Brace Jovanovich, Inc.

All rights reserved. No part of this publication may be reproduced or transmitted in any form or by any means, electronic or mechanical, including photocopy, recording, or any information storage and retrieval system, without permission in writing from the publisher.

ISBN: 0-15-515624-1
Library of Congress Catalog Card Number: 76-45937

Printed in the United States of America

Preface

In selecting essay anthologies for our own writing courses over the years, we have kept in mind the two-fold goal of most composition courses: to teach students to write skillfully and to read critically. And we have found that to accomplish this objective an anthology should have these three features: (1) carefully chosen selections that can serve as models for student writing and that will nurture thoughtful reading, (2) an "apparatus" that will stimulate student analysis of the selections, and (3) an organization that matches the stages through which students' writing develops. These characteristics, we believe, will be found in our text.

Some selections in this volume will be familiar to teachers of composition; other, less familiar, pieces will complement these standard works. All the selections are reprinted in their entirety or are excerpts capable of standing alone, all are well written, and all will interest students, challenge them to develop critical reading skills, and inspire them to improve their writing in specific ways. We have chosen twentieth-century authors because we believe that students should model their own writing after that of good modern writers. Ethnic minority and women writers are well represented, and, in addition, we have included some humorous pieces.

The apparatus has many distinctive features as well as some more familiar ones. We include questions on meaning, questions on style and structure, and suggestions for writing, some of which ask students to reflect on parallels between their experiences and those of the writers represented. Preceding each work is a Getting Started section that encourages students to start thinking about the selection to follow, often by raising questions that they can keep in mind while reading the essay. This section also includes unusual or unfamiliar words from the essay, with clues that will help to reveal their meanings. Following each selection, these same words are further explored in a section that encourages students to use and become familiar with their dictionaries, to explore the connotations and denotations of words, and to become aware of how contexts shape the meanings of words. In addition to the apparatus, at the very beginning of the anthology there is a brief introduction to paragraph and sentence structure designed to help students understand the later questions on style and structure and to provide a succinct account of some of the basic principles of effective expository prose.

The organization of the text is clear, simple, and logical. The works are grouped in three divisions: Essays Chiefly Personal, Essays Chiefly Informative, and Essays Chiefly Persuasive. These three divisions form a progression that correlates with the kinds of writing assignments and instruction that are provided in most composition courses today. Within each part, the essays advance from short and relatively simple pieces to longer and more complex ones. An alternative table of contents is provided for instructors who desire a classification of the essays under rhetorical headings.

We wish to acknowledge with gratitude the help given us by Lee Shenkman and Abigail Winograd of Harcourt Brace Jovanovich. Above all, we express our appreciation to our students through the years who, by their growth as writers, have helped us crystallize our own thinking about how anthologies can be used to help students master the craft of the essay and have thus indirectly contributed to the shaping of this book.

HALSEY P. TAYLOR
VICTOR N. OKADA

Contents

Preface iii
Rhetorical Table of Contents vii
An Introduction to Paragraph and Sentence Structure 1

ESSAYS CHIEFLY PERSONAL

Helen Keller	From *The Story of My Life*	13
Shirley Dolph	The Eye of a Deer	17
Charles A. Goodrum	The Dog Census	20
Jeanne Wakatsuki Houston and James D. Houston	Shikata Ga Nai	29
Carol Gross	Death Is a Personal Matter	37
Alan B. Rothenberg	Peaceful Coexistence with Rattlesnakes	41
E. M. Forster	My Wood	50
Laurie Lee	First Light	55
George Orwell	The Spike	66
Phyllis McGinley	The Consolations of Illiteracy	75
Charlton Ogburn, Jr.	Trials of a Word-watcher	82
Thomas Sancton	The Silver Horn	91
Lillian Smith	When I Was a Child	102
Richard Rodriguez	Going Home Again: The New American Scholarship Boy	116

ESSAYS CHIEFLY INFORMATIVE

James Lipton	An Exaltation of Larks	133
Alexander Petrunkevitch	The Spider and the Wasp	141
Raymond C. Murray	The Geologist as Private Eye	148
Donald Winks	How to Read an Organization Chart for Fun and Survival	155

Leo Rosten	The Torments of Translation	163
Brian McGinty	The Trouble Began in San Francisco	169
Howard E. Evans	The Intellectual and Emotional World of the Cockroach	179
Jørgen Meldgaard	The Lost Vikings of Greenland	189
William A. Douglass	Lonely Lives under the Big Sky	198
John Hersey	A Noiseless Flash	208
Rachel Carson	The Sunless Sea	221
Frederick Lewis Allen	The Automobile Revolution	236

ESSAYS CHIEFLY PERSUASIVE

Joseph Wood Krutch	The Sloburbs	249
Alice Walker	The Civil Rights Movement: What Good Was It?	256
Marchette Chute	Getting at the Truth	265
Louis J. Halle	The Language of Statesmen	272
Jessica Mitford	From *The American Way of Death*	279
Edwin R. Clapp	Why the Devil Don't You Teach Freshmen to Write?	286
John F. Kennedy	Daniel Webster	296
Martin Luther King, Jr.	Letter from Birmingham Jail	310
Henry Steele Commager	Why History	326
Ruth Mulvey Harmer	Doctors, Dollars, and Dangerous Drugs	338
James Harvey Robinson	On Various Kinds of Thinking	355
Barry Commoner	The Energy Crisis—All of a Piece	371
Barbara W. Tuchman	History as Mirror	382
Arthur M. Schlesinger, Jr.	Politics and the American Language	398

Rhetorical Table of Contents

Note to the instructor: This alternative table of contents is provided for the convenience of those instructors who organize their classes according to rhetorical patterns. We have adopted widely recognized and discrete rhetorical divisions, omitting categories having to do with the author's relationship to his or her subject—categories like "explanation" and "argument"—since these are implicitly covered by the headings for the major divisions of the book. Placement of a work in a particular category is not intended to suggest that the writer uses one rhetorical technique only; rather, it calls the student's attention to the major rhetorical principle according to which the essay is structured.

NARRATION

Helen Keller	From *The Story of My Life*	13
Shirley Dolph	The Eye of a Deer	17
Jeanne Wakatsuki Houston and James D. Houston	Shikata Ga Nai	29
Laurie Lee	First Light	55
Thomas Sancton	The Silver Horn	91

DESCRIPTION

Alexander Petrunkevitch	The Spider and the Wasp	141
Howard E. Evans	The Intellectual and Emotional World of the Cockroach	179
John Hersey	A Noiseless Flash	208
Rachel Carson	The Sunless Sea	221

CLASSIFICATION

James Harvey Robinson	On Various Kinds of Thinking	355

PROCESS ANALYSIS

Raymond C. Murray	The Geologist as Private Eye	148
Donald Winks	How to Read an Organization Chart for Fun and Survival	155
Marchette Chute	Getting at the Truth	265

RHETORICAL TABLE OF CONTENTS

DEFINITION

George Orwell	The Spike	66
Charlton Ogburn, Jr.	Trials of a Word-watcher	82
James Lipton	An Exaltation of Larks	133
Joseph Wood Krutch	The Sloburbs	249

COMPARISON/CONTRAST

Barbara W. Tuchman	History as Mirror	382
Arthur M. Schlesinger, Jr.	Politics and the American Language	398

CAUSE/EFFECT

E. M. Forster	My Wood	50
Phyllis McGinley	The Consolations of Illiteracy	75
Lillian Smith	When I Was a Child	102
Richard Rodriguez	Going Home Again: The New American Scholarship Boy	116
Brian McGinty	The Trouble Began in San Francisco	169
Frederick Lewis Allen	The Automobile Revolution	236
Alice Walker	The Civil Rights Movement: What Good Was It?	256
John F. Kennedy	Daniel Webster	296

PROBLEM/SOLUTION

Charles A. Goodrum	The Dog Census	20
Carol Gross	Death Is a Personal Matter	37
Alan B. Rothenberg	Peaceful Coexistence with Rattlesnakes	41
Edwin R. Clapp	Why the Devil Don't You Teach Freshmen to Write?	286
Martin Luther King, Jr.	Letter from Birmingham Jail	310
Ruth Mulvey Harmer	Doctors, Dollars, and Dangerous Drugs	338
Barry Commoner	The Energy Crisis—All of a Piece	371

ANALYSIS

Leo Rosten	The Torments of Translation	163
Jørgen Meldgaard	The Lost Vikings of Greenland	189
William A. Douglass	Lonely Lives under the Big Sky	198
Louis J. Halle	The Language of Statesmen	272
Jessica Mitford	From *The American Way of Death*	279
Henry Steel Commager	Why History	326

An Introduction to Paragraph and Sentence Structure

In this brief introduction, we will not attempt to present you with a comprehensive discussion of rhetorical principles. For example, we do not discuss such matters as diction, tone, and methods of organizing the whole essay, because we frequently cover such points in the questions that follow each selection. And we do not define such terms as *simile* and *metaphor,* because the definitions for such terms can easily be found in a desk dictionary. Instead, we have deliberately restricted our discussion to paragraph and sentence structure. Following most selections, certain recurring and rather specific questions on these two elements are raised, and a number of terms such as *unity, coherence,* and *emphasis* are regularly employed. You will find that a careful study of this section before you begin reading any of the essays—and quick reviews later—will do much to enhance your appreciation of the works that follow. The more you understand the structural and stylistic elements that make an essay good—and even great—the more you will be able to adapt these techniques to your own ends.

Body Paragraphs

An essayist usually organizes sentences into units of meaning that we call paragraphs. Effective paragraphs are generally characterized by three qualities: unity, coherence, and development. We shall explain and illustrate each concept in turn. For the moment, our discussion is confined to "body" paragraphs—that is, paragraphs that come between the introduction and the conclusion of the essay.

A fundamental quality of a well-structured paragraph is *unity.* A paragraph is unified when every sentence—indeed, every phrase and every word—contributes to the development of a single main idea. Often, the writer signals the main idea to the reader in a *topic statement,* which usually, though not always, is placed at the beginning of the paragraph. Here is an excellent example of a unified paragraph that begins with a topic statement:

> Geologic maps can often be used in crime investigation to outline the areas where rocks and minerals associated with crimes or suspects could have originated. The owner of some valuable gems found chips of common rock instead of precious stones when she opened the cargo box that had been sent by air. Study of the chips indicated that they came from a foreign country

that was a stopover point on the air route. Examination of the geologic map for that area indicated the probable source of the rock chips. This evidence cleared the air-freight handlers at the final destination and led to the apprehension of those responsible for the substitution. (from Raymond C. Murray, "The Geologist as Private Eye")

Another feature of an effective paragraph is *coherence,* a quality that goes hand in hand with unity and with orderly development of the main idea of the paragraph. A paragraph is said to be coherent when each sentence flows smoothly to the next, when there are no awkward gaps between sentences.

One of the most common methods skillful writers use to make their paragraphs coherent is to effect transitions through such markers as *also, but, however, nevertheless,* and *finally.* Note the role that such markers play in keeping the following paragraph coherent:

Do not put much trust in titles: study positions on the chart and who reports to whom. For example, if a vice president suddenly appears as "assistant to" a loftier official, often for "special projects," see if he is still in the same spot on the chart. If so, this is a legitimate assignment. But if he has moved up, down, or sideways, the odds are he will keep on moving right off the chart and out of the company. Conversely, when an executive from *outside* the company is brought in as "assistant to" one of the big brass, he is almost certainly his replacement. (from Donald Winks, "How to Read an Organization Chart for Fun and Survival")

Another technique for achieving paragraph coherence is to use a pronoun consistently, as in the following paragraph:

Still, white liberals and deserting civil rights sponsors are quick to justify their disaffection from the movement by claiming that it is all over. "And since it is over," *they* will ask, "would someone kindly tell me what has been gained by it?" *They* then list statistics supposedly showing how much more advanced segregation is now than ten years ago—in schools, housing, jobs. *They* point to a gain in conservative politicians during the last few years. *They* speak of ghetto riots and of the recent survey that shows that most policemen are admittedly too anti-Negro to do their jobs in ghetto areas fairly and effectively. *They* speak of every area that has been touched by the civil rights movement as somehow or other going to pieces. (from Alice Walker, "The Civil Rights Movement: What Good Was It?")

Still another method that writers frequently employ is to use sentences that are parallel in structure (such sentences are usually easy to spot because they not only frequently begin with the same words but sometimes contain other identical words elsewhere). This method is well illustrated in the next paragraph:

AN INTRODUCTION TO PARAGRAPH AND SENTENCE STRUCTURE

What good was the civil rights movement? *If it* had just given this country Dr. King, a leader of conscience for once in our lifetime, *it would have been enough. If it* had just taken black eyes off white television stories, *it would have been enough. If it* had fed one starving child, *it would have been enough.* (from "The Civil Rights Movement: What Good Was It?")

There are other methods for achieving paragraph coherence, and writers will frequently use a combination of methods in a single paragraph. Whenever you find yourself reading a paragraph that seems to "flow" particularly well, stop to analyze the means by which this quality has been achieved.

The third essential element of a sound paragraph is adequate development. Good prose is concrete and often vivid. The writer explains generalizations with facts, figures, details, illustrations, and so on. Notice the degree to which Martin Luther King, Jr., develops the following paragraph:

We have waited for more than 340 years for our constitutional and God-given rights. The nations of Asia and Africa are moving with jetlike speed toward gaining political independence, but we still creep at horse-and-buggy pace toward gaining a cup of coffee at a lunch counter. Perhaps it is easy for those who have never felt the stinging darts of segregation to say, "Wait." But when you have seen vicious mobs lynch your mothers and fathers at will and drown your sisters and brothers at whim; when you have seen hate-filled policemen curse, kick and even kill your black brothers and sisters; when you see the vast majority of your twenty million Negro brothers smothering in an airtight cage of poverty in the midst of an affluent society; when you suddenly find your tongue twisted and your speech stammering as you seek to explain to your six-year-old daughter why she can't go to the public amusement park that has just been advertised on television, and see tears welling up in her eyes when she is told that Funtown is closed to colored children, and see ominous clouds of inferiority beginning to form in her little mental sky, and see her beginning to distort her personality by developing an unconscious bitterness toward white people; when you have to concoct an answer for a five-year-old son who is asking: "Daddy, why do white people treat colored people so mean?"; when you take a cross-country drive and find it necessary to sleep night after night in the uncomfortable corners of your automobile because no motel will accept you; when you are humiliated day in and day out by nagging signs reading "white" and "colored"; when your first name becomes "nigger," your middle name becomes "boy" (however old you are) and your last name becomes "John," and when your wife and mother are never given the respected title "Mrs."; when you are harried by day and haunted by night by the fact that you are a Negro, living constantly at tiptoe stance, never quite knowing what to expect next, and are plagued with inner fears and outer resentments; when you are forever fighting a degenerating sense of "nobodiness"—then you will understand why we find it difficult to wait. There comes a time when the cup of endurance runs over, and men are no longer willing to be plunged into an abyss of despair. I hope, sirs, you can understand our legitimate and unavoidable impatience. (from "Letter from Birmingham Jail")

Introductory Paragraphs

The length of the introduction should depend upon the length and nature of the paper. Writers often use several paragraphs to introduce a paper of moderate length. Because most of your papers in this class will be fairly brief, a single introductory paragraph will generally be sufficient.

This introductory paragraph must also be unified, coherent, and developed. But because it comes at the beginning of the essay, the paragraph must fulfill at least two functions. First, it must clearly indicate the purpose of the entire essay. It is in their introductory paragraphs that writers usually indicate the subject matter and scope of their essays. Second, the introductory paragraph—like the title—must arouse the readers' interest so that they will want to read further. To fulfill the first goal, writers often incorporate a *thesis statement* in the first paragraph—that is, a statement that explains the primary purpose of the essay. To fulfill the second goal, they may use one of a variety of techniques, some of the most common of which are explained and illustrated here.

One often-used introductory technique is to relate an interesting and pertinent anecdote or event. This technique is used well in the following paragraph:

> Recently I was at a party at which one of the guests spoke of a collision of airplanes in mid air. "Mid air," another of the guests—a magazine editor—repeated with a smile. "Airplanes always collide in *mid* air. One wonders where else in the air they could collide." His manner was amused, off-hand. But I did not miss the working of his jaw-muscles, the clenching of his fists. Here, confronted by a pet abomination, was a fellow-martyr to that condition known by the inadequate and not very descriptive term of *purism,* defined by the *Oxford English Dictionary* as "scrupulous or exaggerated observance of, or insistence upon, purity or correctness, esp. in language or style." (from Charlton Ogburn, Jr., "Trials of a Word-watcher")

A second technique is to begin with an arresting quotation. The quotation need not, of course, be one by a famous writer. The following paragraph begins with two questions from 1 Corinthians:

> O Death, where is thy sting? O grave, where is thy victory? Where, indeed. Many a badly stung survivor, faced with the aftermath of some relative's funeral, has ruefully concluded that the victory has been won hands down by a funeral establish-

ment—in disastrously unequal battle. (from Jessica Mitford, "The American Way of Death")

A third technique is to summarize a commonly held or conventional view toward a particular subject and indicate to the reader that the remainder of the essay will demonstrate the inadequacy of that view. Notice how this paragraph fits the pattern:

> Despite all the outcry and accusation in recent years, despite the growing mass and competence of professional assaults upon the problem, it seems that Johnny still "can't write." One reason is, I think, a misunderstanding, both lay and learned, of what writing means. When the man next to me in the Chicago plane discovers that I teach English, he mumbles something about watching his grammar. When Dr. Stackblower, associate professor of anthropology, bears down on me roaring, "Why the devil don't you teach the freshmen to write?" I know that he has just read some paper rich in orthographical mayhem. If Johnny makes a gross blunder in usage or spelling, both businessman and academic are shocked by his "English." But if Johnny scrambles the logic of his argument, or drifts into irrelevance, or dishes out bland generalizations innocent of support, or winds up in Timbuktu when he sets out for Oshkosh—the man in the plane (or the street) is unlikely to be aware of error. And if Dr. Stackblower is, he will charge it to incompetence in anthropology. That "English" is implicated never crosses either of their minds. (from Edwin R. Clapp, "Why the Devil Don't You Teach Freshmen to Write?")

A fourth technique that can be used to arouse the reader's interest is to explain the specific occasion that gave rise to the essay. Martin Luther King, Jr., begins his "Letter from Birmingham Jail" in this manner:

> While confined here in the Birmingham City Jail, I came across your recent statement calling our present activities "unwise and untimely." Seldom do I pause to answer criticism of my work and ideas. If I sought to answer all of the criticisms that cross my desk, my secretaries would have little time for anything other than such correspondence in the course of the day, and I would have no time for constructive work. But since I feel that you are men of genuine good will and that your criticisms are sincerely set forth, I want to try to answer your statement in what I hope will be patient and reasonable terms.

A fifth technique is to emphasize the importance of the subject matter of the essay—either to the writer or to the reader (and often to both). Here is an illustrative paragraph:

> We live in a time of unending crises. A series of grave, seemingly intractable problems clamor for attention: degradation of

the environment; the rapid growth of world population; the food crisis; the energy crisis—rapidly mounting calamities that may merge into a worldwide economic collapse. And, overshadowing all, war and the threat of war. (from Barry Commoner, "The Energy Crisis—All of a Piece")

It goes without saying that the list of techniques discussed here is far from complete. Moreover, it should be understood that writers will often use a combination of techniques to introduce their essays.

Concluding Paragraphs

How a writer concludes an essay will, of course, depend upon the nature of the material. If the material is complex and developed at some length, the writer may provide a summary of the basic points, and this may be done in more than one paragraph. At other times, the essay may not even have a formal concluding paragraph, ending instead with the last and climactic point. For most of the papers that you write in this course, a single concluding paragraph will generally be appropriate. And because most of these papers will be relatively brief, a summary will usually be unnecessary. What other techniques, then, are available to the writer?

One fairly common method is to point out the implications that grow out of the material that has been developed in the body of the essay. In other words, the writer leaves the reader with an idea to ponder. This technique is particularly well handled in the following paragraph:

> The lesson of the energy crisis is this: to survive on the earth, which is our habitat, we must live in keeping with its ecological imperatives. And if we are to take this course of ecological wisdom we must accept, at last, the wisdom of placing our faith not in production for private gain, but for public good; not in the exploitation of one people by another, but in the equality of all peoples; not in arms which devastate the land and the people and threaten world catastrophe, but in the desire which is shared everywhere in the world—for harmony with the environment, and for peace among the peoples who live in it. (from "The Energy Crisis—All of a Piece")

A second technique is to present an interesting anecdote that provides an appropriate close. Note the manner in which this method is employed in the following conclusion (the two paragraphs could have been combined by the writer):

> And yet the purist—even such as I—has his vindications. Do you know why Mariner I, the "probe" aimed at Mars, went off course into oblivion? I ask you, do you know? Because, in all the complicated instructions fed into its guidance system, one hyphen was inadvertently omitted. One tiny hyphen that requires you only to extend your little finger to the upper right-hand

AN INTRODUCTION TO PARAGRAPH AND SENTENCE STRUCTURE

corner of the keyboard. It cost the American people two million bucks.
And if you ask me, it served them damned well right. (from "Trials of a Word-watcher")

A third technique is to present a relevant and effective quotation, as in this paragraph:

> Ultimately, of course, medical schools will have to do more to educate doctors more completely. Recently, Dr. Donald C. Brodie, associate dean of the School of Pharmacy at the University of California in San Francisco, demanded that an answer be provided to why the physician should be "the dupe of the detail man [salesman]." If a doctor cannot "hold his own" in a five-minute conference with a salesman, he said, "it is certainly an indictment of his profession and of the educational system that produced him." (from Ruth Mulvey Harmer, "Doctors, Dollars, and Dangerous Drugs")

This list of techniques for concluding an essay is no more complete than the list you were given for introducing an essay. And, again, it should be explained that writers will often end an essay with a paragraph that incorporates a number of methods.

Sentence Structure

As you read the essays in this book, you will find a wealth of sentence models, for the authors of these essays are polished writers who structure their sentences for variety and emphasis. Although we cannot, in so brief a guide, present a complete explanation of sentence structure, we can point out some of the patterns that writers regularly use to make their sentences varied and emphatic.

An important principle of sentence structure is that sentences should, if possible, begin with important words and, more important, end with important words. Here are some sentences from John F. Kennedy's profile of Daniel Webster; they will serve to illustrate this fundamental principle (all of the model sentences cited in this discussion of sentence structure are from this work). Following each of Kennedy's sentences, a less effective version is provided so that you can make a comparison.

> a The Senate's main concern, he insisted, was neither to promote slavery nor to abolish it, but to preserve the United States of America.
>
> He insisted that the Senate's main concern was neither to promote slavery nor to abolish it, but to preserve the United States of America.
>
> b In his moments of magnificent inspiration, as Emerson once described him, Webster was truly "the great cannon loaded to the lips."

AN INTRODUCTION TO PARAGRAPH AND SENTENCE STRUCTURE

> In his moments of magnificent inspiration, Webster was truly "the great cannon loaded to the lips," as Emerson once described him.

> c Webster, wrote one of his intimate friends, was "a compound of strength and weakness, dust and divinity," or in Emerson's words "a great man with a small ambition."

> One of his intimate friends wrote that Webster was "a compound of strength and weakness, dust and divinity," and he was "a great man with a small ambition" according to Emerson.

Aside from this basic principle of sentence emphasis, there are several other principles that help to make certain sentences more emphatic than others.

The first principle is that *periodic sentences* are more emphatic than *loose sentences.* Most of the sentences that we ordinarily write are loose ones; in such constructions, the main clause (main idea) comes first and is followed by phrases and subordinate clauses. Periodic sentences are generally more emphatic than loose ones because they are rarer and because the main clause (main idea) is suspended until the end of the sentence. This sentence by Kennedy is periodic:

> For three hours and eleven minutes, with only a few references to his extensive notes, Daniel Webster pleaded the union's cause.

It is more emphatic than the following version, which is loose in its structure:

> Daniel Webster pleaded the union's cause for three hours and eleven minutes, with only a few references to his extensive notes.

A word of caution regarding your own use of periodic sentences: they should be used judiciously. A paper that is overburdened with periodic sentences will sound unnatural.

The second principle is that sentences can be made emphatic by repeating significant words and phrases. This technique is evident in the following sentence by Daniel Webster, which Kennedy quotes:

> I shall oppose *all* slavery extension and *all* increase of slave representation in *all* places, at *all* times, under *all* circumstances, even *against all* inducements, *against all* supposed limitation of great interests, *against all* combinations, *against all* compromises.

Kennedy himself uses the device of repetition in the following sentence:

> Summoning for the last time that spell-binding oratorical ability, he *abandoned* his previous opposition to slavery in the territories, *abandoned* his constituents' abhorrence of the Fugitive

Slave Law, *abandoned* his own place in the history and hearts of his countrymen and *abandoned* his last chance for the goal that had eluded him for over twenty years—the Presidency.

The third principle is that an inverted sentence is more emphatic than a sentence in normal word order. The usual word order of the English sentence is subject-verb-complement: I (subject) must meet (verb) that girl who moved here from Philadelphia (complement). A sentence that departs from this pattern is usually more emphatic than one that does not: That girl who moved here from Philadelphia (complement) I (subject) must meet (verb). Kennedy quotes this inverted sentence by Alexander Stephens: "A dismemberment of this Republic I now consider inevitable." Stephens's sentence is much more emphatic than the following version: "I now consider a dismemberment of this Republic inevitable." Like periodic sentences, inverted sentences should be used sparingly and only for a special effect.

The fourth principle is that when a sentence contains a series of phrases or clauses—particularly at the end—they should be positioned in order of increasing importance so that the last item will be climactic. Kennedy observes this principle in the following passage: "Tensions mounted, plots unfolded, disunity was abroad in the land."

The fifth principle is that a short sentence that follows longer sentences often acquires considerable emphasis, particularly when this sentence is at the end of a paragraph. Study this paragraph:

> But whatever his faults, Daniel Webster remained the greatest orator of his day, the leading member of the American Bar, one of the most renowned leaders of the Whig party, and the only Senator capable of checking Calhoun. And thus Henry Clay knew he must enlist these extraordinary talents on behalf of his Great Compromise. Time and events proved he was right.

The preceding comments on paragraph and sentence structure will, we hope, prove helpful in analyzing the essays in this anthology. They are not intended to be prescriptive but, rather, descriptive. Slavish and mechanical imitation of these techniques you should avoid, but we hope that you will experiment with them as you seek, in this and subsequent courses, to develop your own unique style.

ESSAYS CHIEFLY PERSONAL

From
The Story of My Life
HELEN KELLER

Getting Started

With Ideas

You will probably recognize "Helen Keller" as the name of the remarkable blind and deaf woman who, about the turn of the century, showed the world that a severely handicapped person was capable of acquiring a college education. And you may know the story of her childhood discovery of the meaning of language, a story that provides the climax for the play *The Miracle Worker*. In this chapter of her autobiography, Helen Keller tells that story simply and movingly.

With Words

1 languor (2*)—from the Latin word meaning "to feel faint."
2 plummet (3)—think of "*plumb* line."

[1] The most important day I remember in all my life is the one on which my teacher, Anne Mansfield Sullivan, came to me. I am filled with wonder when I consider the immeasurable contrast between the two lives which it connects. It was the third of March, 1887, three months before I was seven years old.

[2] On the afternoon of that eventful day, I stood on the porch, dumb, expectant. I guessed vaguely from my mother's signs and from the hurrying to and fro in the house that something unusual was about to happen, so I went to the door and waited on the steps. The afternoon sun penetrated the mass of honeysuckle that covered the porch, and fell on my upturned face. My fingers lingered almost unconsciously on the familiar leaves and blossoms which had just come forth to greet the sweet southern spring. I did not know what the future held of marvel or surprise for me. Anger and bitterness had preyed upon me continually for weeks and a deep languor had succeeded this passionate struggle.

[3] Have you ever been at sea in a dense fog, when it seemed as if a tangible white darkness shut you in, and the great ship, tense and anx-

---

Helen Keller, *The Story of My Life*, New York: Doubleday, 1954.

* The numbers in parentheses refer to paragraph numbers.

ious, groped her way toward the shore with plummet and sounding-line, and you waited with beating heart for something to happen? I was like that ship before my education began, only I was without compass or sounding-line, and had no way of knowing how near the harbour was. "Light! give me light!" was the wordless cry of my soul, and the light of love shone on me in that very hour.

[4] I felt approaching footsteps. I stretched out my hand as I supposed to my mother. Some one took it, and I was caught up and held close in the arms of her who had come to reveal all things to me, and, more than all things else, to love me.

[5] The morning after my teacher came she led me into her room and gave me a doll. The little blind children at the Perkins Institution had sent it and Laura Bridgman had dressed it; but I did not know this until afterward. When I had played with it a little while, Miss Sullivan slowly spelled into my hand the word "d-o-l-l." I was at once interested in this finger play and tried to imitate it. When I finally succeeded in making the letters correctly I was flushed with childish pleasure and pride. Running downstairs to my mother I held up my hand and made the letters for doll. I did not know that I was spelling a word or even that words existed; I was simply making my fingers go in monkey-like imitation. In the days that followed I learned to spell in this uncomprehending way a great many words, among them *pin, hat, cup* and a few verbs like *sit, stand* and *walk*. But my teacher had been with me several weeks before I understood that everything has a name.

[6] One day, while I was playing with my new doll, Miss Sullivan put my big rag doll into my lap also, spelled "d-o-l-l" and tried to make me understand that "d-o-l-l" applied to both. Earlier in the day we had had a tussle over the words "m-u-g" and "w-a-t-e-r." Miss Sullivan had tried to impress it upon me that "m-u-g" is *mug* and that "w-a-t-e-r" is *water,* but I persisted in confounding the two. In despair she had dropped the subject for the time, only to renew it at the first opportunity. I became impatient at her repeated attempts and, seizing the new doll, I dashed it upon the floor. I was keenly delighted when I felt the fragments of the broken doll at my feet. Neither sorrow nor regret followed my passionate outburst. I had not loved the doll. In the still, dark world in which I lived there was no strong sentiment or tenderness. I felt my teacher sweep the fragments to one side of the hearth, and I had a sense of satisfaction that the cause of my discomfort was removed. She brought me my hat, and I knew I was going out into the warm sunshine. This thought, if a wordless sensation may be called a thought, made me hop and skip with pleasure.

[7] We walked down the path to the well-house, attracted by the fragrance of the honeysuckle with which it was covered. Some one was drawing water and my teacher placed my hand under the spout. As the cool stream gushed over one hand she spelled into the other the word *water,* first slowly, then rapidly. I stood still, my whole attention fixed upon the motions of her fingers. Suddenly I felt a misty consciousness as of

FROM *THE STORY OF MY LIFE*

something forgotten—a thrill of returning thought; and somehow the mystery of language was revealed to me. I knew then that "w-a-t-e-r" meant the wonderful cool something that was flowing over my hand. That living word awakened my soul, gave it light, hope, joy, set it free! There were barriers still, it is true, but barriers that could in time be swept away.

[8] I left the well-house eager to learn. Everything had a name, and each name gave birth to a new thought. As we returned to the house every object which I touched seemed to quiver with life. That was because I saw everything with the strange, new sight that had come to me. On entering the door I remembered the doll I had broken. I felt my way to the hearth and picked up the pieces. I tried vainly to put them together. Then my eyes filled with tears; for I realized what I had done, and for the first time I felt repentance and sorrow.

[9] I learned a great many new words that day. I do not remember what they all were; but I do know that *mother, father, sister, teacher* were among them—words that were to make the world blossom for me, "like Aaron's rod, with flowers." It would have been difficult to find a happier child than I was as I lay in my crib at the close of that eventful day and lived over the joys it had brought me, and for the first time longed for a new day to come.

Questions on Meaning

1 Why did Helen Keller break her doll? Why did she later feel remorse about this act when she expressed no remorse at the time?

2 When Helen's teacher brought her her hat (before the experience at the pump), Helen knew she was going out into the sun. In a sense, then, the hat "meant" to her a trip outdoors. Is there a difference between this kind of meaning and the meaning she experienced at the pump? Explain.

3 What does the author mean when she says that the word *water,* once she understood its meaning, "awakened my soul, gave it light, hope, joy, set it free"?

Questions on Style and Structure

1 Which of the techniques discussed in the Introduction to Paragraph and Sentence Structure does Keller use to introduce this selection?

2 In paragraph 3, Keller explains the way she felt about her life before she met Anne Sullivan by comparing herself with a ship "at sea in a dense fog." This device of explanation through comparison is called *analogy.* Do you find the analogy effective? Why or why not? With what else might the author have compared herself?

3 How successful is Keller in keeping her paragraphs unified and coherent? Study, for example, paragraph 5. Around what central idea is it unified? What devices does she use to make the paragraph coherent?

4 How effective is the concluding paragraph?

Exploring Words

1 *languor.* Your dictionary probably lists more than one meaning for the word *languor.* Which of these meanings applies to Helen Keller's use of the word?

2 *plummet.* You will find a verb form of this word listed in your dictionary as well as the noun form, which Helen Keller uses. What relationship in meaning do you find between these two forms of the word?

Suggestions for Writing

1 Discuss the most important day in your life. Try to be as concrete as Keller.

2 Discuss a discovery you have made that has helped you resolve a communication problem of your own. Perhaps, for instance, you have finally learned how to understand your father or your English teacher or your mechanic or someone else who "speaks another language." Or you may have recently discovered the best way to read a daily newspaper, a lyric poem, or the racing news. Show both what you have learned and how you learned it.

3 Many people take the language they speak for granted, perhaps because they cannot remember the period in their lives when they had not yet learned to speak. Consider, for a moment, the importance of language to your life, and write an essay in which you discuss the role that words play in your life. For example, you might think of the ways in which language has helped to make you more human or more aware of your surroundings. Or you might wish to comment on a word or words to which you react strongly, showing the reasons for your reaction.

The Eye of a Deer
SHIRLEY DOLPH

Getting Started

With Ideas

You should find it encouraging to know that this essay was written by a student in response to an assignment in a composition class.

With Words

1 inexplicable (1)—(pronounced in-ex'-pli-ca-ble) relate it to *explain,* and remember that *in* often means "not."
2 ignominiously (8)—the Latin parts from which this word comes mean "ignore" and "name," but the context will be even a better clue to the meaning of this word.

[1] Red caps and heavy black leather boots, soggy and muddy, were strewn about the entry shed. I gingerly picked my way through them and glanced apprehensively around for signs of blood. Several rifles leaned against the back wall, and a handful of shells lay scattered on top of the woodbox. In the fading light the puddles forming around the boots on the old wooden floor were dark and murky. I felt small and lonely, with an inexplicable sense of losing something. I stared at the puddles for a moment and, realizing I was shivering, I quickly slipped out of my white snow boots and went into the house.

[2] The family was sitting around the big kitchen table waiting for dinner. The pleasant conversation and the warmth of the kitchen combined with the smell of bread baking soon salved my wounded mood.

[3] In excited tones my older brothers were recounting their day's adventure in the woods. They had tracked a big white-tailed buck and had come upon him suddenly, unexpectedly. Stan, the youngest, was the only one in a firing position. An older brother swore, "Damn kid, froze on the trigger! Let a ten-pointer get clean away! That's what happens when you let a boy try to do a man's job." A small sigh of relief escaped me, unnoticed by the others. I searched Stan's eyes for a message, but he fixed them on the floor in an intent stare.

[4] I exulted silently, "He couldn't do it—I knew he wouldn't!"

Reprinted by permission of the author.

Stan, at twelve, was two years older than I, and, when he wasn't teasing me to the point of tears, he was my best friend. When our father died, Stan and I had become especially close. He shared my reverence for all living things, especially animals. Together we had raised, loved, and played with a variety of pets, mostly cats, dogs, and rabbits. We delighted in hanging over the rails to watch the squealing baby pigs. We'd climb trees in the woods and watch squirrels and chipmunks and imitate birds. Stan was marvelous at splinting broken wings and coaxing abandoned baby animals to eat from an eye dropper. If one of his tiny patients succumbed, we would hold a sad funeral, always with a stone-ringed grave, a small stick cross, and tenderly planted wild flowers.

[5] Stan and I both hated the sight of blood and never watched the slaughtering of the pigs or cows on the farm. We avoided the chicken coop when we knew one of those unfortunate fowl was about to lose its head to an ax. It would run wildly about, headless, for several seconds like an unearthly creature, screaming noiselessly.

[6] The men were eating ravenously now and talking about their plans for the next day's hunting. Stan was quiet and still avoiding my eyes. I picked at my dinner, and my thoughts went back to three months earlier. Stan and I were in a tree at the far edge of the cow pasture when Stan grabbed my arm and motioned for me to be quiet. There, cautiously edging towards a salt lick block, was the most magnificent animal I had ever seen. It was a male white-tailed deer. It stood regally, its fuzzy brown antlers resembling a velvet crown. I looked at Stan. His eyes were wide with awe and admiration, and he was holding his breath. The buck raised his head, and we could see his huge dark eyes. He sensed our presence then, and in two graceful leaps he was back in the woods. Stan let out his breath in a low whistle, "Whooeeee, wasn't he something!" I nodded eagerly, and Stan took my hand to help me down the tree.

[7] My mother's concerned voice brought me back to the dinner table. I assured her that I was feeling fine and started to help clear the dishes.

[8] The next day, while my brothers hunted, I tried to read and keep busy but could not keep my attention focused on anything. When I heard the old Ford coming up the road earlier than expected, I knew. Hesitantly I looked out of my window at the once proud and graceful buck, now draped ignominiously over the fender of the car, its eyes staring sightlessly and its antlers still threatening. My tears were tears of pity—for the killed deer and for my brother, Stan, who had been forced to watch it be killed.

[9] The men came in triumphantly. This had been a clever one, they said. But they had finally tracked him down. Several of them had a bead on him, but it was Stan's bullet that brought him down. Stan's bullet! I couldn't believe it. The men were slapping Stan on the back and saying something about his growing up. Stan looked flushed and pleased. Then he saw the confusion and questioning in my eyes and said harshly, "You're

THE EYE OF A DEER

just a kid. A girl. A man's gotta put food on the table—can't you understand that?"

[10] I saw my dark, heavy sadness mirrored in the great staring eyes of the deer. I had lost my best friend.

Questions on Meaning

1 Why is the title particularly appropriate for this selection?

2 In what sense does the last paragraph sum up the idea of the essay?

Questions on Style and Structure

1 Which of the sentences in the first paragraph comes closest to expressing the central idea of this essay?

2 Which sentence in paragraph 4 serves as the topic statement?

3 *Oxymoron* is a literary device in which contradictory terms or ideas are combined. "Screaming noiselessly" in paragraph 5 is an example of this device. Where else does the author use oxymoron? Do you find the phrases effective? Write a sentence of your own in which you use oxymoron.

4 In paragraph 10, Dolph uses the phrase "dark, heavy sadness." What do the two adjectives contribute to the meaning?

Exploring Words

1 *inexplicable.* Although *inexplicable* is from the same root as *explain,* and although *in* means "not," *unexplainable* would probably not be as satisfactory a word as the one the author chose. What connotations (implied or suggested meanings) does *inexplicable* have that *unexplainable* does not have?

2 *ignominiously.* Consult your dictionary, and then try using *ignominiously* in a sentence of your own.

Suggestions for Writing

1 Describe an experience that made you disillusioned about someone or something. To what degree did the experience contribute to your growing up?

2 Write about an experience that made you aware that you and a member of your family (or a close friend) differed on a fundamental value or attitude. Show how this discovery affected your relationship with the person.

The Dog Census
CHARLES A. GOODRUM

Getting Started

With Ideas

If you were offered a summer job conducting a "dog census," what duties would you anticipate?

With Words

1 consecration (3)—you are probably familiar with the word *consecrate* as it is used in Lincoln's "Gettysburg Address": "But, in a larger sense, we cannot dedicate—we cannot *consecrate*—we cannot hallow—this ground." Recall this passage when you come upon Goodrum's use of *consecration*.
2 euphemism (21)—from the Greek *eu,* meaning "good," as in *eulogy, euthanasia,* and *eugenics.*
3 pique (21)—from the French word meaning "to prick or sting." In English, the word is usually applied to feelings.
4 opacity (36)—associate it with *opaque.*
5 rueful (37)—the quotation that follows this word should help you determine its meaning.

[1] One of the major traumas of my formative years was a strange little episode involving a dog census. I am now a civil servant, and looking back on it, I realize that this was my first brush with both the Bureaucracy and the Public. My sympathies were with the Public all the way, but as is so often the case in these great moral issues, the money came from the government, and I needed money.

[2] I had successfully completed my freshman year of college in Wichita, Kansas, and it was already clear that my future lay in political science. I had conveyed this idea to the proper profs, and it was therefore manifest justice that my name should be among the select few who would be offered summer jobs at city hall. Here we would see real municipal government at work.

[3] I recall our consecration by the head of the department, who urged us to "take this opportunity to serve, to observe, to apply and see applied the principles of public administration you have studied so well

"The Dog Census" appeared in *The Atlantic Monthly,* March 1963. Copyright 1963 by Charles A. Goodrum. Reprinted by permission of the author.

THE DOG CENSUS

through the past year." How true, I thought (and the money will buy the fall tuition).

[4] On the first of June we assembled at city hall in the office of the comptroller, where we were in turn divided into teams and reassigned to our specific tasks throughout the municipal departments. It was thus with some surprise that my roommate and I learned that our assignment did not fall in the civic center, but that we were to report to an unfamiliar address in the business district.

[5] We sought out the number and found it to be a two-chair barbershop off Main Street, where we were soon joined by four other youths of eighteen or nineteen, like ourselves. The first-chair barber lined us up along the wall and proceeded with the orientation.

[6] "Boys, you're about to take a dog census. I'm gonna give you a bunch of slips of paper, and every time you find a dog and can get the name and address of the guy he belongs to, you'll get ten cents. Don't think you can kid me, see, because I've been running these things ever' four years since before you was born. Ever' one of the papers is got a number on it, and I expect to get ever' one back, see? And don't go making up names, hear? Now, you got two weeks to do the job in. You'll get your money at the end, but you come in here ever' day or so and I'll give you some more slips and some more streets. I'll give you slips and streets as fast as you need 'em, but you hit ever' house, see, and don't think you can kid me, because—" et cetera.

[7] My roommate, Al Munroe, and I were to work as a team, each to take one side of a street, the streets to be assigned four at a time, running from city limit to city limit. The assault was to begin the next morning and continue for fourteen days; how far and how fast we would go were up to us.

[8] We went back to the dorm somewhat mystified, but intrigued at the possibilities of the operation. This was in the late thirties, when most of our friends were taking summer jobs in stores at $16.50 a week or on construction projects for $20. To match their $16.50 would require 165 dogs apiece. Surely in a week we could each find 165 dogs; but how could you discover whose they were? And just how would the owners react to the official presentation prescribed by our leader? We looked to the next morning with mild concern.

[9] Following an early breakfast, we took a bus to the southern extremity of town, walked two blocks to the limit of our first assigned street, and started toward the other end, five miles to the north. Elm-shaded and peaceful, it looked like an early summer *Saturday Evening Post* cover. I took the west side, and Munroe the east. Pursuing instructions to the letter, I went up the walk of the first house, mounted the porch, and knocked at the door. The sound of a chair being pushed back was followed by the head of the house approaching in undershirt and pants. He peered through the screen door and said, "Yeah?"

[10] I lifted the pad and pencil to present arms and declared, as

instructed, "Good morning, sir. I'm from the police department, and we're taking a dog census. Is there a dog in this household?"

[11] "The hell you say," he said.

[12] "Yes, sir. What I mean is, do you have a dog here, sir?"

[13] "You're kidding, huh?"

[14] "No! No, sir. You don't have a dog, I suppose?"

[15] "A dog census! Hah! I'll be goddamned. A dog census. I'll be go-to-hell. How about that? A dog census—" By this time he'd turned around and disappeared into the house, leaving me peering through the screen.

[16] I turned around myself and walked back toward the street, where I found Munroe already waiting. "Did yours have one?" I asked.

[17] "I don't think so."

[18] "What'd they say?"

[19] "I'm not sure. I don't think they were up yet, and the lady was pretty short."

[20] We reversed our fields and looked at the next houses on our respective sides. The thing was even more complicated than we had thought, and we both were nearly as scared of finding a dog as we were of being laughed at. The real threat to the program was our little pad of paper slips, yellow ones for the householders and white receipts for the barber, carbons in between. The slips read:

CITY OF WICHITA, KANSAS

To: (name)
Of: (address)

SUMMONS

You are hereby ordered to appear in Police Court within five days to receive sentence for failure to secure dog license. Sentence shall not exceed thirty days nor fifty dollars fine. Such action may be forestalled by the payment of $2.00 (male) or $3.50 (female) each to license all dogs found in your custody. Such payment may be made at the Department of Licenses, City Hall, from 9:00 to 5:00, Monday through Saturday.

[21] It had quickly become apparent to all of us, even back in the barbershop, that the word "census" was at best a euphemism. One of the others had asked the barber if this notice might not pique some of the citizens, and he had replied, with a strange smile, "Yep! Some of 'em get a bit exercised all right."

[22] Munroe had asked, "What if they've already licensed the dog? Shouldn't we ask them before we fill out the slip?"

[23] And the barber had replied, "Nope. Ain't hardly anybody that has, so it ain't likely you'll run into 'em. If you ask 'em if they've got a license, they'll all say they have, and you'll never have no excuse for filling out the slip and shoving it on 'em. You only get paid on the slip, you know.

THE DOG CENSUS

If they scream and yell too loud after you give it to 'em, you can tell 'em that the license bureau will check 'em all, and if they really have paid, they can forget it. You won't hardly ever find anybody who has, so you needn't worry—much." Even at the time, the slight hesitation in his otherwise forthright delivery had disturbed us.

[24] I climbed the porch of the second house. Much knocking. Nobody home. Went up to the third house. A grandmotherly-looking lady came out, and I tried the official approach. She looked puzzled, decided she had misunderstood, started to ask again, and decided against it. "No," she said, and shut the door. I abandoned porch three for porch four.

[25] Or, rather, stoop four. This house had the look of belonging to a carpenter or someone in the building trade. It had no porch, but had a fan-shaped brick and concrete veranda and a neat, newly painted doorway. Everything about the place looked alert and well cared for. I pressed the doorbell and precipitated a peal of chimes inside. A large man of about fifty came to the door with a massive hound of some variety beside him. The beast woofed a couple of times and then looked curiously at me through the screen door.

[26] "Good morning, sir," I recited. "I'm from the police department, and we're taking a dog census. I see you have one there! Ha, ha, ha." Striking the man-to-man approach.

[27] "You betcha, son. This is George. George is just like one of the family. He's three years old, and I'll swear he's still growing."

[28] "He's a good one, all right!" I tried to keep it friendly and nonchalant. "Let's see now, let me make a note of this. This is 3639 South Topeka, isn't it? And your name, sir, is—?"

[29] "Alexander Strean. S-t-r-e-a-n."

[30] "Thank you, sir. Here's this little slip of paper, and thank you for your courtesy." He opened the screen door, took the paper, and began to read. His face clouded as he progressed.

[31] "Go get him, George," he said in a flat voice, and the dog scrambled past him and shot out the open door with a machine-gun-like roar of barks, growls, and woofs all mixed together. His ears were down and his hair up.

[32] I backed down the steps as fast as I could go without falling over backward, and as I treadled toward where I thought the street must be, I could remember that the secret of dealing with either dogs or horses was not to let them know you were afraid. So as I staggered backward I fixed the hound with what I hoped was a stern expression and wheezed, "Now, George. Down, boy. Down. George! Stop it, boy. Down, George. Down! Down!"

[33] At this moment I found the street, fell over the curb, and landed in a skidding arc on my back. I wrenched forward to protect myself against the expected lunge and was startled to find George, with his front feet precisely on the edge of the grass in front of the curb, laying down a barrage of noise but not moving an inch. I had just learned the first great

truth on which we built the next two weeks: If You Can Make It to the Nearest Property Line, You Are in the Clear.

[34] By this time, Munroe had rushed over to help me up, and we stood there in the street, contemplating the situation. I had just earned ten cents and aged six months. In one block we had both been laughed at and ignored. Munroe had been lied to, and I had been assaulted. We had to decide whether to abandon the whole thing or mount a formal campaign. We weighed pride, limbs, the authority of the state, and ten cents a dog into the balance and decided we would give battle. The first thing we needed was arms.

[35] We retraced our steps to the bus line and rode back downtown to an office supply store. We entered and asked to see their selection of clipboards—the larger the better. They produced a choice that exceeded our wildest hopes. Munroe invested the equivalent of twenty dogs in a doubled aluminum job which was about the size of a snow shovel (it was intended as a wallboard for an automobile parts department), and I sunk fifteen dogs' worth in a massive wooden model which was as thick as my thumb and weighed well over three pounds. It was capped with a huge steel clip on top and two mounting hinges on the back, which gave it a beautiful heft. We stood there in the store practicing knee-high sweeps with these, like golf pros selecting a set of woods. In the ensuing days we became marvelously skilled with these weapons. My backhand was always my best. I could sweep that board from a writing position down, across, and up the side of the head of a charging chow or schnauzer like Manolete in his prime. With little snapping terriers and bulldogs, a fast wrist action not unlike a sculling stroke over the stern of a rowboat permitted me to back to the property line with complete aplomb, leaving the dogs breathless and faintly confused as to their bearings.

[36] Munroe maintained his dignity throughout. His metal board would drop from chest high with a single firm forehand, catching boxers and German shepherds across the skull, between the ears. A momentary opacity would cross their eyes, and you could almost hear their heads ringing. By the time they were in focus and ready to spring, Munroe would have withdrawn to the next lot, walking backward with all the assurance of the chancellor leaving the Queen.

[37] We snapped our little pads into our new boards and headed back for South Topeka Street. From there on, we abandoned the official approach and developed our own. If the householder was a young woman, we played the rueful innocent: "Lady, you aren't going to believe this, but the city is paying us ten cents for any dog we can find. Do you have a dog?" When she had finished laughing and admitted she *did* have a little specimen in the garage, we'd say, "Now, some knothead at city hall has written up the worst possible way of reminding you, but this is supposed to be a notice telling you it's time to get a dog license. Just ignore what it says, but get downtown before too long and get everybody off your neck."

THE DOG CENSUS

With this approach we wouldn't get the dog sicced on us more than three times out of five.

[38] Elderly ladies never understood what we were doing no matter how we phrased it. We finally got so we abandoned all formality, and when one would open the door we'd just say, "Good morning, ma'am, do you have a dog?" If she would say yes, we would ask her name, fill out the slip, fold it, and hand it to her closed over, saying, "Please give this to your husband when he comes home. Thank you." It wasn't that we were trying to deceive them, but bitter experience convinced us they never seemed able to understand, no matter how carefully we explained.

[39] All men under fifty arrived at the door mad before they even knew what we wanted, so we snapped out our question as nastily as they had saluted us, and although we would get the dog after us five times out of five, we at least retained our pride.

[40] In this manner we worked our way up and down the streets of Wichita. We would start off at seven thirty in the morning and keep at it till nine at night, when we would take a late bus back to the dorm, tender of knuckle and leg-weary. Inasmuch as we were backing out of about one yard in three, we not only found muscles we had never noticed; we were wearing out soles faster than heels. But we did find dogs. To this day I stand in amazement at the way they appeared everywhere in every size and shape. By the end of the first day, I had flushed out over a hundred and eighty specimens, and had netted eighteen dollars for the day. This beat grading papers or carrying roofing paper all hollow.

[41] In the ensuing days, we increased our unit production as well. We found that if you scuffed your feet on the way to the porch, whistled loudly, and rattled the screen door ever so slightly before knocking on it, you could rouse the family dog to a fury long before the householder could swear he had never had a pet of any kind. Similarly, we found we could increase our efficiency by locating the neighborhood grouch. She would give herself away at once by snapping, "No, I don't have a dog, and the city ought to shoot every one they find. The least people could do is to keep theirs tied up." To this we would reply, all innocence, "Oh, is there one next door?"

[42] This would usually elicit, "No, not them, but the next ones down have a big nasty one that's always in my roses. Then the people in that yellow house there have two that run loose all day." Having sold out her fellowman, she felt better, and we could head directly to pay dirt.

[43] Everything seemed to be going well for the first few days, and although Munroe inexplicably found about 15 percent more dogs on his side of the street than I did, there were plenty for all, and we progressed block after block through the city, spreading interruption and fury as we passed. We stopped washing machines, telephone calls, baths, lawn mowers, vacuum sweepers, and infant feedings. As I look back on it now, I think it is a miracle we weren't lynched.

[44] By the second week, however, our daily haul, which had been climbing nicely, began to decline. Not only did we find fewer dogs, but people seemed less and less astonished to be interviewed regarding a dog census. It soon became clear that the three small teams, although apparently lost in a town of 115,000, were beginning to be known. Ruth had phoned Margaret, who had warned the Pattersons, and by the time we arrived, all we got was the lady of the house looking us straight in the eye and saying, "We've never had a dog," with the nine-year-old whispering from the kitchen, "Hold her a little longer—he's still here."

[45] By the time we made our final trip back to the barbershop, I had recorded 1650 dogs and Munroe had identified 1948. I remember to the penny the $165.00 and the $194.80 we took in. It was fifteen years and a world war later before I again made so much money for two weeks' work.

[46] All this came back to me a few weeks ago when I was visiting my Wichita relatives. One morning, while we were at the breakfast table, the doorbell rang. My seven-year-old rushed out to see who it was, and through the living room came an adolescent treble, "I'm from the police department, and we're taking a dog census. Do you have a dog?"

[47] Chris replied curtly, "No," and shut the door.

[48] "Hold it!" I yelled, and dashed to the front door. I called out to the departing guest, "Wait a minute, son. I once took a dog census myself, and I'd love to hear how it's done now. What do they pay you per slip?"

[49] The youngster was alert and courteous, and he replied cheerfully, "We get ten cents a dog, and twenty-five cents for every four chickens or one cow."

[50] "Great Scott!" I remonstrated. "Even twenty years ago all the chickens and cows had disappeared!"

[51] "Yes, I know. We haven't found a one."

[52] "May I see the slip?"

[53] "Sure," and he handed me the yellow pad. It read:

CITY OF WICHITA, KANSAS

Name:
Address:

You are hereby reminded that the fee for licensing of dogs is $2.00. If your dog has already been licensed, please ignore this notice.

[54] I sped him on his way. Twenty-two years later, the ten cents was the same, the license fee was the same, discrimination because of sex had been eliminated, and the slip had been worked over by the public relations consultant. As a civil servant, I rejoiced. You can't ask for more than that: no inflation for a generation, and the state has learned to keep a civil tongue in its head.

THE DOG CENSUS

Questions on Meaning

1 Both the main idea and the tone of this essay are introduced in the first sentence. If you are not entirely familiar with current uses of the word *trauma*, check your dictionary, noting especially the usage labeled *psychiatric*. How serious is Goodrum in saying that the dog census job was one of the "major traumas" of his youth? What other words in the first paragraph help establish his tone?

2 This work could be regarded as having two major divisions: the writer's discovery of the problem his summer job presented and his working out a solution to that problem. The first section, then, would end with the sentence "I had just learned the first great truth on which we built the next two weeks: If You Can Make It to the Nearest Property Line, You Are in the Clear." Trace the author's changing attitude to his job up to this time, noting particularly his conversation with his department chairman in paragraph 3 (what language in that paragraph suggests that the author expects the job to be a rather dignified one?), his introduction in the barbershop to the duties of the job (is he given any reason to be suspicious there? is he suspicious?), and his initiation the first working day (does the word *trauma* fit that day's experience?).

3 What does Goodrum mean when he says in paragraph 21 "It had quickly become apparent to all of us, even back in the barbershop, that the word 'census' was at best a euphemism"? Why do you suppose the city administration kept the designation "dog census" even after they made the significant changes described in the last few paragraphs?

4 State the main idea of the essay in your own words. Is that idea expressed directly anywhere in the work? (That is, does the essay contain a thesis sentence?)

Questions on Style and Structure

1 Do you find the title eye-catching? Try to invent other titles that would be equally effective.

2 In the first paragraph appears the tongue-in-cheek phrase "these great moral issues." Where else is such language used? How does it contribute to Goodrum's tone?

3 In paragraph 7, Goodrum uses the term *assault,* a word frequently used in warfare. Where else does he use such war-related words? How do these words contribute to his tone?

4 In written English dialogue, it is conventional to begin a new paragraph each time there is a new speaker—which is exactly what Goodrum has done in paragraphs 10 through 19. What quality would be lost if the author had summarized the incident, eliminating the quotations?

Exploring Words

1 *consecration*. When you consult the dictionary treatment of this word, you will see that the context in which Lincoln used the word is more typical than Goodrum's context. Why do you suppose Goodrum used it to refer to a conversation with a faculty member about a summer job? What does *consecrate* have in common with such words as *sacrament, sacred, sacrilege,* and even *sacrifice*?

2 *euphemism*. Check your dictionary to be sure that the meaning you deduced from the context and the etymological clue you were given is a correct one. Then think of common *euphemisms* that are used in American society. Names of occupations are good examples (*mortician* for *undertaker*, *cosmetologist* for *hairdresser*, and so on).

3 *pique*. Your dictionary will probably list more than one definition for this word when it is used as a verb. Which one comes closest to Goodrum's use?

4 *opacity*. Among the several meanings your dictionary gives for *opaque*, one meaning will probably be a metaphorical extension of the original sense of the word. The practice of metaphorical extension is very common in English (think, for example, of *cradle* in "the cradle of western civilization" or *avalanche* in "an avalanche of mail"). Which of the several meanings for *opaque* is the metaphorical one, and how do you think this meaning arose?

5 *rueful*. Which of the meanings your dictionary gives for *rueful* best fits Goodrum's context?

Suggestions for Writing

1 Describe your own experiences on a job that turned out differently from the way you expected. Did you learn something on the job anyway?

2 Discuss the most unusual activity in which you have ever been involved. Try to be as concrete as Goodrum. Try experimenting with dialogue.

Shikata Ga Nai

JEANNE WAKATSUKI HOUSTON
AND JAMES D. HOUSTON

Getting Started

With Ideas

This selection is Chapter Two of the Houstons' account of Jeanne's childhood experiences at Manzanar, one of the relocation centers to which most Japanese-Americans (American citizens for the most part) were sent during the Second World War. You will find it helpful to know from the beginning that "Shikata ga nai" translates "It cannot be helped."

With Words

1 translucent (8)—from the Latin prefix *trans-*, meaning "through" or "across," and the Latin word *lucere*, meaning "to shine."
2 ironic (14)—this word and the related word *irony* appear in many of the essays in this anthology. Note carefully the context in which the Houstons use *ironic*; it makes a basic meaning of this important word especially clear.

[1] In December of 1941 Papa's disappearance didn't bother me nearly so much as the world I soon found myself in.

[2] He had been a jack-of-all-trades. When I was born he was farming near Inglewood. Later, when he started fishing, we moved to Ocean Park, near Santa Monica, and until they picked him up, that's where we lived, in a big frame house with a brick fireplace, a block back from the beach. We were the only Japanese family in the neighborhood. Papa liked it that way. He didn't want to be labeled or grouped by anyone. But with him gone and no way of knowing what to expect, my mother moved all of us down to Terminal Island. Woody already lived there, and one of my older sisters had married a Terminal Island boy. Mama's first concern now was to keep the family together; and once the war began, she felt safer there than isolated racially in Ocean Park. But for me, at age seven, the island was a country as foreign as India or Arabia would have been. It was the first time I had lived among other Japanese, or gone to school with them, and I was terrified all the time.

[3] This was partly Papa's fault. One of his threats to keep us

From *Farewell to Manzanar* by Jeanne Wakatsuki Houston and James D. Houston. Copyright © 1973 by James D. Houston. Reprinted by permission of Houghton Mifflin Company.

younger kids in line was "I'm going to sell you to the Chinaman." When I had entered kindergarten two years earlier, I was the only Oriental in the class. They sat me next to a Caucasian girl who happened to have very slanted eyes. I looked at her and began to scream, certain Papa had sold me out at last. My fear of her ran so deep I could not speak of it, even to Mama, couldn't explain why I was screaming. For two weeks I had nightmares about this girl, until the teachers finally moved me to the other side of the room. And it was still with me, this fear of Oriental faces, when we moved to Terminal Island.

[4] In those days it was a company town, a ghetto owned and controlled by the canneries. The men went after fish, and whenever the boats came back—day or night—the women would be called to process the catch while it was fresh. One in the afternoon or four in the morning, it made no difference. My mother had to go to work right after we moved there. I can still hear the whistle—two toots for French's, three for Van Camp's—and she and Chizu would be out of bed in the middle of the night, heading for the cannery.

[5] The house we lived in was nothing more than a shack, a barracks with single plank walls and rough wooden floors, like the cheapest kind of migrant workers' housing. The people around us were hardworking, boisterous, a little proud of their nickname, *yo-go-re*, which meant literally *uncouth one*, or roughneck, or dead-end kid. They not only spoke Japanese exclusively, they spoke a dialect peculiar to Kyushu, where their families had come from in Japan, a rough, fisherman's language, full of oaths and insults. Instead of saying *ba-ka-ta-re*, a common insult meaning *stupid*, Terminal Islanders would say *ba-ka-ya-ro*, a coarser and exclusively masculine use of the word, which implies gross stupidity. They would swagger and pick on outsiders and persecute anyone who didn't speak as they did. That was what made my own time there so hateful. I had never spoken anything but English, and the other kids in the second grade despised me for it. They were tough and mean, like ghetto kids anywhere. Each day after school I dreaded their ambush. My brother Kiyo, three years older, would wait for me at the door, where we would decide whether to run straight home together, or split up, or try a new and unexpected route.

[6] None of these kids ever actually attacked. It was the threat that frightened us, their fearful looks, and the noises they would make, like miniature Samurai, in a language we couldn't understand.

[7] At the time it seemed we had been living under this reign of fear for years. In fact, we lived there about two months. Late in February the navy decided to clear Terminal Island completely. Even though most of us were American-born, it was dangerous having that many Orientals so close to the Long Beach Naval Station, on the opposite end of the island. We had known something like this was coming. But, like Papa's arrest, not much could be done ahead of time. There were four of us kids still young enough to be living with Mama, plus Granny, her mother, sixty-five then,

speaking no English, and nearly blind. Mama didn't know where else she could get work, and we had nowhere else to move *to*. On February 25 the choice was made for us. We were given forty-eight hours to clear out.

[8] The secondhand dealers had been prowling around for weeks, like wolves, offering humiliating prices for goods and furniture they knew many of us would have to sell sooner or later. Mama had left all but her most valuable possessions in Ocean Park, simply because she had nowhere to put them. She had brought along her pottery, her silver, heirlooms like the kimonos Granny had brought from Japan, tea sets, lacquered tables, and one fine old set of china, blue and white porcelain, almost translucent. On the day we were leaving, Woody's car was so crammed with boxes and luggage and kids we had just run out of room. Mama had to sell this china.

[9] One of the dealers offered her fifteen dollars for it. She said it was a full setting for twelve and worth at least two hundred. He said fifteen was his top price. Mama started to quiver. Her eyes blazed up at him. She had been packing all night and trying to calm down Granny, who didn't understand why we were moving again and what all the rush was about. Mama's nerves were shot, and now navy jeeps were patrolling the streets. She didn't say another word. She just glared at this man, all the rage and frustration channeled at him through her eyes.

[10] He watched her for a moment and said he was sure he couldn't pay more than seventeen fifty for that china. She reached into the red velvet case, took out a dinner plate and hurled it at the floor right in front of his feet.

[11] The man leaped back shouting, "Hey! Hey, don't do that! Those are valuable dishes!"

[12] Mama took out another dinner plate and hurled it at the floor, then another and another, never moving, never opening her mouth, just quivering and glaring at the retreating dealer, with tears streaming down her cheeks. He finally turned and scuttled out the door, heading for the next house. When he was gone she stood there smashing cups and bowls and platters until the whole set lay in scattered blue and white fragments across the wooden floor.

[13] The American Friends Service helped us find a small house in Boyle Heights, another minority ghetto, in downtown Los Angeles, now inhabited briefly by a few hundred Terminal Island refugees. Executive Order 9066 had been signed by President Roosevelt, giving the War Department authority to define military areas in the western states and to exclude from them anyone who might threaten the war effort. There was a lot of talk about internment, or moving inland, or something like that in store for all Japanese Americans. I remember my brothers sitting around the table talking very intently about what we were going to do, how we would keep the family together. They had seen how quickly Papa was removed, and they knew now that he would not be back for quite a while.

Just before leaving Terminal Island Mama had received her first letter, from Bismarck, North Dakota. He had been imprisoned at Fort Lincoln, in an all-male camp for enemy aliens.

[14] Papa had been the patriarch. He had always decided everything in the family. With him gone, my brothers, like councilors in the absence of a chief, worried about what should be done. The ironic thing is, there wasn't much left to decide. These were mainly days of quiet, desperate waiting for what seemed at the time to be inevitable. There is a phrase the Japanese use in such situations, when something difficult must be endured. You would hear the older heads, the Issei, telling others very quietly, *"Shikata ga nai"* (It cannot be helped). *"Shikata ga nai"* (It must be done).

[15] Mama and Woody went to work packing celery for a Japanese produce dealer. Kiyo and my sister May and I enrolled in the local school, and what sticks in my memory from those few weeks is the teacher—not her looks, her remoteness. In Ocean Park my teacher had been a kind, grandmotherly woman who used to sail with us in Papa's boat from time to time and who wept the day we had to leave. In Boyle Heights the teacher felt cold and distant. I was confused by all the moving and was having trouble with the classwork, but she would never help me out. She would have nothing to do with me.

[16] This was the first time I had felt outright hostility from a Caucasian. Looking back, it is easy enough to explain. Public attitudes toward the Japanese in California were shifting rapidly. In the first few months of the Pacific war, America was on the run. Tolerance had turned to distrust and irrational fear. The hundred-year-old tradition of anti-Orientalism on the west coast soon resurfaced, more vicious than ever. Its result became clear about a month later, when we were told to make our third and final move.

[17] The name Manzanar meant nothing to us when we left Boyle Heights. We didn't know where it was or what it was. We went because the government ordered us to. And, in the case of my older brothers and sisters, we went with a certain amount of relief. They had all heard stories of Japanese homes being attacked, of beatings in the streets of California towns. They were as frightened of the Caucasians as Caucasians were of us. Moving, under what appeared to be government protection, to an area less directly threatened by the war seemed not such a bad idea at all. For some it actually sounded like a fine adventure.

[18] Our pickup point was a Buddhist church in Los Angeles. It was very early, and misty, when we got there with our luggage. Mama had bought heavy coats for all of us. She grew up in eastern Washington and knew that anywhere inland in early April would be cold. I was proud of my new coat, and I remember sitting on a duffel bag trying to be friendly with the Greyhound driver. I smiled at him. He didn't smile back. He was befriending no one. Someone tied a numbered tag to my collar and to the duffel bag (each family was given a number, and that became our official

designation until the camps were closed), someone else passed out box lunches for the trip, and we climbed aboard.

[19] I had never been outside Los Angeles County, never traveled more than ten miles from the coast, had never even ridden on a bus. I was full of excitement, the way any kid would be, and wanted to look out the window. But for the first few hours the shades were drawn. Around me other people played cards, read magazines, dozed, waiting. I settled back, waiting too, and finally fell asleep. The bus felt very secure to me. Almost half its passengers were immediate relatives. Mama and my older brothers had succeeded in keeping most of us together, on the same bus, headed for the same camp. I didn't realize until much later what a job that was. The strategy had been, first, to have everyone living in the same district when the evacuation began, and then to get all of us included under the same family number, even though names had been changed by marriage. Many families weren't as lucky as ours and suffered months of anguish while trying to arrange transfers from one camp to another.

[20] We rode all day. By the time we reached our destination, the shades were up. It was late afternoon. The first thing I saw was a yellow swirl across a blurred, reddish setting sun. The bus was being pelted by what sounded like splattering rain. It wasn't rain. This was my first look at something I would soon know very well, a billowing flurry of dust and sand churned up by the wind through Owens Valley.

[21] We drove past a barbed-wire fence, through a gate, and into an open space where trunks and sacks and packages had been dumped from the baggage trucks that drove out ahead of us. I could see a few tents set up, the first rows of black barracks, and beyond them, blurred by sand, rows of barracks that seemed to spread for miles across this plain. People were sitting on cartons or milling around, with their backs to the wind, waiting to see which friends or releatives might be on this bus. As we approached, they turned or stood up, and some moved toward us expectantly. But inside the bus no one stirred. No one waved or spoke. They just stared out the windows, ominously silent. I didn't understand this. Hadn't we finally arrived, our whole family intact? I opened a window, leaned out, and yelled happily. "Hey! This whole bus is full of Wakatsukis!"

[22] Outside, the greeters smiled. Inside there was an explosion of laughter, hysterical, tension-breaking laughter that left my brothers choking and whacking each other across the shoulders.

[23] We had pulled up just in time for dinner. The mess halls weren't completed yet. An outdoor chow line snaked around a half-finished building that broke a good part of the wind. They issued us army mess kits, the round metal kind that fold over, and plopped in scoops of canned Vienna sausage, canned string beans, steamed rice that had been cooked too long, and on top of the rice a serving of canned apricots. The Caucasian servers were thinking that the fruit poured over rice would make a good dessert. Among the Japanese, of course, rice is never eaten with

sweet foods, only with salty or savory foods. Few of us could eat such a mixture. But at this point no one dared protest. It would have been impolite. I was horrified when I saw the apricot syrup seeping through my little mound of rice. I opened my mouth to complain. My mother jabbed me in the back to keep quiet. We moved on through the line and joined the others squatting in the lee of half-raised walls, dabbing courteously at what was, for almost everyone there, an inedible concoction.

[24] After dinner we were taken to Block 16, a cluster of fifteen barracks that had just been finished a day or so earlier—although finished was hardly the word for it. The shacks were built of one thickness of pine planking covered with tarpaper. They sat on concrete footings, with about two feet of open space between the floorboards and the ground. Gaps showed between the planks, and as the weeks passed and the green wood dried out, the gaps widened. Knotholes gaped in the uncovered floor.

[25] Each barracks was divided into six units, sixteen by twenty feet, about the size of a living room, with one bare bulb hanging from the ceiling and an oil stove for heat. We were assigned two of these for the twelve people in our family group; and our official family "number" was enlarged by three digits—16 plus the number of this barracks. We were issued steel army cots, two brown army blankets each, and some mattress covers, which my brothers stuffed with straw.

[26] The first task was to divide up what space we had for sleeping. Bill and Woody contributed a blanket each and partitioned off the first room: one side for Bill and Tomi, one side for Woody and Chizu and their baby girl. Woody also got the stove, for heating formulas.

[27] The people who had it hardest during the first few months were young couples like these, many of whom had married just before the evacuation began, in order not to be separated and sent to different camps. Our two rooms were crowded, but at least it was all in the family. My oldest sister and her husband were shoved into one of those sixteen-by-twenty-foot compartments with six people they had never seen before—two other couples, one recently married like themselves, the other with two teenage boys. Partitioning off a room like that wasn't easy. It was bitter cold when we arrived, and the wind did not abate. All they had to use for room dividers were those army blankets, two of which were barely enough to keep one person warm. They argued over whose blanket should be sacrificed and later argued about noise at night—the parents wanted their boys asleep by 9:00 p.m.—and they continued arguing over matters like that for six months, until my sister and her husband left to harvest sugar beets in Idaho. It was grueling work up there, and wages were pitiful, but when the call came through camp for workers to alleviate the wartime labor shortage, it sounded better than their life at Manzanar. They knew they'd have, if nothing else, a room, perhaps a cabin of their own.

[28] That first night in Block 16, the rest of us squeezed into the second room—Granny, Lillian, age fourteen, Ray, thirteen, May, eleven, Kiyo, ten, Mama, and me. I didn't mind this at all at the time.

SHIKATA GA NAI

Being youngest meant I got to sleep with Mama. And before we went to bed I had a great time jumping up and down on the mattress. The boys had stuffed so much straw into hers, we had to flatten it some so we wouldn't slide off. I slept with her every night after that until Papa came back.

Questions on Meaning

1. When Jeanne Wakatsuki Houston says in the first sentence of this selection that "Papa's disappearance didn't bother me nearly as much as the world I soon found myself in," she prepares the reader for an account of a time of troubles, regarded from a child's point of view. What attitude or feelings about the changes that were occurring in her young life does the author recall in this selection, and what behavior of hers does she recount that demonstrates these feelings and attitudes?

2. The authors do treat, at least incidentally, the attitudes of the adults in Jeanne's childhood world toward the forced changes in the conditions of their lives. What deeply rooted values and living habits of the Japanese people were disrupted by their "relocation" (according to this account), and what methods did these people use to cope with these disruptions?

3. In what sense is the title an appropriate one for this selection?

Questions on Style and Structure

1. This selection begins with a one-sentence paragraph. Is this introduction adequate?

2. Paragraphs in personal narratives often are more loosely unified than paragraphs in other kinds of writing. Choose four paragraphs from this selection at random and test each one for unity. Are they as unified as the paragraph from Raymond C. Murray's "The Geologist as Private Eye" that is cited in the Introduction to Paragraph and Sentence Structure (pp. 1–2)?

3. Paragraph 19 begins with this sentence: "I had never been outside Los Angeles County, never traveled more than ten miles from the coast, had never even ridden on a bus." Would the three sentence elements be as effective in any other order?

4. Much of this chapter is written from the point of view of a child. Are there any places where the point of view changes to that of an adult? Where?

Exploring Words

1. *translucent.* Check your dictionary for the meaning or meanings of *translucent.* List the objects you can think of that could be described by this term.

2 *ironic.* Which of the several meanings your dictionary lists for *irony* applies to the Houstons' use of *ironic?* Write a sentence of your own using the word in the same sense.

Suggestions for Writing

1 The authors explain the meaning of the Japanese expression "Shikata ga nai" in paragraph 14. After rereading that paragraph, discuss one or more experiences in your life for which the expression "Shikata ga nai" would have been appropriate.

2 Write about an event of your childhood that was important to you, contrasting your feelings about that event with the feelings you thought you perceived in the adults who shared it with you.

Death Is a Personal Matter
CAROL GROSS

Getting Started

With Ideas

You will find the tone and the subject of this selection quite different from those of any other piece in this book. It is included here becase it treats a universal human concern with dignity and compassion. When it appeared in the "My Turn" column of *Newsweek* magazine, a number of readers responded with letters commenting on the author's unusually moving treatment of a somber but significant subject.

With Words

1 biopsy (3)—from the Greek prefix *bi-* (*bio*), meaning "life," and the Greek root *opsy,* meaning "examination."
2 inured (17)—from the Latin prefix meaning "within" and the Latin word meaning "use" or "custom."

---

[1] My father sleeps. I sit writing . . . trying to get something on paper I know is there, but which is as elusive and slippery as the life that's ending before me.

[2] My father has cancer. Cancer of the sinuses, and as the autopsy will show later, of the left occipital lobe, mastoid, cerebellum.

[3] His head lies at an awkward angle on the pillow because of a lump on his neck grown to grapefruit size—the visible sign that, for some reason, was not considered worthy of biopsy for ten doctor-to-doctor-running months. The invisible is worse.

[4] My imagination enters the chamber of horrors of overgrown sinus passages, and I wince at the thought of the excruciating pain my father has borne for so long. Occasionally the pain rips through the veil of drugs and, still asleep, he reaches out a skinny white arm and grips the bed railing with a hand, gnarled, but still warm and amazingly strong.

[5] I watch his rickety body shudder from the bombarding agonies. I cry and pray and gently wipe the glistening sweat from his forehead, sit again and watch, not quite sure what I am watching for. I have

---

"Death Is a Personal Matter" appeared in *Newsweek,* January 12, 1976. Copyright 1976 by Newsweek Inc. All rights reserved. Reprinted by permission.

no measure of previous days and nights. I have only been here a few hours.

A PAINFUL BURDEN

[6] When I came in, he didn't know me. I wrote my name on a card with the words, "I'm here, Dad." And he tried to understand, but couldn't. Later, when a friend arrived, he managed introductions of the lovely lady "who looks just like my daughter" to "my good friend, Oskar." Then, joking and being gracious, he made Oskar and me laugh, enjoy ourselves and feel comfortable. And we felt love. Now it is night, and I do not know whether the fitful sleep is appropriate and whether tomorrow he will wake and have time to joke and be gracious again.

[7] I have not seen my father for nine months, when the lump was still a secret below his ear. A few months later I heard about it and headaches, and then from time to time all the diagnoses of arthritis, a cyst, sinusitis . . . even senility. Then finally—the lump now a painful burden to be carried—he was subjected to nine days of tests of bowels, bladder, blood. And on the last day a hollow needle was inserted into the growth; the cells gathered, magnified, interpreted and pronounced cancer. Immediate surgery and/or cobalt treatment indicated.

[8] They were told, my mother and father, the day after his 75th birthday party. Then, after panic and the trauma of an old World War I rifle that would not fire, with my mother—ordered outside the bedroom—hearing the click, click, click . . . and a plastic bag, tucked around my father's face in one last act of stricken, singular loyalty and cooperation by my mother, to be clawed away at the last moment . . . and spilled pills . . . and falling . . . and weeping . . . and holding each other . . . and finally giving in, my father reluctantly left his own bed and was taken to the hospital.

"LET ME ALONE"

[9] And after the trauma of no dentures, no hearing aid and one unexpected cobalt treatment, triumphant that his mind functioned and his voice was firm, he stated unfalteringly: "Let me alone. No more treatments. I am 75. I have had an excellent life. It is time for me to die in my own way." His decision was not met with approval.

[10] These things I learned later, but now I hear him moan and watch his face contort and his bony fingers press his forehead. And I go down the night corridors of the hospital and ask for another shot for my father. All the nurses look at me, and I at them. We do not speak. It is not necessary. The air is filled with the serene mystery of tacit agreements. Another doctor is in charge now, and the orders written on the chart are clear and kind.

[11] After the shot is given, my father's breathing changes. There are longer intervals between each breath. I time them with my own breathing, and feel the suspense as I wait to exhale and take another breath. But even now I do not know I am here for the end. I am not familiar with dying. I pray again he will not suffer long. I anticipate weeks because his heart is that of a lion.

[12] I pet him, and hold his hand and kiss it. I wipe away the urine from between his wasted legs, knowing he would be terribly embarrassed if he knew. But I am grateful to minister to him with love at the end of his life.

[13] In the morning, another friend comes in to relieve me. I go for breakfast. A head nurse severely scolds me for wearing a cotton nightgown smock over my slacks as certainly not appropriate to wear in my father's room. I shrug and order coffee.

[14] Later on, washed and clean, my father rests peacefully on his side. I take his hand. He wakens, and now with only one eye functioning, but it blue and clear, he smiles a sweet gentle smile, and says, "Holy smokes . . . it's Carol." The last child has come and he is happy. Then for a moment he looks puzzled . . . Carol all the way from Buffalo? . . . and then he understands. He tells me he would like to rest now and squeezes my hand. His eyes close, and as though a shade were being pulled back from his face, the pain moves from chin to nose to forehead and disappears. He sleeps and breathes softly. I smile at his peace. I leave.

[15] My mother returns to the hospital to take my place. The phone rings 30 minutes later. Gently and quietly my father has died with her last kiss upon his lips.

JOYOUS FREEDOM

[16] As the family drives back to the hospital, I sense a great elation as if someone were flying with arms flung out in total freedom. I chuckle because the joyous, almost gleefully alive, feeling, is so strong. Yes, old man . . . Pop . . . I'm glad for you. Enjoy, enjoy and Godspeed.

[17] Death is not easy under any circumstances, but at least he did not suffer tubes and IV's and false hope, and we did not suffer the play-acting, the helpless agonies of watching a loved one suffer to no purpose, finally growing inured to it all or even becoming irritated with a dying vegetable that one cannot relate to any longer. In the end, I have learned, death is a very personal matter between parents and offspring, husbands and wives, loving neighbors and friends, and between God or symbols of belief and the dying ones and all who care about them.

[18] There comes a point where it is no longer the business of the courts, the American Medical Association, the government. It is private business. And I write now publicly only because it needs to be said again, and my father would have agreed.

[19] So, Pop, I say it for you, for all of us still here. Wish us well and God bless.

Questions on Meaning

1 Gross makes considerable use of flashbacks and abrupt time shifts here. How do these variations of the usual chronological pattern of narration contribute to the development of the underlying idea of the essay, that is, of the basic attitude it expresses? What is that idea or that attitude?

2 Comment on the appropriateness of the last paragraph, considering its relationship to all that has gone before.

Questions on Style and Structure

1 Although there are many shifts of time in this piece, the essay is written principally in the present tense. What effect does Gross accomplish by choosing the present tense as the basic method for telling her story?

2 What effect is achieved by the frequent use of the ellipsis (. . .) in paragraph 8?

3 Gross's sentences are often very short, and they often begin with subject and verb, as in the following series: "And I go down the night corridors of the hospital and ask for another shot for my father. All the nurses look at me, and I at them. We do not speak. It is not necessary. The air is filled with the serene mystery of tacit agreements." What purpose does the author's use of this kind of sentence structure serve?

4 Where does the conclusion of the essay begin? Is it an effective conclusion? Why? Does it make use of any concluding techniques mentioned in the Introduction to Paragraph and Sentence Structure?

Exploring Words

1 *biopsy*. How many words can you find in your dictionary derived from the Greek prefix *bio*? Do you understand how these words are related?

2 *inured*. To what responsibilities or situations have you become *inured*?

Suggestions for Writing

1 In a serious, reflective tone, treat an experience that had special significance for you.

2 Write an essay titled "_____ Is a Personal Matter."

Peaceful Coexistence with Rattlesnakes
ALAN B. ROTHENBERG

Getting Started

With Ideas

This selection could be classified as either an informative piece or as personal writing. The editors chose the "personal" category because of the writer's *tone*—that is, his attitude toward his subject (*tone* may also be used to mean an author's attitude toward his or her audience). What attitude toward his subject does Rothenberg's choice of a title suggest? Note how the opening paragraph carries out that same attitude or tone. You will probably find that the rest of the article tells you more than you ever knew (or perhaps thought you wanted to know) about rattlesnakes. But the information you are given about these creatures is always presented from the special perspective that the author establishes at the beginning.

With Words

1 veritable (2)—from the Latin word meaning "true." Now you will understand why people talk about "the eternal *verities.*"
2 histrionic (2)—if you have ever watched how some professional wrestlers and boxers behave before, during, and after a fight, you will understand how this word is being used.
3 imperturbable (3)—associate it with the verb *perturb:* He *perturbed* me.
4 malevolently (3)—the context and your knowledge that the prefix *mal-* usually means "bad" (as in *malpractice, maladjustment,* and *malfunction*) should provide you with sufficient clues.
5 sinuous (3)—related to the more common word *sinus,* which is the Latin word for "curves."
6 posthumous (3)—again, the context should be helpful, as well as your knowledge of the meaning of *post-* in such words as *postscript, postmortem,* and *postgraduate.*
7 paradox (9)—Charles Caleb Colton (1790?–1832) once wrote, "Man is an embodied *paradox,* a bundle of contradictions."
8 sedentary (17)—from the Latin word meaning "to sit." Another word from this source is *sediment.*

"Peaceful Coexistence with Rattlesnakes" appeared in *Harper's Magazine,* May 1962. Copyright 1962 by *Harper's Magazine.* Reprinted by permission of the author.

[1] In 1944 I acquired my summer place in the hills around Wurtsboro, New York, now less than a two-hour ride from Times Square. Almost at once, old-timers in the country obliged me with tales of giant rattlesnakes in the region. For a while I classed these with stories of mountain lions having roamed up from the South into the Catskills. The very idea that in mid-twentieth century deadly serpents might be permitted to survive on what was virtually the doorstep of New York City was to me unthinkable. There must be laws in New York State, I thought, making rattlesnakes illegal—along with rats, mad dogs, and lions in the streets.

[2] Shortly after I moved into my summer place, our community gardener drove his pickup truck onto my lawn and, with a half-proud laugh (I couldn't tell what was in the other half), invited me and my neighbors to see something "interesting" in the back of his truck. I had a premonition it would be a rattler; I had neither premonition nor preparation for the monster which I beheld. This was a full-grown timber rattler—a veritable serpent, six feet of ponderous, powerful snake. What shocked me more than its length was its muscularity, its solidity. Its neck was like a wrestler's wrist; its middle was round and bulging like a wrestler's forearm. Yet no wrestler (no matter how histrionic) ever entered a ring with that nympholeptic stare, that dragonlike, subhuman hate in its eye.

[3] Of course, this snake was dead. Our imperturbable gardener had pinned its neck down with a pronged weeder and severed it with a blow of his axe. The massive black diamond of a head, lying a full foot from the still-writhing body, glared at me malevolently out of lidless eyes—a stare that seemed to reach me from fifty million years back. The sinuous toiling of the body was slow and majestic, with nothing in it of pain or agony. There was in fact something supernatural about this cold, posthumous fury that Death itself could not still. And then something really horrible happened that sent all of us reeling in a widening ring from the truck. My neighbor's son reached toward the snake and, with a brave giggle, seized the heavy rattles on the still-upright tail and shook them. The whole snake coiled in insult; the headless neck yawned open, revealing the bleeding throat; the thick, headless body reared and struck at its own rattles.

[4] My neighbor's son dropped the tail and fell back. All of us were visibly shaken. I have since learned that, had the boy seized the severed head, it might have tried to bite him. (Raymond L. Ditmars in *Reptiles of North America* gives an account of just such an experience.)

[5] Since census taking among rattlesnakes is difficult, to say the least, no one seems prepared to say how many rattlesnakes there are in the United States. Laurence M. Klauber in his monumental *Rattlesnakes: Their Habits, Life Histories, and Influence on Mankind* (1956) estimates, however, that about 800,000 rattlesnakes are killed each year by automobiles alone. In the face of such numbers, the attitude of the "responsible" agencies remains stoic, if not Spartan. For instance, *U.S. Wildlife Leaflet 345* (reissued in 1958) says, "Snake control has been studied rela-

tively little and the Fish and Wildlife Service does not do research on the subject." Then it adds in a tone that plainly implies that rattlesnakes are my problem and not theirs: "This leaflet has been compiled in response to many inquiries. It describes various procedures that have proved useful under certain conditions. No single method works under all conditions and at times it may be necessary to adapt two or more methods to fit circumstances."

[6] Be it on record that I, for one, did not accept the idea of peaceful coexistence with rattlesnakes. Our gardener had killed that snake some 150 feet from my porch steps, and since I had two young children who liked to roam about our lawn, I decided to report the matter to some "responsible" department of government which would, I felt, send me immediate help.

A QUESTION OF PROTECTION

[7] Game preservation in New York is under state jurisdiction and I began by writing to the Department of Entomology of the University of the State of New York. I described the terrain around my property and my problem with two youngsters playing on the edges of a forest. I received the following reply, signed by Ralph Palmer, Senior Zoologist:

> So far as I know, there is no government agency in this state which will give you aid in ridding your summer residence of rattlers. It is barely possible that the Conservation Department's local game protector might know enough about rattlers to seek them out in the proper habitat and destroy them. You might write to the Conservation Department, Arcade Building, Albany 7, and find out who your local game protector is and whether or not he handles such matters. At the moment I can think of no solution to your problem except, perhaps, constantly being on the watch and killing such rattlers as you see.

[8] This letter left me with a feeling of terrible aloneness. And if Mr. Palmer's suggestion to contact my local game warden offered a hint that New York State did feel a little responsible for its citizens even in "the bush" of Sullivan County, the postscript nullified this impression:

> May I suggest that you look up *Field Book of Snakes* by Schmidt and Davis, 1941 (published by Putnam) and look up pp. 36–43, on snake bite. Your library may have this book. For a snake-bite outfit, I recommend the Dudley Kit, made by Flack-Hendrick Co., San Antonio, Texas. Costs about $2.00.

[9] Though unnerved, I took Ralph Palmer's advice and wrote to the Conservation Department. Their answering letter—I have lost the text

but remember it well—began by informing me that getting rid of rattlesnakes in rough, mountainous country was a difficult problem. And then it said, in effect, "Since rattlesnakes are not protected in New York State, we cannot help you in exterminating them." I concluded that the key to this seeming paradox lay in the word "protected," *i.e.*, that since there was no appropriation in New York State for dealing with rattlesnakes in any shape, manner, or form, they could not ask anyone to take a rattlesnake into "protective custody." The writer went on to say that I could understand how the government could no more help residents with rattlers than with many other pests which went hand in hand with living in the country. But though powerless to act, the Conservation Department wanted to be helpful and so it was referring my letter to my local game warden.

[10] My wife and I were off with the children on an auto trip when a polite, uniformed Conservation man from our local office turned his car into our driveway. He found my mother-in-law alone and unsuspecting on the porch. (We had carefully kept the presence of rattlers from her as well as from the children.)

[11] "Good day, ma'am. I am here to discuss the problem of your rattlesnakes," he began.

[12] "My what?"

[13] The Conservation man hastened to assure her that he'd never known of anyone who'd ever died of snake bite in New York State, but Grandma has never spent another summer with us since. We ourselves discussed putting our house up for sale. Though we dearly loved it and its surroundings, the responsibility of trying to guard our children against so repulsive a foe as the rattler soured our whole feeling about the place.

[14] The problem, with its accompanying uneasiness, lay tabled all winter. Over the Fourth of July the next season (again in the air-conditioned Catskills), I was dozing in a hammock congratulating myself for not having added my car to the weekend's highway toll, when I heard from my neighbor's lawn a woman's muffled shriek, a man's guttural command, and another sound, like that of an electric buzzer.

[15] My neighbor was poking a shovel at something on the grass and bawling to his womenfolk to hurry with a rake or an axe. His daughter-in-law rushed these to him from the garage. With caution and difficulty, he held the snake down with the rake and wounded it with the axe. He waved me away as dangerous interference. After an agonized half-hour of combat, he stunned the snake and then cut off its head. This snake—a four-foot banded rattler as thick as your ankle—remained on display for a day or two on my neighbor's lawn while the whole summer colony trooped by to gasp and shudder. But no one made any suggestion as to how to prevent other rattlers from leaving the woods and invading our precincts.

[16] When a second neighbor killed another large rattler on his property that same summer, I decided to resume my efforts to find outside help. This time I chose the U.S. Department of Agriculture. Again I told

my story and received the following reply—from Waldo L. Schmitt, Head Curator of the Department of Zoology of the Smithsonian Institution:

> Your letter to the Department of Agriculture has been referred to this museum for reply. Dr. Doris M. Cochran, Associate Curator of the Division of Reptiles, says that the total eradication of rattlesnakes in any rocky or mountainous region is a real problem. If you can find out where the snakes hibernate in winter, a charge of explosives might wreck their den and kill most of the inhabitants. [Human or reptile, I wondered.] If the cave or rock ledge where they spend the winter is not too big, cyanide gas (a deadly poison which must be handled with the greatest care) may be pumped into the cave, and thus you would be sure of getting all within range of the gas.
>
> Some animals such as hogs and deer are natural enemies of rattlers, and will trample and kill them at sight. An invasion of thousands of garter snakes was controlled in Manitoba, Canada, by filling bright metal trays with water and nicotine sulphate. After two days the area around the trays was littered with dead snakes. But as the rattler is not as aquatic as the garter snake, this method might not be successful in your case.
>
> It is not likely that a wire fence would be of much use in keeping them out, as rattlers are fairly good climbers. If the dynamiting of the den in winter is not practicable, it is possible that men with stout sticks might get them as they emerge from the den at the first warm days of spring. There would always be some late ones, so the vigil might have to extend over several days.
>
> Snake-bite serum may be secured from any large biological supply house. Most of it is made for our Eastern snakes by Wythe of Philadelphia. Perhaps you might get further suggestion from Mr. Roger Conant of the Philadelphia Zoological Garden, who is a most avid snake hunter.

[17] This letter quite overwhelmed me, but I weighed each point carefully:

(1) *Find out where the rattlers hibernate and wreck their den with a charge of explosives?* My summer home is on top of a thickly forested mountain. In the dead of winter the temperature sometimes drops to 20 or 30 below. I am a sedentary resident of New York City, and know nothing about explosive charges or cyanide gas—even if I could get some.

(2) *Hogs and deer are natural enemies of rattlers and will kill them on sight?* If only I could leave the problem to hogs and deer. There were plenty of deer in the region, but unfortunately hunters were forever depleting their numbers. As for hogs—who would want to turn his lawn into a pigsty even to get rid of rattlers?

(3) *Bright metal trays with water and nicotine sulphate?* Not a bad idea, but the poison might kill every dog in the area, to say nothing of

birds, rabbits, chipmunks, and squirrels which were, alas, *protected* by the Conservation Law.

(4) *Men with stout sticks might get them as they emerge from the den at the first warm days of spring?* Something heroic stirred in my blood at the phrase "men with stout sticks." But where would I get the other men to drop everything in New York City at the first warm days of spring, seize stout sticks, drive up to a hole in the woods of the Catskills, and remain there with arms raised perhaps for days, waiting for the late ones to emerge?

(5) *Snake-bite serum?* This repeated suggestion thoroughly depressed me.

AUNT AIMEE TAKES OVER

[18] Lulled by another winter in fangless New York City, I let several months slip by, neither enlisting men with stout sticks nor buying hogs. Besides, a chance remark of my grocer's in Wurtsboro had done much to lessen my fears. The rattlers we'd caught, he said, were probably stirred out of their natural haunts by the construction of the new road through the woods to Mountaindale. Now that the construction was over, these snakes would slink back into deep forest and not wander near a house for another twenty-five years.

[19] But a friend of mine at a camp in nearby Monroe, New York, wrote that one of the buildings was almost unusable because of rattlesnakes crawling in the foundations. And another friend of mine in Woodstock, New York, wrote that a construction company had refused to build a house on a mountaintop there because of a swarm of rattlers. I could feel the rattlesnake population—in new-born broods of five to seventeen—exploding in the woods of New York State.

[20] Meanwhile, an aunt of mine, Mrs. Aimee B. Mundel, to whom I had confided my concern, decided to carry on the search for help. She wrote to Roger Conant who'd been described so wistfully in my letter from Waldo Schmitt as "an avid snake hunter." She received the following reply:

> Please be advised that there is no known repellent nor no generally accepted method for exterminating these snakes. The only advice I can give you is to be constantly vigilant and to kill the snakes whenever they are discovered. In early spring when they are emerging from hibernation they are apt to be sunning themselves on warm days. Later in the season, when the weather becomes hot, they, like most other snakes, become nocturnal. Actually the risk of being bitten by a rattlesnake is not a serious one. Approximately as many people are struck by lightning every year as are bitten by venomous snakes. For first-aid purposes I would recommend that you purchase an anti-snake-bite kit. . . .

[21] Well, that last letter did it. I bought a snake-bite kit. I also bought something else (my own idea)—a shotgun, and practiced using it. Despite the profundity and kindness in Roger Conant's letter, I found one thing in it disquieting. Whenever there's a thunderstorm, I count the bolts of lightning and wonder who is being bitten by a snake now.

[22] My latest inquiries have again been in Washington, D.C. From the Department of the Interior, I learned of *Wildlife Leaflet 345*, "Control of Snakes." This summarizes in seven pages just about all the known methods of snake control, from snake-proof fences (which are now thought practical) to trapping snakes, gassing their dens, and using hogs to deplete the rattlesnake population. It does not mention, however, a new hope for the rattlesnake-harassed citizen: a new snake-repellent product called "Snake-stop." Within the last few months this has been manufactured by Animal Repellents Inc. of Griffin, Georgia. I am indebted for this recent information to Dr. Doris M. Cochran of the Division of Reptiles of the Smithsonian Institution. "Snake-stop" is, Dr. Cochran reports, granular in character and depends on the odor of civet musk for its effect. (Apparently it makes rattlers think there is a civet cat in the neighborhood, and cats of all kinds have been known to kill large rattlers.) One pound of "Snake-stop" distributed over each 420-square-foot area will, its manufacturers claim, so repel rattlers that this area will be safe from them. I have no idea, of course, whether smelling civet musk is preferable to fighting off rattlers.

THE CROWN OF EVOLUTION

[23] On the theory that knowledge is power, I have continued to read about rattlesnakes. This has not made me love them, but it has increased my respect for them as well-organized, highly specialized creatures who, despite countless raids on their dens by expert snake hunters like A. M. Jackley, continue to flourish over a vast area of our country. Laurence Klauber estimates that about a thousand persons in the U.S. are bitten every year by rattlesnakes—and that about thirty of these die. I now know that neither forest fires nor floods have much effect in reducing their numbers; that they are not easily affected by most poison gases; that they do not go for poisoned bait unless it's still alive. I now know that they have been successfully trapped hundreds at a time, but that I'd have to be far more steel-nerved *and* expert than I am to attempt this myself. I know that the rattler is the crowning achievement in evolution of the entire snake family (Dr. Charles Bogard, Curator of the American Museum of Natural History, has called it "one of the most successful creatures in existence today"), and that since it is still evolving, I may expect it to become even deadlier in the future. I know, further, that living in New York State, I should consider myself fortunate in at least one respect—for the banded rattler, which is my particular woodland companion, has the mildest disposition of all rattlers; he more frequently runs away than stands his ground

at the approach of man—but I shouldn't count on this. Sometimes he stands. I know, too, that the danger of a rattler's bite is in direct proportion to the size of the rattler and in inverse proportion to the body weight of the person bitten. (One of the booby prizes for not dieting these days.)

[24] Last and most important, I am finally convinced that no government agency exists which will offer to destroy rattlers for me as an individual citizen—unless perhaps I live in South Dakota where A. M. Jackley was the first of a series of appointees known as Snake Control Officers.

[25] Peaceful coexistence with rattlesnakes—with all its attendant uneasiness—is therefore the only recourse for one who, like myself, is unwilling to give up his mountain hideaway in New York State during the summer. This means, of course, steering clear of unexplored woods, rocky ledges, and ravines, and hoping that the rattlesnake for his part will stick to his own wild preserves. Of course if he comes right up on my lawn, I have my shotgun, my snake-bite serum, and my civet-scented snake repellent. The situation is not without its international parallels.

Questions on Meaning

1 The author, a former New York City high school teacher, makes clear early in the essay that he had had little to do with rattlesnakes before he bought his summer home in the Catskills. How would you describe his reaction to the snake the gardener shows him a short time after he moves into that home?

2 Throughout the essay, Rothenberg expresses continuing surprise at what he finds as he investigates the problem of rattlesnake control. Contrast the responses he receives from the agencies he writes to with the response he says he expected (see paragraphs 6 and 7). Do you think he is severely criticizing federal and state agencies when he refers to such matters as a pamphlet "with a tone that plainly implies that rattlesnakes are my problem and not theirs" (paragraph 5), a letter that "left me with a feeling of terrible aloneness" (paragraph 8), and another that "quite overwhelmed me" (paragraph 17)? If not, what attitude is he taking toward them?

3 Trace the development of the position Rothenberg finally adopts on the snake-control problem (see the last paragraph). Note especially the shifts in his attitude toward the repeated suggestion that he buy a snake-bite kit (see paragraphs 8, 16, and 20).

Questions on Style and Structure

1 How effective is Rothenberg's title in arousing your curiosity?

2 Is the division between paragraphs 3 and 4 justified? Study the structure of paragraphs 14, 15, and 16. Would you divide the paragraphs differently? Why or why not?

3 Rather than quoting the letters he received from various officials, Rothenberg could have summarized them in his own words. Why do you suppose he quoted from these letters?

4 Through what devices does the author achieve coherence in paragraph 23?

5 Is the last sentence an effective way to conclude the essay?

Exploring Words

1 *veritable.* Consult your dictionary, and then write a sentence using *veritable.*

2 *histrionic.* List three categories of people who are often described as *histrionic.*

3 *imperturbable.* At what kinds of tasks are you often *imperturbable?* Check your dictionary for a precise definition.

4 *malevolently.* You should note that this word is usually used to describe human behavior.

5 *sinuous.* What natural phenomena besides snakes could you describe as *sinuous?*

6 *posthumous.* Be sure that you know how this word should be pronounced. What would you like to be remembered for *posthumously?*

7 *paradox.* Is Rothenberg's use of the word effective here? Check your dictionary.

8 *sedentary.* Do you prefer a *sedentary* life or the opposite kind? If you prefer the opposite, see if you can find a word in the dictionary or thesaurus that describes your life style.

Suggestions for Writing

1 Write about a change in your own attitude toward some form of animal life. Perhaps, for instance, you have learned to live with cats, to appreciate dogs, or to handle laboratory mice unflinchingly.

2 Write about an animal you think is underappreciated or misunderstood by the general public.

3 Write an essay with the title "Peaceful Coexistence with _____." The blank might, for example, be filled in with "My Parents," "My Boyfriend," "My Girlfriend," "My High School English Teacher."

4 Discuss an amusing problem that you once had and the steps you took to solve it.

My Wood
E. M. FORSTER

Getting Started

With Ideas

In this essay, British author E. M. Forster comments on his feelings about being a property owner. You will find it helpful to expect from the beginning these characteristics of Forster's tone and style: (1) he sometimes uses words in senses that are different from the ones you are accustomed to (what do Americans usually call a wooded piece of property instead of referring to it as a "wood"?); (2) he often uses figurative language to express key ideas (be sure, for example, that you understand what he means when he says that owning property makes him feel "heavy"); and (3) he uses many Biblical allusions, some of which you will probably need to check in your dictionary.

With Words

1 asceticism (2)—derived from the Greek *asketes,* meaning a "monk" or "hermit." What kind of life do you associate with such a person?
2 antithesis (2)—from the Latin prefix *anti-* and a Latin root that means to "set" or "place." (If you think of the English word *thesis,* you will also be on the right track.)
3 carnal (5)—from the Latin *caro,* meaning "flesh."

[1] A few years ago I wrote a book which dealt in part with the difficulties of the English in India. Feeling that they would have had no difficulties in India themelves, the Americans read the book freely. The more they read it the better it made them feel, and a cheque to the author was the result. I bought a wood with the cheque. It is not a large wood—it contains scarcely any trees, and it is intersected, blast it, by a public footpath. Still, it is the first property that I have owned, so it is right that other people should participate in my shame, and should ask themselves, in accents that will vary in horror, this very important question: What is the effect of property upon the character? Don't let's touch economics; the effect of private ownership upon the community as a whole is another question—a more important question, perhaps, but another one. Let's keep to psychol-

From *Abinger Harvest.* Copyright 1936, 1964, by E. M. Forster. Reprinted by permission of Harcourt Brace Jovanovich, Inc.

ogy. If you own things, what's their effect on you? What's the effect on me of my wood?

[2] In the first place, it makes me feel heavy. Property does have this effect. Property produces men of weight, and it was a man of weight who failed to get into the Kingdom of Heaven. He was not wicked, that unfortunate millionaire in the parable, he was only stout; he stuck out in front, not to mention behind, and as he wedged himself this way and that in the crystalline entrance and bruised his well-fed flanks, he saw beneath him a comparatively slim camel passing through the eye of a needle and being woven into the robe of God. The Gospels all through couple stoutness and slowness. They point out what is perfectly obvious, yet seldom realized: that if you have a lot of things you cannot move about a lot, that furniture requires dusting, dusters require servants, servants require insurance stamps, and the whole tangle of them makes you think twice before you accept an invitation to dinner or go for a bathe in the Jordan. Sometimes the Gospels proceed further and say with Tolstoy that property is sinful; they approach the difficult ground of asceticism here, where I cannot follow them. But as to the immediate effects of property on people, they just show straightforward logic. It produces men of weight. Men of weight cannot, by definition, move like the lightning from the East unto the West, and the ascent of a fourteen-stone bishop into a pulpit is thus the exact antithesis of the coming of the Son of Man. My wood makes me feel heavy.

[3] In the second place, it makes me feel it ought to be larger.

[4] The other day I heard a twig snap in it. I was annoyed at first, for I thought that someone was blackberrying, and depreciating the value of the undergrowth. On coming nearer, I saw it was not a man who had trodden on the twig and snapped it, but a bird, and I felt pleased. My bird. The bird was not equally pleased. Ignoring the relation between us, it took fright as soon as it saw the shape of my face, and flew straight over the boundary hedge into a field, the property of Mrs. Henessy, where it sat down with a loud squawk. It had become Mrs. Henessy's bird. Something seemed grossly amiss here, something that would not have occurred had the wood been larger. I could not afford to buy Mrs. Henessy out, I dared not murder her, and limitations of this sort beset me on every side. Ahab did not want that vineyard—he only needed it to round off his property, preparatory to plotting a new curve—and all the land around my wood has become necessary to me in order to round off the wood. A boundary protects. But—poor little thing—the boundary ought in its turn to be protected. Noises on the edge of it. Children throw stones. A little more, and then a little more, until we reach the sea. Happy Canute! Happier Alexander! And after all, why should even the world be the limit of possession? A rocket containing a Union Jack, will, it is hoped, be shortly fired at the moon. Mars. Sirius. Beyond which . . . But these immensities ended by saddening me. I could not suppose that my wood was the destined nucleus

of universal dominion—it is so very small and contains no mineral wealth beyond the blackberries. Nor was I comforted when Mrs. Henessy's bird took alarm for the second time and flew clean away from us all, under the belief that it belonged to itself.

[5] In the third place, property makes its owner feel that he ought to do something to it. Yet he isn't sure what. A restlessness comes over him, a vague sense that he has a personality to express—the same sense which, without any vagueness, leads the artist to an act of creation. Sometimes I think I will cut down such trees as remain in the wood, at other times I want to fill up the gaps between them with new trees. Both impulses are pretentious and empty. They are not honest movements towards money-making or beauty. They spring from a foolish desire to express myself and from an inability to enjoy what I have got. Creation, property, enjoyment form a sinister trinity in the human mind. Creation and enjoyment are both very, very good, yet they are often unattainable without a material basis, and at such moments property pushes itself in as a substitute, saying, "Accept me instead—I'm good enough for all three." It is not enough. It is, as Shakespeare said of lust, "The expense of spirit in a waste of shame": it is "Before, a joy proposed; behind, a dream." Yet we don't know how to shun it. It is forced on us by our economic system as the alternative to starvation. It is also forced on us by an internal defect in the soul, by the feeling that in property may lie the germs of self-development and of exquisite or heroic deeds. Our life on earth is, and ought to be, material and carnal. But we have not yet learned to manage our materialism and carnality properly; they are still entangled with the desire for ownership, where (in the words of Dante) "Possession is one with loss."

[6] And this brings us to our fourth and final point: the blackberries.

[7] Blackberries are not plentiful in this meagre grove, but they are easily seen from the public footpath which traverses it, and all too easily gathered. Foxgloves, too—people will pull up the foxgloves, and ladies of an educational tendency even grub for toadstools to show them on the Monday in class. Other ladies, less educated, roll down the bracken in the arms of their gentlemen friends. There is paper, there are tins. Pray, does my wood belong to me or doesn't it? And, if it does, should I not own it best by allowing no one else to walk there? There is a wood near Lyme Regis, also cursed by a public footpath, where the owner has not hesitated on this point. He had built high stone walls each side of the path, and has spanned it by bridges, so that the public circulate like termites while he gorges on the blackberries unseen. He really does own his wood, this able chap. Dives in Hell did pretty well, but the gulf dividing him from Lazarus could be traversed by vision, and nothing traverses it here. And perhaps I shall come to this in time. I shall wall in and fence out until I really taste the sweets of property. Enormously stout, endlessly avaricious, pseudo-creative, intensely selfish, I shall weave upon my forehead the quadruple

crown of possession until those nasty Bolshies come and take it off again and thrust me aside into the outer darkness.

Questions on Meaning

1 In your own words, list the author's four main points about property ownership, using the most direct, straightforward language you can find. Then consider the differences (besides length) between your treatment and Forster's. To what extent has your summary captured the meaning or the purpose of this essay? Why is this so?

2 How serious is Forster in this essay? How do you know?

Questions on Style and Structure

1 Which of the techniques discussed in the Introduction to Paragraph and Sentence Structure does Forster use to introduce this essay?

2 Is the division between paragraphs 3 and 4 justified? How about the division between paragraphs 6 and 7?

3 In paragraph 2, Forster embellishes a Biblical parable, which is reprinted here (King James Version):

Then said Jesus unto his disciples, Verily I say unto you, That a rich man shall hardly enter into the kingdom of heaven.
And again I say unto you, It is easier for a camel to go through the eye of a needle, than for a rich man to enter into the kingdom of God. (Matt. 19:23–24)

How effective is Forster's embellishment?

4 What transitional phrase does the author use to link paragraph 2 to paragraph 1? Where else does he use such phrases?

5 Forster uses illustrations that some people might consider trivial (the bird and blackberries) in order to show the effects of owning property. Are these good illustrations?

6 This essay does not have a separate concluding paragraph. Where does the conclusion begin?

7 Writers usually try to maintain consistent diction; that is, they try to remain at one level. Here are two sentences in which there is a mixture of formal and informal language. Comment on their effectiveness.

   a It is not a large wood—it contains scarcely any trees, and it is intersected, blast it, by a public footpath. (paragraph 1)
   b Enormously stout, endlessly avaricious, pseudo-creative, intensely selfish, I shall weave upon my forehead the quadruple crown of pos-

session until those nasty Bolshies come and take it off again and thrust me aside into the outer darkness. (paragraph 7)

Exploring Words

1 *asceticism.* After you have read the dictionary definition of this word, try to think of some antonyms.

2 *antithesis.* You will probably find a one-word synonym for *antithesis* in your dictionary. Try substituting that word for *antithesis* in the sentence beginning with "Men of weight" (paragraph 2), and then ask yourself what the statement means in the context of the whole paragraph (you will probably also need to look up the British sense of the word *stone*).

3 *carnal.* Check the several dictionary definitions of this word. Which one comes closest to Forster's use?

Suggestions for Writing

1 Discuss your own feelings about property ownership, but focus on your attitudes toward property other than real estate—perhaps a car, a set of tools, a collection of books, a credit card, or a diary. Decide how serious you want to be, and then adopt a tone that fits your purpose.

2 Discuss the effects on yourself of owning property. Perhaps you might want to write a rebuttal to Forster, showing the pleasures of owning a piece of "real" property.

First Light
LAURIE LEE

Getting Started

With Ideas

As you will discover when you read the first two paragraphs of this work, British poet Laurie Lee uses language in distinctive ways as he recalls with surprising sharpness experiences from his very early childhood. Even his title is rich in implications—implications that will become increasingly clear to you if you let Lee tell his story in his own way and are not distracted by unusual expressions or memories that surprise you.

With Words

1 garrulous (11)—from the Latin word for "chatter."
2 inexorable (14)—A frequently mispronounced word (the accent is on the second syllable: in-ex-o-ra-ble). This word is often used in the phrase "*inexorable* fate." Think of this phrase when you come to Lee's "*inexorable* tradition."
3 glutinous (24)—from the Latin word for "glue."

[1] I was set down from the carrier's cart at the age of three; and there with a sense of bewilderment and terror my life in the village began.

[2] The June grass, amongst which I stood, was taller than I was, and I wept. I had never been so close to grass before. It towered above me and all around me, each blade tattooed with tiger skins of sunlight. It was knife-edged, dark and a wicked green, thick as a forest and alive with grasshoppers that chirped and chattered and leapt through the air like monkeys.

[3] I was lost and didn't know where to move. A tropic heat oozed up from the ground, rank with sharp odours of roots and nettles. Snow clouds of elderblossom banked in the sky, showering upon me the fumes and flakes of their sweet and giddy suffocation. High overhead ran frenzied larks, screaming, as though the sky were tearing apart.

[4] For the first time in my life I was out of the sight of humans. For the first time in my life I was alone in a world whose behaviour I could neither predict nor fathom: a world of birds that squealed, of plants that

Reprinted by permission of William Morrow & Co., Inc. from *The Edge of Day* by Laurie Lee. Copyright © 1959 by Laurie Lee.

stank, of insects that sprang about without warning. I was lost and I did not expect to be found again. I put back my head and howled, and the sun hit me smartly on the face, like a bully.

[5] From this daylight nightmare I was wakened, as from many another, by the appearance of my sisters. They came scrambling and calling up the steep rough bank and, parting the long grass, found me. Faces of rose, familiar, living; huge shining faces hung up like shields between me and the sky; faces with grins and white teeth (some broken) to be conjured up like genii with a howl, brushing off terror with their broad scoldings and affection. They leaned over me—one, two, three—their mouths smeared with red currants and their hands dripping with juice.

[6] "There, there, it's all right, don't you wail anymore. Come down 'ome and we'll stuff you with currants."

[7] And Marjorie, the eldest, lifted me into her long brown hair, and ran me jogging down the path and through the steep rose-filled garden, and set me down on the cottage doorstep, which was our home, though I couldn't believe it.

[8] That was the day we came to the village, in the summer of the last year of the First World War. To a cottage that stood in a half-acre of garden on a steep bank above a lake; a cottage with three floors and a cellar and a treasure in the walls, with a pump and apple trees, syringa and strawberries, rooks in the chimneys, frogs in the cellar, mushrooms on the ceiling, and all for three and sixpence a week.

[9] I don't know where I lived before then. My life began on the carrier's cart which brought me up the long slow hills to the village, and dumped me in the high grass, and lost me. I had ridden wrapped up in a Union Jack to protect me from the sun, and when I rolled out of it, and stood piping loud among the buzzing jungle of that summer bank, then, I feel, was I born. And to all the rest of us, the whole family of eight, it was the beginning of a life.

[10] But on that first day we were all lost. Chaos was come in cartloads of furniture, and I crawled the kitchen floor through forests of upturned chairlegs and crystal fields of glass. We were washed up in a new land, and began to spread out, searching its springs and treasures. The sisters spent the light of that first day stripping the fruit bushes in the garden. The currants were at their prime, clusters of red, black and yellow berries all tangled up with wild roses. Here was bounty the girls had never known before, and they darted squawking from bush to bush, clawing the fruit like sparrows.

[11] Our Mother too was distracted from duty, seduced by the rich wilderness of the garden so long abandoned. All day she trotted to and fro, flushed and garrulous, pouring flowers into every pot and jug she could find on the kitchen floor. Flowers from the garden, daisies from the bank, cow parsley, grasses, ferns and leaves—they flowed in armfuls through the cottage door until its dim interior seemed entirely possessed by the world outside—a still green pool flooding with honeyed tides of summer.

[12] I sat on the floor on a raft of muddles and gazed through the

green window which was full of the rising garden. I saw the long black stockings of the girls, gaping with white flesh, kicking among the currant bushes. Every so often one of them would dart into the kitchen, cram my great mouth with handfuls of squashed berries, and run out again. And the more I got the more I called for more. It was like feeding a fat young cuckoo.

[13] The long day crowed and chirped and rang. Nobody did any work, and there was nothing to eat save berries and bread. I crawled about among the ornaments on the unfamiliar floor—the glass fishes, china dogs, shepherds and shepherdesses, bronze horsemen, stopped clocks, barometers, and photographs of bearded men. I called on them each in turn, for they were the shrines and faces of a half-remembered landscape. But as I watched the sun move around the walls, drawing rainbows from the cut-glass jars in the corner, I longed for a return of order.

[14] Then, suddenly, the day was at an end, and the house was furnished. Each stick and cup and picture was nailed immovably in place; the beds were sheeted, the windows curtained, the straw mats laid, and the house was home. I don't remember seeing it happen, but suddenly the inexorable tradition of the house, with its smell, chaos and complete logic, occurred as though it had never been otherwise. The furnishing and founding of the house came like the nightfall of that first day. From that uneasy loneliness of objects strewn on the kitchen floor, everything flew to its place and was never again questioned.

[15] And from that day we grew up. The domestic arrangement of the house was shaken many times, like a snowstorm toy, so that beds and chairs and ornaments swirled from room to room, pursued by the gusty energies of Mother and the girls. But always these things resettled within the pattern of the walls, nothing escaped or changed, and so it remained for twenty years.

[16] Now I measured that first growing year by the widening fields that became visible to me, the new tricks of dressing and getting about with which I became gradually endowed. I could open the kitchen door by screwing myself into a ball and leaping and banging the latch with my fist. I could climb into the high bed by using the ironwork as a ladder. I could whistle, but I couldn't lace my shoes. Life became a series of experiments which brought grief or the rewards of accomplishment: a pondering of patterns and mysteries in the house, while time hung golden and suspended, and one's body, from leaping and climbing, took on the rigid insanity of an insect, petrified, as it were, for hours together, breathing and watching. Watching the grains of dust fall in the sunny room, following an ant from its cradle to the grave, going over the knots in the bedroom ceiling—knots that seemed to dilate and run in the half-light of dawn and form the fluid shapes of monsters, or moved stealthily from board to board; but which settled again in the wax light of day no more monstrous than fossils in coal.

[17] These knots on the bedroom ceiling were the whole range of

a world, and over them my eyes went endlessly voyaging in that long primeval light of waking to which a child is condemned. They were archipelagoes in a sea of blood-coloured varnish, they were armies grouped and united against me, they were the alphabet of a macabre tongue, the first book I ever learned to read.

[18] Radiating from that house, with its crumbling walls, its thumps and shadows, its fancied foxes under the floor, I moved along paths that lengthened inch by inch with my mounting strength of days. From stone to stone in the trackless yard I sent forth my acorn shell of senses, moving through unfathomable oceans like a South Sea savage island-hopping across the Pacific. Antennae of eyes and nose and grubbing fingers captured a new tuft of grass, a fern, a slug, the skull of a bird, a grotto of bright snails. Through the long summer ages of those first few days I enlarged my world and mapped it in my mind: its secure havens, its dust-deserts and puddles, its peaks of dirt and flag-flying bushes. Returning too, dry-throated, over and over again, to its several well-prodded horrors: the bird's gaping bones in its cage of old sticks; the black flies in the corner, slimy dead; dry rags of snakes; and the crowded, rotting, silent-roaring city of a cat's grub-captured carcass.

[19] Once seen, these relics passed within the frontiers of the known lands, to be remembered with a buzzing in the ears, to be revisited when the stomach was strong. They were the first tangible victims of that destroying force whose job I knew went on both night and day, though I could never catch him at it. Nevertheless I was grateful for them. Though they haunted my eyes and stuck in my dreams, they reduced for me the first infinite possibilities of horror. They chastened the imagination with the proof of a limited frightfulness.

[20] From the harbour mouth of the scullery door I learned the rocks and reefs and the channels where safety lay. I discovered the physical pyramid of the cottage, its stores and labyrinths, its centres of magic, and of the green, sprouting island-garden upon which it stood. My Mother and sisters sailed past me like galleons in their busy dresses, and I learned the smells and sounds which followed in their wakes, the surge of breath, air of carbolic, song and grumble, and smashing of crockery.

[21] How magnificent they appeared, full-rigged, those towering girls, with their flying hair and billowing blouses, their white-mast arms stripped for work or washing. At any moment one was boarded by them, bussed and buttoned, or swung up high like a wriggling fish to be hooked and held in their lacy linen.

[22] The scullery was a mine of all the minerals of living. Here I discovered water—a very different element from the green crawling scum that stank in the garden tub. You could pump it in pure blue gulps out of the ground; you could swing on the pump handle and it came out sparkling like liquid sky. And it broke and ran and shone on the tiled floor, or quivered in a jug, or weighted your clothes with cold. You could drink it, draw with it, froth it with soap, swim beetles across it, or fly it in bubbles

in the air. You could put your head in it, and open your eyes, and see the sides of the bucket buckle, and hear your caught breath roar, and work your mouth like a fish, and smell the lime from the ground. Substance of magic—which you could tear or wear, confine or scatter, or send down holes, but never burn or break or destroy.

[23] The scullery was water, where the old pump stood. And it had everything else that was related to water: thick steam of Mondays, edgy with starch; soapsuds boiling, bellying and popping, creaking and whispering, rainbowed with light and winking with a million windows. Bubble, bubble, toil and grumble, rinsing and slapping of sheets and shirts, and panting Mother rowing her red arms like oars in the steaming waves. Then the linen came up on a stick out of the pot, like pastry, or woven suds, or sheets of moulded snow.

[24] Here, too, was the scrubbing of floors and boots, of arms and necks, of red and white vegetables. Walk into the morning disorder of this room and all the garden was laid out dripping on the table. Chopped carrots like copper pennies, radishes and chives, potatoes dipped and stripped clean from their coats of mud, the snapping of tight pea-pods, long shells of green pearls, and the tearing of glutinous beans from their nests of wool.

[25] Grown stealthy, marauding among these preparations, one nibbled one's way like a rat through roots and leaves. Peas rolled under the tongue, fresh cold, like solid water; teeth chewed green peel of apples, acid sharp, and the sweet white starch of swedes. Beaten away by wet hands gloved with flour, one returned in a morose and speechless lust. Slivers of raw pastry, moulded, warm, went down in the shapes of men and women—heads and arms of unsalted flesh seasoned with nothing but a dream of cannibalism.

[26] Large meals were prepared in this room, cauldrons of stew for the insatiate hunger of eight. Stews of all that grew on these rich banks, flavoured with sage, coloured with Oxo and laced with a few bones of lamb. There was, it is true, little meat at those times; sometimes a pound of bare ribs for boiling, or an occasional rabbit dumped at the door by a neighbour. But there was green food of great weight in season, and lentils and bread for ballast. Eight to ten loaves came to the house every day, and they never grew dry. We tore them to pieces with their crusts still warm, and their monotony was brightened by the objects we found in them—string, nails, paper, and once a mouse; for those were days of happy-go-lucky baking. The lentils were cooked in a great pot which also heated the water for the Saturday-night baths. Our small wood fire could heat sufficient water to fill one bath only, and this we shared in turn. Being the youngest but one, my water was always the dirtiest but one, and the implications of this privilege remain with me to this day.

[27] Waking one morning in the white-washed bedroom, I opened my eyes and found them blind. Though I stretched them and stared where

the room should be, nothing was visible but a glare of gold, flat on my throbbing eyelids. I groped for my body and found it there. I heard the singing of birds. Yet there was nothing at all to be seen of the world save this quivering yellow light. Was I dead? I wondered. Was I in heaven? Whatever it was, I hated it. I had wakened too soon from a dream of crocodiles and I was not ready for this further outrage. Then I heard the girls' steps on the stairs.

[28] "Our Marge!" I shouted, "I can't see nothing!" And I began to give out my howl.

[29] A slap of bare feet slithered across the floor, and I heard sister Marjorie's giggle.

[30] "Just look at him," she said. "Pop and fetch a flannel, Doth—'is eyes've got stuck down again."

[31] The cold edge of the flannel passed over my face, showered me with water, and I was back in the world. Bed and beams, and the sun-square window, and the girls bending over me grinning.

[32] " 'Oo did it?" I yelled.

[33] "Nobody, silly. Your eyes got bunged up, that's all."

[34] The sweet glue of sleep; it had happened before but somehow I always forgot. So I threatened the girls I'd bung theirs up too; I was awake, I could see, I was happy. I lay looking out of the small green window. The world outside was crimson and on fire. I had never seen it looking like that before.

[35] "Doth?" I said, "what's happening to them trees?"

[36] Dorothy was dressing. She leaned out of the window, slow and sleepy, and the light came through her nightdress like sand through a sieve.

[37] "Nothing's happening," she said.

[38] "Yes it is then," I said. "They're falling to bits."

[39] Dorothy scratched her dark head, yawning wide, and white feathers floated out of her hair.

[40] "It's only the leaves droppin'. We're in autumn now. The leaves always drop in autumn."

[41] Autumn? In autumn. Was that where we were? Where the leaves always dropped and there was always this smell. I imagined it continuing, with no change, for ever, these wet flames of woods burning on and on like the bush of Moses, as natural a part of this newfound land as the eternal snows of the poles. Why had we come to such a place?

[42] Marjorie, who had gone down to help with the breakfast, suddenly came tumbling back up the stairs.

[43] "Doth," she whispered; she seemed excited and frightened; "Doth . . . 'e's turned up again. 'Elp on Loll with 'is clothes and come on down, quick."

[44] We went down and found him sitting by the fireside, smiling, wet and cold. I climbed up to the breakfast table and stared at him, the stranger. To me he did not so much appear to be a man as a conglomer-

ation of woody things. His face was red and crinkled, brilliant like fungus. There were leaves in his mud-matted hair, and leaves and twigs on his crumbling clothes, and all over him. His boots were like the back pulp you find when you dig under a tree. Mother gave him porridge and bread and he smiled palely at us all.

[45] "It must have been cruel in the wood," said our Mother.

[46] "I've got some sacks, ma'am," he said, spooning his porridge. "They keep out the wet."

[47] They wouldn't; they'd suck it up like a wick and wrap him in it.

[48] "You oughtn't to live like that," said Mother. "You ought to get back to your home."

[49] "No," smiled the man. "That wouldn't do. They'd jump on me before you could say 'knife.' "

[50] Mother shook her head sadly, and sighed, and gave him more porridge. We boys adored the look of the man; the girls, fastidious, were more uncertain of him. But he was no tramp or he wouldn't be in the kitchen. He had four bright medals in his pocket, which he would produce and polish and lay on the table like money. He spoke like nobody else we knew, in fact we couldn't understand many of his words. But Mother seemed to understand him, and would ask him questions, and look at the photographs he carried in his shirt and sigh and shake her head. He talked something of battles and of flying in the air, and it was all wonderful to us.

[51] He was no man from these parts. He had appeared on the doorstep one early morning, asking for a cup of tea. Our Mother had brought him in and given him a whole breakfast. There had been blood on his face and he had seemed very weak. Now he was in a kitchen with a woman and a lot of children, and his eyes shone brightly, and his whiskers smiled. He told us he was sleeping in the wood, which seemed to me a good idea. And he was a soldier, because Mother had said so.

[52] I knew about war; all my uncles were in it; my ears from birth had been full of the talk of it. Sometimes I used to climb into the basket chair by the fire and close my eyes and see brown men moving over a field in battle. I was three, but I saw them grope and die and felt myself older than they.

[53] This man did not look like a soldier. He had a beard and his khaki was torn. But the girls insisted he was a soldier, and said it in whispers, like a secret. And when he came down to our house for breakfast, and sat hunched by the fire, steaming with damp and coated with leaves and dirt, I thought of him sleeping up there in the wood. I imagined him sleeping, then having a go at the battle, then coming down to us for a cup of tea. He was the war, and the war was up there; I wanted to ask, "How's the war in that wood?"

[54] But he never told us. He sat drinking his tea, gulping and gasping, the fire drawing the damp out of his clothes as if ghosts were rising from him. When he caught our eyes he smiled from his beard. And

when brother Jack shot at him with a spoon, saying, "I'm a sodger," he replied softly, "Aye, and you'd make a better one than me, son, any day."

[55] When he said that, I wondered what had happened to the war. Was he in those rags because he was such a bad soldier? Had he lost the war in the wood?

[56] When he didn't come any more, I knew he had. The girls said some policemen had taken him away in a cart. And Mother sighed and was sad over the poor man.

[57] In weather that was new to me, and cold, and loud with bullying winds, my Mother disappeared to visit my father. This was a long way off, out of sight, and I don't remember her going. But suddenly there were only the girls in the house, tumbling about with brooms and dishcloths, arguing, quarrelling, and putting us to bed at random. House and food had a new smell, and meals appeared like dismal conjuring tricks: cold, raw, or black with too much fire. Marjorie was breathless and everywhere; she was fourteen, with all the family in her care. My socks slipped down, and stayed down. I went unwashed for long periods of time. Black leaves swept into the house and piled up in the corners; it rained, and the floors sweated, and washing filled all the lines in the kitchen and dripped sadly on one and all.

[58] But we ate; and the girls moved about in a giggling flurry, exhausted at their losing game. As the days went by, such a tide of muddles mounted in the house that I didn't know which room was which. I lived free, grubbing outside in the mud till I was black as a badger. And my nose ran free, as unchecked as my feet. I sailed my boots down the drain, I cut up sheets for puttees and marched like a soldier through the swamps of leaves. Sensing my chance I wandered far, eating all manner of raw objects: coloured berries, twigs and grubs; sick every day, but with a sickness of which I was proud.

[59] All this time the sisters went through the house, darting upstairs and down, beset on all sides by the rain coming in, boys growing filthier, sheets scorching, saucepans burning, and kettles boiling over. The doll's house became a madhouse, and the girls frail birds flying in a wind of chaos. Doth giggled helplessly, Phyl wept among the vegetables, and Marjorie would say, when the day was over: "I'd lie down and die, if there was a place to lie down in."

[60] I was not at all surprised when I heard of the end of the world. Everything pointed to it. The sky was low and whirling with black clouds; the woods roared night and day, stirring great seas of sound. One night we sat round the kitchen table, cracking walnuts with the best brass candlestick, when Marjorie came in from the town. She was shining with rain and loaded with bread and buns. She was also very white.

[61] "The war's over," she said. "It's ended."

[62] "Never," said Dorothy.

[63] "They told me at the Stores," said Marjorie. "And they were giving away prunes." She gave us a bagful, and we ate them raw.

FIRST LIGHT

[64] The girls got tea and talked about it. And I was sure it was the end of the world. All my life was the war, and the war was the world. Now the war was over. So the end of the world was come. It made no other sense to me.

[65] "Let's go out and see what's happening," said Doth.

[66] "You know we can't leave the kids," Marge said.

[67] So we went too. It was dark, and the gleaming roofs of the village echoed with the buzz of singing. We went hand in hand through the rain, up the bank and down the street. A bonfire crackled in one of the gardens, and a woman jumped up and down in the light of it, red as a devil, a jug in her hand, uttering cries that were not singing. All down the other gardens there were other bonfires too. And a man came up and kissed the girls and hopped in the road and twisted on one toe. Then he fell down in the mud and lay there, working his legs like a frog and croaking a loud song.

[68] I wanted to stop. I had never seen a man like this, in such a wild good humour. But we hurried on. We got to the pub and stared through the windows. The bar seemed on fire with its many lamps. Rose-coloured men, through the rain-wet windows, seemed to bulge and break into flame. They breathed out smoke, drank fire from golden jars, and I heard their great din with awe. Now anything might happen. And it did. A man rose up and crushed a glass like a nut between his hands, then held them out laughing for all to see his wounds. But the blood was lost in the general light of blood. Two other men came waltzing out of the door, locked in each other's arms. Fighting and cursing, they fell over the wall and rolled down the bank in the dark.

[69] There was a screaming woman we could not see. "Jimmy! Jimmy!" she wailed. "Oh, Jimmy! Thee s'll kill 'im! I'll fetch the vicar, I will! Oh, Jimmy!"

[70] "Just 'ark at 'em," said Dorothy, shocked and delighted.

[71] "The kids ought to be in bed," said Marjorie.

[72] "Stop a minute longer. Only a minute. It wouldn't do no 'arm."

[73] Then the schoolhouse chimney caught fire. A fountain of sparks shot high into the night, writhing and sweeping on the wind, falling and dancing along the road. The chimney hissed like a firework, great rockets of flame came gushing forth, emptying the tiny house, so that I expected to see chairs and tables, knives and forks, radiant and burning, follow. The moss-tiles smouldered with sulphurous soot, yellow jets of smoke belched from cracks in the chimney. We stood in the rain and watched it, entranced, as if the sight had been saved for this day. As if the house had been saved, together with the year's bad litter, to be sent up in flames and rejoicing.

[74] How everyone bellowed and scuffled and sang, drunk with their beer and the sight of the fire. But what would happen now that the war was over? What would happen to my uncles who lived in it?—those huge remote men who appeared suddenly at our house, reeking of leather

and horses. What would happen to our father, who was khakied like every other man, yet special, not like other men? His picture hung over the piano, trim, haughty, with a badged cap and a spiked moustache. I confused him with the Kaiser. Would he die now the war was over?

[75] As we gazed at the flaming schoolhouse chimney, and smelt the burning throughout the valley, I knew something momentous was occurring. At any moment I looked for a spectacular end to my already long life. Oh, the end of the war and the world! There was rain in my shoes, and Mother had disappeared. I never expected to see another day.

Questions on Meaning

1 In this selection, which is the first chapter of an autobiographical book, *The Edge of Day,* Lee weaves together several early-childhood impressions—his awareness of contrasting order and chaos in his life, his understanding and misunderstanding of the war, his feeling of closeness to his sisters and to nature. Like any first chapter of a book, this piece has as one of its purposes introducing what comes later. But there is a kind of unity here, a tying together of these several themes. How is it achieved? That is, what dominant impression of the author's early life underlies all that he says here? (Remember his title as you answer the question.)

2 Lee describes in considerable detail his boyhood home and its surroundings. State in your own words the significance Lee finds in this setting as he thinks back on early influences upon his development.

Questions on Style and Structure

1 One of the distinctive features of this selection is the frequent use of similes and metaphors. After consulting your dictionary for definitions of these terms, underline examples you find in Lee's writing. Which ones seem to be particularly effective? Which ones are ineffective? Do any seem to you to be odd or fanciful?

2 Another distinctive feature of this chapter is its vividness and concreteness. For example, all of paragraph 2 is devoted to a description of grass. Identify other passages that are similarly concrete. What would be lost if these passages were more abstract?

3 The first two sentences in paragraph 4 are parallel in structure. Can you find other examples of parallel sentences?

4 How effectively does Lee use dialogue in this autobiographical selection? Would paraphrased versions of the dialogue be as effective?

5 Much of the writing here is descriptive. Thus, the author appeals to the reader's various senses. Find examples of such sensory appeals (hearing, sight, touch, smell).

6 Why is the conclusion of the chapter appropriate? Look again at the first paragraph. How are the introduction and conclusion related?

Exploring Words

1 *garrulous*. Using your dictionary, find three words that mean approximately what *garrulous* means. Then try framing sentences for these words, noting the subtle distinctions your use of each implies.

2 *inexorable*. Look this word up in your dictionary, and then try using it with several different nouns. Then compare your phrases with Lee's "*inexorable* tradition."

3 *glutinous*. Write a sentence of your own using the word *glutinous*.

Suggestions for Writing

1 As Lee does, describe a significant childhood experience. Discuss the experience from both your present perspective and your childhood perspective.

2 In an essay, comment on your relationship with your parents or siblings as you were growing up.

The Spike
GEORGE ORWELL

Getting Started

With Ideas

You have probably not had any experience with, or even previously read about, the institution that gives this essay its title. And you may not find *spike,* in the sense that the word is used here, defined in your dictionary. But Orwell's precise account of an experience in a British spike in the 1930s makes very clear the purpose and the unique characteristics of that institution. As you read the essay, how soon do you become aware of that purpose and those characteristics?

With Words

1 riff-raff (1)—from the Middle English *rif and raf,* meaning "one and all."
2 panacea (13)—from the Greek words for "cure" and "all."
3 ineradicably (14)—from the Latin root meaning "root." What other *radic* words do you know that refer to roots in some sense?
4 iniquities (15)—from the Latin *aequus,* meaning "equal."
5 furtively (16)—the context should make this one clear.
6 ennui (27)—if you are not completely familiar with this word, which is borrowed from French, you should look it up, even in your first reading, because it occurs in a figure of speech that is close to the central meaning of the essay.

---

[1] It was late afternoon. Forty-nine of us, forty-eight men and one woman, lay on the green waiting for the spike to open. We were too tired to talk much. We just sprawled about exhaustedly, with homemade cigarettes sticking out of our scrubby faces. Overhead the chestnut branches were covered with blossom, and beyond that great woolly clouds floated almost motionless in a clear sky. Littered on the grass, we seemed dingy, urban riff-raff. We defiled the scene, like sardine-tins and paper bags on the seashore.

[2] What talk there was ran on the Tramp Major of this spike. He was a devil, everyone agreed, a tartar, a tyrant, a bawling, blasphemous, uncharitable dog. You couldn't call your soul your own when he was

From *The Collected Essays, Journalism and Letters of George Orwell,* Vol. I, edited by Sonia Orwell and Ian Angus, copyright © 1968 by Sonia Brownell Orwell. Reprinted by permission of Harcourt Brace Jovanovich, Inc.

about, and many a tramp had he kicked out in the middle of the night for giving a back answer. When you came to be searched he fair held you upside down and shook you. If you were caught with tobacco there was hell to pay, and if you went in with money (which is against the law) God help you.

[3] I had eightpence on me. "For the love of Christ, mate," the old hands advised me, "don't you take it in. You'd get seven days for going into the spike with eightpence!"

[4] So I buried my money in a hole under the hedge, marking the spot with a lump of flint. Then we set about smuggling our matches and tobacco, for it is forbidden to take these into nearly all spikes, and one is supposed to surrender them at the gate. We hid them in our socks, except for the twenty or so per cent who had no socks, and had to carry the tobacco in their boots, even under their very toes. We stuffed our ankles with contraband until anyone seeing us might have imagined an outbreak of elephantiasis. But it is an unwritten law that even the sternest Tramp Majors do not search below the knee, and in the end only one man was caught. This was Scotty, a little hairy tramp with a bastard accent sired by cockney out of Glasgow. His tin of cigarette ends fell out of his sock at the wrong moment, and was impounded.

[5] At six the gates swung open and we shuffled in. An official at the gate entered our names and other particulars in the register and took our bundles away from us. The woman was sent off to the workhouse, and we others into the spike. It was a gloomy, chilly, lime-washed place, consisting only of a bathroom and dining-room and about a hundred narrow stone cells. The terrible Tramp Major met us at the door and herded us into the bathroom to be stripped and searched. He was a gruff, soldierly man of forty, who gave the tramps no more ceremony than sheep at the dipping-pond, shoving them this way and that and shouting oaths in their faces. But when he came to myself, he looked hard at me, and said:

[6] "You are a gentleman?"

[7] "I suppose so," I said.

[8] He gave me another long look. "Well, that's bloody bad luck, guv'nor," he said, "that's bloody bad luck, that is." And thereafter he took it into his head to treat me with compassion, even with a kind of respect.

[9] It was a disgusting sight, that bathroom. All the indecent secrets of our underwear were exposed; the grime, the rents and patches, the bits of string doing duty for buttons, the layers upon layers of fragmentary garments, some of them mere collections of holes held together by dirt. The room became a press of steaming nudity, the sweaty odours of the tramps competing with the sickly, sub-faecal stench native to the spike. Some of the men refused the bath, and washed only their "toe-rags", the horrid, greasy little clouts which tramps bind round their feet. Each of us had three minutes in which to bathe himself. Six greasy, slippery roller towels had to serve for the lot of us.

[10] When we had bathed our own clothes were taken away from us,

and we were dressed in the workhouse shirts, grey cotton things like nightshirts, reaching to the middle of the thigh. Then we were sent into the dining-room, where supper was set out on the deal tables. It was the invariable spike meal, always the same, whether breakfast, dinner or supper—half a pound of bread, a bit of margarine, and a pint of so-called tea. It took us five minutes to gulp down the cheap, noxious food. Then the Tramp Major served us with three cotton blankets each, and drove us off to our cells for the night. The doors were locked on the outside a little before seven in the evening, and would stay locked for the next twelve hours.

[11] The cells measured eight feet by five, and had no lighting apparatus except a tiny, barred window high up in the wall, and a spyhole in the door. There were no bugs, and we had bedsteads and straw palliasses, rare luxuries both. In many spikes one sleeps on a wooden shelf, and in some on the bare floor, with a rolled-up coat for pillow. With a cell to myself, and a bed, I was hoping for a sound night's rest. But I did not get it, for there is always something wrong in the spike, and the peculiar shortcoming here, as I discovered immediately, was the cold. May had begun, and in honour of the season—a little sacrifice to the gods of spring, perhaps—the authorities had cut off the steam from the hot pipes. The cotton blankets were almost useless. One spent the night in turning from side to side, falling asleep for ten minutes and waking half frozen, and watching for dawn.

[12] As always happens in the spike, I had at last managed to fall comfortably asleep when it was time to get up. The Tramp Major came marching down the passage with his heavy tread, unlocking the doors and yelling to us to show a leg. Promptly the passage was full of squalid shirt-clad figures rushing for the bathroom, for there was only one tub full of water between us all in the morning, and it was first come first served. When I arrived twenty tramps had already washed their faces. I gave one glance at the black scum on top of the water, and decided to go dirty for the day.

[13] We hurried into our clothes, and then went to the dining-room to bolt our breakfast. The bread was much worse than usual, because the military-minded idiot of a Tramp Major had cut it into slices overnight, so that it was as hard as ship's biscuit. But we were glad of our tea after the cold, restless night. I do not know what tramps would do without tea, or rather the stuff they miscall tea. It is their food, their medicine, their panacea for all evils. Without the half gallon or so of it that they suck down a day, I truly believe they could not face their existence.

[14] After breakfast we had to undress again for the medical inspection, which is a precaution against smallpox. It was three-quarters of an hour before the doctor arrived, and one had time now to look about him and see what manner of men we were. It was an instructive sight. We stood shivering naked to the waist in two long ranks in the passage. The filtered light, bluish and cold, lighted us up with unmerciful clarity. No one can imagine, unless he has seen such a thing, what pot-bellied, degen-

erate curs we looked. Shock heads, hairy, crumpled faces, hollow chests, flat feet, sagging muscles—every kind of malformation and physical rottenness were there. All were flabby and discoloured, as all tramps are under their deceptive sunburn. Two or three figures seen there stay ineradicably in my mind. Old "Daddy," aged seventy-four, with his truss, and his red, watering eyes: a herring-gutted starveling, with sparse beard and sunken cheeks, looking like the corpse of Lazarus in some primitive picture: an imbecile, wandering hither and thither with vague giggles, coyly pleased because his trousers constantly slipped down and left him nude. But few of us were greatly better than these; there were not ten decently built men among us, and half, I believe, should have been in hospital.

[15] This being Sunday, we were to be kept in the spike over the weekend. As soon as the doctor had gone we were herded back to the dining-room, and its door shut upon us. It was a lime-washed, stone-floored room, unspeakably dreary with its furniture of deal boards and benches, and its prison smell. The windows were so high up that one could not look outside, and the sole ornament was a set of Rules threatening dire penalties to any casual who misconducted himself. We packed the room so tight that one could not move an elbow without jostling somebody. Already, at eight o'clock in the morning, we were bored with our captivity. There was nothing to talk about except the petty gossip of the road, the good and bad spikes, the charitable and uncharitable counties, the iniquities of the police and the Salvation Army. Tramps hardly ever get away from these subjects; they talk, as it were, nothing but shop. They have nothing worthy to be called conversation, because emptiness of belly leaves no speculation in their souls. The world is too much with them. Their next meal is never quite secure, and so they cannot think of anything except the next meal.

[16] Two hours dragged by. Old Daddy, witless with age, sat silent, his back bent like a bow and his inflamed eyes dripping slowly on to the floor. George, a dirty old tramp notorious for the queer habit of sleeping in his hat, grumbled about a parcel of tommy that he had lost on the road. Bill the moocher, the best built man of us all, a Herculean sturdy beggar who smelt of beer even after twelve hours in the spike, told tales of mooching, of pints stood him in the boozers, and of a parson who had peached to the police and got him seven days. William and Fred, two young ex-fishermen from Norfolk, sang a sad song about Unhappy Bella, who was betrayed and died in the snow. The imbecile drivelled about an imaginary toff who had once given him two hundred and fifty-seven golden sovereigns. So the time passed, with dull talk and dull obscenities. Everyone was smoking, except Scotty, whose tobacco had been seized, and he was so miserable in his smokeless state that I stood him the makings of a cigarette. We smoked furtively, hiding our cigarettes like schoolboys when we heard the Tramp Major's step, for smoking, though connived at, was officially forbidden.

[17] Most of the tramps spent ten consecutive hours in this dreary

room. It is hard to imagine how they put up with it. I have come to think that boredom is the worst of all a tramp's evils, worse than hunger and discomfort, worse even than the constant feeling of being socially disgraced. It is a silly piece of cruelty to confine an ignorant man all day with nothing to do; it is like chaining a dog in a barrel. Only an educated man, who has consolations within himself, can endure confinement. Tramps, unlettered types as nearly all of them are, face their poverty with blank, resourceless minds. Fixed for ten hours on a comfortless bench, they know no way of occupying themselves, and if they think at all it is to whimper about hard luck and pine for work. They have not the stuff in them to endure the horrors of idleness. And so, since so much of their lives is spent in doing nothing, they suffer agonies from boredom.

[18] I was much luckier than the others, because at ten o'clock the Tramp Major picked me out for the most coveted of all jobs in the spike, the job of helping in the workhouse kitchen. There was not really any work to be done there, and I was able to make off and hide in a shed used for storing potatoes, together with some workhouse paupers who were skulking to avoid the Sunday morning service. There was a stove burning there, and comfortable packing cases to sit on, and back numbers of the *Family Herald,* and even a copy of *Raffles* from the workhouse library. It was paradise after the spike.

[19] Also, I had my dinner from the workhouse table, and it was one of the biggest meals I have ever eaten. A tramp does not see such a meal twice in the year, in the spike or out of it. The paupers told me that they always gorged to the bursting point on Sundays, and went hungry six days of the week. When the meal was over the cook set me to do the washing-up, and told me to throw away the food that remained. The wastage was astonishing; great dishes of beef, and bucketfuls of bread and vegetables, were pitched away like rubbish, and then defiled with tealeaves. I filled five dustbins to overflowing with good food. And while I did so my fellow tramps were sitting two hundred yards away in the spike, their bellies half filled with the spike dinner of the everlasting bread and tea, and perhaps two cold boiled potatoes each in honour of Sunday. It appeared that the food was thrown away from deliberate policy, rather than that it should be given to the tramps.

[20] At three I left the workhouse kitchen and went back to the spike. The boredom in that crowded, comfortless room was now unbearable. Even smoking had ceased, for a tramp's only tobacco is picked-up cigarette ends, and, like a browsing beast, he starves if he is long away from the pavement-pasture. To occupy the time I talked with a rather superior tramp, a young carpenter who wore a collar and tie, and was on the road, he said, for lack of a set of tools. He kept a little aloof from the other tramps, and held himself more like a free man than a casual. He had literary tastes, too, and carried one of Scott's novels on all his wanderings. He told me he never entered a spike unless driven there by hunger, sleeping under hedges and behind ricks in preference. Along the south coast he had begged by day and slept in bathing-machines for weeks at a time.

[21] We talked of life on the road. He criticised the system which makes a tramp spend fourteen hours a day in the spike, and the other ten in walking and dodging the police. He spoke of his own case—six months at the public charge for want of three pounds' worth of tools. It was idiotic, he said.

[22] Then I told him about the wastage of food in the workhouse kitchen, and what I thought of it. And at that he changed his tune immediately. I saw that I had awakened the pew-renter who sleeps in every English workman. Though he had been famished along with the rest, he at once saw reasons why the food should have been thrown away rather than given to the tramps. He admonished me quite severely.

[23] "They have to do it," he said. "If they made these places too pleasant you'd have all the scum of the country flocking into them. It's only the bad food as keeps all that scum away. These tramps are too lazy to work, that's all that's wrong with them. You don't want to go encouraging of them. They're scum."

[24] I produced arguments to prove him wrong, but he would not listen. He kept repeating:

[25] "You don't want to have any pity on these tramps—scum, they are. You don't want to judge them by the same standards as men like you and me. They're scum, just scum."

[26] It was interesting to see how subtly he disassociated himself from his fellow tramps. He has been on the road six months, but in the sight of God, he seemed to imply, he was not a tramp. His body might be in the spike, but his spirit soared far away, in the pure aether of the middle classes.

[27] The clock's hands crept round with excruciating slowness. We were too bored even to talk now, the only sound was of oaths and reverberating yawns. One would force his eyes away from the clock for what seemed an age, and then look back again to see that the hands had advanced three minutes. Ennui clogged our souls like cold mutton fat. Our bones ached because of it. The clock's hands stood at four, and supper was not till six, and there was nothing left remarkable beneath the visiting moon.

[28] At last six o'clock did come, and the Tramp Major and his assistant arrived with supper. The yawning tramps brisked up like lions at feeding-time. But the meal was a dismal disappointment. The bread, bad enough in the morning, was now positively uneatable; it was so hard that even the strongest jaws could make little impression on it. The older men went almost supperless, and not a man could finish his portion, hungry though most of us were. When we had finished, the blankets were served out immediately, and we were hustled off once more to the bare, chilly cells.

[29] Thirteen hours went by. At seven we were awakened, and rushed forth to squabble over the water in the bathroom, and bolt our ration of bread and tea. Our time in the spike was up, but we could not go until the doctor had examined us again, for the authorities have a terror of

smallpox and its distribution by tramps. The doctor kept us waiting two hours this time, and it was ten o'clock before we finally escaped.

[30] At last it was time to go, and we were let out into the yard. How bright everything looked, and how sweet the winds did blow, after the gloomy, reeking spike! The Tramp Major handed each man his bundle of confiscated possessions, and a hunk of bread and cheese for midday dinner, and then we took the road, hastening to get out of sight of the spike and its discipline. This was our interim of freedom. After a day and two nights of wasted time we had eight hours or so to take our recreation, to scour the roads for cigarette ends, to beg, and to look for work. Also, we had to make our ten, fifteen, or it might be twenty miles to the next spike, where the game would begin anew.

[31] I disinterred my eightpence and took the road with Nobby, a respectable, downhearted tramp who carried a spare pair of boots and visited all the Labour Exchanges. Our late companions were scattering north, south, east and west, like bugs into a mattress. Only the imbecile loitered at the spike gates, until the Tramp Major had to chase him away.

[32] Nobby and I set out for Croydon. It was a quiet road, there were no cars passing, the blossom covered the chestnut trees like great wax candles. Everything was so quiet and smelt so clean, it was hard to realise that only a few minutes ago we had been packed with that band of prisoners in a stench of drains and soft soap. The others had all disappeared; we two seemed to be the only tramps on the road.

[33] Then I heard a hurried step behind me, and felt a tap on my arm. It was little Scotty, who had run panting after us. He pulled a rusty tin box from his pocket. He wore a friendly smile, like a man who is repaying an obligation.

[34] "Here y'are, mate," he said cordially. "I owe you some fag ends. You stood me a smoke yesterday. The Tramp Major give me back my box of fag ends when we come out this morning. One good turn deserves another—here y'are."

[35] And he put four sodden, debauched, loathly cigarette ends into my hand.

Questions on Meaning

1 Now that you know what a spike is, with which institutions in present-day American society would you compare it? In what ways?

2 Which features of life in a spike did Orwell find most disagreeable? Which did he find most unjust? Why?

3 Contrast Orwell's basic attitude toward the men who stay in spikes with the attitude the operators of these establishments have toward these "tramps."

4 How would you describe Orwell's underlying feeling about the spike as an institution?

THE SPIKE

5 In what sense does the Tramp Major use "gentleman" in paragraph 6? Why does the writer answer, "I suppose so," when asked if he is a gentleman?

Questions on Style and Structure

1 Like other selections in this section, this essay is organized chronologically. What transitional devices does Orwell use to tie the narrative together?

2 What major purpose does the introductory paragraph accomplish? How does it do so?

3 What kinds of sensory appeals does Orwell make in the selection? Which sense(s) does he appeal to most?

4 In paragraph 15, there is an allusion to Wordsworth's sonnet "The World Is Too Much with Us." Read the poem; then decide whether the allusion is appropriate and effective.

The world is too much with us; late and soon,
Getting and spending, we lay waste our powers;
Little we see in Nature that is ours;
We have given our hearts away, a sordid boon!
This sea that bares her bosom to the moon,
The winds that will be howling at all hours,
And are up-gathered now like sleeping flowers,
For this, for everything, we are out of tune;
It moves us not. —Great God! I'd rather be
A Pagan suckled in a creed outworn;
So might I, standing on this pleasant lea,
Have glimpses that would make me less forlorn;
Have sight of Proteus rising from the sea;
Or hear old Triton blow his wreathèd horn.

5 Orwell uses a number of similes in his account (for example, "Our late companions were scattering north, south, east and west, like bugs into a mattress"). Identify these similes and comment on their appropriateness.

6 How does Orwell achieve paragraph unity? Note, for example, paragraphs 9 and 11 and others you find striking in unity.

7 How does Orwell achieve coherence in paragraph 2?

8 Paragraph 2 is devoted to a description of the Tramp Major. He is described as a "devil." What words with similar connotations does Orwell use in that paragraph?

9 Orwell uses a number of British colloquialisms and slang expressions. Which words do you think fit this category? Can you determine their meanings from their contexts?

10 Is the last sentence an appropriate ending for the essay? Why? How is the conclusion tied in with the opening sentence?

Exploring Words

1 *riff-raff.* Look up the origin and development of this word in your dictionary. What relationship do you find between the meaning given for the Middle English expression and that for the modern word? *Riff-raff* is usually considered slang or near-slang. Is it an appropriate expression for Orwell to use here? Look up *hoi polloi* and note the similarity of its development. Can you think of other words that have undergone the same kind of transformation?

2 *panacea.* What connotations do you find in Orwell's use of this term? As you have been discovering, words have different shades of meaning depending on their context. In what contexts have you heard the word *panacea* used?

3 *ineradicably.* Look up the several meanings of the word *radical.* Which would you consider metaphorical? How do these several meanings relate to the Latin root *radic*? Can you think of other words that have undergone similar metaphorical development (for example, *branch* as in "a branch of mathematics")?

4 *iniquities.* Look up *iniquity* and *inequity,* and be prepared to explain how both could have developed from the same root. Do you think Orwell could have used *inequities* here? If so, which word do you prefer in this context?

5 *furtively.* After you have noted Orwell's use of this word and confirmed your impressions of its meaning by checking your dictionary, write a sentence of your own using the word appropriately.

6 *ennui.* Are there any clues in the etymology of *ennui* that suggest why Orwell used this word rather than *boredom*? (Here, of course, he may have used it partly to avoid repetition.)

Suggestions for Writing

1 Think of an "institution" (for example, an organization or a group enterprise of some sort) that you know well through personal experience but that most people have probably never heard of—perhaps a high school club, a college fraternity, a community or church committee, or even an unusual class with a special purpose or instructional plan. The very name of this organization or group project will probably mean a great deal to you but very little to most others. Use this name as the title of a paper and write an account of one experience that name brings to mind. As Orwell did in "The Spike," concentrate on sharing with your readers an attitude you have toward this "institution," letting the attitude come out through your narrative rather than stating it directly.

2 As Orwell does, describe a place as vividly as you can (for example, a nursing home, an institution for the retarded, an Army induction center). Appeal to your readers' sense organs (touch, hearing, and so on). Try to influence their attitudes toward this place through careful word choice. Try your hand, too, at the appropriate use of figurative language (but try to avoid hackneyed language).

The Consolations of Illiteracy
PHYLLIS MCGINLEY

Getting Started

With Ideas

Both the title and the one-sentence first paragraph of this essay suggest that the writer is using an unusual tone. You may find it helpful to know that Phyllis McGinley is a well-known writer of humorous light verse. But while her language here is casual and sometimes exaggerated and her remarks often facetious, much of the time she signals to the thoughtful reader that she means exactly what she says.

With Words

1 decorous (4)—associating the word with *decor* and *decorum* will help you determine its meaning.
2 disparate (9)—associate this word with the noun *disparity*.
3 surfeit (16)—the source of this word means "to overdo."

---

[1] There is something to be said for a bad education.

[2] By any standards mine was deplorable; and I deplored it for years, in private and in public. I flaunted it as if it were a medal, a kind of cultural Purple Heart which both excused my deficiencies and lent luster to my mild achievements. But as time goes on I murmur against it less. I find that even ignorance has its brighter side.

[3] For if I grew up no better instructed about the world of books than was Columbus about global geography, I had in store for me, as he did, the splendors of discovery. There is such a thing as a literary landscape; to that, to nearly the whole length and breadth of classic English writing, I came as an astonished stranger. No one who first enters that country on a conducted tour can have any notion what it is like to travel it alone, on foot, and at his own pace.

[4] I am not exaggerating. My education really was bad. As a child I lived on a ranch in Colorado with the nearest one-room schoolhouse four miles away and the roads nearly impassable in winter. Sometimes there

"The Consolations of Illiteracy" appeared in *Saturday Review*, August 1, 1953. Copyright 1953 by *Saturday Review*. Reprinted by permission of *Saturday Review*.

was no teacher for the school, sometimes my brother and I were the only pupils. If there was a public library within practical distance I never learned of it. We were a reading family but my father's library ran chiefly to history and law and the collected works of Bulwer-Lytton. I wolfed down what I could but found a good deal of it indigestible. In my teens neither the public high school of a very small Western town nor the decorous boarding school I later attended made much effort to mend the damage. It seems to me now that we were always having to make reports on "Ivanhoe" or repeat from memory passages from Burke's "Speech on Conciliation." I think in two separate English classes we spent most of the year parsing "Snowbound."

[5] However, it was at college I seriously managed to learn nothing. My alma mater was one of those universities founded and supplied by the state which in the West everybody attends as automatically as kindergarten. There are—or were then—no entrance examinations. Anybody could come and everybody did, for the proms and the football games; and they sat under a faculty which for relentless mediocrity must have outstripped any in the land. So by putting my mind to it, I was able to emerge from four years there quite uncorrupted by knowledge. Let me amend that to literary knowledge. Somewhere along the line, out of a jumble of courses in Sociology, Household Chemistry, Hygiene, Beginner's German, I remember picking up bits and pieces of learning designed to enrich my life: the Theory of Refrigeration; the fact that Old German and Anglo-Saxon were two languages balefully akin and equally revolting; and the law about no offspring's having eyes darker than the eyes of the darker of his two parents. I had also, in one semester, been made to bolt Shakespeare entire, including the sonnets; and the result of such forced feeding had left me with an acute allergy to the Bard I was years getting over. Otherwise, few Great Books had impinged on my life. Through a complicated system of juggling credits and wheedling heads of departments, I had been able to evade even the Standard General Survey of English Literature.

[6] I had read things, of course. I was even considered quite a bookworm by my sorority sisters, who had given up going to the library after polishing off "The Wizard of Oz." But it was the contemporaries who occupied me. I had read Mencken but not Marlowe, Atherton but not Austen, Hoffenstein but not Herrick, Shaw but not Swift, Kipling but not Keats, Millay but not Marvell. Unbelievable as it may seem to an undergraduate, I had never even read A. E. Housman. Although I had scribbled verses in my notebooks during geology lectures, I had not so much as heard of Herbert or Donne or Gay or Prior or Hopkins. I had shunned Chaucer and avoided Dryden. Oliver Goldsmith I knew by hearsay as the author of a dull novel called "The Vicar of Wakefield." Milton had written solely in order to plague the young with "Il Penseroso." I hadn't read "Vanity Fair" or "Ethan Frome" or "Essay on Man" or "Anna Karenina" or "The Hound of Heaven" or "The Dubliners." (Joyce was a contemporary

but the furore over "Ulysses" was a mist that obscured his younger work.) Almost none of the alleged classics, under whose burden the student is supposed to bow, had I peered into either for pleasure or for credit.

[7] As a consequence, although I came to them late, I came to them without prejudice. We met on a basis completely friendly; and I do not think the well-educated can always claim as much.

[8] I commiserate, indeed, with people for whom "Silas Marner" was once required reading. They tell me it left permanent scars on their childhood; and I am certain they could not approach George Eliot as open-mindedly as I did, only a year or two ago, when I tried "Adam Bede" as one might try for the first time an olive. "But it's magnificent!" I went around exclaiming to my friends. "I've been deceived! You told me Eliot was dull."

[9] I pity the unlucky ones who wrote compositions on "Richardson as the Father of the English Novel." They could never come, relaxed and amused, upon "Pamela" as if it were a brand-new book. The literate may cherish as dearly as I do such disparate joys as "The Deserted Village" or "Pride and Prejudice" or "Old Curiosity Shop" or "The Bostonians." I do not think, however, they feel the same proprietary delight as I do toward them. Behind those pages, for me, hovers no specter of the classroom and the looseleaf notebook. Each is my own discovery.

[10] Often such discoveries have been embarrassing. Once I had begun to read for pleasure in a century not my own, I kept stumbling across treasures new to me only. I remember when I first pulled "Cranford" out of a boarding-house bookcase shortly after I had left college. For weeks I kept buttonholing my friends to insist they taste with me that remarkable and charming tidbit written by some unheard-of wit who signed herself simply "Mrs. Gaskell." And I recall how I blushed to learn they had nearly all read it—and disliked it—as juniors. Although I no longer go about beating the drum for each masterpiece I unearth, neither am I apologetic about someone's having been there before me. After all, Cortez (or Balboa, if one insists on being literal) must have known, when he surveyed the Pacific from that peak in Darien, that generations of Indians had seen it earlier. But the view was new to him. His discovery was important because it came at the right time in his career.

[11] So mine have come. There are books that one needs maturity to enjoy just as there are books an adult can come on too late to savor. I have never, for instance, been able to get through "Wuthering Heights." That I should have read before I was sixteen. I shall never even *try* "Treasure Island," which I missed at twelve.

[12] On the other hand, no child can possibly appreciate "Huckleberry Finn." That is not to say he can find no pleasure in it. He can and does. But it takes a grown-up to realize its wry and wonderful bouquet. Imagine opening it for the first time at forty! That was my reward for an underprivileged youth. For that Mark Twain shall have my heart and hand forever in spite of what he said about Jane Austen. "It's a pity they let her

die a natural death," he wrote to William Dean Howells. Perhaps the young Samuel Clemens read her as part of a prescribed curricula. Otherwise how could even that opinionated and undereducated genius have so misjudged an ironic talent more towering than his own? Had I been younger than thirty when I first happened on Miss Austen I might have found her dry. Had I read her much later I might have been too dry, myself. Her season suited me.

[13] For no matter how enchanting to the young are the realms of gold, maturity makes one a better traveler there. Do not misunderstand me. I wish with all my heart that I had taken to the road earlier—I do not boast because I was provincial so long. But since I began the journey late, I make use of what advantages I have. So for one thing, I capitalize on my lack of impatience. I am not on fire to see everything at once. There is no goal I must reach by any sunset. And how fresh all the landscape is to me! I wander as far afield as I care to, one range of hills opens out into another which I shall explore in due time. I move forward or backward. I retrace my steps when I please. I fall in love with the formal grandeur of the eighteenth century and stop there for as many months as the mood holds. Boswell's "London Journal" leads me back into Johnson himself and into the whole great age. I read Pope and Gray and Goldsmith and backward still through Richardson and Fielding. I read the letters and diaries of Miss Burney because Dr. Johnson calls her his "dear little Fanny." (The view there is unimportant but amusing.) And that leads me forward once more to Jane Austen. I could not proceed at a pace so leisurely were I twenty once more and in haste to keep up with the fashionable cults. I go where I like. I read Gibbon one week and Sarah Orne Jewett the next, with catholic pleasure. Henry James entertains me not because he is in the mode but because he is enthralling, and I continue to prefer "The Bostonians" to "The Golden Bowl." I do not need to praise Kafka; and I can keep Montaigne and Clarence Day and Coleridge on the same bedside stand.

[14] Because I am grown-up I am under no compulsion from either the critics or the professors to like *anything*. If I try "Tristam Shandy" and find it heavy going, I admit it and never open the second volume. If I do not agree with the world that "Moby Dick" is the Great American Novel, studded with the richest possible symbolism, I need not pretend to enjoy Melville. I think Trollope dull. That is nothing against Trollope; I need not dwell in the country he has invented.

[15] And it is wonderful to be a member of no party! I pick my own way among the landmarks. No Baedaker distracts me from the scenery. I can be behind-times enough to like Tennyson and Browning. I can prefer Crawshaw to Donne and Willa Cather to Ronald Firbank. I can read (and disagree with) Virginia Woolf on Monday and on Tuesday begin an amiable quarrel with Newman; nor do I find it a dizzy flight. And so much still to see! Peak upon peak unfolds. But there are also delightful little fenced fields and flowery culverts where I can rest when I do not wish to

climb. I have not yet read "War and Peace." But then I've never ready anything by Rider Haggard, either, or Wilkie Collins, or anything of Mary Webb's except "Precious Bane." I haven't read Pepys's Diary or Katherine Mansfield's. I have "The House of Seven Gables" ahead of me, and I have also "Our Mutual Friend."

[16] For of all my discoveries, nearly the most breathless was Dickens, himself. How many of the educated can even suspect the delights of such a delayed encounter? I think we owned a "Collected Works" when I was a child. But I had tried "David Copperfield" too early and had believed all my life that he was not for me. One night last winter I was sleepless and somehow without a book. From our own shelves I took down "Little Dorrit," which people tell me now is one of the least beguiling of the lot. But Keats first looking on his Homer could have been no more dazzled than I first poring on my Boz. I felt as a treasure-hunter might feel had he tripped over the locked chest that belonged to Captain Kidd. "Oh, my America, my new-found land!" How many novels were there? Thirty-odd? And every one of them still to be possessed! I got as drunk on Dickens for a while as I used to on the Cavalier poets when I first discovered *them*. I read in quick succession, "Great Expectations," "Martin Chuzzlewit," "Oliver Twist," "The Pickwick Papers," the very "David Copperfield" which had once put me off, and then the preposterous, magnificent, exasperating, ridiculous, and utterly engrossing "Bleak House." I stopped there for fear I should have a surfeit; but it's consoling to know the rest of the novels are there waiting for me, none of them grown stale or too familiar for enjoyment.

[17] There is still much to deplore about my education. I shall never read Latin verse in the original or have a taste for the Brontës, and those are crippling lacks. But all handicaps have compensations and I have learned to accept both cheerfully. To have first met Dickens, Austen, and Mark Twain when I was capable of giving them the full court curtsy is beatitude enough for any reader. Blessed are the illiterate, for they shall inherit the Word!

Questions on Meaning

1 Summarize Phyllis McGinley's opinions of her formal schooling, showing what she found lacking in her elementary, secondary, and college programs.

2 What are the "consolations" McGinley finds in the "bad education" she received? Is she recommending bad schools for everyone? What are the values she finds in the kind of literary self-education she has been experiencing?

3 The author compares herself with several explorers. Who are these people and what does she feel she has in common with them?

Questions on Style and Structure

1 One of the distinctive features of this essay is its rich use of figurative language. Underline all the passages containing metaphors and similes. Pay particular attention to the kinds of metaphors and similes that McGinley uses to describe books and the pleasures of reading. You might categorize these under such headings as "Images of Discovery," "Images of Tasting and Eating," and so forth.

2 Reproduced here is Keats's famous sonnet "On First Looking into Chapman's Homer," which McGinley alludes to in paragraph 10. Where else does she allude to the poem? Why are these allusions appropriate?

> Much have I traveled in the realms of gold,
> And many goodly states and kingdoms seen;
> Round many western islands have I been
> Which bards in fealty to Apollo hold.
> Oft of one wide expanse had I been told
> That deep-browed Homer ruled as his demesne;
> Yet did I never breathe its pure serene
> Till I heard Chapman speak out loud and bold:
> Then felt I like some watcher of the skies
> When a new planet swims into his ken;
> Or like stout Cortez when with eagle eyes
> He stared at the Pacific—and all his men
> Looked at each other with a wild surmise—
> Silent, upon a peak in Darien.

George Chapman was a translator of Homer's *The Iliad* and *The Odyssey*. Keats's poem contains an error; it was Balboa who "stared at the Pacific" from "a peak in Darien."

3 Is the division between paragraphs 1 and 2 justified?

4 Like other authors represented in this anthology, McGinley is careful to unify her paragraphs. Note, for example, paragraph 5. What is her topic statement? What other paragraphs do you find particularly unified? Would you agree that her paragraphs are concretely developed?

5 What is the topic statement of paragraph 6?

6 In paragraph 6, what technique for emphasis does the author use in the following passage? "I had read Mencken but not Marlowe, Atherton but not Austen, Hoffenstein but not Herrick, Shaw but not Swift, Kipling but not Keats, Millay but not Marvell." Account for the particular manner in which she has paired the authors (why not, for example, "Kipling but not Swift"?).

7 The first sentence of paragraph 5 is ostensibly paradoxical: "However, it was at college I *seriously* managed to *learn nothing.*" Are there other paradoxical statements in that paragraph?

Exploring Words

1 *decorous*. What kinds of activities did you engage in recently that someone might consider *decorous* or *indecorous*. See your dictionary's definition of both words.

2 *disparate*. Write a sentence about your current course work using the adjective *disparate*.

3 *surfeit*. Check your dictionary, and then think of at least three things of which you have recently had a *surfeit* (besides dictionary work).

Suggestions for Writing

1 Write an essay—humorous or serious—pointing out a strength or a weakness in your own education.

2 Discuss the pleasures you have found in reading, focusing perhaps on one type of reading you especially enjoy.

3 Write an essay entitled "The Consolations of ———."

Trials of a Word-watcher
CHARLTON OGBURN, JR.

Getting Started

With Ideas

In his opening paragraphs, Ogburn admits (by implication) that he is a "purist" and a "word-watcher." After you have read the first two paragraphs, ask yourself what *tone* the writer is adopting, that is, what attitude he is expressing toward the behavior he describes. Does he recommend "word-watching" as a hobby, or is he laughing at himself for engaging in it? Then read on to see how he develops his point, using the special tone he has established at the beginning.

With Words

1 abomination (1)—think of the so-called *"Abominable* Snowman."
2 flatulent (4)—from the Latin word *flatus* ("act of blowing"). Note that though physicians use the word to refer to gases produced in the bowels, Ogburn is using the word in a metaphorical sense.
3 travesty (5)—you are probably familiar with the use of this word in the phrase "a *travesty* of justice."
4 philatelist (7)—the context should be helpful here. What would an American collect that issues from Mauritius, a tiny island in the Indian Ocean?
5 vainglory (7)—what would you expect a word based upon the adjective form of *vanity* and the word *glory* (as related to *glorify*) to mean?
6 heinous (13)—from the Middle English word for *hateful.*
7 extirpated (14)—the context and your familiarity with the prefix *ex-* should make the meaning clear.
8 colloquial (26)—the middle portion of this word is related to *loquacious* and *locution.*

---

[1] Recently I was at a party at which one of the guests spoke of a collision of airplanes in mid air. "Mid air," another of the guests—a magazine editor—repeated with a smile. "Airplanes always collide in *mid* air. One wonders where else in the air they could collide." His manner was

"Trials of a Word-watcher," copyright © 1965 by Charlton Ogburn, Jr. Appeared originally in *Harper's Magazine*, April 1965. Reprinted by permission of McIntosh and Otis, Inc.

amused, off-hand.[1] But I did not miss the working of his jaw-muscles, the clenching of his fists. Here, confronted by a pet abomination, was a fellow-martyr to that condition known by the inadequate and not very descriptive term of *purism*, defined by the *Oxford English Dictionary* as "scrupulous or exaggerated observance of, or insistence upon, purity or correctness, esp. in language or style."

[2] Until that moment I had employed the expression *mid air* with contentment and assurance. I now felt that all my life my intelligence had been insulted by it. I experienced the exhilaration of an obsessive collector who unexpectedly acquires a prize. At the same time, my heart sank as I recognized that I had taken on another distraction, an increment to a burden under which I was already staggering. A sultan who has added a notable beauty to a harem already ruinous in its demands upon him would know what I mean.

[3] Purism is like alcoholism or drug-addiction. Once it takes hold, the victim's most heroic efforts of will to combat it are likely to prove inadequate. I had found this out during the years I spent in the government. I was supposed to be an official charged (in government terminology) with substantive responsibilities. Yet all the while, possibly because of the kind of thing I had to spend my time reading, I found myself falling ever more deeply under the sway of an ever-proliferating array of bugaboos of syntax and vocabulary and becoming a mere compulsive proof-reader. "Cannot help but believe new regime certain grow disenchanted its present internatl assocs," I would read in a telegram from an overseas post, but instead of considering whether my superiors should not be "alerted" (ugh!) to the opportunities such a development would open for the U.S., I would be sent off on a tangent by the reporting officer's English. "It is not enough that he cannot but believe," I would mutter. "It is not enough that he cannot help believing. Nothing will do but that he *cannot help but* believe!"

[4] One does not, of course, have to be a fetishist about words to be put off by the flatulent jargon endemic in bureaucracies. ("Prior to implementation of approved directives, all concerned agencies will consult as to appropriate instrumentalities.") But worse than that, to one who suffers from morbid inflammation of the word-consciousness, are the affronts to grammar habitually employed in the government with an air of professionalism—such as, for example, "hopefully" used to mean "I hope" or "it is to be hoped." You read, "Hopefully, the government of X will see the error of its present course in time," and your morning is ruined. You start imagining where the precedent could lead: "Fearfully, the government of X will not see its error in time. . . . Expectfully, the U.S. will have to bail it out."

[5] Then there is that "effective immediately" routine, with which notices begin. I used to have a day-dream in which I got back at my superiors who, among their other trying ways, permitted this travesty of Eng-

---

[1] The author's system of hyphenation has been followed faithfully throughout this article.

lish. In it, I would appear before them to reply to the charge of having failed to comply with an order stating, for example, *Effective immediately, all chairmen of inter-agency committees will keep this office informed of all meetings held and of the action taken.* "I am not," I would say with devastating trenchancy, "an immediately effective chairman."

[6] While my colleagues were striving to forge new links with our partners in the Free World (working out "agreed positions" to be set forth in "agreed texts"—as if you *could* agree a position or a text!) I was fighting the battle of "presently." The government had been swept by a vogue for this word. "Now" was becoming almost as rare in official disseminations as "eftsoons." In a carefully controlled voice, I would explain in a drafting committee, as if I had not done so in a score of others, that "presently" did not mean "at present." It meant "in the immediate future." Not only were the results of my efforts disappointing, to say the least, but one of my associates whom I *had* impressed came to me one day with an aggrieved air and a tale of having lost a dollar by betting that "presently" had just the sense I had said only to find that "at present" loomed as large as any other among the meanings given in his dictionary. He had, if you please, looked it up in *Webster's*! I had patiently to explain that *Webster's* would accept any usage if enough word-slingers gave it currency.

PRESERVED FROM VAINGLORY

[7] The pathological word-watcher, it should be made clear, is no more apt to rejoice in his fixation than is the book-keeper who cannot see a row of figures on a license-plate or railroad-car without adding them up. He can hardly help realizing that just as a philatelist who devotes his life to Mauritian issues is likely to become fairly expert in his field, so is a person who gives the better part of his attention to the pitfalls of English—even if his family goes in want, as it is apt to. Actually, if he is like me—I being one who as a child was sent to progressive schools, where I was taught no formal grammar—he may be unable to parse "The cat sat on the mat" or guess what is being talked about when hanging participles or gerunds are brought up. He may, like me, be unable to spell and have to depend upon his wife to catch mistakes in what he writes, usually the same ones over and over again. (Says mine, "Absense isn't going to make *my* heart grow fonder until you learn that it ends with an 's-e,' not a 'c-e.'"[2]) The word-watcher is also preserved from vainglory by the lack of conspicuous popular demand for what he has to offer.

[8] "Will I type this up in triplicate?" my secretary used to ask. She was an Irish-American lass from New Hampshire. "I don't know," I would reply. "Shall you?" Her eyes would travel to the bronze paper-cutter

---

[2] She says I have got it wrong again. It seems only honest for me to leave it as it is, however.—C. O., Jr.

on my desk. Before she came finally to sink it in my neck, however, she married a military attaché on home leave from Helsinki and that was the last I saw of her.

[9] It is difficult to administer correctives in such a way as to make them appreciated; that is the point. I have heard purists resort to the device of repeating the offender's erring statement in correct form, reflectively, as if unaware that they had altered the expression but trusting him to benefit from the example. Thus, when he hears the sentence, "If the information would leak out we'd be in trouble," the purist will, after thinking it over, muse, "Umm. Yes. If it should leak out, that would be too bad." But possibly because a slight stress on the *should* is almost unavoidable, this may provoke the testy retort, "What's the matter, did I say something wrong again?"

[10] An alternative method is for the purist to pretend to be a partner of the offender's in fallibility and interestedly speculate upon the unseemly locution as upon one he himself might well have employed. "Whether we go or not depends upon the weather," he repeats with a faint smile at the ceiling, weighing the words. "Curious, isn't it, how we put in that 'or not' after 'whether' even when it is subsumed under the word 'whether' itself; that is to say [*chuckle*], regardless of *whether or not* it is needed." I have never heard anyone get away with this.

[11] I do not mean to imply that the purist is motivated primarily by the desire for gratitude in setting others to rights. In the case of a reiterated corruption of the language it is a matter of self-preservation. I discovered the limits of what one can take in connection with the policy papers put out by the National Security Council, the nation's supreme policy-making body in foreign affairs. For years I steeled myself to the notation at the head of these papers. It read, "The President approves NSC 168 [or whatever] and directs its implementation." But human nerves can bear just so much. In a meeting with the Secretary of the Council something inside me finally snapped. "The President directs its implementation, you say? He does nothing of the kind!" I cried. "His subordinates do that!" My voice was shrill. "What you mean is, 'The President directs that it be implemented.' Good God, man! What . . . what . . ." I threw up my hands. It was held that the prolonged crisis in Southeast Asia had been too much for me.

[12] Why does anyone fall into this "exaggerated observance of . . . correctness, esp. in language or style"? Psychologists tell us that excessive concern with detail is a form of escapism originating in a basic sense of insecurity. They are no doubt right. So are most human pursuits—coin-collecting, cigarette-smoking, reading, drinking, big-game-hunting, girl-chasing, money-making, probably even psychology-studying. Anyone who has not got a basic sense of insecurity and an over-riding desire to escape has fewer brains than a rabbit. As for why the compulsion leads in some persons to purism instead of to some less generally irritating and more socially acceptable extravagance, my guess is that it is a matter

of the influences one comes under in one's formative years.

[13] One of my early memories is of my grandfather's refusing to attend the local Methodist church any longer because of the minister's abuse of English. " '*That* much,' '*that* important,' " he scoffed. "Are we to have 'that' foisted upon us as an adverb? Is the minister's time *that* important that he cannot say 'as important as that'?" To have moved my grandparent—otherwise the gentlest, most forbearing of men—to such impatience, the offense, I judged, must have been heinous. Indeed, I conceived the notion at an early age that violations of the canons of English were almost as reprehensible as violations of the moral code, and that there were canons to right of us, canons to left of us, canons in front of us.

[14] That does not mean I learned easily. I can still hear my father saying, time after time, "Not different *than*. Different *from*." And, "Not *in back of. Back of,* or *behind*." It must have taken years for such delinquencies to be extirpated from my juvenile prattle, with my mother working at it as conscientiously as my father. I remember from boyhood the astonishment in the face of a friend of mine when, upon my asking if I had to "stay home," my mother replied that I could not stay home now or ever. "Home is not an adverb. You stay *at* home." Her condemnation of the use of "place" for "where" in "eat some place" or "going some place" was (and still is) so unsparing—how can you eat a place or go a place?—that I cannot meet with the usage without a sense of imminent disaster, and I can never speak of church-goers or theater-goers without a twinge of conscience. Can you go a church? Should there not be a "to" in there somewhere? To-church-goers? Go-to-churchers?

[15] I must be at least as hard on my children as my parents were on me. I sometimes wonder that they have not given up talking altogether, for they seldom get three sentences out consecutively without being brought up short by their mother or father. (They catch it from both sides, for the wife of a purist is either another purist or a good prospect for a divorce-lawyer.)

[16] "Not 'I did it already.' Say, 'I've already done it.' "

[17] "Not '*Robin* Hood.' 'Robin *Hood*.' You wouldn't say '*John* Smith.' "

[18] "Not 'They're both alike.' 'They're alike.' It wouldn't be possible for just one of them to be alike."

[19] "Not 'The Matthews.' 'The Matthewses.' . . . Yes, I know they've got 'The Matthews' on their mailbox. It's still wrong. One Matthews, two Matthewses."

[20] "Not 'I feel badly.' That would mean that your sense of feeling is impaired. Say, 'I feel bad.' "

[21] " 'Escapers,' not 'escapees.' . . . I don't care what they say in school or in the newspapers. 'Employees' are persons who are employed. 'Payees' are persons who are paid. 'Escapees' would be persons who are escaped—the guards, that is."

I JUST KNOW IT—THAT'S ALL

[22] The two girls get their own back, however. Not only do I hear them correcting their friends, but they correct me.

[23] "Why do you say 'idear' and 'Canader'?" one of the sprites asks.

[24] "Well, it's this way," I explain. "New Englanders and Southerners, like President Kennedy and your father—and like the English—don't sound *r*'s except when they precede vowels. We say . . . let's see. . . . We say 'Baltimo*ah*, Maryland,' but 'Baltimo*rr r*and Ohio.' We separate the vowel sounds by sounding the *r*. So when we get two vowel sounds in succession, one at the end of one word, one at the beginning of the next, we tend to put in an *r* from force of habit, even when it doesn't belong there. We say 'the ide*ah* wasn't mine,' but then we're apt to say 'the ide*arr* is a good one.' Same with Canada. 'Canad*ah* goose' but 'Canad*arr* ale.'"

[25] "But it's wrong, isn't it?"

[26] "You could say it's colloquial."

[27] "Wrong."

[28] "Well, yes."

[29] The girls are just beginning to learn that relying on my authority has its risks. For example, I know that "Do you have?" means "Do you ordinarily have?" or "Do you make a practice of having?" whereas "Have you?" or "Have you got?" means "Are you in possession of the object at present?" I know it is incorrect to say, "Do you have a pencil with you?" It is just as incorrect as it would be to say, "Have you [or have you got] a good time in the country?" But I cannot cite any rules of syntax that make this so. I just know it, that's all. I know by the way it sounds and because I've had it on good authority. To insist upon what you know is right, tolerating no divergent opinion, when you cannot say why it is right, takes character. But it does not always win arguments.

[30] There is the further complicating fact that, like any confirmed word-watcher, I supplement the accepted rules of English with others of my own devising. Or, as I prefer to think of it, I discover hitherto unformulated principles. One of these is my law of A-or-An-Before-H. This law states that "a" shall be used before a word beginning with "h" if the accent is on the first syllable of that word (provided the "h" is sounded) but that if the accent is on a subsequent syllable, "an" shall be used. Thus we are to speak of *a* history but *an* historical novel, *a* hexagon, but *an* hexagonal figure. Neat, isn't it? I should add that the law permits no exception. True, "an hotel" may sound a little affected or precious, but a people which has the Saviour in the Sermon on the Mount speaking of "an hill" (the translators of the King James Bible having of course lacked the benefit of my law) should certainly have the resolution to say "an hotel" in a clear, unfaltering voice. I demand nothing less from my offspring—who, by the way, regard the word "hotel" as a queer derivative of "motel"—and the fact that nobody but me recognizes my law does not move me.

THE HYPHEN, ALAS!

[31] It is the misfortune of the purist to appear arrogant when all he is doing is being right. Perhaps much may be forgiven him in recognition of his being committed to a losing cause. Poor sod, as the British would say, he is driven on the one hand to pursue a perfection perhaps unattainable this side of the grave (at least the ugly suspicion insinuates itself that the only purity of speech is to be found in total silence, of which language is in its entirety a corruption) and on the other to cling to positions that irresistibly are eroded away beneath him; for, like the noblest headlands, destined to be undermined by the remorseless seas, it is the fate of language to deteriorate. (I am aware that some would say evolve.) I, for example, have given the best years of my life to the hyphen—and to what end?

[32] The hyphen is being done away with—indefensibly, ruthlessly, as if a conspiracy had been formed against it. And we must understand that if the hyphen goes, so does the very conception of the structure of English.

[33] The hyphen permits us to shorten "a railroad operated by the state" to "a state-operated railroad." But in National Intelligence Estimates costing tens of thousands of dollars each we may read "a state operated railroad" or even "a state owned and operated railroad"—a phrase in which the parts of speech are impossible to identify and one devoid of meaning. We may read of "Western oriented regimes," which can mean only Western regimes facing east, and of "white collar workers," which could mean either workers with white collars or white men who work on collars.

[34] Writers who should know better do not show it. John Hersey gives us *The Child Buyer,* apparently believing that a child buyer is one who buys children, whereas in fact it is a child who buys. And Joseph W. Alsop in his book *From the Silent Earth* (his exciting book, I must admit) may think he is describing a helmet encrusted with boar's tusks in his phrase "a boar's tusk-encrusted helmet" but what he is actually describing is a tusk-encrusted helmet belonging to a boar. (He did use one hyphen, though.)

[35] Where is this leading? It has already led, as I can report from my own observation, to a headline reading "Child Chasing Fox Found Rabid" and to an advertisement suggesting "For the pet lover on your Christmas list, a perfect little four-poster bed for the corner of the living room."

[36] One would expect the nation to draw back from the brink while there is time, but I am pessimistic. The hyphen is disappearing, and neither the purist's outrage nor his lamentations will save it, I fear, or retard the degeneration of the English language into mouthfuls of words indiscriminately spewed forth. He pounds the table till his wattles shake, and it does no good.

[37] And yet the purist—even such as I—has his vindications. Do you know why Mariner I, the "probe" aimed at Mars, went off course into

oblivion? I ask you, do you know? Because, in all the complicated instructions fed into its guidance system, one hyphen was inadvertently omitted. One tiny hyphen that requires you only to extend your little finger to the upper right-hand corner of the keyboard. It cost the American people two million bucks.

[38] And if you ask me, it served them damned well right.

Questions on Meaning

1. Now that you have read the whole essay, how would you describe Ogburn's attitude toward his own "purism"? Through his tone, is he apologizing for his obsession, defending it, or taking some other stance?

2. Mention some examples Ogburn gives of his own behavior that fit the *Oxford English Dictionary* definition of "purism" as "exaggerated observance of purity . . . in language or style."

3. Make a list of the expressions Ogburn says he objects to or that he quotes other purists objecting to. Which of these expressions do you usually try to avoid yourself? Which ones did the author convince you you should try to avoid? Which ones seem completely correct and appropriate despite Ogburn's criticisms (or the criticisms of someone he refers to)? What are your criteria?

Questions on Style and Structure

1. Ogburn introduces his essay with an anecdote. Did you find it amusing and effective? Do you agree that "mid air" is a redundant expression? Can you think of other examples that the author could have used (for example, "consensus of opinion")?

2. In paragraph 2, how do the following words shape the author's tone: *insulted, exhilaration, obsessive, prize, burden,* and *staggering*? How should the reader react to such words? How does the analogy in the last sentence of the paragraph contribute to the tone? Analyze the other paragraphs of this essay for tone, paying particular attention to the author's choice of words.

3. The last sentence of paragraph 2, as explained in the preceding question, presents an analogy. The first sentence of paragraph 3 also draws an analogy between purism and alcoholism or drug-addiction. Where else does the author use analogies? Why does he use so many?

4. Study the structure of Ogburn's paragraphs. Is each one unified and developed?

5. Why do you suppose he devotes so much attention to the hyphen? Why does he discuss it last?

6. Does the essay have an adequate conclusion?

Exploring Words

1. *abomination.* To which institutions, customs, or practices in American society would you apply *abomination?* Check your dictionary to be sure you understand the way the word is used.

2. *flatulent.* After checking your dictionary, make a list of roughly synonymous words that are more commonly used to convey this idea.

3. *travesty.* Use your dictionary to study the development of the words *travesty* and *transvestite,* and consider the relationships between the two words.

4. *philatelist.* Using your dictionary, discover what *philatelist* has in common with *philander, philanthropist, philharmonic, philologist,* and *philosopher.*

5. *vainglory.* Can this word be applied to you? If so, in what ways?

6. *heinous.* Check the pronunciation of this word (it is often mispronounced), and write a sentence using it.

7. *extirpated.* Write a sentence in which you use the word *extirpated* accurately.

8. *colloquial.* After checking your dictionary's definition of this word, list six words that might be considered *colloquial* in a freshman essay.

Suggestions for Writing

1. Write a paper on "The Trials of a _____," choosing as your topic one of the "human pursuits" with which Ogburn compared word-watching in paragraph 12. (Or, if you are not given to any of these "pursuits," choose one that is included in your life style.) You may wish to show how whatever activity you are dealing with is "a form of escapism originating in a basic sense of insecurity."

2. If you are like most Americans, you are probably unfamiliar with some of the "distractions" about which Ogburn complains (for example, his grief over the current usage of *hopefully*). Go to the library and browse through one of the following reference books on usage:

   Bergen Evans and Cornelia Evans, *A Dictionary of Contemporary American Usage.*
   Wilson Follett, *Modern American Usage.*
   William and Mary Morris, *Harper Dictionary of Contemporary Usage.*
   Margaret Nicholson, *A Dictionary of American-English Usage.*

   Then present some of your most interesting discoveries in a brief paper.

3. As Ogburn does, write an essay in which you excoriate those usages that annoy you.

The Silver Horn
THOMAS SANCTON

Getting Started

With Ideas

What kind of subject matter and treatment do you expect to find in an autobiographical essay with the title "The Silver Horn"? Is there any reason to think this title may be symbolic? If so, of what? (Consider, for example, your personal associations with the word *silver*. Were there any "silvery" moments in your own early life?) The first paragraph makes clear, in a general way, the direction the rest of the essay will take. But as you read on, you will want to keep in mind possible implications of the title. Its full significance does not come out until the last paragraph.

With Words

1 servile (14)—associate this word with *servant* and *servitude*.
2 circumscribed (15)—the context together with your familiarity with the prefix *circum-* will help you with the meaning of this word.
3 embryonic (34)—from the root *embryo*.
4 amalgams (34)—relate it to *amalgamation* and *Amalgamated* Steel.
5 consummate (35)—you are probably familiar with the verb form of this word, but note that Sancton uses the word as an adjective.
6 Gothic (39)—this term, which is from the name of an ancient Germanic people, is now used in many different senses (for example, it is used in discussing architecture and novels), but note that Sancton uses it to apply to a mood or feeling.

[1] The scene is a Boy Scout summer camp, thickly grown with pines and cypress. There is a row of green clapboard cabins, with clean floors and neat double-decker bunks; there is an open field and a flag hanging still in the heavy air; and at the field's edge the land drops down a little to the dark water of a bayou. I spent five summers here, from the time I was twelve until I entered college. I did my first real living and my first real thinking in this camp.

[2] And I think of it now. Like some reader of a long novel who turns back through the pages to find a forgotten part of the plot, and who

---

"The Silver Horn" appeared in *Harper's Magazine*, February 1944. Copyright 1944 by *Harper's Magazine*. Reprinted by permission of Russell and Volkening, Inc., as agents for the author.

comes with a flash of recognition across old scenes and dialogues, and characters who have gone out of the narrative but whose personalities and substance once filled pages and pages, I have gone turning back through the pages of my life. When was it and where was it—I have been asking— that I first began to believe what I now believe about the Southern world I left not many years ago, about Negroes, about democracy, about America, about life and death, about men and all their curious fates? This search has been long and turning. Often it has led me back to the years of my early teens and to the summers I spent in the camp.

[3] I was born to the sidewalks and asphalt of the largest city and the widest street in the South. In New Orleans, broad Canal Street was never empty of speeding automobiles and streetcars, even late at night, and of people walking by, their footsteps echoing on the sidewalk. But here on the bayou another world existed. In the morning it was the strange, thin call of a bugle that broke into our sleep. Almost before we were awake we could smell the wet exercise field and the forest. Birds popped from tree to tree, plump and colorful, bluejays, mockingbirds, cardinals, flickers—Audubon had painted in these woods. Rabbits ran into the bushes. Snakes we had no fear of, long thick blue racers and speckled king snakes, slid through the weeds at our approach.

[4] Standing in the wet grass, still yawning and sleepy, we took the morning exercises. Night chill was in the air, but behind our backs the sun was rising, and its warmth crept onto our shoulders. After the exercises we raced along a wagon road to the swimming pool, and as we ran up, shouting and excited, two or three startled frogs made tremendous leaps and plumped beneath the glassy surface of the water. After the swim we dried our skinny sunburned bodies and ran to the mess hall.

[5] Most of us in the camp were poor boys, or boys who were almost poor. It was not a welfare camp, but the fees were low, less than a dollar a day for a camper. As a consequence it was filled with boys from modest New Orleans neighborhoods and also from the tough ones. There was always a smattering of the democratic rich: the son of the traction company president came every summer. So did his cousin from Texas, a wild, hard towhead with plenty of money and the soul of a true picaroon. He fascinated and dominated the rest of us. He was the first colorful outlaw I ever knew. But most of the well-to-do families sent their boys to camps in the Maine woods or the North Carolina mountains. Our camp was only forty miles from the city. Department store clerks, streetcar motormen, little grocers could afford the fees.

[6] We had no saddle horses, no golf course, and only a weed-grown tennis court which no one used. For diversion we fell back on nature. In the morning we performed a work detail, cutting a patch of weeds or hauling dirt in wheelbarrows to mend a road. After this we were free to swim, to paddle on the bayou in slender little Louisiana boats called pirogues, to fish for the boisterous black bass and yellow perch and fat

blue catfish, and to work for our Boy Scout medals and merit badges, tracking through the grassy cut-over pine lands, cooking dough and bacon on sweet-gum spits, bandaging one another with first-aid splints.

[7] These little medals and bits of colored ribbon meant a great deal to us. We wrote home enthusiastic letters about our progress, describing in detail how we had passed the tests, forwarding the comments of some eighteen-year-old camp officer as though it really mattered. Our parents, most of whom did not have very big events happening in their own lives, were just as eager and simple-hearted about these things, and one or two of the fathers were foolishly ambitious to have their sons win the highest number of merit badges in the area.

[8] Little things that happened during these years seemed of great importance. I remember that in my first year at camp I wore an ill-fitting Boy Scout hat. One of the councillors, a boy five years my senior who seemed to me to belong already to the grown-up world of brilliance and authority, began, in a pleasant way, to tease me about the hat. Every morning for a week he led us to the abandoned logging road and clocked us as we walked and trotted a measured mile. My hat was anchored down by a heavy chin strap; it flopped and sailed about my head as I ran to the finish line. The boy began to laugh at me. He waved his arms and called out, "Come on, you rookie!" The other kids took it up and Rookie became my first nickname. I loved it. I tingled when someone called it out. I painted it on my belt, carved it in my packing case, inked it into my hatband, and began to sign it to my letters home. Years later when we were grown I knew this camp officer again. The gap between our ages had vanished and in real life now he seemed to me a rather colorless young lawyer. He did not remember about the hat.

[9] At mealtime we ate ravenously in the mess hall. There were steaming platters of pork and beans and cabbage and stew. As we walked to the long clapboard building with our hair freshly combed and water glistening on our faces, which we washed at the flowing pipe of a big artesian well, we existed in a transport of driving hunger. In the steamy fragrance of the mess hall we set up a clatter of knives and forks and china, and afterward we went to our cabins and flopped on the bunks in a state of drowsy satisfaction. Somehow, fat never formed on our skinny frames. We ran too much. We paddled in the boats. We swam. We cut firewood and played softball after supper. When there was nothing else to do we climbed in the rafters of our cabins, trying to invent complicated monkey swings that no one else could do. Every year some campers broke their arms.

II

[10] A giant Negro named Joe did the camp's heavy work. He cut and trimmed the big trees, dug the deep post holes, mixed the cement, cleaned out the underbrush. His strength was a never-ending fascination for the rest of us. Joe was a light-eyed Negro, with a tan cast of skin and a

huge bald dome of a head. One of his grandparents must certainly have been a white man. He lived half a mile down the bayou with his large and hazily defined family, in an old "plantation house."

[11] Actually it was not, and never had been, a pretentious place, and I do not know what kind of plantation could have been there. The ground round it was alternately sandy and swampy and there are no plantations where pine trees grow. Pines mean sandy land. In slave days the Negroes had boiled Southern history down to a couplet:

Cain't make a living on sandy lan'—
Ruther be a nigger den a po' white man.

[12] Joe's place stood on a cleared bend in the bayou. The weatherboards and shingles were green with age. The house rested on high slender pillars and there were patches of bright red brick where the covering mortar had fallen away. The yard was shaded by two enormous water oaks, hung with gray Spanish moss, and an iron kettle stood beneath the trees where women did the washing. At the bank of the bayou five or six towering cypress trees leaned heavily toward the water, for the slow currents of a century had washed their roots completely bare of soil. To get a new anchorage on the land the trees had sent out a forest of gnarled roots and stubby knees along the shoreline. The house seemed beautiful and somber in these surroundings as we paddled past it on our expeditions down the bayou to the lake.

[13] Obviously a white man had built this place long ago, and if he had not been a plantation owner, he had at least been a man of substance. Perhaps this had been the summer home for some wealthy old New Orleans Frenchman in years gone by. Sometimes the camp officers spoke of Joe as "caretaker" on the place. But that was hardly possible. He and his family inhabited every room; chickens roamed freely, and washing hung on lines stretched across the wide porch. It was clear to us that the Negro giant was no caretaker here. He possessed this place, to have and to hold. How he got it and why we never asked him; and his presence there did not seem a very curious thing to us. Already a dark, subjective understanding of Louisiana's history was in our blood and bones.

[14] Joe smoked strong cigarettes and chewed tobacco. His teeth were rotted stumps. We delighted in bringing him supplies of smokes from the nearby town on Saturdays to win his quick and genuine appreciation. There were two or three measures of a Cajun French ditty he used to sing, dancing and stomping the ground, waving his hat and swaying his heavy shoulders with real grace. The words and the stomping finished together, with two hard accents. He would do this every time in exchange for a gift. Yet he did it in such a way that we knew always that this was nothing more than a grown-up man doing monkeyshines for children. He enjoyed making us laugh. There was nothing servile about it.

[15] He got to be one of the people I liked best of all—not only in the camp but in my whole circumscribed world. I liked Joe very simply

because he was a nice man. He recognized me every year when I returned to the camp, and after the second or third year I could tell that he considered me a real friend and was glad to have me back. We talked together often, equally and easily, and when I was sixteen and seventeen and by then a councillor in the camp, Joe would do me the honor of becoming quite serious with me and of placing our whole friendship on a mature plane. I do not remember many of the things we talked about, but I do remember that a conversation with him was a reassurance and a satisfaction; that it was always good to find him walking on the road and to fall in with him.

[16] I saw a brief notice in the paper, some years after I had stopped going to the camp, that Joe had died of blood poisoning in the New Orleans Charity Hospital. I thought of those stumps of teeth, and of the many years they had been seeping infection into his system. I thought also of the tall trees I had seen him fell, and that now Joe too had come toppling to the earth. And, though I felt a quiet sorrow, I felt no anguish. Life grew rank and lush along the bayou. His old house was teeming with the spawn of his years. The sun would beat upon the water forever, the trout would break the surface, the rushes would grow thick and green. Joe had done his share of hauling and of digging. Now he could lie down in the warm and sun-drenched earth and sleep.

III

[17] During those summers in camp a love grew up in me for the rhythms of nature, for tropical rains that came sweeping through the pines and oaks, for the fiery midday sun, for long evenings, and the deep black nights. Great campfires were lit beside the bayou and a rushing column of luminous smoke and sparks ascended to the cypress trees. Fire gleamed in the water where bass were sleeping in the stumps. Campers wandered toward the meeting place, their flashlights swinging in the woods. We sat about the fire, singing, beating deep rumbling tom-toms made of hollowed oak logs, performing an ageless repertoire of skits and mimicry. And after these sessions one leader took the Protestant boys and another the Catholics and, standing in the open fields, in our separate groups, we prayed aloud.

[18] My heart had strayed already from the formal, repetitious praying. A towering pine tree at the field's edge made a silhouette in the starry sky. I knew the constellations, the Giant, the Dipper, the Bear. I looked for the two inseparable stars, Misar and Alcar, horse and rider, and sensed the fact that Arabs named these stars a thousand years before me, and even in my boy's ignorance I felt aware of man's long and varied time upon the earth. I knew this night-filled wilderness had stretched beneath these stars for endless ages before Frenchmen had come in boats to build New Orleans. I thought of the Indians who had fished and hunted here, whose bones and broken pottery we sometimes found in grassy mounds. I felt worshipful of the earth, the pine tree, the night itself.

[19] Sometimes we packed provisions and tents and mosquito bars and paddled down the bayou to the lake, ten miles away. The lake was a great inland finger of the Gulf of Mexico, twenty miles long, ten wide. Twenty miles below us, in prehistoric times, the mouth of the Mississippi river had built up new land, and these watery prairies had pinched off the small inland gulf and made a lake of it, but it connected still through a series of passes with the Mexican Gulf. The lake teemed with croakers, catfish, shrimp, and big blue-clawed crabs. At the northern end, where we camped, a network of tributary bayous emptied into the lake. For the last mile or so of their crooked lengths, where the brackish water of the lake crept into the slow-moving bayous, fish and small life were abundant, bass fed in the rushes, and muskrats built their cities of the plains.

[20] There was a relatively high, sandy point near the mouth of the bayou, where we camped. The sun went down red into the lake and left a long, clear twilight. A few stars came out. A salty wind blew in from the Mexican Gulf; it came out of the south every night. The breeze swept over the rushes and made small waves break on the sandy, grassy shore. There was a red beacon light on weather-beaten piles out in the lake and its long reflection shimmered in the water. We sprayed our mosquito netting with citronella and built up a driftwood fire and lay down on canvas bedrolls spread upon the thin, tough grass and sand. The trade wind blew through our tents throughout the night. We listened to the waves. We could smell the vast salt marshes far below us. A yellow moon came out of the gulf. Far down the lake we could see the lights of a railroad bridge. We felt the beauty of this wilderness like a hunger.

[21] After two days of fishing and swimming in the lake, our shoulders and faces darker from the sun, we paddled back up the winding bayou.

IV

[22] One summer when I was sixteen a party of us, paddling upstream to buy some candy at a crossroads store, came upon three young girls who were bathing in a sandy cove. There were four of us in the long pirogue, all of an age. For a long moment we were speechless. At last we said hello, and they answered in warm gay voices. We drifted the boat into the cove and began to speak to them. Two of the girls were sisters. The three of them had come to visit a relative who kept a fine summer lodge in the woods across the bayou from the camp. One of the sisters was fifteen and the others were seventeen. They were aglow with fresh and slender beauty, and their bathing suits were bright flags of color. Their impact upon us was overwhelming. We grew silly, tongue-tied, said foolish things we did not mean to say, shoved one another about in the boat, and finally overturned it. The loreleis laughed musical little laughs. They seemed unbearably beautiful. We had no idea what to do about it.

[23] The girls had been at the lodge for a week. They missed their beaux in New Orleans, they missed the dating and the dancing and the

music. It was a gay town in the summertime. The older girls looked upon us as children; but still—they must have reflected—we were not such children at that. The younger sister, a slender child with thick brown hair and heavily crimsoned lips, sat on the bank and regarded us with a happy open face.

[24] At last we took courage and asked if we could call on them that night.

[25] "Oh, yes!" they cried eagerly. Life at that moment was dazzling.

[26] Making this rendezvous was an impulsive thing to do, for it was midweek and we should have to steal away after taps and walk down a path without flashlights through a snake-infested lowland and—because the boats were counted and chained at nightfall—swim across the bayou, holding our clothes above our heads.

[27] We crept from our cabins at ten o'clock that night and met in the pine woods. One of us intoned a counting-out rhyme; the loser had to walk first down the path through the snake hole. He cut a long gum sapling and rattled it down the path ahead of us. We walked bunched tightly together, tense with fear, giggling at our own unbelievable audacity, trembling in our eagerness. At the bayou's edge we slipped out of our shorts and shirts and sneakers and, holding them above our heads with one hand, we felt our way round the knees and along the sunken roots of a cypress tree, and pushed off into the bayou and began to swim.

[28] The moon had not yet risen. We had only the silhouettes of trees to guide us. We swam closely together, cautioning one another to silence, bursting into convulsive squeals as water lilies brushed against our bodies or when a fish broke the surface near us. We swam upstream from the camp, past two bends, and waded from the water in the cove where we had met the girls. Now we were laughing with relief and excitement, and popping one another on the backsides. We scraped the glistening water from our bodies, dressed, and combed our wet hair and hurried off down the wagon path into the woods. Long ago the cove had been a landing stage for small schooners which came to load pine firewood for New Orleans.

[29] The girls were waiting for us, dressed in bright print cotton dresses and wearing hair ribbons. The soft light gave age and mystery to their youthful shoulders, to their slender bodies; and, like nameless night-blooming vines in the woods about us, they bore a splendid fragrance all their own, a fragrance of youth and cleanliness and fresh cosmetics. They were playing a phonograph on the wide porch of the lodge. This was the summer of Maurice Chevalier's great success in American movies. The little sister sang his song, rolling her eyes, turning out her soft pink lip:

If ze night-ting gail
Cood zing lak you . . .

[30] And she sang another:

> . . . you make me feel so grand
> I want to hand the world to you.
> You seem to understand
> Each foolish little dream I'm dreaming, scheme I'm
>   scheming . . .

[31] I was so in love with her I could hardly catch my breath. I was in love with the other sister too, and with their friend. All of the boys were in love with all of the girls; the girls—so they said—had crushes on each of us. Our hearts were afire.

[32] We walked hand in hand down the wagon trail to the cove and built a bonfire. We stretched out on blankets, laughing, singing. We sang the songs that people always sing by rivers and campfires, "There's a Long, Long Trail A-winding," "The Sweetheart of Sigma Chi," all the rest. We kissed the girls and they held fast to us. Before this night we had been only boys, holding hands with girls in movies, not quite sure why we pursued them and acted silly. Now, lying beneath the open sky, for the first time we understood the poignance and the beauty of the human heritage.

[33] Every night for two weeks we came to see them. And when they told us good-by the last kiss was as much a discovery as the first, and we knew that love was a thing that could never grow old. After they had gone we would steal from our cabins to sit on the back porch of the camp hospital, on a hill, where we could see the bayou and the cove and the woods where we had found them; and we sat there talking late into the night, like daemon lovers in the ballads of old. I never passed the cove again, even years later when I would paddle down the bayou fishing, without remembering our meetings with a suddenly racing heart. First love is unforgettable.

V

[34] I had no lessons to do in those summer months of camp life. There was plenty of time to think. I was living a communal life with other boys. Among us were embryonic bullies, scoundrels, cheats, promoters, Babbitts, Christers, and stuffed shirts; and there were also the boys of good heart, the unselfish, the humorous, the courageous, boys who were the salt of the earth, but who, often in their later lives, would be misled and preyed upon and set against one another by the sharp ones. One and all we lived together, ate together, slept together. Our personalities clashed, fermented, or formed amalgams. Sitting together at night in the lamplit cabins, with darkness and towering woods closing in upon us, we had our first grave talks about religion, about death, about sex. The future stretching before us was wide and fathomless. And all about us, in the grass, in the underbrush, in towering summer skies, we beheld the face of nature and the earth's wide harmonies as they had never been revealed in our city

lives. At night we could stretch out upon the field, observe the stars, and grasp the first time the fact that some were vastly deeper in space than others. In our star-study courses we heard phrases like "light years." It began to seep into the consciousness of many of us that a hundred years or the life of an individual had little meaning in the total universe; and from this point some of us began our first gropings after moral philosophy, gropings for a belief that could give the total universe a meaning in our own lives.

[35] There was a bugler in our camp who was the first consummate expert, in any field, that I had known. He had no other talent but his music. He was a good-natured, chubby, curly-headed Italian boy, rather lazy, and when he was not back in the woods practicing his cornet he walked round with a dreamy look, as though our own handicrafts could not possibly be of interest to him.

[36] Paolo had a silver trumpet and he preferred it to the bugle. He wanted to be a great musician. He would take his horn and music back into a pine clearing a quarter of a mile from the camp and all day long we could hear him practicing the runs. He blew the trumpet with a clear, sweet tone. We had supreme confidence as we stood at attention on the parade grounds and the flag came down the creaking flagpole pulley in the late afternoon sunlight, and Paolo stood alone, with everyone watching, and bugled. We were proud of him when visitors came. He had that ability of experts to create a sense of possessiveness in others.

[37] It was at bedtime that Paolo gathered up into his clear, thin music all the ineffable hungering of our awakening lives. At ten o'clock he climbed a high ladder to a life-guard platform we had nailed into the branches of a tall cypress tree beside the bayou. Paolo lived for this moment and, with the whole camp silent and listening below him in the darkness, he blew taps with a soft and ghostly beauty all his own. Somehow the music spoke for us, uttered the thing we knew but had no words for, set up a wailing in the pine trees of the brevity and splendor of human life. Lying in our bunks in the darkness of the cabin, some of us fell into sleep; but some lay in silence thinking longer, alive to the night, and I was of these.

[38] One night some ten years later I entered a smoke-filled tavern in another city where Paolo was playing in a band. By this time he had made a small reputation as a boy with a hot trumpet. I watched his now older face as he tore through the hot routines. He was tired. The silver horn made noise but, though I knew little about it, I could see that he was not a great jazz musician.

[39] I did not go to see him any more. I wanted to remember Paolo before he had lost something, before any of us had lost it, a kind of innocence. I wanted to remember him in the land of our first discoveries, when he had climbed into a cypress tree to blow his horn, and there was a kind of Gothic night-drench in our lives.

Questions on Meaning

1 After finishing the essay, do you find that the title has the general meaning you expected it to have? Does it have a more specific meaning? Is it intended as a symbol?

2 What is the writer's feeling about Paolo, the bugler, when he rediscovers him in later life? Does an emphasis on this feeling make an appropriate ending for the essay? Why?

3 What other people at the camp make especially strong impressions on Sancton? Compare his reaction to each of these people with his reaction to the boy Paolo. Why does he give special attention to all of these people in this work?

Questions on Style and Structure

1 Sancton's essay is divided into five numbered sections. What is the unifying idea of each section? What would be the effect of switching the order of sections IV and V?

2 The author's paragraphs are worthy of close attention. Most of them are tightly unified (look, for example, at paragraphs 7, 10, 15, and 16). Are there any paragraphs that could be improved?

3 Note how Sancton achieves coherence in paragraph 18 through the regular use of the pronoun *I*. Can you find other paragraphs in which pronouns are similarly used to achieve coherence?

4 Section IV, which is devoted to the subject of first love, may perhaps strike some readers as oversentimental. How does it strike you? Why?

5 Sancton at times repeats words very effectively for emphasis ("One and all we lived *together,* ate *together,* slept *together,*" instead of "One and all we lived, ate, and slept together"). Can you find other examples?

Exploring Words

1 *servile.* Note the analogous use of the *-ile* suffix in such words as *juvenile, puerile,* and *infantile.* Can you think of other such words?

2 *circumscribed.* How many other words beginning with *circum-* can you think of, and what is the relationship between these words?

3 *embryonic.* You will note that Sancton's use of *embryonic* is metaphorical. What other nouns can you think of with which the word *embryonic* could be used? Several other terms dealing with reproduction are frequently used metaphorically (such as "pregnant idea"). How many of these can you think of?

4 *amalgams.* Which of the meanings listed in your dictionary applies to Sancton's use of the word? Write a sentence of your own using the term in the same sense.

5 *consummate.* What relationship do you find between the meaning your dictionary gives for the verb and adjective forms of this word?

6 *Gothic.* Check your dictionary for the various usages of *Gothic.* Does any entry fit Sancton's use of the term? If so, which one?

Suggestions for Writing

1 Have you had the experience of encountering someone you once knew well and finding that that person or you (or both of you) have changed so much that you no longer have anything in common? Write about the experience, making sure that you help your reader to understand: (1) what the person was like when you knew him or her before; (2) what kind of relationship the two of you had (meaning, probably, what you did together); (3) what the person seemed like on the second meeting; and (4) how you felt about the change.

2 Choose a place where you spent a considerable portion of your childhood (it could be a campground, a summer camp, a neighborhood clubhouse, a church, or maybe just a tree house in your own backyard) and show the effects of your experiences there on your own development. Because your piece will be considerably shorter than Sancton's, it will need a sharper focus. One way to achieve this focus is first to provide a specific *physical description* of the place and then to show your *activities* there, concluding with a comment on why the memory of the place is important to you.

3 Write a paper on the topic "The First Time I ———."

When I Was a Child
LILLIAN SMITH

Getting Started

With Ideas

Lillian Smith is well known for both her novels and her nonfiction. Her writings often concern the social tensions of the South in which she grew up, the South of the early twentieth century. In this selection from her autobiography, *Killers of the Dream,* she speaks in the first paragraph of a "trouble" in the South that even the children growing up there know about. As you read the rest of the essay, it will be a good idea to keep in mind the question: just what is this "trouble" that is "bigger than they [the children], bigger than their family, bigger than their church, so big that people turn away from its size"?

With Words

1 dissonant (9)—from the Latin prefix *dis-* ("apart") and the root for *sound* (think, for example, of *supersonic*). But check the context to avoid misunderstanding the way the Latin prefix and root are used in this word. You may know the antonym, *consonant,* and you probably know the synonym *discordant.*
2 decorums (9)—related to *decor* and *decorous.* See also "The Consolations of Illiteracy" (p. 75).
3 modulations (10)—from the Latin word meaning "small measure."
4 peremptory (11)—from the Latin word meaning "destructive." But this clue will help you get only a very general sense of Smith's meaning. Watch the context for further clues.
5 malaise (19)—you probably know some other *mal* words—*malicious,* for example. The variant spelling, *malease,* may give you a further clue.

[1] Even its children know that the South is in trouble. No one has to tell them; no words said aloud. To them, it is a vague thing weaving in and out of their play, like a ghost haunting an old graveyard or whispers after the household sleeps—fleeting mystery, vague menace, to which each responds in his own way. Some learn to screen out all except the soft and the soothing; others deny even as they see plainly, and hear. But all know that under quiet words and warmth and laughter, under the slow ease and tender concern about small matters, there is a heavy burden on

"When I Was a Child" is reprinted from *Killers of the Dream* by Lillian Smith. By permission of W. W. Norton & Company, Inc. Copyright 1949, © 1961 by Lillian Smith.

all of us and as heavy a refusal to confess it. The children know this "trouble" is bigger than they, bigger than their family, bigger than their church, so big that people turn away from its size. They have seen it flash out like lightning and shatter a town's peace, have felt it tear up all they believe in. They have measured its giant strength and they feel weak when they remember.

[2] This haunted childhood belongs to every southerner. Many of us run away from it but we come back like a hurt animal to its wound, or a murderer to the scene of his sin. The human heart dares not stay away too long from that which hurt it most. There is a return journey to anguish that few of us are released from making.

[3] We who were born in the South call this mesh of feeling and memory "loyalty." We think of it sometimes as "love." We identify with the South's trouble as if we, individually, were responsible for all of it. We defend the sins and sorrows of three hundred years as if each sin had been committed by us alone and each sorrow had cut across our heart. We are as hurt at criticism of our region as if our own name were called aloud by the critic. We have known guilt without understanding it, and there is no tie that binds men closer to the past and each other than that.

[4] It is a strange thing, this umbilical cord uncut. In times of ease, we do not feel its pull, but when we are threatened with change, suddenly it draws the whole white South together in a collective fear and fury that wipe our minds clear of reason and we are blocked off from sensible contact with the world we live in.

[5] To keep this resistance strong, wall after wall has been thrown up in the southern mind against criticism from without and within. Imaginations close tight against the hurt of others; a regional armoring takes place to keep out the "enemies" who would make our trouble different—or maybe rid us of it completely. For it is a trouble that we do not want to give up. We are as involved with it as a child who cannot be happy at home and cannot bear to tear himself away, or as a grown-up who has fallen in love with his own disease. We southerners have identified with the long sorrowful past on such deep levels of love and hate and guilt that we do not know how to break old bonds without pulling our lives down. *Change* is the evil word, a shrill clanking that makes us know too well our servitude. *Change* means leaving one's memories, one's sins, one's ancient prison, the room where one was born. How can we do this when we are tied fast!

[6] The white man's burden is his own childhood. Every southerner knows this. Though he may deny it even to himself, yet he drags through life with him the heavy weight of a past that never eases and is rarely understood, of desire never appeased, of dreams that died in his heart.

[7] In this South I was born and now live. Here it was that I began to grow, seeking my way, as do all children, through the honeycomb cells of our life to the bright reality outside. Sometimes it was as if all doors

opened inward. . . . Sometimes we children lost even the desire to get outside and tried only to make a comfortable home of the trap of swinging doors that history and religion and a war, man's greed and his guilt had placed us in at birth.

[8] It is not easy to pick out of such a life those strands that have to do only with color, only with Negro-white relationships, only with religion or sex, for they are knit of the same fibers that have gone into the making of the whole fabric, woven into its basic patterns and designs. Religion . . . sex . . . race . . . money . . . avoidance rites . . . malnutrition . . . dreams—no part of these can be looked at and clearly seen without looking at the whole of them. For, as a painter mixes colors and makes of them new colors, so religion is turned into something different by race, and segregation is colored as much by sex as by skin pigment, and money is no longer a coin but a lost wish wandering through a man's whole life.

[9] A child's lessons are blended of these strands however dissonant a design they make. The mother who taught me what I know of tenderness and love and compassion taught me also the bleak rituals of keeping Negroes in their place. The father who rebuked me for an air of superiority toward schoolmates from the mill and rounded out his rebuke by gravely reminding me that "all men are brothers," trained me in the steel-rigid decorums I must demand of every colored male. They who so gravely taught me to split my body from my feelings and both from my "soul," taught me also to split my conscience from my acts and Christianity from southern tradition.

[10] Neither the Negro nor sex was often discussed at length in our home. We were given no formal instruction in these difficult matters but we learned our lessons well. We learned the intricate system of taboos, of renunciations and compensations, of manners, voice modulations, words, feelings, along with our prayers, our toilet habits, and our games. I do not remember how or when, but by the time I had learned that God is love, that Jesus is His Son and came to give us more abundant life, that all men are brothers with a common Father, I also knew that I was better than a Negro, that all black folks have their place and must be kept in it, that sex has its place and must be kept in it, that a terrifying disaster would befall the South if ever I treated a Negro as my social equal and as terrifying a disaster would befall my family if ever I were to have a baby outside of marriage. I had learned that God so loved the world that He gave His only begotten Son so that we might have segregated churches in which it was my duty to worship each Sunday and on Wednesday at evening prayers. I had learned that white southerners are a hospitable, courteous, tactful people who treat those of their own group with consideration and who as carefully segregate from all the richness of life "for their own good and welfare" thirteen million people whose skin is colored a little differently from my own.

[11] I knew by the time I was twelve that a member of my family would always shake hands with old Negro friends, would speak gently and graciously to members of the Negro race unless they forgot their place, in which event icy peremptory tones would draw lines beyond which only the desperate would dare take one step. I knew that to use the word "nigger" was unpardonable and no well-bred southerner was quite so crude as to do so; nor would a well-bred southerner call a Negro "mister" or invite him into the living room or eat with him or sit by him in public places.

[12] I knew that my old nurse who had patiently cared for me through long months of illness, who had given me refuge when a little sister took my place as the baby of the family, who comforted me, soothed, fed me, delighted me with her stories and games, let me fall asleep on her deep warm breast, was not worthy of the passionate love I felt for her but must be given instead a half-smiled-at affection similar to that which one feels for one's dog. I knew but I never believed it, that the deep respect I felt for her, the tenderness, the love, was a childish thing which every normal child outgrows, that such love begins with one's toys and is discarded with them, and that somehow—though it seemed impossible to my agonized heart—I too, must outgrow these feelings. I learned to give presents to this woman I loved, instead of esteem and honor. I learned to use a soft voice to oil my words of superiority. I learned to cheapen with tears and sentimental talk of "my old mammy" one of the profound relationships of my life. I learned the bitterest thing a child can learn: that the human relations I valued most were held cheap by the world I lived in.

[13] From the day I was born, I began to learn my lessons. I was put in a rigid frame too intricate, too complex, too twisting to describe here so briefly, but I learned to conform to its slide-rule measurements. I learned that it is possible to be a Christian and a white southerner simultaneously; to be a gentlewoman and an arrogant callous creature in the same moment; to pray at night and ride a Jim Crow car the next morning and to feel comfortable in doing both. I learned to believe in freedom, to glow when the word *democracy* is used, and to practice slavery from morning to night. I learned it the way all of my southern people learn it: by closing door after door until one's mind and heart and conscience are blocked off from each other and from reality.

[14] I closed the doors. Or perhaps they were closed for me. Then one day they began to open again. Why I had the desire or the strength to open them or what strange accident or circumstance opened them for me would require in the answering an account too long, too particular, too stark to make here. And perhaps I should not have the insight or wisdom that such an analysis would demand of me, nor the will to make it. I know only that the doors opened, a little; that somewhere along that iron corridor we travel from babyhood to maturity, doors swinging inward began to swing outward, showing glimpses of the world beyond, of that clear bright thing we call "reality."

[15] I believe there is one experience in my childhood which pushed these doors open, a little. And I am going to tell it here, although I know well that to excerpt from a life and family background one incident and name it as a "cause" of a change in one's life direction is a distortion and often an irrelevance. The profound hungers of a child and how they are filled have too much to do with the way in which experiences are assimilated to tear an incident out of a life and look at it in isolation. Yet, with these reservations, I shall tell it, not because it was in itself so severe a trauma, but because it became for me a symbol of buried experiences that I did not have access to. It is an incident that has rarely happened to other southern children. In a sense, it is unique. But it was an acting-out, a special private production of a little script that is written on the lives of most southern children before they know words. Though they may not have seen it staged this way, each southerner has had his own dramatization of the theme.

[16] I should like to preface the account by giving a brief glimpse of my family and background, hoping that the reader, entering my home with me, will be able to blend the ragged edges of this isolated experience into a more full life picture and in doing so will see that it is, in a sense, everybody's story.

[17] I was born and reared in a small Deep South town whose population was about equally Negro and white. There were nine of us who grew up freely in a rambling house of many rooms, surrounded by big lawn, back yard, gardens, fields, and barn. It was the kind of home that gathers memories like dust, a place filled with laughter and play and pain and hurt and ghosts and games. We were given such advantages of schooling, music, and art as were available in the South, and our world was not limited to the South, for travel to far places seemed a simple, natural thing to us, and usually there was one of the family in a remote part of the earth.

[18] We knew we were a respected and important family of this small town but beyond this knowledge we gave little thought to status. Our father made money in lumber and naval stores for the excitement of making and losing it—not for what money can buy nor the security which it sometimes gives. I do not remember at any time wanting "to be rich" nor do I remember that thrift and saving were ideals which our parents considered important enough to urge upon us. Always in the family there was an acceptance of risk, a mild delight even in burning bridges, an expectant "what will happen now!" We were not irresponsible; living according to the pleasure principle was by no means our way of life. On the contrary we were trained to think that each of us should do something that would be of genuine usefulness to the world, and the family thought it right to make sacrifices if necessary, to give each child adequate preparation for this life's work. We were also trained to think learning important, and books, but "bad" books our mother burned. We valued music and art and crafts-

manship but it was people and their welfare and religion that were the foci around which our lives seemed naturally to move. Above all else, the important thing was what we "planned to do with our lives." That each of us must do something was as inevitable as breathing for we owed a "debt to society which must be paid." This was a family commandment.

[19] While many of our neighbors spent their energies in counting limbs on the family tree and grafting some on now and then to give symmetry to it, or in reliving the old bitter days of Reconstruction licking scars to cure their vague malaise, or in fighting each battle and turn of battle of that Civil War which has haunted the southern conscience so long, my father was pushing his nine children straight into the future. "You have your heritage," he used to say, "some of it good, some not so good; and as far as I know you had the usual number of grandmothers and grandfathers. Yes, there were slaves, far too many of them in the family, but that was your grandfather's mistake, not yours. The past has been lived. It is gone. The future is yours. What are you going to do with it?" Always he asked this question of his children and sometimes one knew it was but an echo of the old question he had spent his life trying to answer for himself. For always the future held my father's dreams; always there, not in the past, did he expect to find what he had spent his life searching for.

[20] We lived the same segregated life as did other southerners but our parents talked in excessively Christian and democratic terms. We were told ten thousand times that status and money are unimportant (though we were well supplied with both); we were told that "all men are brothers," that we are a part of a democracy and must act like democrats. We were told that the teachings of Jesus are real and important and could be practiced if we tried. We were told also that to be "radical" is bad, silly too; and that one must always conform to the "best behavior" of one's community and make it better if one can. We were taught that we were superior not to people but to hate and resentment, and that no member of the Smith family could stoop so low as to have an enemy. No matter what injury was done us, we must not injure ourselves further by retaliating. That was a family commandment too.

[21] We had family prayers once each day. All of us as children read the Bible in its entirety each year. We memorized hundreds of Bible verses and repeated them at breakfast, and said "sentence prayers" around the family table. God was not someone we met on Sunday but a permanent member of our household. It never occurred to me until I was fourteen or fifteen years old that He did not see every act and thought and chalk up the daily score on eternity's tablets.

[22] Despite the strain of living so intimately with God, the nine of us were strong, healthy, energetic youngsters who filled our days with play and sports and music and books and managed to live much of our lives on the careless level at which young lives should be lived. We had our times of profound anxiety of course, for there were hard lessons to be learned

about the body and "bad things" to be learned about sex. Sometimes I have wondered how we ever learned them with a mother so shy with words.

[23] She was a wistful creature who loved beautiful things like lace and sunsets and flowers in a vague inarticulate way, and took good care of her children. We always knew this was not her world but one she accepted under duress. Her private world we rarely entered, though the shadow of it lay at times heavily on our hearts.

[24] Our father owned large business interests, employed hundreds of colored and white laborers, paid them the prevailing low wages, worked them the prevailing long hours, built for them mill towns (Negro and white), built for each group a church, saw to it that religion was supplied free, saw to it that a commissary supplied commodities at a high price, and in general managed his affairs much as ten thousand other southern businessmen manage theirs.

[25] Even now, I can hear him chuckling as he told my mother how he won his fight for Prohibition. The high point of the campaign was election afternoon, when he lined up the entire mill force of several hundred (white and black), passed out a shining silver dollar to each one of them, marched them in and voted liquor out of our county. It was a great day in his life. He had won the Big Game, a game he was always playing with himself against all kinds of evil. It did not occur to him to scrutinize the methods he used. Evil was a word written in capitals; the devil was smart; if you wanted to win you outsmarted him. It was as simple as that.

[26] He was a practical, hardheaded, warmhearted, high-spirited man born during the Civil War, earning his living at twelve, struggling through bitter decades of Reconstruction and post-Reconstruction, through populist movement, through the panic of 1893, the panic of 1907, on into the twentieth century accepting his region as he found it, accepting its morals and its mores as he accepted its climate, with only scorn for those who held grudges against the North or pitied themselves or the South; scheming, dreaming, expanding his business, making and losing money, making friends whom he did not lose, with never a doubt that God was always by his side whispering hunches as to how to pull off successful deals. When he lost, it was his own fault. When he won, God had helped him.

[27] Once while we were kneeling at family prayers the fire siren at the mill sounded the alarm that the mill was on fire. My father did not falter from his prayer. The alarm sounded again and again—which signified that the fire was big. With quiet dignity he continued his talk with God while his children sweated and wriggled and hearts beat out of their chests in excitement. He was talking to God—how could he hurry out of the presence of the Most High to save his mills! When he finished his prayer, he quietly stood up, laid the Bible carefully on the table. Then, and only then, did he show an interest in what was happening in Mill Town.

WHEN I WAS A CHILD

... When the telegram was placed in his hands telling of the death of his beloved favorite son, he gathered his children together, knelt down, and in a steady voice which contained no hint of his shattered heart, loyally repeated, "God is our refuge and strength, a very present help in trouble. Therefore will we not fear, though the earth be removed, and though the mountains be carried into the midst of the sea." On his deathbed, he whispered to his old Business Partner in Heaven: "I have fought the fight; I have kept the faith."

[28] Against this backdrop the drama of the South was played out one day in my life:

[29] A little white girl was found in the colored section of our town, living with a Negro family in a broken-down shack. This family had moved in only a few weeks before and little was known of them. One of the ladies in my mother's club, while driving over to her washerwoman's, saw the child swinging on a gate. The shack, as she said, was hardly more than a pigsty and this white child was living with ignorant and dirty and sick-looking colored folks. "They must have kidnapped her," she told her friends. Genuinely shocked, the clubwomen busied themselves in an attempt to do something, for the child was very white indeed. The strange Negroes were subjected to a grueling questioning and finally grew frightened and evasive and refused to talk at all. This only increased the suspicion of the white group, and the next day the clubwomen, escorted by the town marshal, took the child from her adopted family despite their tears.

[30] She was brought to our home. I do not know why my mother consented to this plan. Perhaps because she loved children and always showed tenderness and concern for them. It was easy for one more to fit into our ample household and Janie was soon at home there. She roomed with me, sat next to me at the table; I found Bible verses for her to say at breakfast; she wore my clothes, played with my dolls and followed me around from morning to night. She was dazed by her new comforts and by the interesting activities of this big lively family; and I was as happily dazed, for her adoration was a new thing to me; and as time passed a quick, childish, and deeply felt bond grew up between us.

[31] But a day came when a telephone message was received from a colored orphanage. There was a meeting at our home, whispers, shocked exclamations. All afternoon the ladies went in and out of our house talking to Mother in tones too low for children to hear. And as they passed us at play, most of them looked quickly at Janie and quickly looked away again, though a few stopped and stared at her as if they could not tear their eyes from her face. When my father came home in the evening Mother closed her door against our young ears and talked a long time with him. I heard him laugh, heard Mother say, "But Papa, this is no laughing matter!" And then they were back in the living room with us and my mother was pale and my father was saying, "Well, work it out, honey, as best you can. After all, now that you know, it is pretty simple."

[32] In a little while my mother called my sister and me into her bedroom and told us that in the morning Janie would return to Colored Town. She said Janie was to have the dresses the ladies had given her and a few of my own, and the toys we had shared with her. She asked me if I would like to give Janie one of my dolls. She seemed hurried, though Janie was not to leave until next day. She said, "Why not select it now?" And in dreamlike stiffness I brought in my dolls and chose one for Janie. And then I found it possible to say, "Why? Why is she leaving? She likes us, she hardly knows them. She told me she had been with them only a month."

[33] "Because," Mother said gently, "Janie is a little colored girl."

[34] "But she can't be. She's white!"

[35] "We were mistaken. She is colored."

[36] "But she looks——"

[37] "She is colored. Please don't argue!"

[38] "What does it mean?" I whispered.

[39] "It means," Mother said slowly, "that she has to live in Colored Town with colored people."

[40] "But why? She lived here three weeks and she doesn't belong to them, she told me she didn't."

[41] "She is a little colored girl."

[42] "But you said yourself that she has nice manners. You said that," I persisted.

[43] "Yes, she is a nice child. But a colored child cannot live in our home."

[44] "Why?"

[45] "You know, dear! You have always known that white and colored people do not live together."

[46] "Can she come over to play?"

[47] "No."

[48] "I don't understand."

[49] "I don't either," my young sister quavered.

[50] "You're too young to understand. And don't ask me again, ever again, about this!" Mother's voice was sharp but her face was sad and there was no certainty left there. She hurried out and busied herself in the kitchen and I wandered through that room where I had been born, touching the old familiar things in it, looking at them, trying to find the answer to a question that moaned in my mind like a hurt thing. . . .

[51] And then I went out to Janie, who was waiting, knowing things were happening that concerned her but waiting until they were spoken aloud.

[52] I do not know quite how the words were said but I told her that she was to return in the morning to the little place where she had lived because she was colored and colored children could not live with white children.

[53] "Are you white?" she said.

[54] "I'm white," I replied, "and my sister is white. And you're colored. And white and colored can't live together because my mother says so."

[55] "Why?" Janie whispered.

[56] "Because they can't," I said. But I knew, though I said it firmly, that something was wrong. I knew my father and mother whom I passionately admired had done that which did not fit in with their teachings. I knew they had betrayed something which they held dear. And I was shamed by their failure and frightened, for I felt that they were no longer as powerful as I had thought. There was something Out There that was stronger than they and I could not bear to believe it. I could not confess that my father, who had always solved the family dilemmas easily and with laughter, could not solve this. I knew that my mother who was so good to children did not believe in her heart that she was being good to this child. There was not a word in my mind that said it but my body knew and my glands, and I was filled with anxiety.

[57] But I felt compelled to believe they were right. It was the only way my world could be held together. And, like a slow poison, it began to seep through me: *I was white. She was colored. We must not be together. It was bad to be together. Though you ate with your nurse when you were little, it was bad to eat with any colored person after that. It was bad just as other things were bad that your mother had told you. It was bad that she was to sleep in the room with me that night. It was bad. . . .*

[58] I was suddenly full of guilt. For three weeks I had done things that white children are not supposed to do. And now I knew these things had been wrong.

[59] I went to the piano and began to play, as I had always done when I was in trouble. I tried to play Paderewski's *Minuet* and as I stumbled through it, the little girl came over and sat on the bench with me. Feeling lonely, lost in these deep currents that were sweeping through our house that night, she crept closer and put her arms around me and I shrank away as if my body had been uncovered. I had not said a word, I did not say one, but she knew, and tears slowly rolled down her little white face. . . .

[60] And then I forgot it. For more than thirty years the experience was wiped out of my memory. But that night, and the weeks it was tied to, worked its way like a splinter, bit by bit down to the hurt places in my memory and festered there. And as I grew older, as more experiences collected around that faithless time, as memories of earlier, more profound hurts crept closer and closer drawn to that night as if to a magnet, I began to know that people who talked of love and Christianity and democracy did not mean it. That is a hard thing for a child to learn. I still admired my parents, there was so much that was strong and vital and sane and good about them and I never forgot this; I stubbornly believed in their sincerity, as I do to this day, and I loved them. Yet in my heart they were under suspicion. Something was wrong.

[61] Something was wrong with a world that tells you that love is good and people are important and then forces you to deny love and to humiliate people. I knew, though I would not for years confess it aloud, that in trying to shut the Negro race away from us, we have shut ourselves away from so many good, creative, honest, deeply human things in life. I began to understand so slowly at first but more and more clearly as the years passed, that the warped, distorted frame we have put around every Negro child from birth is around every white child also. Each is on a different side of the frame but each is pinioned there. And I knew that what cruelly shapes and cripples the personality of one is as cruelly shaping and crippling the personality of the other. I began to see that though we may, as we acquire new knowledge, live through new experiences, examine old memories, gain the strength to tear the frame from us, yet we are stunted and warped and in our lifetime cannot grow straight again any more than can a tree, put in a steel-like twisting frame when young, grow tall and straight when the frame is torn away at maturity.

[62] As I sit here writing, I can almost touch that little town, so close is the memory of it. There it lies, its main street lined with great oaks, heavy with matted moss that swings softly even now as I remember. A little white town rimmed with Negroes, making a deep shadow on the whiteness. There it lies, broken in two by one strange idea. Minds broken in two. Hearts broken. Conscience torn from acts. A culture split in a thousand pieces. That is segregation. I am remembering: a woman in a mental hospital walking four steps out, four steps in, unable to go further because she has drawn an invisible line around her small world and is terrified to take one step beyond it. . . . A man in a Disturbed Ward assigning "places" to the other patients and violently insisting that each stay in his place. . . . A Negro woman saying to me so quietly, "We cannot ride together on the bus, you know. It is not legal to be human in Georgia."

[63] Memory, walking the streets of one's childhood . . . of the town where one was born.

Questions on Meaning

1 In your own words, explain what you think Smith means by each of the following statements. As you do so, think about how the ideas expressed in these statements relate to each other. Think of the impact of the essay as a whole as you work with each statement.

   a The white man's burden is his own childhood. Every southerner knows this. Though he may deny it even to himself, yet he drags through life with him the heavy weight of a past that never eases and is rarely understood. . . . (paragraph 6)

WHEN I WAS A CHILD

  b Sometimes it was as if all doors opened inward. . . . Sometimes we children lost even the desire to get outside and tried only to make a comfortable home of the trap of swinging doors that history and religion and a war, man's greed and his guilt had placed us in at birth. (paragraph 7)

  c I began to understand so slowly at first but more and more clearly as the years passed, that the warped, distorted frame we have put around every Negro child from birth is around every white child also. (paragraph 61)

  d I began to see that though we may, as we acquire new knowledge, live through new experiences, examine old memories, gain the strength to tear the frames from us, yet we are stunted and warped and in our lifetime cannot grow straight again any more than can a tree, put in a steel-like twisting frame when young, grow tall and straight when the frame is torn away at maturity. (paragraph 61)

2 What personality and character traits in her father does Smith depict here? Why do you think she pays so much attention to these qualities in this essay? How does what she says about her father relate to the main idea she is developing throughout?

3 Commenting on the Janie incident, Smith says: "I knew my father and mother, whom I passionately admired, had done that which did not fit in with their teachings. I knew they had betrayed something which they held dear." What other specific examples and what general behavior patterns does the author mention that develop her point that the southern people of her period were torn between conflicting principles?

4 What connection do you find between the three examples with which Smith closes her essay? "A woman in a mental hospital walking four steps out, four steps in, unable to go further because she has drawn an invisible line around her small world and is terrified to take one step beyond it. . . . A man in a Disturbed Ward assigning 'places' to the other patients and violently insisting that each stay in his place. . . . A Negro woman saying to me so quietly, 'We cannot ride together on the bus, you know. It is not legal to be human in Georgia.' " Why do you think the author chose to end her piece with these particular examples?

Questions on Style and Structure

1 Where does the introduction of this essay end? What is the function of the introduction?

2 This essay is rich in figurative language. Discuss what each of the following examples contributes to the author's tone and purpose.

  a To them, it is a vague thing weaving in and out of their play, like a ghost haunting an old graveyard or whispers after the household sleeps—fleeting mystery, vague menace, to which each responds in his own way. (paragraph 1)

ESSAYS CHIEFLY PERSONAL

    b Here it was that I began to grow, seeking my way, as do all children, through the honeycomb cells of our life to the bright reality outside. (paragraph 7)

    c I know only that the doors opened, a little; that somewhere along that iron corridor we travel from babyhood to maturity, doors swinging inward began to swing outward, showing glimpses of the world beyond, of that clear bright thing we call "reality." (paragraph 14)

    d It never occurred to me until I was fourteen or fifteen years old that He did not see every act and thought and chalk up the daily score on eternity's tables. (paragraph 21)

    e But that night, and the weeks it was tied to, worked its way like a splinter, bit by bit down to the hurt places in my memory and festered there. (paragraph 60)

    f A little white town rimmed with Negroes, making a deep shadow on the whiteness. (paragraph 62)

3 In the first paragraph, the author repeats a word for emphasis: "The children know this 'trouble' is *bigger* than they, *bigger* than their family, *bigger* than their church, so big that people turn away from its size." Find another sentence in which emphasis is achieved through such repetition.

4 What technique does Smith use to make paragraph 3 coherent? How about paragraphs 9 and 13?

5 Many of the sentences in this selection have been carefully structured for emphasis and variety. Compare the pairs of sentences below (the first of each pair is Smith's); be prepared to explain the superiority of her version.

    a But all know that under quiet words and warmth and laughter, under the slow ease and tender concern about small matters, there is a heavy burden on all of us and as heavy a refusal to confess it. (paragraph 1)

        But all know that there is a heavy burden on all of us and as heavy a refusal to confess it under quiet words and warmth and laughter, under the slow ease and tender concern about small matters.

    b In this South I was born and now live. (paragraph 7)

        I was born and now live in this South.

    c While many of our neighbors spent their energies in counting limbs on the family tree and grafting some on now and then to give symmetry to it, or in reliving the old bitter days of Reconstruction licking scars to cure their vague malaise, or in fighting each battle and turn of battle of that Civil War which has haunted the southern conscience so long, my father was pushing his nine children straight into the future. (paragraph 19)

        My father was pushing his nine children straight into the future while many of our neighbors . . .

    d Her private world we rarely entered, though the shadow of it lay at times heavily on our hearts. (paragraph 23)

We rarely entered her private world, though the shadow of it lay at times heavily on our hearts.

6 In paragraphs 32 through 48, the author presents a long conversation between her and her mother. Should she have summarized it instead? Why or why not?

7 Smith, in paragraph 16, speaks of presenting "a brief glimpse" of her family and background. Would you agree that that "brief glimpse" is essential to the essay? If so, in what way?

Exploring Words

1 *dissonant*. Note that Smith uses the term in a metaphorical sense (she is obviously not writing about sounds). Can you think of some other metaphorical uses of this word?

2 *decorums*. What *decorums* do you remember observing when you were a child. (You should know that this word is usually used in the singular form as in "standards of *decorum*.")

3 *modulations*. What do the following words have in common: *modulate, modest, modify, module, moderate* (the adjective form), and *modicum*? Confirm your intuitions by checking your dictionary.

4 *peremptory*. In your dictionary you will probably find several rather different meanings listed for *peremptory*. Which one of these applies to Smith's use of the term? What relationship do you find between these meanings?

5 *malaise*. Would a more precise term fit here? Check your dictionary.

Suggestions for Writing

1 In paragraph 14, Smith writes of her own experiences, "I know only that the doors opened, a little; that somewhere along that iron corridor we travel from babyhood to maturity, doors swinging inward began to swing outward, showing glimpses of the world beyond, of that clear bright thing we call 'reality.'" Write a concretely developed essay dealing with one of the doors that swung outward in your own life.

2 Write a paper showing the effect of the town or region in which you grew up on the development of your personality.

Going Home Again: The New American Scholarship Boy
RICHARD RODRIGUEZ

Getting Started

With Ideas

At the time this article was originally published, Richard Rodriguez was on the faculty at the University of California at Berkeley. Prior to that time, he had been what he calls a "new American scholarship boy." As you read the essay, watch for his definition of this phrase and look also for the metaphorical significance of the first part of the title: "Going Home Again."

With Words

1 juxtaposition (2)—from the Latin *juxta* ("near") and the English word *position*.
2 gregarious (5)—from the Latin word meaning "belonging to a flock."
3 parochialism (17)—think of *parochial* schools, but recognize that this word is used in a metaphorical sense, as it often is.
4 paradoxically (26)—if you consider the context of this word here and recall the way *paradox* was used in "Peaceful Coexistence with Rattlesnakes" (p. 41), you will be close to Rodriguez's meaning.
5 atrophied (26)—from the Greek *a* ("not") and the Greek *trephein* ("to nourish"). Note Rodriguez's metaphorical use of the word.
6 voyeur (28)—"Peeping Tom" is often considered a slang synonym, but again you will see Rodriguez uses the term figuratively.
7 tenuously (29)—from the Latin word meaning "thin" or "slight."

[1] At each step, with every graduation from one level of education to the next, the refrain from bystanders was strangely the same: "Your parents must be so proud of you." I suppose that my parents were proud, although I suspect, too, that they felt more than pride alone as they watched me advance through my education. They seemed to know that my education was separating us from one another, making it difficult to

Reprinted from *The American Scholar*, Volume 44, Number 1, Winter 1974–75. Copyright © 1974 by the United Chapters of Phi Beta Kappa. By permission of the publishers.

resume familiar intimacies. Mixed with the instincts of parental pride, a certain hurt also communicated itself—too private ever to be adequately expressed in words, but real nonetheless.

[2] The autobiographical facts pertinent to this essay are simply stated in two sentences, though they exist in somewhat awkward juxtaposition to each other. I am the son of Mexican-American parents, who speak a blend of Spanish and English, but who read neither language easily. I am about to receive a Ph.D. in English Renaissance literature. What sort of life—what tensions, feelings, conflicts—connects these two sentences? I look back and remember my life from the time I was seven or eight years old as one of constant movement away from a Spanish-speaking folk culture toward the world of the English-language classroom. As the years passed, I felt myself becoming less like my parents and less comfortable with the assumption of visiting relatives that I was still the Spanish-speaking child they remembered. By the time I began college, visits home became suffused with silent embarrassment: there seemed so little to share, however strong the ties of our affection. My parents would tell me what happened in their lives or in the lives of relatives; I would respond with news of my own. Polite questions would follow. Our conversations came to seem more like interviews.

[3] A few months ago, my dissertation nearly complete, I came upon my father looking through my bookcase. He quietly fingered the volumes of Milton's tracts and Augustine's theology with that combination of reverence and distrust those who are not literate sometimes show for the written word. Silently, I watched him from the door of the room. However much he would have insisted that he was "proud" of his son for being able to master the texts, I knew, if pressed further, he would have admitted to complicated feelings about my success. When he looked across the room and suddenly saw me, his body tightened slightly with surprise, then we both smiled.

[4] For many years I kept my uneasiness about becoming a success in education to myself. I did so in part because I wanted to avoid vague feelings that, if considered carefully, I would have no way of dealing with; and in part because I felt that no one else shared my reaction to the opportunity provided by education. When I began to rehearse my story of cultural dislocation publicly, however, I found many listeners willing to admit to similar feelings from their own pasts. Equally impressive was the fact that many among those I spoke with were *not* from nonwhite racial groups, which made me realize that one can grow up to enter the culture of the academy and find it a "foreign" culture for a variety of reasons, ranging from economic status to religious heritage. But why, I next wondered, was it that, though there were so many of us who came from childhood cultures alien to the academy's, we voiced our uneasiness to one another and to ourselves so infrequently? Why did it take *me* so long to acknowledge publicly the cultural costs I had paid to earn a Ph.D. in Renaissance English literature? Why, more precisely, am I writing these words only

now when my connection to my past barely survives except as nostalgic memory?

[5] Looking back, a person risks losing hold of the present while being confounded by the past. For the child who moves to an academic culture from a culture that dramatically lacks academic traditions, looking back can jeopardize the certainty he has about the desirability of this new academic culture. Richard Hoggart's description, in *The Uses of Literacy*, of the cultural pressures on such a student, whom Hoggart calls the "scholarship boy," helps make the point. The scholarship boy must give nearly unquestioning allegiance to academic culture, Hoggart argues, if he is to succeed at all, so different is the milieu of the classroom from the culture he leaves behind. For a time, the scholarship boy may try to balance his loyalty between his concretely experienced family life and the more abstract mental life of the classroom. In the end, though, he must choose between the two worlds: if he intends to succeed as a student, he must, literally and figuratively, separate himself from his family, with its gregarious life, and find a quiet place to be alone with his thoughts.

[6] After a while, the kind of allegiance the young student might once have given his parents is transferred to the teacher, the new parent. Now without the support of the old ties and certainties of the family, he almost mechanically acquires the assumptions, practices, and style of the classroom milieu. For the loss he might otherwise feel, the scholarship boy substitutes an enormous enthusiasm for nearly everything having to do with school.

[7] How readily I read my own past into the portrait of Hoggart's scholarship boy. Coming from a home in which mostly Spanish was spoken, for example, I had to decide to forget Spanish when I began my education. To succeed in the classroom, I needed psychologically to sever my ties with Spanish. Spanish represented an alternate culture as well as another language—and the basis of my deepest sense of relationship to my family. Although I recently taught myself to read Spanish, the language that I see on the printed page is not quite the language I heard in my youth. That other Spanish, the spoken Spanish of my family, I remember with nostalgia and guilt: guilt because I cannot explain to aunts and uncles why I do not answer their questions any longer in their own idiomatic language. Nor was I able to explain to teachers in graduate school, who regularly expected me to read and speak Spanish with ease, why my very ability to reach graduate school as a student of English literature in the first place required me to loosen my attachments to a language I spoke years earlier. Yet, having lost the ability to speak Spanish, I never forgot it so totally that I could not understand it. Hearing Spanish spoken on the street reminded me of the community I once felt a part of, and still cared deeply about. I never forgot Spanish so thoroughly, in other words, as to move outside the range of its nostalgic pull.

[8] Such moments of guilt and nostalgia were, however, just

that—momentary. They punctuated the history of my otherwise successful progress from *barrio* to classroom. Perhaps they even encouraged it. Whenever I felt my determination to succeed wavering, I tightened my hold on the conventions of academic life.

[9] Spanish was one aspect of the problem, my parents another. They could raise deeper, more persistent doubts. They offered encouragement to my brothers and me in our work, but they also spoke, only half jokingly, about the way education was putting "big ideas" into our heads. When we would come home, for example, and challenge assumptions we earlier believed, they would be forced to defend their beliefs (which, given our new verbal skills, they did increasingly less well) or, more frequently, to submit to our logic with the disclaimer, "It's what we were taught in our time to believe. . . ." More important, after we began to leave home for college, they voiced regret about how "changed" we had become, how much further away from one another we had grown. They partly yearned for a return to the time before education assumed their children's primary loyalty. This yearning was renewed each time they saw their nieces and nephews (none of whom continued their education beyond high school, all of whom continued to speak fluent Spanish) living according to the conventions and assumptions of their parents' culture. If I was already troubled by the time I graduated from high school by that refrain of congratulations ("Your parents must be so proud. . . ."), I realize now how much more difficult and complicated was my progress into academic life for my parents, as they saw the cultural foundation of their family erode, than it was for me.

[10] Yet my parents were willing to pay the price of alienation and continued to encourage me to become a scholarship boy because they perceived, as others of the lower classes had before them, the relation between education and social mobility. Lacking the former themselves made them acutely aware of its necessity as prerequisite for the latter. They sent their children off to school in the hopes of their acquiring something "better" beyond education. Notice the assumption here that education is something of a tool or license—a means to an end, which has been the traditional way the lower or working classes have viewed the value of education in the past. That education might alter children in more basic ways than providing them with skills, certificates of proficiency, and even upward mobility, may come as a surprise for some, but the financial cost is usually tolerated.

[11] Complicating my own status as a scholarship boy in the last ten years was the rise, in the mid-1960s, of what was then called "the Third World Student Movement." Racial minority groups, led chiefly by black intellectuals, began to press for greater access to higher education. The assumption behind their criticism, like the assumption of white working-class families, was that educational opportunity was useful for economic and social advancement. The racial minority leaders went one

step further, however, and it was this step that was probably most revolutionary. Minority students came to the campus feeling that they were representative of larger groups of people—that, indeed, they were advancing the condition of entire societies by their matriculation. Actually, this assumption was not altogether new to me. Years before, educational success was something my parents urged me to strive for precisely because it would reflect favorably on *all* Mexican-Americans—specifically, my intellectual achievement would help deflate the stereotype of the "dumb Pancho." This early goal was only given greater currency by the rhetoric of the Third World spokesmen. But it was the fact that I felt myself suddenly much more a "public" Mexican-American, a representative of sorts, that was to prove so crucial for me during these years.

[12] One college admissions officer assured me one day that he recognized my importance to his school precisely as deriving from the fact that, after graduation, I would surely be "going back to [my] community." More recently, teachers have urged me not to trouble over the fact that I am not "representative" of my culture, assuring me that I can serve as a "model" for those still in the *barrio* working toward academic careers. This is the line that I hear, too, when being interviewed for a faculty position. The interviewer almost invariably assumes that, because I am racially a Mexican-American, I can serve as a special counselor to minority students. The expectation is that I still retain the capacity for intimacy with "my people."

[13] This new way of thinking about the possible uses of education is what has made the entrance of minority students into higher education so dramatic. When the minority group student was accepted into the academy, he came—in everyone's mind—as part of a "group." When I began college, I barely attracted attention except perhaps as a slightly exotic ("Are you from India?") brown-skinned student; by the time I graduated, my presence was annually noted by, among others, the college public relations office as "one of the fifty-two students with Spanish surnames enrolled this year." By having his presence announced to the campus in this way, the minority group student was unlike any other scholarship boy the campus had seen before. The minority group student now dramatized more publicly, if also in new ways, the issues of cultural dislocation that education forces, issues that are not solely racial in origin. When Richard Rodriguez *became* a Chicano, the dilemmas he earlier had as a scholarship boy were complicated but not decisively altered by the fact that he had assumed a group identity.

[14] The assurance I heard that, somehow, I was being useful to my community by being a student was gratefully believed, because it gave me a way of dealing with the guilt and cynicism that each year came my way along with the scholarships, grants, and, lately, job offers from schools which a few years earlier would have refused me admission as a student. Each year, in fact, it became harder to believe that my success had anything to do with my intellectual performance, and harder to resist the

conclusion that it was due to my minority group status. When I drove to the airport, on my way to London as a Fulbright Fellow last year, leaving behind cousins of my age who were already hopelessly burdened by financial insecurity and dead-end jobs, momentary guilt could be relieved by the thought that somehow my trip was beneficial to persons other than myself. But, of course, if the thought was a way of dealing with the guilt, it was also the reason for the guilt. Sitting in a university library, I would notice a janitor of my own race and grow uneasy; I was, I knew, in a rough way a beneficiary of his condition. Guilt was accompanied by cynicism. The most dazzlingly talented minority students I know today refuse to believe that their success is wholly based on their own talent, or even that when they speak in a classroom anyone hears them as anything but *the* voice of their minority group. It is scarcely surprising, then, though initially it probably seemed puzzling, that so many of the angriest voices on the campus against the injustices of racism came from those not visibly its primary victims.

[15] It became necessary to believe the rhetoric about the value of one's presence on campus simply as a way of living with one's "success." Among ourselves, however, minority group students often admitted to a shattering sense of loss—the feeling that, somehow, something was happening to us. Especially from students who had not yet become accustomed, as by that time I had, to the campus, I remember hearing confessions of extreme discomfort and isolation. Our close associations, the separate dining-room tables, and the special dormitories helped to relieve some of the pain, but only some of it.

[16] Significant here was the development of the ethnic studies concept—black studies, Chicano studies, et cetera—and the related assumption held by minority group students in a number of departments that they could keep in touch with their old cultures by making these cultures the subject of their study. Here again one notices how different the minority student was from other comparable students: other scholarship boys—poor Jews and the sons of various immigrant cultures—came to the academy singly, much more inclined to accept the courses and material they found. The ethnic studies concept was an indication that, for a multitude of reasons, the new racial minority group students were not willing to give up so easily their ties with their old cultures.

[17] The importance of these new ethnic studies was that they introduced the academy to subject matter that generally deserved to be studied, and at the same time offered a staggering critique of the academy's tendency toward parochialism. Most minority group intellectuals never noted this tendency toward academic parochialism. They more often saw the reason for, say, the absence of a course on black literature in an English department as a case of simple racism. That it might instead be an instance of the fact that academic culture can lose track of human societies and whole areas of human experience was rarely raised. Never asking such a question, the minority group students never seemed to wonder ei-

ther if as teachers their own courses might suffer the same cultural limitations other seminars and classes suffered. Consequently, in a peculiar way the new minority group critics of higher education came to justify the academy's assumptions. The possibility that academic culture could encourage one to grow out of touch with cultures beyond its conceptual horizon was never seriously considered.

[18] Too often in the last ten years one heard minority group students repeat the joke, never very funny in the first place, about the racial minority academic who ended up sounding more "white" than white academics. Behind the scorn for such a figure was the belief that the new generation of minority group students would be able to avoid having to make similar kinds of cultural concessions. The pressures that might have led to such conformity went unexamined.

[19] For the last few years my annoyance at hearing such jokes was doubtless related to the fact that I was increasingly beginning to sense that I was the "bleached" academic the minority group students found so laughable. I suppose I had always sensed that my cultural allegiance was undergoing subtle alterations as I was being educated. Only when I finished my course work in graduate school and went off to England for my dissertation year did I grasp how far I had traveled from my cultural origins. My year in England was actually my first opportunity to write and reflect upon the kind of material that I would spend my life producing. It was my first chance, too, to be free simultaneously of the distractions of course-work and of the insecurities of trying to find my niche in academic life. Sitting in the reading room of the British Museum, I no longer doubted that I had joined academic society. Ironically, this feeling of having finally arrived allowed me to look back to the community whence I came. That I was geographically farther away from my home than I had ever been lent a metaphorical resonance to the cultural distance I suddenly felt.

[20] But the feeling was not pleasing. The reward of feeling a part of the world of the British Museum was an odd one. Each morning I would arrive at the reading room and grow increasingly depressed by the silence and what the silence implied—that my life as a scholar would require self-absorption. Who, I wondered, would find my work helpful enough to want to read it? Was not my dissertation—whose title alone would puzzle my relatives—only my grandest exercise thus far in self-enclosure? The sight of the heads around me bent over their texts and papers, many so thoroughly engrossed that they wouldn't look up at the silent clock overhead for hours at a stretch, made me recall the remarkable noises of life in my family home. The tedious prose I was writing, a prose constantly qualified by footnotes, reminded me of the capacity for passionate statement those of the culture I was born into commanded—and which, could it be, I had now lost.

[21] As I remembered it during those gray English afternoons, the past rushed forward to define more precisely my present condition. Re-

membering my youth, a time when I was not restricted to a chair but ran barefoot under a summer sun that tightened my skin with its white heat, made the fact that it was only my mind that "moved" each hour in the library painfully obvious.

[22] I did need to figure out where I had lost touch with my past. I started to become alien to my family culture the day I became a scholarship boy. In the British Museum the realization seemed obvious. But later, returning to America, I returned to minority group students who were still speaking of their cultural ties to their past. How was I to tell them what I had learned about myself in England?

[23] A short while ago, a group of enthusiastic Chicano undergraduates came to my office to ask me to teach a course to high school students in the *barrio* on the Chicano novel. This new literature, they assured me, has an important role to play in helping to shape the consciousness of a people currently without adequate representation in literature. Listening to them I was struck immediately with the cultural problems raised by their assumption. I told them that the novel is not capable of dealing with Chicano experience adequately, simply because most Chicanos are not literate, or are at least not yet comfortably so. This is not something Chicanos need to apologize for (though, I suppose, remembering my own childhood ambition to combat stereotypes of the Chicano as mental menial, it is not something easily admitted). Rather the genius and value of those Chicanos who do not read seem to me to be largely that their reliance on voice, the spoken word, has given them the capacity for intimate conversation that I, as someone who now relies heavily on the written word, can only envy. The second problem, I went on, is more in the nature of a technical one: the novel, in my opinion, is not a form capable of being true to the basic sense of communal life that typifies Chicano culture. What the novel as a literary form is best capable of representing is solitary existence set against a large social background. Chicano novelists, not coincidentally, nearly always fail to capture the breathtakingly rich family life of most Chicanos, and instead often describe only the individual Chicano in transit between Mexican and American cultures.

[24] I said all of this to the Chicano students in my office, and could see that little of it made an impression. They seemed only frustrated by what they probably took to be a slick, academic justification for evading social responsibility. After a time, they left me, sitting alone. . . .

[25] There is a danger of being misunderstood here. I am not suggesting that an academic cannot reestablish ties of any kind with his old culture. Indeed, he can have an impact on the culture of his childhood. But as an academic, one exists by definition in a culture separate from one's nonacademic roots and, therefore, any future ties one has with those who remain "behind" are complicated by one's new cultural perspective.

[26] Paradoxically, the distance separating the academic from his nonacademic past can make his past seem, if not closer, then clearer. It is

possible for the academic to understand the culture from which he came "better" than those who still live within it. In my own experience, it has only been as I have come to appraise my past through categories and notions derived from the social sciences that I have been able to think of Chicano life in cultural terms at all. Characteristics I took for granted or noticed only in passing—the spontaneity, the passionate speech, the trust in concrete experience, the willingness to think communally rather than individually—these are all significant phenomena to me now as aspects of a total culture. (My parents have neither the time nor the inclination to think about their culture as a culture.) Able to conceptualize a sense of Chicano culture, I am now also more attracted to that culture than I was before. The temptation now is to try to preserve those traits of my old culture that have not yet, in effect, atrophied.

[27] The racial self-consciousness of minority group students during the last few years evident in the ethnic costumes, the stylized gestures, and the idiomatic though often evasive devices for insisting on one's continuing membership in the community of the past, are also indications that the minority group student has gained a new appreciation of the culture of his origin precisely because of his earlier alienation from it. As a result, Chicano students sometimes become more Chicano than most Chicanos. I remember, for example, my father's surprise when, walking across my college campus one afternoon, we came upon two Chicano academics wearing serapes. He and my mother were also surprised—indeed offended—when they earlier heard student activists use the word "Chicano." For them the term was a private one, primarily descriptive of persons they knew. It suggested intimacy. Hearing the word shouted into a microphone by a stranger left them bewildered. What they could not understand was that the student activist finds it easier than they to use "Chicano" in a more public way, for his distance from their culture and his membership in academic culture permits a wider and more abstract view.

[28] The Mexican-Americans who begin to call themselves Chicanos in this new way are actually forming a new version of what it means to be a Chicano. The culture that didn't see itself as a culture is suddenly prized and identified for being one. The price one pays for this new self-consciousness is the knowledge of just that—it is *new*—and this knowledge is not available to those who remain at home. So it is knowledge that separates as well as unites people. Wanting more desperately than ever to assert his ties with the newly visible culture, the minority group student is tempted to exploit those characteristics of that culture that might yet survive in him. But the self-consciousness never allows one to feel completely at ease with the old culture. Worse, the knowledge of the culture of the past often leaves one feeling strangely solitary. At home, I hear relatives speak and find myself analyzing too much of what they say. It is embarrassing being a cultural anthropologist in one's own family's kitchen. I keep feeling myself little more than a cultural voyeur. I often come away from family gatherings suspecting, in fact, that what conceptions of my

culture I carry with me are no more than illusions. Because they were never there before, because no one back home shares them, I grow less and less to trust their reliability: too often they seem no more than mental bubbles floating before an academic's eye.

[29] Many who have taught minority group students in the last decade testify to sensing characteristics of a childhood culture still very much alive in these students. Should the teacher make these students aware of these characteristics? Initially, most of us would probably answer negatively. Better to trust the unconscious survival of the past than the always problematical, sometimes even clownish, re-creations of it. But the cultural past cannot be assured of survival; perhaps many of its characteristics are lost simply because the student is never encouraged to look for them. Even those that do survive do so tenuously. As a teacher, one can only hope that the best qualities in his minority group students' cultural legacy aren't altogether snuffed out by academic education.

[30] More easy to live with and distinguishable from self-conscious awareness of the past are the ways the past unconsciously survives—perhaps even yet survives in me. As it turns out, the issue becomes less acute with time. With each year, the chance that the student is unaware of his cultural legacy is diminished as the habit of academic reflectiveness grows stronger. Although the culture of the academy makes innocence about one's cultural past less likely, this same culture, and the conceptual tools it provides, increases the desire to want to write and speak about the past. The paradox persists.

[31] Awaiting the scholarship boy who finally acknowledges the fact that his perceptions of reality have changed is the dilemma of action. The sentimental reaction to this knowledge entails merely a refusal to renew contact with one's nonacademic culture lest one contaminate it. The problem, however, with this sentimental solution is that it overlooks the way academic culture renders one capable of dealing with the transactions of mass society. Academic culture, with its habits of conceptualization and abstraction, allows those of us from other cultures to deal with each other in a mass society. In this sense academic culture does have a profound political impact. Although people intent upon social mobility think of education as a means to an end, education does become an end: its culture allows one to exist more easily in a society increasingly anonymous and impersonal. The truth is, the academic's distance from his own experience brings the capacity for communicating with bureaucracies and understanding one's position in society—a prerequisite for political action.

[32] If the sentimental reaction to nonacademic culture is to fear changing it, the political response, typical especially of working-class and lately minority group leaders, is to see higher education solely in terms of its political and social possibilities. Its cultural consequences, in this view, are disregarded. At this time when we are so keenly aware of social and economic inequality, it might seem beside the point to warn those who are

working to bring about equality that education alters culture as well as economic status. And yet, if there is one main criticism that I, as a minority group student, must make of minority group leaders in their past attacks on the "racism" of the academy, it is that they never distinguished between my right to higher education and the desirability of my actually entering the academy—which is another way of saying again that they never recognized that there were things I could lose by becoming a scholarship boy.

[33] Certainly, the academy changes those from alien cultures more than it is changed by them. While minority groups had an impact on higher education, largely because of their advantage in coming as a group, within the last few years students such as myself, who finally ended up certified as academics, also ended up sounding very much like the academics we found when we came to the campus. I do not enjoy making such admissions. But perhaps now the time has come when questions about the cultural costs of education ought to be delayed no longer. Those of us who have been scholarship boys know in our bones that our education has exacted a large price in exchange for the large benefits it has conferred upon us. And what is sadder to consider, after we have paid that price, we go home and casually change the cultures that nurtured us. My parents today understand how they are "Chicanos" in a large and impersonal sense. The gains from such knowledge are clear. But so, too, are the reasons for regret.

Questions on Meaning

Here are some key quotations from different parts of the essay, each followed by a question. Answer the questions, and then think about the ways the ideas expressed in them fit together. Be ready to state in your own words the main idea of the whole essay (either in a paragraph or in a brief oral statement).

1 "For the child who moves to an academic culture from a culture that dramatically lacks academic traditions, looking back can jeopardize the certainty he has about the desirability of this new academic culture." (paragraph 5) What examples of the conflict between the academic culture (school, college, and graduate school) and of the culture from which he came does Rodriguez mention?

2 "Now without the support of the old ties and certainties of the family, he [the young student] almost mechanically acquires the assumptions, practices, and style of the classroom milieu." (paragraph 6) Mention some instances Rodriguez reports that show how this problem affected his relationships with his family.

3 ". . . I was already troubled by the time I graduated from high school by that refrain of congratulations ('Your parents must be so proud. . . .'). . . ."

(paragraph 9) Why was he "troubled" when people said they thought his parents must be proud of him?

4 "When Richard Rodriguez *became* a Chicano, the dilemmas he earlier had as a scholarship boy were complicated but not decisively altered by the fact that he had assumed a group identity." (paragraph 13) Explain this statement in your own words, paying particular attention to the fact that *became* is in italics.

5 ". . . academic culture can lose track of human societies and whole areas of human experience. . . ." (paragraph 17) What do you think Rodriguez means by this? Note his preceding comments on the value of ethnic study programs.

6 "That I was geographically farther away from my home than I had ever been lent a metaphorical resonance to the cultural distance I suddenly felt." (paragraph 19) What does he mean by a "metaphorical resonance"? Why did his period of study abroad have the effect he describes here?

7 "It is embarrassing being a cultural anthropologist in one's own family's kitchen." (paragraph 28) Explain this statement.

8 ". . . if there is one main criticism that I, as a minority group student, must make of minority group leaders in their past attacks on the 'racism' of the academy, it is that they never distinguished between my right to higher education and the desirability of my actually entering the academy. . . ." (paragraph 32) Show how this comment sums up the idea of the entire essay.

Questions on Style and Structure

1 Where does the introduction of this essay end? How would you justify your answer?

2 If you were to outline this selection, how many main sections (which would be indicated by Roman numerals) would it have? What would the heading of each section be?

3 Paragraph 4 serves as a good example of the author's concern with paragraph unity and coherence. What is the central idea of the paragraph? Underline the words that make the paragraph coherent. What other paragraphs did you find to be particularly effective?

4 Writers frequently overuse quotation marks around words. When Rodriguez surrounds a word with quotation marks, he does so for a particular reason. After examining the context in which each of the following sentences appears, explain why the quotation marks are appropriate.

  a The expectation is that I still retain the capacity for intimacy with "my people." (paragraph 12)
  b It became necessary to believe the rhetoric about the value of one's presence on campus simply as a way of living with one's "success." (paragraph 15)

c But as an academic, one exists by definition in a culture separate from one's nonacademic roots and, therefore, any future ties one has with those who remain "behind" are complicated by one's new cultural perspective. (paragraph 25)

d It is possible for the academic to understand the culture from which he came "better" than those who still live within it. (paragraph 26)

5 Analyze the following examples of figurative language. How does such language contribute to the author's purpose?

a . . . I realize now how much more difficult and complicated was my progress into academic life for my parents, as they saw the cultural foundation of their family erode, than it was for me. (paragraph 9)

b For the last few years my annoyance at hearing such jokes ["about the racial minority academic who ended up sounding more 'white' than white academics"] was doubtless related to the fact that I was increasingly beginning to sense that I was the "bleached" academic the minority group students found so laughable. (paragraph 19)

c I keep feeling myself little more than a cultural voyeur. (paragraph 28)

d Because they [suspicions "that what conceptions of my culture I carry with me are no more than illusions"] were never there before, because no one back home shares them, I grow less and less to trust their reliability: too often they seem no more than mental bubbles floating before an academic's eye. (paragraph 28)

6 Rodriguez uses a rich variety of sentence patterns in this essay. Construct several sentences that duplicate the structure of the italicized portions of each of the following pairs of sentences.

a *That it might instead be an instance of the fact that academic culture can lose track of human societies and whole areas of human experience* was rarely raised. (paragraph 17)

That I was geographically farther away from home than I had ever been lent a metaphorical resonance to the cultural distance I suddenly felt. (paragraph 19) [The noun clauses, which are underlined, serve as the subjects of these two sentences.]

b *However much he would have insisted that he was "proud" of his son for being able to master the texts,* I knew, if pressed further, he would have admitted to complicated feelings about my success. (paragraph 3)

By the time I began college, visits home became suffused with silent embarrassment: there seemed so little to share, *however strong the ties of our affection.* (paragraph 2)

7 Frequently, the sentences that the author uses depart from the usual word order of English sentences. Here are several sentences from the essay, each followed by another version that conforms to the usual word order. Carefully compare the two versions, and be prepared to explain why Rodriguez's sentences are superior.

a Equally impressive was the fact that many among those I spoke with were *not* from nonwhite racial groups, which made me realize that one can grow up to enter the culture of the academy and find it a "foreign" culture for a variety of reasons, ranging from economic status to religious heritage. (paragraph 4)

The fact that . . . was equally impressive.

b For the loss he might otherwise feel, the scholarship boy substitutes an enormous enthusiasm for nearly everything having to do with school. (paragraph 6)

The scholarship boy substitutes an enormous enthusiasm for nearly everything having to do with school for the loss he might otherwise feel.

c To succeed in the classroom, I needed psychologically to sever my ties with Spanish. (paragraph 7)

I needed psychologically to sever my ties with Spanish to succeed in the classroom.

d That other Spanish, the spoken Spanish of my family, I remember with nostalgia and guilt. . . . (paragraph 7)

I remember the other Spanish, the spoken Spanish of my family, with nostalgia and guilt. . . .

e Especially from students who had not yet become accustomed, as by that time I had, to the campus, I remember hearing confessions of extreme discomfort and isolation. (paragraph 15)

I remember hearing confessions of extreme discomfort and isolation especially from students who had not yet become accustomed to the campus as I had by that time.

f Awaiting the scholarship boy who finally acknowledges the fact that his perceptions of reality have changed is the dilemma of action. (paragraph 31)

The dilemma of action awaits the scholarship boy who finally acknowledges the fact that his perceptions of reality have changed.

8 What basic technique does Rodriguez use to conclude this essay?

Exploring Words

1 *juxtaposition.* After examining your dictionary's definition of the word, write a sentence of your own using it.

2 *gregarious.* Although the Latin word from which *gregarious* comes refers to animals that flock together, the English word is usually applied to human behavior, as it is in Rodriguez's essay. Check your dictionary's definition, and then write a sentence using *gregarious* to describe the behavior of an individual or group you know.

3 *parochialism.* This word, like *provincial,* has taken on a negative meaning as it has developed (linguists call this process "pejoration"). Think of other words that have undergone this kind of change. One example is "the establishment."

4 *paradoxically*. Why do you suppose Rodriguez chose *paradoxically* rather than *strangely, oddly enough,* or *remarkably*?

5 *atrophied*. Check your dictionary, and then use *atrophied* in its literal sense.

6 *voyeur*. Consult your dictionary to be sure you understand the literal sense of this word, and then write a sentence using the term figuratively as Rodriguez does.

7 *tenuously*. Rodriguez speaks of people who "survive . . . *tenuously*" outside the *barrio*. What relationships of your own fit the meaning of *tenuously* that you find in your dictionary? You will also see the term used with *arguement*. Can you think of a *tenuous arguement* you have heard recently?

Suggestions for Writing

1 Write a paper showing how your experiences in school, in college, in church, or in another institution or organization have influenced the development of an attitude you hold or a value system to which you subscribe.

2 Have you ever been in a "foreign" culture in which you had to make difficult adjustments of the sort that Rodriguez had to make when he entered the English-speaking classrooms? If so, describe those experiences in a paper.

ESSAYS CHIEFLY INFORMATIVE

An Exaltation of Larks
JAMES LIPTON

Getting Started

With Ideas

If you are a hunter, you may know some of the terms in English for groups of animals and birds, but you almost certainly will not know all that are covered here. What, for instance, does one call a group of wild boars encountered on a hunt? And what is a hunter's term for three or more foxes? For a "flock" of pheasants? Lipton tells you, and he also explains how these terms came into the language.

With Words

1. tutelage (1)—you are probably familiar with the related word *tutor*.
2. disquisition (2)—a Latin word that means "inquiry." The context should also be helpful.
3. exultantly (22)—this word is derived from the Latin word for "leap out or up," and the word *exult* once meant "to leap for joy."
4. philologists (26)—from the Greek prefix *phil-*, meaning "love," and the Greek root *logos*, one meaning of which is "word."
5. cogent (28)—from the Latin word meaning "to drive together or collect."
6. disingenuous (28)—when you read this word, be sure you pronounce it correctly (dis-in-gen'-u-ous). Also, be sure you do not confuse the meaning of *ingenuous* with that of *ingenious*.
7. motley (see "A Rafter of Turkeys," p. 137)—the context will probably be helpful here.
8. doggedly (see "A Siege of Herons," p. 137)—yes, it is related to *dog*, but when you come to *doggedly* in this text you will need to think a bit before you understand the relationship in meaning of the two words.

[1] In 1906, having rid himself once and for all of Holmes and Watson, Sir Arthur Conan Doyle returned to the literary form with which he had begun his career fifteen years earlier, producing an historical novel, *Sir Nigel*. In it the young Nigel comes under the tutelage of Sir John Buttesthorn, the Knight of Dupplin, head huntsman to the King, and England's greatest authority on the hunt. In Chapter XI, the sublimely immodest old knight says to Nigel: "I take shame that you are not more

From *An Exaltation of Larks* by James Lipton. Copyright © 1968 by James Lipton. Reprinted by permission of Grossman Publishers.

skilled in the mystery of the woods, seeing that I have had the teaching of you, and that no one in broad England is my master at the craft. I pray you to fill your cup again whilst I make use of the little time that is left to us."

[2] There follows a lengthy disquisition on the chase, "with many anecdotes, illustrations, warnings and exceptions, drawn from his own great experience" and finally the knight says, "But above all I pray you, Nigel, to have a care in the use of the terms of the craft, lest you should make some blunder at table, so that those who are wiser may have the laugh of you, and we who love you may be shamed."

[3] "Nay Sir John," said Nigel. "I think that after your teaching I can hold my place with the others."

[4] The old knight shook his white head doubtfully. "There is so much to be learned that there is no one who can be said to know it all," said he. "For example, Nigel, it is sooth that for every collection of beasts of the forest, and for every gathering of birds of the air, there is their own private name so that none may be confused with another."

[5] "I know it, fair sir."

[6] "You know it, Nigel, but . . . none can say that they know all, though I have myself pricked off eighty and six for a wager at court, and it is said that the chief huntsman of the Duke of Burgundy has counted over a hundred . . . Answer me now, lad, how would you say if you saw ten badgers together in the forest?"

[7] "A cete of badgers, fair sir."

[8] "Good, Nigel—good, by my faith! And if you walk in Woolmer Forest and see a swarm of foxes, how would you call it?"

[9] "A skulk of foxes."

[10] "And if they be lions?"

[11] "Nay, fair sir, I am not like to meet several lions in Woolmer Forest."

[12] "Ay, lad, but there are other forests besides Woolmer, and other lands besides England, and who can tell how far afield such a knight errant as Nigel of Tilford may go, when he sees worship to be won? We will say that you were in the deserts of Nubia, and that afterward at the court of the great Sultan you wished to say that you had seen several lions . . . How then would you say it?"

[13] ". . . Surely, fair sir, I would be content to say that I had seen a number of lions, if indeed I could say aught after so wondrous an adventure."

[14] "Nay, Nigel, a huntsman would have said that he had seen a pride of lions, and so proved that he knew the language of the chase. Now, had it been boars instead of lions?"

[15] "One says a singular of boars."

[16] "And if they be swine?"

[17] "Surely it is a herd of swine."

[18] "Nay, nay, lad, it is indeed sad to see how little you know . . . No man of gentle birth would speak of a herd of swine; that is the peasant

speech. If you drive them it is a herd. If you hunt them it is other. What call you them then, Edith?"

[19] "Nay, I know not."

[20] ". . . But you can tell us, Mary?"

[21] "Surely, sweet sir, one talks of a sounder of swine."

[22] The old knight laughed exultantly. "Here is a pupil who never brings me shame! . . . Hark ye! Only last week that jack-fool, the young Lord of Brocas, was here talking of having seen a covey of pheasants in the wood. One such speech would have been the ruin of a young squire at court. How would you have said it, Nigel?"

[23] "Surely, fair sir, it should be a nye of pheasants."

[24] "Good Nigel—a nye of pheasants, even as it is a gaggle of geese or a badling of ducks, a fall of woodcock or a wisp of snipe. But a covey of pheasants! What sort of talk is that?"

[25] What sort indeed! This quotation from Conan Doyle makes, for me, the central point . . . the terms you will discover here are genuine and authentic; that is, each of them, as fanciful—and even frivolous—as some of them may seem, was at one time either in general use as the *only* proper term for a group of whatever beast, fish, fowl or insect it designated, or had acquired sufficient local currency to warrant its inclusion in a list with the well-established hunting terms.

[26] Bear in mind that most of these terms were codified in the fifteenth century, a time when the English language was in the process of an expansion—or more accurately, explosion—that can only be compared in importance and scope to the intellectual effusions of Periclean Greece or cinquecento Italy. *The Egerton Manuscript,* the earliest surviving list of them, dates from about 1450; *The Book of St. Albans,* the most complete and important of the early lists (and the seminal source for most subsequent compilations), appeared in 1486. I have avoided giving a single, comprehensive collective term to these collective terms. That is because there isn't any. Oddly enough, the compilers of the numerous lists of these words, though obviously enthusiastic philologists, have never felt compelled to settle on a group term for them. The explorer in this field will find these words variously referred to as "nouns of multitude," "company terms," "nouns of assemblage," "collective nouns," "group terms," and "terms of venery." This last seems to me best and most appropriate, and itself warrants some explanation.

[27] "Venery" and its adjective, "venereal," are most often thought of, of course, as signifying love, and more specifically physical love. From *Venus* we have the Latin root *ven* which appears in the word *venari,* meaning "to hunt game." Eric Partridge, in his etymological dictionary *Origins,* asserts that the *ven* in *venari* has its original meaning: "to desire (and therefore) to pursue," and he sees a close connection between it and the word "win," from the Middle English *winnen,* and even the Sanskrit *vanoti,* "he conquers." It is in this sense that venery came to signify the hunt, and it was so used in all the early works on the chase, including the

earliest known on the subject of English hunting, *Le Art* [sic] *de Venery,* written in Norman French in the 1320's by the huntsman of Edward II, Master William Twici.

[28] So, if all the earlier and far greater experts in this field have left it to someone of the twentieth century to select the proper term for these proper terms, I (cautiously and with boundless and well-founded humility) pick up the gauntlet and declare for "terms of venery"; if for no more cogent reason than that it allows of such disingenuous derivative delights as "venereal," "venerealize," and "venerealization." The fact that many of the terms of venery have slipped out of our common speech can only, I think, be described as lamentable. There is little enough poetry in our speech (and lives) to continue to ignore a vein as rich as this. My purpose is to try, in an admittedly modest measure, to redress the balance. My thesis can be summed up very simply: when a group of ravens flaps by, you should, if you want to refer to their presence, say, "There goes an unkindness of ravens." Anything else would be wrong.

A SCHOOL OF FISH
A PRIDE OF LIONS
A HERD OF ELEPHANTS
A LITTER OF PUPS
A FLOCK OF SHEEP
A BAND OF MEN
Hence also band *for a group of musicians.*
A SLATE OF CANDIDATES
Doubtless deriving from the time when nominees' names were chalked on one.
A SWARM OF BEES
A BROOD OF HENS
A STRING OF PONIES
A LABOR OF MOLES
A COVEY OF PARTRIDGES
Here is an interesting etymological journey: the Latin cubare *means "to be lying down" (both* concubine, *to be lying down* with, *and* incubate, *to be lying down* on, *also derive from this root). It becomes* cover *in Old French, whence* cove *or* covy *in Middle English. Thus it refers to nesting habits.*
A PLAGUE OF LOCUSTS
A COLONY OF ANTS
A PASSEL OF BRATS
An American term, of course. J. Donald Adams went looking for this one, finding it finally in Wentworth's American Dialect Dictionary *as "hull passel of young ones," "a passel o' hogs," etc., but no etymology is given. My Southern friends assure me, however, that* passel *is simply "parcel" in a regional accent.*
A MURDER OF CROWS
A KINDLE OF KITTENS

Kin, kindred, *and the German* Kinder *are related to this word from the ME* kindlen. *To* kindle *literally means "to give birth."*

A COWARDICE OF CURS

A POD OF SEALS

The derivation of this word is obvious, since a pod *contains several peas. It was borrowed by sailors to describe groups of seals.*

A SLOTH OF BEARS

A RAFTER OF TURKEYS

Probably not what you think, if you see birds sitting on a beam. The term is related to raft *in the sense of "a large and often motley collection of people and things, as a* raft *of books," according to Webster. It is also related to* raff, *which means a collection of things, and appears in some interesting variations in* riffraff *and* raffish.

A PACE OF ASSES

From the Latin passus, *a step or stride.*

A WALK OF SNIPE

A GAM OF WHALES

A whaling voyage could last as long as three years, so when two whalers encountered each other on some remote sea, it called for a gam, *an exchange of crews via whaleboats and the "gamming chair." It was a happy time for a whaleman and, obviously, the whales' habit of sporting playfully on the surface of the sea gave rise to this fanciful term.*

A NEST OF RABBITS

A GANG OF ELK

A LEAP OF LEOPARDS

A FALL OF WOODCOCKS

A DULE OF DOVES

A corruption of the French deuil, *mourning. The soft, sad ululation of the dove has always evoked an association with mourning.*

A SKULK OF FOXES

A DISSIMULATION OF BIRDS

A PEEP OF CHICKENS

A BUSINESS OF FERRETS

A PITYING OF TURTLEDOVES

A PADDLING OF DUCKS *on water*

A BEVY OF ROEBUCKS

When applied to roes there would seem to be some support for the argument that it stems from the French word for drinking, since roes would frequently be seen together at a watering place.

A SIEGE OF HERONS

From the way the heron doggedly waits for its prey in the shallows at its feet.

A SHOAL OF BASS

A DRIFT OF HOGS

A TRIP OF GOATS

A CHARM OF FINCHES

A SKEIN OF GEESE *in flight*
A GAGGLE OF GEESE *on water*
A CETE OF BADGERS
A CAST OF HAWKS
A DECEIT OF LAPWINGS
AN OSTENTATION OF PEACOCKS
A DROVE OF CATTLE
A PARLIAMENT OF OWLS
A SINGULAR OF BOARS

It seems an odd term for a company, but who are we to argue with Sir John Buttesthorn, the Knight of Dupplin?

A TIDINGS OF MAGPIES
A BOUQUET OF PHEASANTS
A CONGREGATION OF PLOVERS
A TROOP OF KANGAROOS
AN UNKINDNESS OF RAVENS
A BUILDING OF ROOKS

From their nesting habits.

A RICHNESS OF MARTENS
A HOST OF SPARROWS
A KNOT OF TOADS
A DESCENT OF WOODPECKERS
A SOUNDER OF SWINE
A MUSTERING OF STORKS
A CLUTCH OF EGGS
A DRAY OF SQUIRRELS

A Middle English word for their nests.

AN ARMY OF CATERPILLARS
A CRASH OF RHINOCEROSES
A FLIGHT OF SWALLOWS
A CLOWDER OF CATS

A truly marvelous venereal term that somehow conveys the essence of cats in a group. Hodgkin, in Proper Terms, *says that it is probably the same word as "clutter."*

A WATCH OF NIGHTINGALES
A BARREN OF MULES

The term seems to refer to their sterility, but Hodgkin suspects that barren (*or, as it appears in most of the lists,* baren) *was a corruption of the ME* berynge, *"bearing," and, in the same sense,* The Egerton Manuscript *has "a Burdynne of Mulysse."*

A SHREWDNESS OF APES
A ROUTE OF WOLVES
A MURMURATION OF STARLINGS
A SPRING OF TEAL
A SMACK OF JELLYFISH

AN EXALTATION OF LARKS

A HARRAS OF HORSES
Hara *in Latin meant a pigsty, hence any enclosure for animals.*
AN EXALTATION OF LARKS

Questions on Meaning

1 Although the purpose of this piece is clearly to present information on a subject most people know little about, it is nevertheless written in a tone that is not strictly informative. Find examples of language that suggest the author is gently spoofing the custom he describes here.

2 Why do you think Lipton chose for his title the expression "exaltation of larks" rather than any of the other "terms of venery" he mentions?

Questions on Style and Structure

1 What technique does the author use to introduce this essay? Is the length of the introduction (in proportion to the remainder of the essay) justified?

2 Study the manner in which the dialogue from Doyle's novel is set up. Following the conventional practice, Doyle starts a new paragraph whenever there is a shift in speakers. Write a brief dialogue between two or more people.

3 In paragraph 28, the author uses the phrase "pick up the gauntlet." The expression is usually considered a cliché. Why is it appropriate in the context of this essay? When were gauntlets worn?

4 What method does Lipton use to conclude his essay (paragraph 28)? Is the final sentence of the essay meant to be taken seriously?

Exploring Words

1 *tutelage.* In which activities could you offer *tutelage?*

2 *disquisition.* What word might you substitute for *disquisition* in Lipton's sentence?

3 *exultantly.* Be sure that you do not confuse *exult* and *exalt,* in meaning or in pronunciation. Check your dictionary for the difference.

4 *philologists.* From your dictionary, find out what the following words have in common: *Philadelphia, philodendron,* and *Philip.*

5 *cogent.* Look up this word in your dictionary, and compose a sentence using it appropriately.

6 *disingenuous.* Check your dictionary for the definition, and then write a sentence using this word.

7 *motley.* The word is often used with *collection* or *array.* What kinds of "collections" (besides the one Lipton mentions) or "arrays" can you think of to which the word *motley* could be applied? See your dictionary for the definition.

8 *doggedly.* What qualities in the domestic *dog* do you suppose have given us the word *doggedly?* Check your dictionary for a precise definition. Does your dictionary's definition suggest that the word has either negative or positive connotations, or does it imply that it can be used neutrally? Try writing some sentences using *doggedly,* and then compare the connotations of your use of the word with those of your classmates' uses. Can you think of other words that are derived from the names of animals (*outfox* is one example)?

Suggestions for Writing

1 Write a paper discussing a special vocabulary used by people you have been associated with—for example, fellow hobbyists, members of a particular occupation, or just people who live together and have developed their own slang (like members of a family or a fraternity). Be sure to use a consistent tone throughout.

2 Lipton discusses an interesting feature of the English language in this essay. Write a paper in which you discuss any feature of the language that has amused or intrigued you. For example, you might wish to explore the many slang expressions we have for *drunk,* analyze different kinds of euphemisms that Americans habitually employ, or explain the difficulties of mastering spelling.

The Spider and the Wasp
ALEXANDER PETRUNKEVITCH

Getting Started

With Ideas

If you saw this title anywhere except in this section of "informative" works, you might assume that you should interpret it symbolically, for we often compare people and groups of people (such as nations) with spiders and with wasps. And in the first sentence, by using the word *reasoning,* the writer does suggest that he will make some comparisons of insect and spider behavior with human behavior. But where in the first paragraph does he make completely clear that his purpose throughout this article will be to provide information about a sub-human biological relationship?

With Words

1 progeny (1)—from the Latin word *progignere,* which means "to beget."
2 analogies (1)—you may be familiar with this word, but because it is used in a special biological sense in the first sentence of the article, it will probably be a good idea to look up in your dictionary the meaning labeled *Biol.* before you read the rest of the selection.
3 gargantuan (9)—from the name given a giant in a satire by Rabelais.
4 olfactory (14)—unless you have encountered this word before, you will need to look it up. Although technical-sounding, it is a useful term to know because there is really no synonym for it.

[1] In the feeding and safeguarding of their progeny the insects and spiders exhibit some interesting analogies to reasoning and some crass examples of blind instinct. The case I propose to describe here is that of the tarantula spiders and their arch-enemy, the digger wasps of the genus Pepsis. It is a classic example of what looks like intelligence pitted against instinct—a strange situation in which the victim, though fully able to defend itself, submits unwittingly to its destruction.

[2] Most tarantulas live in the Tropics, but several species occur in the temperate zone and a few are common in the southern U. S. Some varieties are large and have powerful fangs with which they can inflict a

From "The Spider and the Wasp," which appeared in *Scientific American,* August 1952. Reprinted with permission. Copyright © 1952 by Scientific American, Inc. All rights reserved.

deep wound. These formidable looking spiders do not, however, attack man; you can hold one in your hand, if you are gentle, without being bitten. Their bite is dangerous only to insects and small mammals such as mice; for a man it is no worse than a hornet's sting.

[3] Tarantulas customarily live in deep cylindrical burrows, from which they emerge at dusk and into which they retire at dawn. Mature males wander about after dark in search of females and occasionally stray into houses. After mating, the male dies in a few weeks, but a female lives much longer and can mate several years in succession. In a Paris museum is a tropical specimen which is said to have been living in captivity for 25 years.

[4] A fertilized female tarantula lays from 200 to 400 eggs at a time; thus it is possible for a single tarantula to produce several thousand young. She takes no care of them beyond weaving a cocoon of silk to enclose the eggs. After they hatch, the young walk away, find convenient places in which to dig their burrows and spend the rest of their lives in solitude. Tarantulas feed mostly on insects and millepedes. Once their appetite is appeased, they digest the food for several days before eating again. Their sight is poor, being limited to sensing a change in the intensity of light and to the perception of moving objects. They apparently have little or no sense of hearing, for a hungry tarantula will pay no attention to a loudly chirping cricket placed in its cage unless the insect happens to touch one of its legs.

[5] But all spiders, and especially hairy ones, have an extremely delicate sense of touch. Laboratory experiments prove that tarantulas can distinguish three types of touch: pressure against the body wall, stroking of the body hair and riffling of certain very fine hairs on the legs called trichobothria. Pressure against the body, by a finger or the end of a pencil, causes the tarantula to move off slowly for a short distance. The touch excites no defensive response unless the approach is from above where the spider can see the motion, in which case it rises on its hind legs, lifts its front legs, opens its fangs and holds this threatening posture as long as the object continues to move. When the motion stops, the spider drops back to the ground, remains quiet for a few seconds and then moves slowly away.

[6] The entire body of a tarantula, especially its legs, is thickly clothed with hair. Some of it is short and woolly, some long and stiff. Touching this body hair produces one of two distinct reactions. When the spider is hungry, it responds with an immediate and swift attack. At the touch of a cricket's antennae the tarantula seizes the insect so swiftly that a motion picture taken at the rate of 64 frames per second shows only the result and not the process of capture. But when the spider is not hungry, the stimulation of its hairs merely causes it to shake the touched limb. An insect can walk under its hairy belly unharmed.

[7] The trichobothria, very fine hairs growing from disklike membranes on the legs, were once thought to be the spider's hearing organs, but we now know that they have nothing to do with sound. They are sensi-

tive only to air movement. A light breeze makes them vibrate slowly without disturbing the common hair. When one blows gently on the trichobothria, the tarantula reacts with a quick jerk of its four front legs. If the front and hind legs are stimulated at the same time, the spider makes a sudden jump. This reaction is quite independent of the state of its appetite.

[8] These three tactile responses—to pressure on the body wall, to moving of the common hair and to flexing of the trichobothria—are so different from one another that there is no possibility of confusing them. They serve the tarantula adequately for most of its needs and enable it to avoid most annoyances and dangers. But they fail the spider completely when it meets its deadly enemy, the digger wasp Pepsis.

[9] These solitary wasps are beautiful and formidable creatures. Most species are either a deep shiny blue all over, or deep blue with rusty wings. The largest have a wing span of about four inches. They live on nectar. When excited, they give off a pungent odor—a warning that they are ready to attack. The sting is much worse than that of a bee or common wasp, and the pain and swelling last longer. In the adult stage the wasp lives only a few months. The female produces but a few eggs, one at a time at intervals of two or three days. For each egg the mother must provide one adult tarantula, alive but paralyzed. The tarantula must be of the correct species to nourish the larva. The mother wasp attaches the egg to the paralyzed spider's abdomen. Upon hatching from the egg, the larva is many hundreds of times smaller than its living but helpless victim. It eats no other food and drinks no water. By the time it has finished its single gargantuan meal and become ready for wasphood, nothing remains of the tarantula but its indigestible chitinous skeleton.

[10] The mother wasp goes tarantula-hunting when the egg in her ovary is almost ready to be laid. Flying low over the ground late on a sunny afternoon, the wasp looks for its victim or for the mouth of a tarantula burrow, a round hole edged by a bit of silk. The sex of the spider makes no difference, but the mother is highly discriminating as to species. Each species of Pepsis requires a certain species of tarantula, and the wasp will not attack the wrong species. In a cage with a tarantula which is not its normal prey the wasp avoids the spider, and is usually killed by it in the night.

[11] Yet when a wasp finds the correct species, it is the other way about. To identify the species the wasp apparently must explore the spider with her antennae. The tarantula shows an amazing tolerance to this exploration. The wasp crawls under it and walks over it without evoking any hostile response. The molestation is so great and so persistent that the tarantula often rises on all eight legs, as if it were on stilts. It may stand this way for several minutes. Meanwhile the wasp, having satisfied itself that the victim is of the right species, moves off a few inches to dig the spider's grave. Working vigorously with legs and jaws, it excavates a hole 8 to 10 inches deep with a diameter slightly larger than the spider's girth. Now

and again the wasp pops out of the hole to make sure that the spider is still there.

[12] When the grave is finished, the wasp returns to the tarantula to complete her ghastly enterprise. First she feels it all over once more with her antennae. Then her behavior becomes more aggressive. She bends her abdomen, protruding her sting, and searches for the soft membrane at the point where the spider's leg joins its body—the only spot where she can penetrate the horny skeleton. From time to time, as the exasperated spider slowly shifts ground, the wasp turns on her back and slides along with the aid of her wings, trying to get under the tarantula for a shot at the vital spot. During all this maneuvering, which can last for several minutes, the tarantula makes no move to save itself. Finally the wasp corners it against some obstruction and grasps one of its legs in her powerful jaws. Now at last the harassed spider tries a desperate but vain defense. The two contestants roll over and over on the ground. It is a terrifying sight and the outcome is always the same. The wasp finally manages to thrust her sting into the soft spot and holds it there for a few seconds while she pumps in the poison. Almost immediately the tarantula falls paralyzed on its back. Its legs stop twitching; its heart stops beating. Yet it is not dead, as is shown by the fact that if taken from the wasp it can be restored to some sensitivity by being kept in a moist chamber for several months.

[13] After paralyzing the tarantula, the wasp cleans herself by dragging her body along the ground and rubbing her feet, sucks the drop of blood oozing from the wound in the spider's abdomen, then grabs a leg of the flabby, helpless animal in her jaws and drags it down to the bottom of the grave. She stays there for many minutes, sometimes for several hours, and what she does all that time in the dark we do not know. Eventually she lays her egg and attaches it to the side of the spider's abdomen with a sticky secretion. Then she emerges, fills the grave with soil carried bit by bit in her jaws, and finally tramples the ground all around to hide any trace of the grave from prowlers. Then she flies away, leaving her descendant safely started in life.

[14] In all this the behavior of the wasp evidently is qualitatively different from that of the spider. The wasp acts like an intelligent animal. This is not to say that instinct plays no part or that she reasons as man does. But her actions are to the point; they are not automatic and can be modified to fit the situation. We do not know for certain how she identifies the tarantula—probably it is by some olfactory or chemo-tactile sense—but she does it purposefully and does not blindly tackle a wrong species.

[15] On the other hand, the tarantula's behavior shows only confusion. Evidently the wasp's pawing gives it no pleasure, for it tries to move away. That the wasp is not simulating sexual stimulation is certain, because male and female tarantulas react in the same way to its advances. That the spider is not anesthetized by some odorless secretion is easily

shown by blowing lightly at the tarantula and making it jump suddenly. What, then, makes the tarantula behave as stupidly as it does?

[16] No clear, simple answer is available. Possibly the stimulation by the wasp's antennae is masked by a heavier pressure on the spider's body, so that it reacts as when prodded by a pencil. But the explanation may be much more complex. Initiative in attack is not in the nature of tarantulas; most species fight only when cornered so that escape is impossible. Their inherited patterns of behavior apparently prompt them to avoid problems rather than attack them. For example, spiders always weave their webs in three dimensions, and when a spider finds that there is insufficient space to attach certain threads in the third dimension, it leaves the place and seeks another, instead of finishing the web in a single plane. This urge to escape seems to arise under all circumstances, in all phases of life and to take the place of reasoning. For a spider to change the pattern of its web is as impossible as for an inexperienced man to build a bridge across a chasm obstructing his way.

[17] In a way the instinctive urge to escape is not only easier but often more efficient than reasoning. The tarantula does exactly what is most efficient in all cases except in an encounter with a ruthless and determined attacker dependent for the existence of her own species on killing as many tarantulas as she can lay eggs. Perhaps in this case the spider follows its usual pattern of trying to escape, instead of seizing and killing the wasp, because it is not aware of its danger. In any case, the survival of the tarantula species as a whole is protected by the fact that the spider is much more fertile than the wasp.

Questions on Meaning

1 Why is it an oversimplification to say that Petrunkevitch stresses the digger wasp's "intelligence" and the tarantula's "stupidity" (even though he does use these words in discussing the unusual relationship of the two creatures)?

2 What explanation does Petrunkevitch give for the tarantula's behavior? If the tarantula is "stupid," why has it survived so long and thrived so successfully?

3 Why does the writer consider the relationship he describes here to be especially important and interesting from a biologist's point of view?

Questions on Style and Structure

1 Are Petrunkevitch's paragraphs generally unified? Examine paragraphs 3 and 4. Are they unified around topic sentences? Which paragraphs seem to be particularly unified? Which ones could be improved?

2 What is the principle of paragraph division in paragraphs 5, 6, and 7? Could you improve upon this division?

3 How effectively does Petrunkevitch manage coherence between paragraphs? What kinds of transitional devices does he use? Study the first sentence of each paragraph after paragraph 1.

4 Note the use of temporal terms (*first,* and so on) to make paragraph 12 coherent. What additional device for coherence does Petrunkevitch use in paragraph 13? Also study paragraph 14. How is it tied together?

5 Analyze the concluding paragraph. How effective is it?

Exploring Words

1 *progeny.* What other words do you know that are derived from the root *gen-*? What relationship do you find between their meanings and the meaning of *progeny?*

2 *analogies.* A frequently used argumentative technique is argument by *analogy.* In this kind of reasoning, a speaker or writer implies a far-reaching similarity between two things or ideas (or between an idea and a thing), one that supports a point he or she wants to make and that is based upon an observable surface similarity. For example, a politician might draw an *analogy* between life in a particular section of a city and life in a jungle. Petrunkevitch uses the term *analogies* in a similar but more specialized sense. Look up the biological meaning of the term in your dictionary, and be ready to comment on the connection between Petrunkevitch's use and the example given here.

3 *gargantuan.* Look up the word *Gargantua.* What qualities does your dictionary attribute to the character in the Rabelais story? Why is the word *gargantuan* appropriate in Petrunkevitch's context? What other words can you think of whose meanings are derived from the names of characters in works of fiction (one example is *Lilliputian*)?

4 *olfactory.* Using your dictionary, translate into plain English the pompous statement "My *olfactory* nerves detect the savory aroma of applied culinary art."

Suggestions for Writing

1 Describe an interesting relationship between two or more people—perhaps the way two maiden aunts of yours who live together get along (or do not get along), or the problems you have living with your little brother, or even the way a teacher you admire relates to his or her class. Give specific examples of the relationship. For example, are the people sarcastic to each other? Angry? Cooperative? Is one clearly dominant? If so, what do they say or do that reveals these attitudes?

2 Select a particular animal that you can use to symbolize a certain kind of human behavior. Show as concretely as you can similarities you find be-

tween the animal's behavior and that of a human being. Are there any differences?

3 Read an encyclopedia article describing a common (or uncommon) animal (for example, a boa constrictor, a squirrel, an ant, a grasshopper). Then, after looking at an actual representative of the species, compare your own observations with the encyclopedia description. In your paper, stress the differences between what you see and what you read in the article. Try to avoid using the technical terms of the encyclopedia article.

The Geologist as Private Eye
RAYMOND C. MURRAY

Getting Started

With Ideas

The title and the first sentence of this selection suggest that it will treat the role that geologists play in solving crimes. These signals also show you that the tone of the article will be informal and straightforward and that its purpose is to provide information to the general public on a little-known topic. You will want to read this piece, then, with particular attention to *who, what, when, where,* and *how* questions.

With Words

1 forensic (1)—Murray uses this word in the phrase *"forensic* geology." If you associate the word with *forensics,* the study of debate in school or college, you may be able to determine why geologists chose *forensic* to describe the geologic specialty with which Murray is concerned here.
2 exonerating (2)—the fact that Murray balances the phrase *"exonerating* the innocent" with "convicting the guilty" should provide a clear contextual clue.
3 subvert (8)—associate this word with the noun *subversion.*

[1] All geologists are detectives. Most use their knowledge about the earth to trace the movement of global plates, uncover the origin of ancient rocks, or locate hidden deposits of metals and fossil fuels. The microscopic clues present in fossil debris provide the material for determining the path of evolution. The evidence for the history of the moon has come from the study of rocks brought back by the astronauts. A small but increasing number of earth scientists, however, are applying their talents and tools not only to science and technology but also to one of the most important societal goals—justice. Forensic geology is the name given to that branch of the earth sciences that uses rocks, minerals, fossils, soils, and related materials and ideas to provide evidence in criminal investigations and trials.

Reprinted, with permission, from *Natural History* Magazine, February 1975. Copyright © The American Museum of Natural History, 1975.

THE GEOLOGIST AS PRIVATE EYE

[2] The modern criminologist employs fingerprints, tool marks, paint, glass, hair and fibers, firearms identification, and other physical evidence. In general this type of evidence assists an investigation either by providing clues that lead to a suspect or by subsequently assisting in convicting the guilty or exonerating the innocent.

[3] The use of geology in crime detection began, as did many of the other kinds of physical evidence, with Sherlock Holmes. Sir Arthur Conan Doyle, who wrote the Holmes series between 1887 and 1893, had his fictional detective suggest many of the methods that were later developed and applied by professional scientists in real cases. Dr. Watson, like all the latter-day Holmes fans, knew that the great detective could "tell at a glance from which part of London the various splashes of soil on his trousers had been picked up." In 1893 Hans Gross, an Austrian professor of criminology, published the *Handbook for Examining Magistrates*. This volume was to have a profound effect on the development and use of science in criminal investigation. Although no actual cases involving forensic geology had appeared at the time of publication, Gross made the prophetic statement, "Dirt on shoes can often tell us more about where the wearer of those shoes had last been than toilsome inquiries." With the idea appearing in print, in both fiction and the professor's *Handbook,* it was not long before minerals, rocks, and fossils in the hands of a geologist would become clues and evidence in an actual criminal case.

[4] In October, 1904, Georg Popp, a chemist, microscopist, and earth scientist in Frankfurt, Germany, was asked to examine the evidence in a murder case in which a seamstress named Eva Disch had been strangled in a bean field with her own scarf. A filthy handkerchief had been left at the scene of the crime and the nasal mucus on the handkerchief contained bits of coal, particles of snuff, and most interesting of all, grains of minerals, particularly hornblende. A prime suspect was known to work both in a coal-burning gasworks and at a local gravel pit. Popp found coal and mineral grains, including hornblende, under the suspect's fingernails. It was also determined that the suspect used snuff. Examination of soil removed from the suspect's trousers revealed that minerals in a lower layer in contact with the cloth matched those of a soil sample taken from the place where the victim's body had been found. Encrusted on this lower layer, a second soil type was found. Examination of the minerals in the upper layer revealed a mineralogy and size of particle, particularly crushed mica grains, that Popp determined were comparable with soil samples collected along the path that led from the murder scene to the suspect's home. From these data it was concluded that the suspect picked up the lower soil layer at the scene of the crime and that this lower and thus earlier material was covered by splashes of mica-rich mud from the path on his return home. When confronted with the soil evidence the suspect admitted the crime, and the Frankfurt newspapers of the day carried such headlines as, "The Microscope as Detective."

[5] It is impossible to determine from the distance of three-

quarters of a century how a contemporary forensic geologist or a jury would evaluate the geologic evidence amassed by Popp. Nevertheless, one fact is evident. Minerals had been used in an actual case, fulfilling Gross's prophecy and providing a real-life example worthy of Holmes. Popp worked on many other criminal cases and made substantial contributions to forensic science. He probably should be considered the founder of forensic geology.

[6] In 1906 Conan Doyle became involved in an actual criminal case during which he applied some of the methods of his fictional creation Holmes. An English solicitor was accused and convicted of killing and mutilating horses and cows. After serving three years in prison he was released but not given a pardon despite some evidence that he was actually innocent of the crimes. Doyle observed that the soil on the shoes worn by the convicted man on the day of the crime was black mud and not the yellow, sandy clay found in the field where the animals had been killed. This observation, combined with other evidence, ultimately led to a full pardon and contributed to the creation of a court of appeals in England.

[7] Today, rocks, minerals, fossils, and other natural and synthetic materials are studied in connection with the thousands of criminal cases tried each year. The Federal Bureau of Investigation laboratory in Washington, D.C., one of the first forensic laboratories in the United States to have geologists study soils and related material as physical evidence, is a worldwide leader in forensic geology. Several other major laboratories, such as that of the New Jersey State Police; the Virginia Bureau of Forensic Sciences; the famous Centre for Forensic Sciences in Toronto, Canada; and the Home Office, Central Research Establishment, at Aldermaston, England, employ geologists. They have made many contributions to the science of forensic geology and thus to justice. Regretfully, there are also many public and private laboratories where lack of trained scientists and equipment or simply the investigators' ignorance of the value of earth materials as evidence has led to the overlooking or misuse of important geologic clues.

[8] Physical evidence, unlike human evidence, cannot subvert the criminal justice system through a combination of memory, emotion, or outright lying. But the integrity and competence of the scientific expert in a criminal case must be equal to the challenge. Physical evidence is divided into two general types, individual items and class items. Fingerprints, some tool marks, and spent ammunition are said to be individual items, meaning they have only one possible source. But most physical evidence—for example, blood, paint, glass, and hair—is grouped under the heading of class items and could come from a variety of sources. The value of a class item in general depends on how common that item is. Forty-three percent of the population has type O blood, whereas only 3 percent of the population has type AB. Type AB blood would thus be a more valuable bit of evidence than type O. Similarly, the paint from a 1932 Rolls Royce would be more valuable as evidence than that from a 1970 Ford.

THE GEOLOGIST AS PRIVATE EYE

[9] Although geologic materials can seldom be considered as truly individual items, there are exceptions. One such was a vandalism case in which a concrete block was broken into fragments that were thrown through a number of store windows from a moving car. In that instance it was possible to piece together the fragments found in the stores and those remaining in the car to reconstruct the original block. Not only did the pieces fit together but individual mineral grains lined up across the pieces and all the fragments were shown to be of the same kind of concrete.

[10] In most examples, geologic material is class evidence, but its value lies in the fact that the different kinds and combinations of rocks, minerals, fossils, and related materials are almost limitless. The evidential potential of geologic materials is therefore greater than that of almost all the other kinds of physical evidence of the class type.

[11] There are more than 2,200 different minerals, many of which are not common. Almost all of these minerals exist in a wide range of compositions, with the result that there is an almost unlimited number of recognizable kinds of minerals. More than a million different kinds of fossils have been identified. Most fossiliferous rocks have populations of fossils that commonly reflect the environment or deposition in which the rock was formed. These groups of fossils provide a very large number of possible combinations.

[12] Almost all rocks—igneous, sedimentary, and metamorphic—are composed of minerals. In any given igneous or metamorphic rock, the kinds and amounts of minerals, their size and texture, represent a wide range of variations. The possible combinations of minerals, the sizes and shapes of minerals, and the kinds and amounts of cement between the grains in sedimentary rocks offer an almost unending diversity. The weathering processes that break up rocks and produce soil add new dimensions to the possible variations. Also, in most urban areas the soils contain particles contributed by man, which further increase the complexity and diversity.

[13] Anyone who has seen the Grand Canyon, noticed the variety of pebbles in a stream bed, or simply observed the color differences in the soils of his own backyard can appreciate the variety and rapid changes that exist in natural earth materials.

[14] In a case of a rape in an eastern United States city, the victim reported that the crime took place in a vacant lot, which was underlain by the beach sands of an ancient glacial lake. The suspect had sand in the cuffs of his trousers. Study of the sand from the cuffs and samples collected at the crime scene showed that the two sands were comparable. Both contained the same minerals and rock grains in the same amounts. Thus it was established with a high degree of probability that the two samples could have come from a common source. One of the rock types was fragments of anthracite coal. These fragments were very common but were not natural to the area. Coal fragments are widely found in the soils of most of our older cities. In this case, however, there was too much coal

in the sand. Further investigation revealed that sixty years before the crime the site had been the location of a coal pile for a laundry. Although the minerals involved in this case might have been duplicated in other places, the presence of the coal became a crucial factor in greatly increasing the probability of a single common source. This geologic evidence, when combined with other evidence and testimony by the victim, led to the conviction of the suspect.

[15] Many man-made and commercially manufactured mineral products such as face powder, cleaning powder, abrasives, masonry, and wallboard become the study material for the forensic geologist. Hundreds of criminals have been brought to justice because of the minerals found on their burglary tools or clothing.

[16] Most interesting is the insulation material used in safes and strong boxes. When fire-resistant safes are broken into by drilling, blowing, cutting, or prying, the fire insulating material that fills the space between the outer and inner metal walls is disrupted. It commonly clings to the tools and clothing of the safe breaker. There is a classic case in which a man was arrested and brought to the police station on a routine minor charge. An observant detective, noticing that the suspect appeared to have a severe case of dandruff, examined his hair. The substance found was, not dandruff, but diatoms, the microscopic fossils that make up the diatomaceous earth used to insulate some safes. On further examination it was learned that the diatoms in the suspect's hair were of the same species as those present in the insulation of a safe that had been blown the previous day. The suspect was accordingly charged with the burglary.

[17] Geologic maps can often be used in crime investigation to outline the areas where rocks and minerals associated with crimes or suspects could have originated. The owner of some valuable gems found chips of common rock instead of precious stones when she opened the cargo box that had been sent by air. Study of the chips indicated that they came from a foreign country that was a stopover point on the air route. Examination of the geologic map for that area indicated the probable source of the rock chips. This evidence cleared the air-freight handlers at the final destination and led to the apprehension of those responsible for the substitution.

[18] Even topographic maps, which record contour lines and indicate the elevation of land, have made their contribution. An informer reported that an illegal still was located somewhere between two towns in southern New Jersey in an area of swamps and higher gravel ridges and that the water well at the site of the still reputedly had a water level twenty feet below the ground. Since the groundwater table and the swamps were on approximately the same level, to find the still it was necessary to find a place on a ridge twenty feet above the local swamp level. A study of the topographic maps of the area showed there was only one place on one ridge where the elevation met that requirement. A church occupied that location. A warrant was obtained and the still was found in the church cellar.

[19] Geology can thus be seen to have made many contributions to crime detection and justice. These contributions will undoubtedly increase and become even more significant as imaginative criminal investigators realize the value of geologic material as evidence and make use of competent forensic geologists.

Questions on Meaning

1. What is the thesis sentence of the article?
2. What role did the fictitious Sherlock Holmes and his creator play in the development of forensic geology?
3. Explain in your own words the difference between individual and class evidence, and indicate the potential usefulness of forensic geology in providing both types.
4. What are some of the synthetic materials that forensic geologists find useful as evidence?

Questions on Style and Structure

1. As writers, we often pay insufficient attention to the choosing of titles. How effective is Murray's title in arousing your interest? Would a title like "Forensic Geology" be as good? Can you think of an even better title than Murray's?
2. What principle of organization explains the arrangement of paragraphs 3, 4, 5, and 6?
3. Study paragraphs 3, 4, 8, and 18. Are they equally unified? If not, which one is the most unified? Which one is the least unified?
4. Can you justify the separation of paragraphs 15 and 16? Would you have combined them? Why?
5. What technique does Murray use to conclude his essay? How effective is the conclusion?

Exploring Words

1. *forensic.* Now that you have read the article and checked your dictionary's treatment of this word, explain in your own words why *"forensic* geology" is an appropriate label for the specialty it describes.
2. *exonerating.* Which of the meanings your dictionary lists for *exonerate* applies to Murray's use of the word? What relationship do you find between this meaning and the meaning of the Latin word that is its source?

3 *subvert.* What relationship in meaning do you find between these words: *subvert, introvert, extrovert, conversion, convertible, verse?* Explain how the meaning of each of these words is related to the meaning of the Latin word from which they are all derived.

Suggestions for Writing

1 Here is a chance to match your ingenuity against that of a forensic geologist (on paper, at least). Plot an interesting crime, and explain what precautions you would take to foil the would-be Sherlock Holmes.

2 Think of some common objects that could be put to unusual or unconventional uses. (For example, pumpkins are made into jack-o'-lanterns for Halloween celebrations in this country.) Then write an essay in which you explain these uses.

3 Think of an activity or a body of knowledge that has a usefulness most people are unaware of. It might be a hobby, a college major (one you expect will lead to a career most people do not associate with this study), or simply a way of arranging your day. Write a paper showing the usefulness you have found in this activity or interest.

How to Read an Organization Chart for Fun and Survival
DONALD WINKS

Getting Started

With Ideas

The title of this selection suggests a dual purpose. If you ever expect to be in a position that places you on a company's organizational chart, you may be interested in the "survival" function of the information provided here. But whether you do or not, you will probably appreciate the "fun" the author has reading the boxes and lines that comprise what he calls an "Orgchart." Note how the tone of the article matches the tone of the title.

With Words

1 astute (1)—derived from the Latin word meaning "craft" or "cunning."
2 enigma (1)—have you ever heard that Leonardo da Vinci's famous *Mona Lisa* has an *enigmatic* smile?
3 semantics (1)—have you ever heard a person involved in an argument say, "It's only a matter of *semantics*"?
4 genesis (11)—what is the book of *Genesis* in the Old Testament about?
5 tantamount (16)—a roughly synonymous expression appears in the same sentence in which this word is used.
6 *de facto* (17)—this term appears frequently in articles about segregation. Two contextual clues appear later in the sentence in which this word is used.
7 equivocal (21)—though you may be unfamiliar with this word, you may know *equivocate* and *equivocation,* two related words. The context is also rich in clues.
8 prefigure (24)—John the Baptist is said to have *prefigured* Christ (you will remember that the prefix *pre-* means "before").
9 hapless (27)— think for a moment of how the word *happy* functions in the phrase *"happy*-go-lucky," and you will be close to the meaning of *hapless.*

[1] Although there are many kinds of organizations, the same type of organization chart is used to describe them all. This is the familiar pyra-

"How to Read an Organization Chart for Fun and Survival" appeared in *Harper's Magazine,* May 1962. Copyright 1962 by *Harper's Magazine.* Reprinted by permission of Russell and Volkening, Inc., as agents for the author.

mid of lines and boxes arranged in ascending order of importance. Astute management people find this standard Orgchart wholly satisfying, but it remains an enigma to those most directly concerned. This is because few executives have pursued the sort of analytic study necessary to understand the variable semantics of the Orgchart.

[2] On the surface, all Orgcharts look alike. There at the apex is the board chairman, just atop the president. Below, vice presidents, general managers, and assorted staff minions are ranked in rows like pinstriped cherubim and seraphim. Each is represented by a box labeled with his title and area of responsibility, and each box is linked by a solid black line to the box of his superior. The visual effect is of an upside-down family tree. Each vice president, in turn, has an Orgchart for his own area—in which he occupies the top box. Similarly his division and department heads have *theirs*. Indeed, the Orgcharts of any large corporation fill a fat manual, but the principle is the same whether the company is General Motors or Gaîté Brassieres. The lines and boxes tell you who is who, who is responsible for what, and how the Org is organized. That is the theory, anyway.

[3] Unfortunately, it seldom works out so neatly. For one thing, corporations today are constantly expanding, diversifying, acquiring other corporations, and merging. This often makes it necessary to issue revised charts every quarter or even every month. Consequently, charts are ever more complex, and there are more of them. But this is the lesser problem. The real difficulty lies in the fact that it is not organizations but people that are being reorganized; and the sensitivity of executives to their position on the chart defies belief.

[4] For example, in one major financial institution all its top executives insisted on having their boxes appear to the right of the president. The problem was resolved only by promising all the left-hand people that they would be moved to the right on the next chart. The size and shape of the box, the thickness of the line linking one to another, and even the typeface cause keen concern to those involved. All executives abhor dotted lines since they indicate less than absolute authority. An unobservant manager recently transferred to a new district was sacked not long ago for firing four salesmen. Headquarters informed him afterward that they did not report to him. He had not noticed that the lines were dotted, but then neither had the men who were fired.

[5] The true purpose of the Orgchart today is a reversal of the Bauhaus *obiter dictum* that form follows function; it is designed and distributed to induce function to follow form, being—in itself—an instrument of change. If this were not so, it would be no more worthy of study than the corporate telephone directory.

[6] In fact, the Orgchart is commonly used to deal with promotions and demotions, transfers of authority, personality clashes, and even dehiring—that is, showing an unwanted executive the door without actu-

ally throwing him out of it. An Orgplanner for a large chemical company who chooses to remain anonymous revealed how this can happen.

[7] "We had a top vice president who had been with the company for many years, but who simply didn't fit in any more," he said. "It was impossible to fire him, and he didn't want to retire. So we moved him off the chart. As each new chart appeared his box moved higher up, closer and closer to the president, and at the same time further and further to the left of the page. He didn't suspect a thing; in fact, he was flattered. But one day, just as his box reached the edge of the page, he got the idea. By then it was too late to do anything but quietly resign."

[8] Though this is an extreme case, the knowledgeable executive scans each new chart with the avidity of a race tout studying the morning line. It tells him whether his own position has changed and, if so, in what direction. He can also get a reading on how well or badly his rivals are doing. Has a straight line been replaced by one with an angle to it? Or worse, has it become dotted? Does Bill now report directly to J. B. instead of to Harry? Is product development under sales now instead of, as formerly, manufacturing?

[9] If you know how to find them, the answers are in the chart. In fact, the Orgchart—properly studied—will disclose much that you did not know before, including things top management does not want you to know. Such information can be helpful in planning a career—or a dignified exit.

[10] Unfortunately, at the present time no university or executive development program offers a practical course in Orgchart reading. This may be because either (a) the subject is not considered worthy of serious academic attention; or (b) management is reluctant to have attention drawn to its true significance. Research suggests the latter to be the case. This essay is a modest first step toward an understanding in depth of the science and semantics of the Orgchart.

[11] Most organization charts are drawn by a clerk or a draftsman on loan from the engineering section. Like Saint Matthew with the angel hovering nearby to dictate the Gospel, he merely records what has come down from a higher source, but these days this exalted being is seldom the company president. In the last few years organization planning has become a full-fledged management specialty whose members have evolved their own language, their own theory, and their own hierarchy. Most large corporations harbor at least one Orgplanner, and some have an entire department devoted to analyzing the needs of the enterprise and devising suitable organizational structures. Necessarily, the Orgplanner works closely with the president in a sort of doctor-patient relationship. He helps the chief executive diagnose organizational ills and prescribe the proper remedies, including amputation where necessary. C. A. Efferson, an Orgplanner of national renown, has lucidly described the genesis of an Orgchart:

[12] "First," he said, "you study the work to be done, the functions, the long-range goals, and then draw the ideal organizational structure, forgetting personalities. The next step is to take the ideal structure to top management and determine what compromises have to be made—mainly because of personalities. However, the ideal structure is not thrown away when the official chart is published. It is kept and continually updated so that future planning does not run counter to the ideal structure, compounding mistakes and necessitating further compromises."

[13] Knowing that the chart is essentially a compromise from the moment of publication, the really astute executive keeps a copy of his company's Orgchart in his desk drawer. Then he keeps modifying it as he finds out whom you actually have to see to get things done. This is the real—or, in Orgplanner's language, "shadow"—organization, as opposed to the official version on the wall, and chances are it bears more than a passing resemblance to the ideal chart in the Orgplanner's office.

[14] In recent years, as companies have grown more gigantic and less comprehensible, Orgplanners have tried to refine their methods and develop new techniques. They argue about whether boxes should be square, in keeping with historical precedent, or oblong, to accommodate in full names like Feinmanhartsberger or Smythe-Forthingay. Should color codes be used to identify line and staff functions? Should staff assistants be shown in the same box as their superior? Prickly though these questions are, they are less controversial than one current theory which holds that the ideal chart should be circular. Supporters of this theory are mainly academicians, who object to the hierarchic rigidity of the conventional squares and oblongs. They want lines of authority and communication to have "a functional and dynamic flow" freeing all members of the organization from artificial restraints. While circular charts do exist, there is no practical purpose to be served in trying to understand them because they cannot be understood. They can only be described.

[15] It is an axiom of Orgplanning that the mere preparation of an accurate chart will reveal unsuspected organizational weaknesses—as, for example, whether there are "too many levels of authority," "overextended spans of control," "unclear lines of accountability," and "duplication of function." These phrases conceal such common-sensical notions as not letting too many cooks spoil the broth, giving each chief only as many Indians as he can keep an eye on, letting the Indians know who their chiefs *are,* and avoiding situations in which ten people—or divisions of departments—are assigned the same task.

[16] A number of corporations resolutely refuse to issue Orgcharts at all on the grounds that they are "artificially restricting." This is roughly equivalent to the belief of certain primitive tribes that snapping a photograph is tantamount to stealing the subject's soul. Other corporations prepare charts but do not circulate them outside of top management—to whom, presumably, the information comes as no surprise and for whom it can have little practical value. Still others circulate charts on which posi-

tions but not individuals are named. Professor Chris Argyris of Yale, a leading theorist on Orgplanning and a sworn enemy of the pyramidal chart, found the practice of one large company especially interesting. Several executives were moved up but were instructed not to tell anyone they had been promoted until the news could be diplomatically broken to the old-timers they were replacing. As a result the Orgchart showed clearly who was who, except he wasn't.

[17] This is not a unique situation. Some companies deliberately issue charts designed to keep the peace rather than picture reality. Even those that try to keep their charts reasonably up-to-date are plagued by ambiguity. Often a corporation may decide on some management changes, but postpone issuing a new Orgchart out of a peculiar sense of delicacy. Thus although everyone knows Bill has been promoted to vice president, they are spared the painful sight of their former peer alone at the apex with everyone reporting to him. Or, an executive being politely demoted is given a fancier title but the new Orgchart does not appear for a few months when the *de facto* situation has established itself and he can face the reality of his true level in the hierarchy.

[18] The nation's top Orgplanners all belong to the Council on Organization Planning of the National Industrial Conference Board, which meets twice annually to discuss broad policy questions such as "Centralization or Decentralization," "Relationships Between Line and Staff," and "Automation: Its Effects." At these gatherings they also exchange information on what each other's Orgcharts *really* mean. The broad policy questions are amply reported in the publications of the NICB. But to find out what was actually said at a Council meeting—including how to read a specific Orgchart—is next to impossible.

[19] This is because the Council—whose members represent such corporate giants as U. S. Steel, Alcoa, RCA, Kaiser Aluminum & Chemical, Chase Manhattan Bank, IBM, Union Carbide, and General Electric—holds its meetings under security restrictions that would do credit to the CIA. Only members are admitted, no transcript of the proceedings is made, no guests are permitted at any time; and when professors from university business schools are invited to give papers, they are invited to leave before the regular session resumes. "Our group is so tightly knit," one member said confidentially, "that I can call another member and he will tell me details of his corporation's organization planning that he would not dare reveal to a high-ranking insider."

[20] It should by now be plain that the only infallible way to read an Orgchart is in the company of the executive who designed it. And at each doubtful point you should demand what the hell he meant by *that*. Unfortunately, Council membership is restricted to twenty-seven Orgplanners, all of them sworn to secrecy.

[21] However, the average executive should not despair. Imprecise, ambiguous, equivocal or even downright misleading though they are, Orgcharts can—if properly understood—cast much light on what is really

transpiring within a large organization. In addition to the general guidelines implicit in what has gone before, there are seven rules which will help you to chart your way safely through the Orgchart. Success will come, not from memorizing the rules but from applying them wisely to your specific situation.

[22] *Rule 1*—There is absolutely no point in studying any chart but your own. Time spent poring over manuals of organization charts or attending classes in organization planning is time wasted. All you can learn from an alien organization chart is the name of someone to phone to ask what it really means. This is exactly what Orgplanners do when they are not exchanging such information directly in secret conclave.

[23] *Rule 2*—The present chart must not be studied *in vacuo;* it takes on meaning only in the context of previous charts. Gather all the charts issued over the past few years and study them. In other words, chart the charts. Trace how things came to be the way they are, develop a knowledge of your organization's structural and verbal euphemisms. Here, as elsewhere, the past illuminates the present.

[24] *Rule 3*—The ideal organization tends to become real before it is officially charted. As we have seen, the chart is a compromise from the moment of publication. However, since both president and planner are agreed on an ideal structure—a master Orgplan—each new chart will logically prefigure future changes. By carefully plotting changes as they appear on new charts, the alert student can often divine the shape of things to come, thereby getting the jump on his corporate peers.

[25] *Rule 4*—Do not put much trust in titles: study positions on the chart and who reports to whom. For example, if a vice president suddenly appears as "assistant to" a loftier official, often for "special projects," see if he is still in the same spot on the chart. If so, this is a legitimate assignment. But if he has moved up, down, or sideways, the odds are he will keep on moving right off the chart and out of the company. Conversely, when an executive from *outside* the company is brought in as "assistant to" one of the big brass, he is almost certainly his replacement.

[26] *Rule 5*—Count the horizontal lines on the chart. If there are more than seven levels of authority between the president and the operating managers, give the chart up as a hopeless case; and, ideally, the job too. Too many levels bespeak a self-perpetuating top management and opportunities for promotion will dwindle as inefficiencies mount. Keep in mind that General Motors has only four levels of authority. Is your company bigger?

[27] *Rule 6*—Study not only the headquarters chart, but also those of all divisions and departments, and keep a keen eye out for disappearing boxes. When one or more vanishes from your chart, don't assume that the hapless occupants have been thrown out on their ears. They may well crop up on another chart. *If this trend continues, the company is decentralizing, and before long all you chaps at headquarters will be regarded as overhead.*

[28] *Rule 7*—In addition to the official chart on your wall, keep

working on another copy. Draw new lines, cross out boxes, add and delete names on the basis of your personal observation. When you have perfected a chart of the shadow organization, throw it away. A new official chart will be along momentarily.

Questions on Meaning

1 Remembering examples the article gives of the ways companies make use of organization charts, explain the statement: "... it [the Orgchart] is designed and distributed to induce function to follow form, being—in itself—an instrument of change." (paragraph 5)

2 Explain the relationship of an actual organization chart, the "ideal organizational structure" the planners come up with first, and the "shadow organization." (paragraphs 12 and 13)

3 Show how the statement, "The real difficulty lies in the fact that it is not organizations but people that are being reorganized," (paragraph 3) is developed throughout the article.

4 Why does Winks stress the fact that one must always read an organization chart with attention to how it differs from previous charts of the same organization?

Questions on Style and Structure

1 Which sentence in paragraph 1 could be said to be the thesis statement?

2 Paragraph 2 is tightly unified (the first sentence is the topic sentence), well-developed, and coherent (note the manner in which Winks achieves transition from sentence to sentence). What other paragraphs do you feel are particularly worthy of emulation?

3 Are there any paragraphs that could be combined?

4 Explain the effectiveness of the following examples of figurative language:

   a Below, vice presidents, general managers, and assorted staff minions are ranked in rows like pinstriped cherubim and seraphim. (paragraph 2)

   b Like Saint Matthew with the angel hovering nearby to dictate the Gospel, he [a clerk or draftsman who draws Orgcharts] merely records what has come down from a higher source, but these days this exalted being is seldom the company president. (paragraph 11)

5 In paragraph 15, Winks deflates the pretentious jargon used by some Orgplanners (for example, "overextended spans of control"). Does Winks ever lapse into such jargon in discussing the "science" of the Orgchart? What kinds of jargon have you come across recently? Why do you suppose people use such language?

6 What transitional devices does the writer use to make paragraph 16 coherent?

7 In paragraph 20, Winks writes, "And at each doubtful point you should demand what the hell he meant by *that.*" What does "the hell" contribute to the sentence?

8 Would the conclusion be just as effective had the author ended with a rule other than Rule 7? Why or why not?

Exploring Words

1 *astute.* List the synonyms that you find in your dictionary. You will note that some of these words have distinctly positive and others distinctly negative connotations. *Astute* generally has positive connotations, as it does in Winks's essay. In what matters are you *astute*?

2 *enigma.* What *enigmas* have you been faced with recently?

3 *semantics.* In the example cited in the Getting Started section, the word *semantics* is used rather loosely. What more precise definitions does your dictionary provide?

4 *genesis.* What is the relationship between *genesis* and *genetics*? Why are *geneticists* so called?

5 *tantamount.* You should note that this word is followed by the word *to.* Get acquainted with this useful word by employing it in a sentence of your own.

6 *de facto.* If you are not familiar with the antonym *de jure,* you should look it up in the dictionary too. Be sure you understand the sense in which both words are used.

7 *equivocal.* Winks uses *imprecise, ambiguous,* and *misleading* in the same sentence in which he uses *equivocal.* Check your dictionary to find the different shades of meaning that these words have.

8 *prefigure.* After checking your dictionary to be sure you know how the word is to be used, write a sentence about your life in which you work in the word *prefigure.*

9 *hapless.* Use your dictionary to find the relationship between *happy, happen,* and *haphazard.*

Suggestions for Writing

1 Write a "How to Read _____" paper showing what you have learned to find between the lines (or beneath the lines) of a topographical map, a TV guide, the stock market report, the sports or comics section of a newspaper, or some other specialized form of reading matter.

2 Write an essay on the following topic: "How to _____ for _____ and _____."

The Torments of Translation
LEO ROSTEN

Getting Started

With Ideas

If you have any knowledge of a language other than English, a good way to get started with this article is to think of expressions you know in that second language that lose much of their force and accuracy when they are translated directly into English.

With Words

1 *Weltanschauung* (2)—pronounced velt-an-shang (the last syllable rhymes with *song*). A word that has been borrowed from the German; the literal translation is "world view."
2 mordant (2)—from the Latin word meaning "to bite."
3 cognates (2)—the following are German *cognates* of familiar English words: *Wasser* ("water"), *Wagen* ("wagon"), *Buch* ("book").
4 onomatopoeia (10)—one example of *onomatopoeia* is the line from a song from the period of the Second World War, *"Bloop bleep, bloop bleep*—the faucet keeps a-drippin' and I just can't sleep."
5 dictum (17)—from the Latin word for "to say."
6 nuances (18)—a word borrowed from the French. A literal translation is "shades of color."
7 empathy (18)—from the Latin word meaning "emotion."

[1] Each language spoken by man (there are over 2,800) is honeycombed with uniqueness. Human languages are as different as peas in a pod (if you examined them under a microscope). What human tongues have in common is only purpose: the use of words to try to describe, understand, and communicate the measureless sensations of existence, the swarm of impressions on the self, the marvelous symbolic productions of the human mind, the infinite fantasies of the imagination, the divine and the wretched parameters of the human condition.

[2] A language is a *Weltanschauung*. Even languages very close in

"The Torments of Translation" appeared in *Harper's Magazine,* June 1972. Copyright © by Leo Rosten. Reprinted by permission of the author.

origin, history, and structure develop surprising differences. The English "conscience" is not the same as the French *conscience* (which means consciousness or conscientiousness). German had no word for "bully" until the twentieth century (a mordant comment on Teutonic values) and can only render the Englishman's idea of "fair play" as *"fair" Spielen*. If this be true of tongues so close to each other in birth, so laden with cognates, so cross-fertilized by usage and literature, how much more does it intrude when one tries to translate Yiddish or Hebrew into any of them?

[3] Translation is not simply a matter of dexterity in transferring synonyms. Translation does not contend with words, but with meanings. To translate is to decode: to transpose one mode of thinking, feeling, fearing, appraising into the word-patterns of another. No language can be separated from its historical skeleton, its psychological skin, or its sociological garments. Languages are acculturated verbalizations of experience and thought.

[4] Christian missionaries in the Orient, for instance, were sorely perplexed because Chinese has neither a word for "word" nor a word for, or an idea of, "sin." (The closest is *tsui*, which means "crime.") And in Africa or Polynesia, the Christian messengers of the Lord found bewildering difficulty in trying to communicate the idea of God—i.e., one supreme deity—to people mystified by such an impoverished theology. In language, which is a system of "culturally ordained categories," each of us "builds the house of his consciousness." [1]

[5] When an English or American speaker in the United Nations says, "I assume," interpreters render it in French as "I deduce" and in Russian as "I consider."

[6] It is hard for us truly to believe that each culture teaches its people what to say about what that culture has taught them to think, feel, see, or even hear. The pioneering studies of Edward Sapir (whom I was fortunate enough to know) and Benjamin Lee Whorf have forced us to consider the surprising degree to which our sensations, our thoughts, even our actions are influenced by the particular system of sounds and symbols we inherit. We all assume that we are experiencing the real world; "but in many cases we are free only to experience the possibilities and limitations of grammar." [2]

[7] For instance: do you think dogs go "woof-woof," "bow-wow," or "arf-arf"? In English prose, they bark that way. But in German, dogs go "wau-wau"; in Chinese, "wang-wang"; in Vietnamese, "gau-gau"; and in Japanese, "wan-wan." In Yiddish, dogs go "how-how," and there is a saying: "The dog who barks 'ho-ho' is not dangerous, but the one who growls 'how-how' is." (I cannot help wondering how a Laplander or Litvak would translate "going to the dogs.")

---

[1] John L. Mish, *The World of Translation* (New York: The PEN Conference, 1970), pp. 241–47.

[2] Walter Nash, *Our Experience of Language* (London: Battsford, 1971), p. 18.

[8] In German, frogs are said to croak "quak-quak," which would confuse an American duck. Scottish roosters would surely be flabbergasted to learn that French roosters go "cocorico" (at least in French novels). As for Arabian donkeys, which Arabian writers tell us go "ham-ham," I quail to think of what they would think if they learned that, in Rumanian, it is dogs who go "ham-ham."

[9] Any sensible American will tell you that scissors go "snip-snip," "snip-snap," or "snap-snap." But to a Greek, believe it or not, scissors go "kritz-kritz." And to a Chinese, scissors hiss "su-su." As for Spaniards, Italians, and Portuguese, their scissors retain as marked a national identity as any other, being written respectively as "ri-ri," "kri-kri," and "terre-terre." [3]

[10] All this may disturb your comfortable assumption that in onomatopoeia, at least, there is universal agreement; that everyone, whether Choctaw or Irish or Cypriot, produces the same oral renditions of and for the same heard sounds; that different languages must employ the same vocalizations for objectively uniform acoustics.

[11] But the notion that onomatopoeia crosses the frontiers of language rests on the misconception that verbal allusions accurately mirror "real" sounds: they do not; they record and reflect those sounds our culture has instructed us to hear, or predisposed us *not* to hear. A German child is taught to hear the buzzing of a bee not as "bzz-bzz" (which English bees do, apparently in order to validate our word "buzzing") but as "sum-sum." If you will repeat "sum-sum" for a while, you may come to prefer it to "bzz-bzz"—or you may, in the interest of world peace, henceforth describe all bees as going "bzz-bzz sum-sum."

[12] Do you think that in every society men grow so angry they "see red?" Well, "our classification of the spectrum into . . . red, orange, yellow, green, blue and violet is culturally arbitrary, and persons in other cultures divide the spectrum quite differently. Perception itself is an aspect of human *behavior*." [4]

[13] Optical recordings often express learned ways of seeing and inferring. I once wrote: "We see things as *we* are, not as they are." Professor E. H. Gombrich tells us that ancient artists drew eyelashes on the lower lids of horses' eyes (the drawings *they* had seen and studied showed eyelashes on horses' lower lids); but lower eyelashes do not happen to exist on real, undrawn horses. As Degas once blurted: "Drawing is not what one sees, but what others must be made to see."

[14] Have I wandered? Only to illustrate, I hope, how complicated simple things become if we examine them with care. The mere change of sound, in translating, can alter the sensual glow and hum of the original. I

---

[3] Helmut Braem, "Languages Are Comparable Yet Unique," *The World of Translation,* pp. 121–34.
[4] M. Segall, D. Campbell, M. J. Herskovits, *The Influence of Culture on Visual Perception* (Indianapolis: Bobbs-Merrill, 1966), pp. 37, 213.

commend to you Bernard Berenson's appraisal of critics: they break a watch into its parts, to hear how it ticks. Changing one word's *position* can alter meaning drastically: "What is harder than getting a pregnant elephant in a Volkswagen? Getting an elephant pregnant in a Volkswagen."

[15] The most tormenting aspect of translation is this: what is idiomatic in one tongue is idiotic in another. Think for a moment of what happens if a translator of English does not realize that "tell it to Sweeney" is a rebuff, not a request; that "a Northern Spy" may have been an undercover agent for Ulysses S. Grant—or is only a variety of apple; that Ockham never used his razor for shaving, any more than Cleopatra used her needle for sewing; that "jack-in-the-pulpit" does not mean the preacher's name is Jack; that "behind the eight ball" is gibberish in nine-tenths of the world; and that when athletes engage in a "rhubarb" they do not sit down to consume a legume.

[16] It gives me the greatest pleasure to inform you that Russian physicists believe that the first nuclear atomic pile in history was constructed in a pumpkin field—that being their natural translation of "squash court," the site in the concrete bowels of the stadium (Stagg Field) of the University of Chicago.

[17] As for poetry, I can do no better than give you Chaim Bialik's despairing dictum: "Reading poetry in translation is like kissing a woman through a veil."

[18] I cannot help feeling that where a translator, however fine a scholar, is not a writer, translation starts under a deadly handicap. For if a writer is anything, he is one who is more sensitive than others to words, who loves their texture, their nuances, their conceptual echoes and ideational overtones. An empathy for language—which is to say, a refined and heightened sensitivity to words—is simply a *sine qua non* (how do you say that in English?) for translators. The man who cannot echo the *beat* of a word, much less a sentence, or who is insensitive to simile and metaphor, or who does not savor parallel construction, or who is word-blind and cadence-deaf, is bound to butcher his task. A seventeenth-century man of letters, John Denham, bristled:

> Such is our pride, our folly and our fate
> That only those who cannot write, translate.

[19] The Bill of Rights composed by the 1971 International Conference on Literary Translation reads:

> The translator's chief obligation is to create the work in a new language with the appropriate music and the utmost response to the silences of the original.[5]

---

[5] *The World of Translation*, p. 8.

As an admirer of the manifesto, I wish that its writers had said "another," not "a new," language: translators are surely not obliged to invent a tongue from scratch.

[20] "A good translation," said Benedetto Croce, "is a work of art."

Questions on Meaning

1. Why does Rosten devote so much attention to the way different languages represent nonverbal sounds (like the "buzzing" of a bee)? What is the technical term for this kind of mimicry? What major point does Rosten mean to establish by showing that different languages imitate the same sounds in different ways?

2. In paragraph 14 the author asks, "Have I wandered?" Has he? Note that in paragraph 13 he got on the subject of the way artists of different periods have drawn the eyelashes of horses whereas in the preceding paragraphs he had been concerned with onomatopoeia and "seeing red." Is there any connection between these two topics?

3. What is the main idea of the article? Where is it stated most directly? Is there a thesis sentence here?

Questions on Style and Structure

1. Examine the figurative language in paragraph 1 and comment on its appropriateness and effectiveness.

2. This statement appears in paragraph 3: "No language can be separated from its historical skeleton, its psychological skin, or its sociological garments." How effective is the figurative language? Are the adjectives interchangeable? Would "sociological skin," for example, work as well?

3. Some of Rosten's paragraphs are brief (5, 17, and 20). Should they be combined and unified with other paragraphs? Why or why not?

4. In paragraphs 7, 8, and 9, Rosten cites examples to demonstrate that people who speak different languages do not "hear" the same sounds. He then cites still another example in paragraph 11. Should he have presented the examples in consecutive paragraphs?

5. In paragraph 14, the author says that "The mere change of sound, in translating, can alter the sensual glow and hum of the original." Why do you suppose he used the phrase "sensual glow and hum"? Do you understand what he means? Should he have written "sensuous glow"?

6. Examine the following sentence from paragraph 2: "If this be true of tongues so close to each other in birth, so laden with cognates, so cross-fertilized by usage and literature, how much more does it intrude when one

tries to translate Yiddish or Hebrew into any of them?" What technique for emphasis does the author use in this sentence?

Exploring Words

1 Weltanschauung. Look up the definition of this term, and then explain in your own words what Rosten means when he says, "A language is a *Weltanschauung.*" Consider the context of the entire paragraph.

2 *mordant.* Can you think of a television comedian whose humor could be described as *mordant?*

3 *cognates.* Think of some *cognates* of English words in a second language of which you have some knowledge. The base *cog-* is found in *cognition* and *recognition.* Are you *cognizant* of a relationship between the meanings of these words?

4 *onomatopoeia.* Make up some *onomatopoetic* expressions for common household sounds (for example, the flushing of a toilet).

5 *dictum.* After consulting your dictionary, think of another word that could be used instead of *dictum* in Rosten's sentence in paragraph 17. Which word do you think is more effective? Why?

6 *nuances.* Think of several words that have different *nuances* according to the ways in which they are used.

7 *empathy.* Which of the definitions cited in your dictionary comes closest to Rosten's use? Does any one fit Rosten's use exactly? Write two sentences using *sympathy* and *empathy* accurately, distinguishing between the meanings.

Suggestions for Writing

1 If you have ever traveled abroad or met someone from a foreign country, you may have encountered difficulties in communication. Write an essay in which you explain those difficulties.

2 Analyze some of the obstacles to successful communication between different groups of Americans (for example, "establishment types" and "counterculture types").

The Trouble Began in San Francisco
BRIAN MCGINTY

Getting Started

With Ideas

You will find that this article provides, entertainingly, some little-known information on Mark Twain's early writing career. As you read it, think about different ways in which the title applies to the material presented.

With Words

1 torpid (7)—from the Latin word meaning "to be stiff or numb."
2 fortuitous (8)—related to *fortunate* (but not exactly the same in meaning).
3 despicable (12)—think of *despise*.
4 undulating (21)—from the Latin word meaning "wave."
5 prodigious (30)—related to *prodigy* as in "child *prodigy*."
6 sinuosities (32)—see *sinuous* in "Peaceful Coexistence with Rattlesnakes" (p. 41).
7 variegated (32)—related to *various*.

---

[1] When Samuel L. Clemens arrived in San Francisco in June of 1864, he harbored no ambitions to become a writer. For nearly two years, he had worked as a reporter for the *Territorial Enterprise* of Virginia City, Nevada, but he had tired of the drudgery of daily writing—as he had tired of the dry winds and alkali dust of Nevada. In San Francisco he hoped to put down his pen and make some money in silver stocks.

[2] Finances in the Pacific metropolis—as in Virginia City, its "mining suburb"—were free and easy, punctuated, as always, by frenzies of speculation. Clemens wrote that "bankers, merchants, lawyers, doctors, mechanics, laborers, and even the very washerwomen and servant-girls, were putting up their earnings on silver stocks, and every sun that rose in the morning went down on paupers and rich men beggared. What a gambling carnival it was!"

[3] Clemens was no stranger to speculation—nor to San Francisco—when he and his friend, the printer Jim Gillis, registered at the

---

"The Trouble Began in San Francisco," by Brian McGinty, reprinted from *American History Illustrated.* Copyright © 1975 The National Historical Society.

city's Occidental Hotel on June 8. The former Mississippi River pilot had visited San Francisco at least three times in 1863, coming down from his perch in the mountains of Nevada to enjoy the comforts of "Heaven on the half shell"—the luxurious Occidental. On one visit to the city, he had stayed two months, enjoying a "butterfly idleness . . . nothing to do, nobody to be responsible to, and untroubled with financial uneasiness." Back in Nevada, he remembered Eldorado's capital fondly: "Ah me! Summer girls and summer dresses, and summer scenes at the 'Willows,' Seal Rock Point, and the grim sea lions wallowing in the angry surf; glimpses through the haze of stately ships far away at sea, a dash along the smooth beach, and the exhilaration of watching the white waves come surging ashore . . . home again in a soft twilight, oppressed with the odor of flowers—home again to San Francisco, drunk, perhaps, but not disorderly." By the time of his permanent move to the city, Clemens calculated that he knew at least a thousand local residents, and when he walked down Montgomery Street shaking hands it was "just like being in Main Street in Hannibal and meeting the old familiar faces."

[4] Though Clemens hoped to make a fortune in silver stocks, his financial position in June 1864 was markedly worse than it had been the year before, in the days of his "butterfly idleness." Then his investments had shown signs that they might carry him to an early and comfortable wealth. But early in 1864 the market began to decline, and by midsummer it broke sharply. Clemens wrote later: "The bubble scarcely left a microscopic moisture behind it. I was an early beggar and a thorough one. My hoarded stocks were not worth the paper they were printed on."

[5] Even before the final break, Clemens found himself short of cash, and to remedy the situation, he looked for a job as soon as he arrived in San Francisco. While living in Virginia City, he had sent occasional snatches of Nevada news to San Francisco magazines and newspapers. The contributions—written under the pseudonym of "Mark Twain"—had given him a local reputation of sorts, and he was relieved to learn that the *Morning Call,* one of the newspapers that had published his work, was willing to hire him as a reporter.

[6] The job called for a different kind of writing than any other he had done before. Promptly at nine o'clock each morning, he appeared at the police court to report the squabbles of the night before. "They were usually between Irishmen and Irishmen, and Chinamen and Chinamen," he wrote, "with now and then a squabble between the two races for a change. Each day's evidence was substantially a duplicate of the evidence of the day before, therefore the daily performance was killingly monotonous." At night he visited each of the city's six theaters, glimpsing bits of plays and operas and writing reviews of the performances for the morning papers. "It was fearful drudgery," he said, "soulless drudgery, and almost destitute of interest. It was an awful slavery for a lazy man, and I was born lazy."

[7] Though there were very few stories for which he could muster any interest, he occasionally happened on one which aroused his enthusiasm. Strolling one Sunday afternoon, he came across a band of hoodlums who were chasing a Chinese laundryman and pelting him with stones. A policeman watched the scene with amusement. Outraged, Twain returned to his office and wrote an indignant account of the story. "Usually I didn't want to read in the morning what I had written the night before; it had come from a torpid heart. But this item had come from a live one. There was fire in it and I believed it was literature—and so I sought for it in the paper the next morning with eagerness. It wasn't there." The editor, George Barnes, explained that he had cancelled the story because the *Call* was a paper of the poor, chiefly the Irish, who hated the Chinese, and it couldn't afford to offend its readers. "Such an assault as I had attempted could rouse the whole Irish hive and seriously damage the paper," Twain noted. "The *Call* could not afford to publish articles criticizing the hoodlums for stoning Chinamen."

[8] The *Call*'s offices on Commercial Street were located next door to the United States Branch Mint. Since its opening ten years before, the Mint had been sorely overcrowded, and to provide additional space for its operations, the superintendent had rented offices for himself and his secretary in the adjoining *Call* building. The arrangement was a fortuitous one for Twain, enabling him to kindle a friendship with the superintendent's secretary, a handsome young man with Dundreary whiskers who doubled as one of San Francisco's leading writers. Bret Harte was about the same age as Mark Twain, but his early literary efforts had met with more spectacular success. Twain spent many hours in Harte's office, listening to stories, seeking advice on style and writing techniques. Harte's experience and critical instincts, which he generously shared, were to prove invaluable to the young *Call* reporter. "He trimmed and trained and schooled me patiently," Twain later wrote, "until he changed me from an awkward utterer of coarse grotesqueness to a writer of paragraphs and chapters that have found a certain favor in the eyes of even some of the very decentest people in the land."

[9] Though his job at the *Call* was far from satisfying, there was little doubt that Mark Twain liked San Francisco. "I fell in love with the most cordial and sociable city in the Union," he remembered later. "After the sage-brush and alkali deserts of Washoe, San Francisco was a paradise to me." In September 1864 he sent a photograph of himself to his mother and sister in St. Louis and wrote: "You can see by my picture that this superb climate agrees with me. And it ought, after living where I was never out of sight of snow peaks twenty-four hours during three years. Here we have neither snow nor cold weather; fires are never lighted, and yet summer clothes are never worn—you wear spring clothes the year round."

[10] In a Turkish bath in the historic Montgomery Block, he

struck up an acquaintance with a man named Tom Sawyer, with whom he liked to play penny ante. Long afterward, the man remained convinced that he had inspired Twain's famous tale of boyhood life along the Mississippi. Outside his tavern at Third and Mission Streets, he proudly hung a sign: "Ale and Spirits! The Original Tom Sawyer, Prop."

[11] Twain had grown so fond of the city that the thought of leaving it hardly occurred to him, even when he was fired from his job at the *Call*. He later admitted he had grown lazy after a hulking clerk from the newspaper's counting room, one "Smiggy McGlural," was hired as his assistant, and it soon became plain that the assistant could do the whole job. "Mr. Barnes discharged me," Twain remembered. "It was the only time in my life that I have ever been discharged and it hurts yet. . . . I was on the world now, with nowhere to go. By my Presbyterian training I knew that the *Morning Call* had brought disaster upon itself. I knew the ways of Providence and I knew that this offense would have to be answered for. I could not foresee when the penalty would fall or what shape it would take but I was as certain it would come, sooner or later, as I was of my own existence."

[12] For two months he was without employment. He bought nothing, avoided paying his board, and "became very adept at 'slinking.' I slunk from back street to back street, I slunk away from approaching faces that looked familiar, I slunk to my meals, ate them humbly and with a mute apology for every mouthful I robbed my generous landlady of, and at midnight, after wanderings that were but slinkings away from cheerfulness and light, I slunk to my bed. I felt meaner, and lowlier and more despicable than the worms."

[13] In December 1864 he beat a retreat from the city, repairing to the Sierra foothills above Sonora, California, where he found refuge in a cabin occupied by Steve Gillis, Jim's brother. The reasons for Twain's move to the mountains are unclear. That he was in financial distress and needed a hospitable roof over his head was reason enough for the trip, but Twain's biographers have hinted at other motives. Steve Gillis had been arrested in a barroom brawl, and Twain had posted a bond for his release. When Gillis failed to appear for his trial, Twain—who didn't have the money to cover the bond—became something of a wanted man. Already, the writer was far from popular with the San Francisco police, who resented his constant insinuations of stupidity, brutality, and corruption among the men in blue. It was even rumored that Police Chief Martin Burke had threatened Twain with legal action for his supposed libels of the constabulary.

[14] Whatever the reasons for his departure, Twain found the Sierra foothills congenial. He tried his hand at pocket mining and spent long hours listening to miners' tales. By February 1865, when he was ready to return to San Francisco, he had filled a notebook with impressions of his mountain sojourn. One of the notebook's references was to a yarn he

had heard in the foothills, a story about a jumping contest between two frogs—one of whose bellies had covertly been filled full of shot.

[15] Twain was still broke when he returned to San Francisco, but his fortunes soon improved. In March he began a series of articles for the *Californian,* a literary journal founded the previous year by Charles Webb and Bret Harte, and soon after he began to write occasional pieces for the *Golden Era* and the *Dramatic Chronicle.* In October he was engaged by the *Territorial Enterprise* as its San Francisco correspondent, and in the same month he became dramatic critic for the *Chronicle.*

[16] As a free-lance writer, Twain enjoyed more freedom than he had ever had as a newspaper reporter. With growing zest he wrote about fashions and theaters, prize fights and operas, politicians and newspaper critics. A friend persuaded him to make a pre-dawn visit to the Cliff House, on the rocky western edge of the San Francisco peninsula. "No, the road was not encumbered by carriages—," Twain wrote after his return, "we had it all to ourselves. I suppose the reason was, that most people do not like to enjoy themselves too much, and therefore they do not go out to the Cliff House in the cold and fog, and the dread silence and solitude of four o'clock in the morning. They are right. The impressive solemnity of such a pleasure trip is only equalled by an excursion to Lone Mountain in a hearse." He wrote an account of the trip for the *Golden Era,* which he prefaced with two quotations:

[17] " 'Early to bed, early to rise, makes a man healthy, wealthy and wise.'—Benjamin Franklin.

[18] " 'I don't see it.'—George Washington.

[19] "Now both of these are high authorities—," Twain continued, "very high and respectable authorities—but I am with General Washington first, last and all the time on this proposition.

[20] "Because I don't see it either."

[21] Few of San Francisco's characteristics escaped Twain's notice. He was introduced to the phenomenon of earthquakes by a prolonged series of tremors which shook the city during the summer of 1864. "I have tried a good many of them here, and of several varieties," he wrote of the quakes, "some that came in the form of a universal shiver; others that gave us two or three sudden upward heaves from below; others that swayed grandly and deliberately from side to side; and still others that came rolling and undulating beneath our feet like a great wave of the sea." The strongest tremor felt by Twain occurred on Sunday, October 8, 1865, as he strolled peacefully along Third Street. The quake was strong enough to destroy the Merchants Exchange building and badly damage the City Hall. Though old-timers belittled the quake, it frightened enough of the more recent arrivals to create a kind of bedlam in the city, on which Twain was eager to report.

[22] "The 'curiosities' of the earthquake were simply endless," he wrote. "Gentlemen and ladies who were sick, or were taking a siesta, or

had dissipated till a late hour and were making up lost sleep, thronged into the public streets in all sorts of queer apparel, and some without any at all. One woman who had been washing a naked child, ran down the street holding it by the ankles as if it were a dressed turkey. Prominent citizens who were supposed to keep the Sabbath strictly, rushed out of saloons in their shirt-sleeves, with billiard cues in their hands. . . . A prominent editor flew downstairs, in the principal hotel, with nothing on but one brief undergarment—met a chambermaid, and exclaimed: 'Oh, what *shall* I do! Where shall I go!'

[23] "She responded with naive serenity: 'If you have no choice, you might try a clothing-store!'"

[24] According to Twain, the tremor toppled several large organ pipes in a church where the minister was just closing the service. Looking up, the cleric hesitated for a moment, then announced that the benediction would be "omitted." "The next instant," Twain added, "there was a vacancy in the atmosphere where he had stood."

[25] A woman sitting in her parlor when the quake struck "saw the wall part at the ceiling, open and shut twice, like a mouth, and then drop the end of a brick on the floor like a tooth. She was a woman easily disgusted with foolishness, and she arose and went out of there."

[26] Twain's literary career received its greatest boost when the popular humorist, Artemus Ward, asked him to contribute a story to an anthology Ward planned to publish. Twain chose to write up the frog story he had heard in the Sierra. In the end, Ward did not use the piece, but "Jim Smiley and His Jumping Frog" was published in the New York *Saturday Press* on November 18, 1865, and reprinted the following month in San Francisco's *Californian*. At first, Twain was astonished by the success of the "Jumping Frog," grumbling that it was no more than a "villainous backwoods squib." But he was glad enough when the sketch was made the nucleus of a little book printed in New York and bearing the title, *The Celebrated Jumping Frog of Calaveras County, and Other Sketches*. He was offered an outright payment of ten thousand dollars for the volume, but he preferred to take a royalty. In the years to come he would compliment himself many times on this decision.

[27] From March until August of 1866 Twain was in Hawaii, writing sketches of island life for the Sacramento *Union*. When he returned to San Francisco, he tried his hand at lecturing, a pursuit which in the years ahead was to be nearly as important to him as writing. He claimed to be surprised that there was a full house in Maguire's Academy of Music when he made his first appearance there on October 2, 1866. But Mark Twain was already a San Francisco favorite, and there was little doubt that his followers would be out in force. Not even his foreboding advertisement could keep them away: "Doors open at 7 o'clock . . . The trouble to begin at 8. . . ."

[28] Twain later remembered his first night before the footlights of the Academy: "The trouble certainly did begin at eight, when I found

myself in front of the only audience I had ever faced, for the fright which had pervaded me from head to foot was paralyzing. It lasted two minutes and was as bitter as death; the memory of it is indestructible but it had its compensations, for it made me immune from timidity before audiences for all time to come."

[29] The lecture was well enough received to land Twain a booking on a tour of California and Nevada towns, where he spoke with ever-increasing assurance. Appearing once or twice more in San Francisco, he retired from the field "rich—for me—and laid out a plan to sail westward from San Francisco and go around the world."

[30] En route he wrote travel letters which were printed in the San Francisco *Alta California*. In 1868 he returned to the city, and in two months of prodigious work turned the letters into a book called *The Innocents Abroad,* his first full-length volume. *The Innocents Abroad* was an instant success, selling more copies than any other American book since *Uncle Tom's Cabin*.

[31] The remainder of Mark Twain's life was spent in the literary centers of the Eastern Seaboard, and in a brilliant series of tours across America, Europe, and Asia. The literary light kindled on the rough frontier of the American West traveled high in the firmament of letters before its flame at last flickered and died. Despite his growing reputation, Mark Twain never forgot San Francisco, nor his years of apprenticeship as a writer on its sandy, wind-blown streets.

[32] "If I were to tell some of my experience," he wrote in a letter to the Society of California Pioneers, "you would recognize California blood in me; I fancy the old, old story would sound familiar no doubt. . . . I have been through the California mill, with all its 'dips, spurs and angles, variations and sinuosities.' I have worked there at all the different trades and professions known to the catalogues. . . . But you perceive that although I am not a Pioneer, I have had a sufficiently variegated time of it to enable me to talk Pioneer like a native, and feel like a Forty-Niner."

[33] He was 71 when another earthquake struck San Francisco. It was 1906, and Twain read of the destruction in the newspaper in his home in New York City. His thoughts returned to the city of his youthful labors. He remembered a peaceful Sunday when the earth trembled beneath his feet and San Francisco's streets were filled with a confused disarray of half-dressed citizens. He thought of the day, long past, when he was fired from his job as a reporter for the *Morning Call,* and he recalled his premonition that the "offense" would have to be "answered for."

[34] So he was not surprised to see in the newspapers of that April 1906, pictures of the magnificent new *Call* building on Market Street, "towering out of the city like a Washington Monument; and the body of it was all gone and nothing was left but the iron bones! It was then I said, 'How wonderful are the ways of Providence!' I had known it would happen. I had known it for forty years."

[35] When he came to San Francisco in 1864, Mark Twain did not

know his life's work would be writing. But he knew it full well when he left the city four years later, the completed manuscript of his first full-length book packed in his bags. The unhappy memory of his departure from the *Call* could do nothing to cloud that certainty. In the future, piloting Mississippi River boats and speculating in Nevada silver stocks would be no more than fond memories for Samuel L. Clemens. Mountains of foolscap and hosts of lecture platforms were henceforth to be his window on the world. It was a wide and wonderful window, crowded with memorable scenes and wise observations. And the window was, perhaps, a little brighter because it had first been opened in the fresh, clean air of San Francisco.

Questions on Meaning

1 One of the reasons that Mark Twain's "San Francisco period" was important in his development as an artist was that it provided scenes and characters for his fiction. What are some examples the article mentions?

2 In what other ways did Mark Twain's experiences in and around San Francisco influence his artistic and professional development?

3 During this period, as in other times of his life, Mark Twain's writing successes and financial failures were closely connected. Trace the changes in his financial status in the period covered by this essay, and show how these changes affected his writing career.

Questions on Style and Structure

1 Explain why the title of this selection is appropriate.

2 McGinty includes many quotations by Mark Twain in this essay. In what ways would the piece be different had the author consistently paraphrased and summarized Twain's remarks? Try paraphrasing one of Twain's comments (for example, the one quoted in question 6 of this section), and compare your passage with the original. Also, note the skill with which McGinty incorporates quotations within his essay.

3 McGinty is careful to unify his paragraphs. Paragraphs 6 and 7, for example, are tightly unified. Which other paragraphs do you find particularly well unified? Are there any that could be improved?

4 Which phrase in the first sentence of paragraph 3 embodies the main idea of that paragraph?

5 Some essays are organized deductively; that is, the thesis is first stated and is then followed by the particulars that support it. Other essays are organized inductively; that is, the thesis is stated at the end, after the particulars

have been cited. In other words, the generalization grows out of the details that have preceded it. How would you characterize the organization of this essay?

6 In paragraph 12, McGinty quotes Twain: "I slunk from back street to back street, I slunk away from approaching faces that looked familiar, I slunk to my meals, ate them humbly and with a mute apology for every mouthful I robbed my generous landlady of, and at midnight, after wanderings that were but slinking away from cheerfulness and light, I slunk to bed." What device is Twain using for emphasis?

7 The author uses figurative language in paragraphs 31 ("literary light") and 35 ("window on the world"). How effective are these passages?

8 Which of the techniques discussed in the Introduction to Paragraph and Sentence Structure does McGinty use to conclude his essay?

Exploring Words

1 *torpid.* What antonyms can you think of or find for *torpid?* The noun *torpor* is used as often as—perhaps more often than—the adjective *torpid.* Check your dictionary, and then write sentences using both of these words.

2 *fortuitous.* See your dictionary for the subtle but important distinction between *fortuitous* and *fortunate.* The two terms can sometimes fit the same context. Write a sentence in which *fortuitous* fits but *fortunate* does not.

3 *despicable.* Check your dictionary, and write a sentence using the word *despicable* appropriately.

4 *undulating.* Mark Twain uses the word *undulate* to refer to the movement of the earth in an earthquake; it is also used sometimes to describe the movement of tall grasses in the wind. What other kinds of movement can you think of that could be described as *undulating?*

5 *prodigious.* This word is often used with the noun *task.* (Note that Mark Twain uses it with a similar word—*work.*) What are some *prodigious* tasks you have performed recently?

6 *sinuosities.* What do you suppose is meant by the *sinuosities* of "the California mill"? Note that there are other examples of figurative language in the sentence. (See also *sinuous* in the Exploring Words section of "Peaceful Coexistence with Rattlesnakes," p. 49.)

7 *variegated.* Check your dictionary, and note the distinctions indicated between *variegated* and *varied.* Write a sentence in which *variegated* would be appropriate but *varied* would not be.

Suggestions for Writing

1 Discuss your experiences at a place you have visited or grown up in. Which activities and events stand out most in your memory? Do you suppose those

experiences have had any influence on your later life? Be sure that your paper has sufficient focus.

2 Take one period of your life—perhaps a part of your childhood or the opening weeks of your first year in college—and show how this period influenced your later development.

3 Take one period of the life of someone you know well, such as a brother or good friend, and show how this period influenced his or her later development.

The Intellectual and Emotional World of the Cockroach
HOWARD E. EVANS

Getting Started

With Ideas

The fictitious cockroach who is mentioned in the first sentence of this unusual article was the creation of a newspaper columnist in the 1920s. Don Marquis had his cockroach hero tell his own story—and the story of the adventures of his best friend, mehitabel, the cat—using a newspaper office typewriter after working hours. But there was one problem: the cockroach was too small to reach the shift bar; therefore he signed his name "archy." None of this has much to do with what this article is really about. But Evans's reference to archy in the first sentence does help establish the tone of the essay, which is humorous and, at the same time, informative. Thus you will probably find that the information that biologist-author Evans gives about the structure and life-style of the cockroach is much easier to take in than you might have expected it to be.

With Words

1 ken (1)—from the Old English word meaning "to know."
2 veritable (3)—from the Latin word meaning "true."
3 encroachment (6)—though Evans's pun may seem to indicate that this word is related to *roach*, it has nothing to do with insects. It is from a Middle English word meaning "to get" or "to seize."
4 traverse (12)—from the Latin word meaning "to cross."
5 phonetics (19)—think of the meaning of *phon-* in words such as *telephone*, *phonograph*, and *phonics*, and the meaning of *-etics* in such words as *genetics* and *dietetics*, and you will be close to the meaning of this word.
6 predators (25)—from the Latin word for "plunderer" or "hunter."

[1] Ever since archy stopped jumping on the keys of Don Marquis' typewriter in the offices of the New York *Sun*, cockroaches have passed from the ken of most of us. It is a pity. Ours is a world of insec-

"The Intellectual and Emotional World of the Cockroach" appeared in *Harper's Magazine*, December 1966. Copyright 1966 by Howard E. Evans. Reprinted by permission of the author.

ticides, rodenticides, herbicides, and etceticides. As archy complained, on reading an advertisement for a roach exterminator:

> the human race little knows
> all the sadness it
> causes in the insect world . . .[1]

[2] Of course, a biologist will tell you that insects are unlikely to experience sadness. But the human species is bereaved when it is unable to appreciate the world of small and creeping things. I heartily recommend cockroaches. Unlike archy, the average roach has little or no poetry in his soul. But he is a marvelous beast nonetheless. He must, of course, be met on his own terms, in his own world. He has been inhabiting that world successfully for somewhat more than 250 million years. The earliest fossil cockroaches look so much like contemporary species that one can almost imagine them freshly crushed by some irate housewife. But the first housewife was still more than 249 million years in the future. Any creature so adept at survival would seem to be worth our attention; survival is a subject we can stand to learn a lot more about.

[3] Cockroaches are primarily creatures of the tropics and subtropics; in temperate regions we know them mainly from a few species that have found an easy living in our homes, stores, and restaurants. These domestic species include among others the American, German, Oriental, Surinam, and Cuban cockroach (a house my family once rented in Florida was a veritable United Nations of roachdom). A few years ago a cockroach was served to me in an order of beefsteak and onions in Texas (I believe it was American, but accurate identification of fried specimens is difficult). I was ravenously hungry after a day in the desert, so I ate everything except the cockroach, which I spread out neatly in the center of the empty plate, arranging his antennae and legs as best I could. The expression on the waiter's face when he cleared the table was ample compensation for the health risk I took. Although cockroaches are basically clean animals, they do track about a good deal of human filth; some carry bacteria responsible for various intestinal disorders, as well as polio virus and even hookworm.

[4] The names of our domestic roaches are largely the result of chance. When the Swedish naturalist Linnaeus received a roach from America he called it *americana*, while a roach from Asia he called *orientalis*. Even by that time (1758) most domestic cockroaches had spread over much of the globe, and modern transportation has finished the job. The late James A. G. Rehn, of the Academy of Natural Sciences of Philadelphia, revealed that the American roach and its close relative the Australian roach belong to a group which occurs in the wild, primarily in tropical Africa. He felt that these species, along with the Madeira roach and several others, came to America at an early date on slave ships. The Oriental roach

---

[1] From *archy and mehitabel*, by Don Marquis, published by Doubleday & Company, Inc.

also has wild relatives in Africa, but it arrived in Europe very long ago, perhaps on Phoenician vessels. Later it apparently traveled to South America on Spanish galleons and to North America on English ships.

[5] The German roach, according to Rehn, came from North Africa. As it spread across Europe it was called the "Prussian roach" by the Russians, the "Russian roach" by the Prussians, thus paralleling the history of syphilis, which was known as the "French disease" throughout much of Europe, but as the "Italian disease" in France. The first outbreak of syphilis in the British colonies, by the way, occurred in Boston twenty-six years after the landing of the *Mayflower*. Evidently that noble ship and its immediate followers carried a good many things besides bluebloods, including, no doubt, the German roach, long an inhabitant of Boston slums but now fighting a rearguard action against urban renewal and the more recently arrived brown-banded cockroach.

[6] America does, of course, have native roaches, but few of them have become domesticated, perhaps a reflection of the fact that man himself had his origins in Africa, thus giving the African roaches a big head start. The so-called Surinam roach apparently did not come originally from that Dutch colony in South America; Rehn found its closest relatives in the Orient, whence the species apparently spread into Africa and then joined several other species in slave ships traveling to that brave new world, America. Only one species, the so-called pale-bordered cockroach, has reversed the usual direction of immigration (may I say encroachment?) and reached the Canary Islands from its home in the West Indies.

[7] Biologists are always on the lookout for animals easy to rear in the laboratory, and what could be easier than cockroaches, which are usually there to start with anyway. Most species require no more than a warm and cozy cage, a little water, and an occasional dog biscuit. Best of all, cockroaches—whom no one seems to love greatly—are exempt from most if not all of the bills pending in Congress which attempt to regulate and restrict the use of laboratory animals.

[8] Scientists have used cockroaches in basic studies of animal behavior, nutrition, and metabolism, and even in cancer research. Dr. Berta Scharrer of the Albert Einstein College of Medicine found that when she cut certain nerves in the Madeira roach they developed tumors in some of the organs supplied by those nerves. Other workers have found tumors resulting from hormonal imbalance after transplanting endocrine glands in roaches. The application of these findings to the understanding of cancer in humans remains to be seen.

[9] Behavior studies suggest that roaches are among the "brighter" insects. This was demonstrated in 1912, by C. H. Turner of Sumner Teachers College in Saint Louis, whose ingenious studies of animal behavior, often with homemade equipment, earned him a reputation as one of the leading Negro biologists of his time. Turner, for example, tried "teaching machines" on cockroaches long before they came to be used for humans. He put roaches in cages containing two compartments,

one lighted and one dark. True to their well-known preference, Turner's roaches regularly headed for the dark compartment. However, when he wired it in such a way that they received an electric shock upon entering, they soon learned to go straight into the lighted compartment. (The males, he found, learned somewhat more quickly than the females.)

[10] Turner also taught his cockroaches to run mazes successfully, a trick few insects can master. He rigged up a complex pattern of pathways made of copper strips supported over a pan of water. At the end of one runway was an inclined plane leading to the jelly glass that was "home" to that particular roach. After only five or six trials at half-hour intervals, most roaches reached their jars faster and faster and made fewer errors en route. In the course of a day the number of errors declined to almost zero. Turner's Oriental roaches had short memories and had to be retrained every day, but another worker found that American roaches remembered and even improved from day to day. Another researcher tried running two or three roaches together to see if they could solve a maze more rapidly in company—as certain fishes can. Exactly the opposite occurred. Apparently extracurricular distractions conflict with serious training even among roaches.

[11] Lest anyone be inclined to dub the roaches "eggheads," I hasten to add that roaches *without* their heads are able to learn some things well. Recently Professor G. A. Horridge, of St. Andrews University in Scotland, arranged a decapitated roach in such a way that the legs received electric shocks every time they fell below a certain level. After about thirty minutes the roach changed its behavior in such a way that the legs were raised and few shocks were received. A decapitated roach, by the way, often lives for several days, although it eventually starves to death.

THE MECHANICS OF COWARDICE

[12] Doubtless the learning abilities of roaches have something to do with their success in putting up with the shenanigans of mankind. Other reasons for their success are to be found in their ability to scuttle off rapidly into crevices where they remain remarkably alert to peril. The roach's alarm system consists of long and active antennae on his head, and a pair of similar but shorter structures at the other end of the body, called *cerci* (from the Greek word for tails). These cerci are highly sensitive structures, and a light puff of air directed at one will send the roach scurrying. The cerci are covered with tiny hairs that bend when a current of air strikes them. Deflection of the hairs stimulates some of the many nerves in the cerci, which send a message to two clusters of nerve cells at their base. Here the message is transferred to giant fibers many times larger than ordinary nerve fibers, which carry nerve impulses more than ten times as fast as ordinary nerves (the rate is more than 15 feet per second which means that an impulse can traverse a giant fiber of the American roach in

less than .003 seconds). These fibers carry the impulse directly to the nerves and muscles of the legs and produce the immediate escape response so characteristic of roaches.

[13] To study the evasive behavior of the cockroach Professor Kenneth Roeder of Tufts University rigged up a treadmill attached to a very sensitive recording device. Behind the roach on the treadmill, he placed a small tube through which a jet of air could be blown at the cerci. At the same time the air jet would strike a small paper flag, also connected to the recording device, such that the interval between air jet and leg movement was registered. The cockroaches were fairly uncooperative, as experimental animals often are, and frequently cleaned themselves or made other unscheduled movements. But eventually Roeder obtained twenty-three good measurements which averaged out to about .05 seconds from air puff to leg movements. In subsequent experiments he found out why, although transmission over the giant fibers requires only about .003 seconds, another .047 seconds, more or less, are required for the final response. Some of the difference was caused by "synaptic delays," that is, the time taken for the impulse to cross from one nerve to another.

[14] Synapses are the switchboards of the nervous system and provide the major means of sorting and directing messages. They do slow things down. Because giant fibers bypass many synapses, they speed up the response. A number of ordinary nerve fibers might handle more information than one giant fiber but at the cost of several thousandths of a second. In the course of evolution, this small gain in speed of escape from enemies outweighed the importance of carrying more detailed messages.

[15] Our own human warning systems operate on much the same principle: emphasis is on rapid transmission of simple messages ("missile approaching") rather than much slower transmission of analytical reports. Such a system may have enhanced the survival of roaches as a group by millions of years, for their response is quick escape, and if the source of stimulation is in fact harmless, nothing is lost. *Our* problem, since we have no place to escape to, is to avoid an inappropriate response to meaningless information.

[16] In addition to their gift for speedy retreat some roaches have developed effective defense mechanisms. They can spray would-be predators with repellent chemicals. Dr. Thomas Eisner of Cornell University has found that one spray—known as a quinone—caused attacking ants and beetles to retreat and to undergo "a series of abnormal seizures, during which leg movements became discoordinated and ineffectual." (Quinones similar to those produced by certain cockroaches have bactericidal properties, and may some day conceivably find a role as medical antibiotics.)

[17] At least one roach has wholly abandoned cowardice in favor of aggression. This roach, with the suitably frightening name *Gromphadorhina portentosa,* not only produces an odor but makes a loud, hissing sound when disturbed. The males are sometimes as much as four inches long and have a pair of thick horns just behind their heads. When males

chance upon one another they charge and push each other back and forth with their horns, all the while hissing loudly. This roach is a native of Madagascar and has not become domesticated, thank God; it is not the sort of thing one would want to encounter on his kitchen shelf.

[18] The lives of cockroaches are remarkably automated. Apparently they don't even have to rely on their senses to decide when to go out on their nightly prowls. This was demonstrated by Dr. Janet Harker of Cambridge University, England, who found that American roaches kept in constant darkness nevertheless became more active when it was night outside, at least for a period of several days. Apparently a hormone is released from a group of cells in the head every twenty-four hours and "tells" the roach to bestir itself. A beheaded cockroach can't tell the time of day—not because he has no eyes but because he has lost the glands which produce this hormone. When Dr. Harker implanted a gland that was producing hormone rhythmically, she could restore the rhythm of activity in the headless roach. By subjecting the gland to temperatures close to freezing she was able to "reset the clock." However, this could be done only with a transplanted gland; when left in the original roach, the gland resets itself. It isn't quite clear why cockroaches need a system for "instrument take-offs" when they can tell when it is dark simply by looking out of their crevices.

THE CHEMISTRY OF LOVE

[19] Like other insects, roaches have no hormones produced by their sex organs. They hardly need them, adult insects being designed for reproduction and not much else. They do have certain built-in inhibiting devices, however; insects cannot afford to spend *all* their waking hours in sex, phonetics notwithstanding. We know that certain endocrine glands in the head of a female roach have much influence on the formation of her eggs. In some species, if these glands are removed soon after the female becomes sexually mature, she fails to produce a chemical—known as a pheromone—which attracts males, and is therefore very likely doomed to spinsterhood. But if she is doused with sex attractant taken from normal females, she can attract males and mates in the usual manner. When a female Surinam roach is pregnant, pressure of the developing eggs sends a nervous impulse to the head which suppresses these same glands and thus stops production of the sex attractant until the eggs are laid.

[20] Many other insects produce pheromones, and the study of their chemistry and effects is currently a very active field of biology. In some cockroaches, the male must actually contact the female before being stimulated, while in other cases the pheromone attracts males from a distance.

[21] The German roach has paid for its intimacy with man by having its sex life analyzed in great detail. When a male detects the phero-

mone of a female, he faces his intended spouse and the pair begin to "fence" with their antennae. Shortly thereafter he turns completely around and faces away from her, at the same time raising his wings at about a 90-degree angle. Through this gesture he is offering her his own chemical attractants, which exude from glands on his back. If courtship is proceeding well, the female climbs upon his back and begins to feed on these exudates, which lure her into copulating position. After a few seconds the male begins to push himself farther back beneath the female, at the same time extruding his genital organs. These are extraordinary structures, resembling nothing so much as a Boy Scout jacknife, with its various blades and bottle and can openers. With the longest of these hooks the male clamps onto a small crescent-shaped plate at the tail end of the female. Then he moves out from under her and turns about facing away from her. Other, smaller hooks are then attached to other structures on the female, who is literally "hooked" for the hour or two required for copulation.

[22] Dr. Louis Roth, of the U.S. Army Laboratories in Natick, Massachusetts, has found important differences in the reproductive behavior of various species. The American roach is more direct than the German, the male pushing himself beneath the female with hardly any preliminaries. In this species and in many others, males are greatly stimulated by female sex pheromone even in the absence of females. If filter paper is taken from the bottom of a cage of females and placed in a cage of males, the latter become greatly excited, flutter their wings, and attempt to mate with the paper. Workers at the United States Department of Agriculture have succeeded in isolating the sex attractant of the American roach by passing a stream of air through jars containing thousands of females, collecting the vapor by freezing it with dry ice. In nine months, they obtained 12.2 milligrams (about .0004 ounces) of this substance, which proved to be intensely exciting to males.

[23] Dr. Robert Barth of the University of Texas, who has become something of a Sigmund Freud to the roach world, finds that homosexuality is rare among roaches. However, he reports that when female pheromone is introduced into a cage of male Cuban roaches, they tear about their cage and proceed to court one another furiously. All steps in heterosexual courtship can be seen, except of course for the final hooking together of the genitalia. We still know very little about the actual nature of these potent sex attractants. Perhaps it is just as well.

[24] The eggs of roaches are produced in neat little packets which, in our homes and laboratory cages, are simply dropped on the floor, to hatch some time later if they do not dry up or become food for another roach. But we now know that this behavior is the result of an abnormal environment. In their natural habitats most roaches safeguard the next generation by concealing their eggs.

[25] I watched one method in a Florida state park on a warm spring evening several years ago. Around me were several female giant Florida roaches—a brown, wingless, and rather odorous species that has

not become domesticated to any extent. Each had an egg case protruding from the end of her body, and each was digging a hole in the sand or at least looking for a place to dig. When she had selected a suitable spot she made a series of backward strokes with her head, piling the sand beneath and behind her. After the hole was about a third of an inch deep, she dribbled saliva into it, picked up the moistened sand grains with her mouth and eventually molded a trough-shaped cavity of proper size and shape to fit the egg capsule. Next she straddled the pit, released the egg case, and slid it into the hole with movements of her abdomen, turning around and making final adjustments with her mandibles. Then she plastered moistened sand over the top of the egg case and smoothed it over. Finally after more than an hour of hard work, she wandered off into the darkness, having effectively protected against predators, parasites, and desiccation offspring she would never see herself.

[26] In laboratory cages, this same roach, like other species, merely drops her egg cases on the floor. But if she is provided with sand, she will act out her normal egg-burying behavior (to a bleary-eyed audience, sometime in the middle of the night).

WORTH LIFETIMES OF STUDY

[27] Other roaches have quite different methods of protecting their eggs. The German roach, for example, carries her egg case around, projecting from the end of her body, and even transfers water to it. She drops it when the eggs are ready to hatch. The female Madeira and Surinam roaches, after extruding the egg case, draw it back into the body, where it occupies a special brood sac until hatching occurs. These roaches are unique in being "born twice," since the eggs first leave the body of the female and are then drawn back in, to emerge a second time as young roaches. In the brood sac, the eggs are thoroughly protected and are supplied with water and, in at least one case, with nutriment. The Surinam roach has even dispensed with the nuisance of having a male sex; one strain of this species consists entirely of females which produce live female young, which grow up to produce live female young, and so on *ad infinitum*. If there is a more efficient reproductive mechanism, the roaches will undoubtedly find it.

[28] When a scientist is asked what good his research is, the classic answer (and a good one) is a shrug of the shoulders. To a student of roaches, it is self-evident that any creature so beautifully adapted and adaptable is worth lifetimes of study. If there are any underlying principles of long-term survival, surely they are evidenced by the roaches. Of the 3,500 species now living fewer than 5 per cent have been studied in any detail. What we do know suggests that every species is a story in itself, and that even our best-known species have still to yield final answers on many details of body function. The study of roaches may lack the aesthetic

values of bird-watching and the glamour of space flight, but nonetheless it would seem to be one of the more worthwhile human activities. In fact, as I scan the evening paper, I wonder if it may not be more worthwhile than most of them.

Questions on Meaning

1 Evans's thesis concerns his reason for thinking that the cockroach deserves the intensive scientific investigation it has been given. What is that reason? Where is it stated specifically?

2 What is the principal support Evans gives for his thesis?

Questions on Style and Structure

1 How successful is the title in arousing your interest? Why is the title effective or ineffective?

2 Generally, how unified are the paragraphs? Which paragraphs do you find striking in their unity? Which ones might be made more unified?

3 The third sentence of the essay contains this string of nouns: "insecticides, rodenticides, herbicides, and etceticides." The last item reveals an author who loves to play with words. Where else does Evans reveal this fondness? How effective is he at this kind of wit?

4 Compare the tone of this essay with that of Petrunkevitch's "The Spider and the Wasp" (p. 141). Why is the tone of each piece appropriate to its purpose and subject matter?

5 What basic technique does Evans use to conclude his essay?

Exploring Words

1 *ken.* Which definitions of this word does your dictionary label *Obsolete?*

2 *veritable.* How are *veritable, verify, verily, verity, veracity,* and *verisimilitude* related in meaning?

3 *encroachment.* Can you think of two activities or phenomena in which *encroachment* may take place?

4 *traverse.* After looking up this word, use it in a sentence about your own experiences.

5 *phonetics.* Does your dictionary cite a definition that precisely fits Evans's use of the word?

6 *predators.* Think of some animals that are *predators.* What is the prey of each? Then think of some human *predators.* Upon whom do they prey?

Suggestions for Writing

1 Write an essay on "The Intellectual and Emotional World of _____" (fill in the blank with the name of any other animal from which humans can learn much).

2 Observe a natural phenomenon closely for at least twenty minutes. This could be the food gathering of ants in your backyard, the flitting of butterflies in your garden, or—if you don't like insects—the attempts of a cat to catch unwary birds (or any other interaction of creatures with their environment). Write about what you observe in as clear, objective, and interesting a way as you can.

The Lost Vikings of Greenland
JØRGEN MELDGAARD

Getting Started

With Ideas

To prepare yourself for this account of the first European settling of a part of the world you may not have thought much about recently, it will probably be a good idea to locate both Greenland and Norway on a large, easy-to-read map.

With Words

1 unsavory (1)—*savory* comes from the Latin word for "taste."
2 fjords (3)—you will probably be able to determine an approximate meaning for this word if you remember what the coast of Norway looks like on a map.
3 reconnoitered (9)—you probably are familiar with the noun *reconnaissance*, as in the phrase *"reconnaissance* patrol."
4 ecclesiastical (20)—from the Latin word for "church."

[1] Eric the Red, the Norse chieftain who discovered and colonized Greenland in about A.D. 985, and his son Leif, also known as Leif the Lucky, who discovered America about the year 1000, are Scandinavian heroes. Legends of their courage and adventurousness form a part of the history in which we take justifiable pride and serve as a welcome counterbalance to the unsavory reputation the Vikings acquired in western Europe in the early Middle Ages.

[2] During the ninth and tenth centuries, the years of the Viking era, the then pagan Norsemen repeatedly raided the Christian countries of England, France, Germany, and Ireland, where they pillaged, burned, and killed, leaving behind a wake of hatred and fear. Wild warriors whose passion for battle transported them into frenzies during which they were said to bite their shields, foam at the mouth, and howl like wolves or growl like bears, the Vikings were called "berserkers" by their peers. That appellation has survived in the English language in the word *berserk*.

[3] Before the end of the Viking era, these adventurers had sailed

Reprinted, with permission, from *Natural History* Magazine, May, 1973. Copyright © The American Museum of Natural History, 1973.

from the fastness of their northern fjords through the Strait of Gibraltar into the Mediterranean and had penetrated south to the Black Sea via the Russian waterways. Despite their intelligence and superb navigational skills, the Vikings were deemed so barbaric by their contemporaries that a special prayer for protection against them was offered in European churches: "God deliver us from the fury of the Northmen."

[4] There was, however, a more constructive side to the Vikings. When they voyaged to places not yet settled, such as Iceland, Greenland, and Vinland, as they called North America, they developed their own culture and demonstrated a capacity for government and peaceful community organization.

[5] Our main sources of information about the 500-year Viking colonization of Greenland and the Scandinavian voyages to Vinland are the sagas of Old Norse literature. But these fragmentary, ancient accounts of the lives of kings, the feuds of chieftains, and the exploits of venturesome men crossing the sea in open boats are often dismissed as nothing more than fables. Now, with the publication during the last decade of Yale University's pre-Columbian Vinland map and the archeological discoveries in Greenland, some of the material in the sagas has been corroborated. The shadowy centuries of Viking settlement in Greenland have become more concrete and our knowledge of what the life of Norse common folk was like during the Middle Ages has been augmented. The sagas can be read without reservation as lively and exciting period descriptions. They give in broad outline an authentic picture of the times and usually correct information about personages and events.

[6] Two sagas in particular tell of Norse adventures in Greenland: *The Saga of the Greenlanders* and *Eric the Red's Saga*. All the sagas, of which there are many, were originally communicated orally. It is not certain when these spoken tales were first written down, but the classic sagas are thought to have been transcribed in Iceland in the thirteenth century and later incorporated into more comprehensive manuscripts. *The Saga of the Greenlanders* is thus found in the *Flatey Book,* an extensive late-fourteenth-century codex. *Eric the Red's Saga* is contained in two documents: the *Hauk's Book* and the *Skalholt Book,* both of which appear to be based on a common source dating back to the end of the thirteenth century.

[7] Greenland is the world's largest island. It lies mainly within the Arctic Circle, closer to the North American continent than to Scandinavia. Most of its 840,000 square miles is steeply mountainous plateau, covered by an ice cap 1,000 or more feet thick. Numerous fjords indent its coasts.

[8] This sizable land mass was first sighted by a European in about the year 900, when a Viking sailor voyaging from Norway to Iceland was driven westward off his course by storms. All he saw of the island on the distant horizon was its inhospitable, ice-packed east coast ringed with rock outcroppings. He did not go ashore, but he did carry back to Iceland word of a new land to the west, and the story persisted for generations.

[9] Iceland had been settled in the mid-ninth century by Norsemen fleeing the domination and oppressive taxation of King Harold I of Norway. Among the colonists living there toward the end of the tenth century was Eric the Red, named for the color of his hair and beard. In 982, Eric was banished from Iceland for three years as punishment for killing several fellow Norsemen in a feud. Recalling the report of a land to the west, he set out to find and explore it during his banishment. For three years Eric systematically reconnoitered Greenland's ice-free southwestern coast, milder and more fertile than the island's forbidding eastern shore, looking for a suitable place for settlement.

[10] The climate of Greenland in Eric's time, like that of the rest of the earth, was more benevolent than it was later to become. There is no mention in the sagas that he encountered ice drifts, now common in far northern waters. On his return to Iceland, Eric told of a land of fertile pastures, which he called "Greenland" in order to entice farmers to join him there in colonization.

[11] In the summer of 985, thirty-five ships carrying 300 to 400 men, women, and children, together with cows, horses, sheep, and household effects, set sail from Iceland for a new home in Greenland. According to the sagas, only fourteen ships arrived safely, some being wrecked in passage and others being driven back to Iceland by wind and weather. A colony known as the East settlement was founded on the Greenland coast near the present Julianehaab, and shortly after, a second colony known as the West settlement was formed about 250 miles northwest near today's Godthaab. The distance between the two settlements was calculated as being a six-day row in a six-oared boat. Eric the Red built his own farmstead at Brattahlid in the center of the East settlement and near the present town of Narssaq.

[12] It was from Brattahlid some time after the year 1000 that the celebrated Vinland expeditions to the northeast coast of the American Continent set forth, voyages of discovery associated with the name of Eric's son Leif. On those expeditions, the Vikings first encountered Indians and Eskimo, the Norsemen called them "Skraellings." In Greenland, the colonists found traces at their two settlements of the presence of Eskimo on the huge island, but the native inhabitants lived far to the north and there is no record that the two populations met for several centuries.

[13] Despite the hazardous voyage from Iceland and Norway to the Greenland settlements, more and more Viking families made the journey, seeking land and a measure of independence. These enterprising and hardworking colonizers built houses, cultivated farms, bred cattle, wove cloth, hunted, fished, traded with Europeans, and generally prospered. What kind of people were these kinsmen of the Vikings who had earlier been the scourge of Europe? A mid-thirteenth-century Norwegian document known as *The King's Mirror,* written by an anonymous scholar in the form of a conversation between a father and son, has this to say about the Greenland settlers:

[14] "As you are anxious to know what one looks for in that land,

or why one goes there at such great peril, it is that one is moved to do so by the threefold character of human nature. One part thereof is the spirit of rivalry and the craving for fame; for the nature of many men drives them to go where great danger can be expected, in order to become famous by doing so. The second is the thirst for knowledge; for in man's nature lies that inclination to explore and see things of which he has before been told, in order to know whether it is as he has been told or not. The third thing is the hope of wealth; for men look for that wherever they learn that gain can be expected, regardless that great dangers threaten on the other side."

[15] Like their mainland relatives, the early Greenland Vikings were pagans who worshiped such Norse gods as Odin, Freya, and Thor. But in 1000, the same year that he discovered America, Leif Ericson introduced Christianity to the Greenland settlements.

[16] According to the Icelandic sagas, fourteen years after Eric the Red settled at Brattahlid, he sent his son Leif to Norway to spend time at the court of King Olaf Tryggvason, as was customary for chieftains' sons. Leif's visit came at a time when the king, having been converted himself, "harried the country to Christianity." Olaf destroyed the pagan temples, forbade the practice of sacrifices, forced his subjects to be baptized, and if they resisted, put them to death.

[17] The sagas report: "The king found Leif no problem. He was baptized with all his shipmates, and spent the winter with the king. . . . That same summer [the year 1000] King Olaf sent Leif Ericson to Greenland to preach Christianity there. The king provided him with a priest and various other holy men to baptize folk there and instruct them in the true faith. Leif set sail for Greenland that summer, and while at sea picked up a ship's crew of men who lay helpless there on a wreck. On this same journey he found Vinland the Good [America]. He reached Greenland at the end of the summer and went to lodge at Brattahlid with Eric his father. From this time forward men called him Leif the Lucky, but his father contended that one thing cancelled out the other, in that Leif had rescued a ship's company and saved the men's lives, but had also introduced a man of mischief [as Eric styled the priest] into Greenland."

[18] The sagas continue: "Leif soon preached Christianity throughout the country," but "Eric took coldly to the notion of abandoning his faith." Thjodhild, Leif's mother, embraced Christianity at once. She had a church built behind the brow of a small hill, just out of sight of their farm, and there she "offered up her prayers, along with those men who adopted Christianity, who were many." Because her husband refused to be converted, Thjodhild would not live with Eric as man and wife once she had taken the faith, "a circumstance which vexed him very much."

[19] By 1126, when the Viking population on Greenland numbered about 4,000 to 5,000 colonists working some 280 farms, an ecclesiastical see was established at Gardar, a large farm in the East settlement, and the island got its own bishop. Several ecclesiastical buildings, includ-

ing sixteen parish churches, a cathedral, a monastery, and a nunnery were subsequently built at the settlements.

[20] Greenland had been a republic, but in 1261, the Norwegian crown gained direct control over the island. King Haakon IV imposed taxes on the settlers and a fine for manslaughter, the *wergeld*. There were few oceangoing ships, and in the following century contact between Greenland and Europe steadily diminished. Gradually the colonies declined. By about 1350, the once flourishing West settlement was deserted. The last authenticated historical light on the East settlement comes from ecclesiastical archives. It is a declaration of the solemnization of a marriage that took place on September 16, 1408 at the Hvalsey church. Many of those who attended the wedding left the settlement in 1410 on the last ship from Greenland of which there is any record. Archeological evidence suggests that the settlement was still inhabited by a few struggling Viking families at the time that Columbus crossed the Atlantic, but by the beginning of the sixteenth century, the East settlement too was deserted. From that time until the start of Danish colonization in the 1700s, the only inhabitants of Greenland were the Eskimo.

[21] We do not know why the Viking colonists became extinct. They may have been exterminated by hungry, marauding bands of Eskimo. The writings of a Norwegian priest, who was made the leader of an expedition from the East settlement to rescue the West settlement in about 1350, say: "when [the expedition] got there, they found no people, neither Christians nor pagans, only wild cattle and sheep." And the *Icelandic Annals,* which occasionally report Greenlandic events, has this 1379 entry: "Skraellings attacked the Greenlanders, killing eighteen of them and carrying two boys off into captivity."

[22] We know that the climate of Greenland deteriorated in the fourteenth century when the whole earth got colder. The general cooling favored the southward migration of the Eskimo tribes. And the buildup of the Greenland ice cap may have partly closed the fjords to navigation and made it difficult, if not impossible, for the Vikings to breed cattle, their principal means of livelihood. A wide band of drift ice now enclosed the coasts of South Greenland. After about 1350 the kings and the merchants back home in the Scandinavian countries found the route to Greenland so perilous and unprofitable that communication gradually ceased.

[23] Some aspects of Norse life in Greenland can be clarified by archeological finds, which supplement the written records. The work of historical reconstruction can be said to have begun in 1721 with the arrival in Greenland of the Norwegian missionary Hans Egede. Dispatched there by royal command to search for traces of the vanished Scandinavian settlements, he traveled to their sites and sent back to Copenhagen descriptions of what he saw. Over the next 150 years similar reports were sent back by Danish officials. These descriptions augmented our knowledge of the topography of the settlments' farms and churches. But the most important source material did not come to light until Capt. Daniel Brunn, a Danish

geographer, started excavations in the East settlement in 1894 and the West settlement in 1903. His diggings established the size of the two settlements and the sites of specific farms and churches and showed for the first time what the farmsteads, sheepfolds, outbuildings, and houses had looked like. Several church ruins were identified and renamed with the help of existing literary sources. Such historical sites as Eric the Red's farm at Brattahlid and the ecclesiastical seat at Gardar were located, along with other ruins deep within the fjords of the Julianehaab district.

[24] Brunn's work wasn't followed up until 1921, when archeologists began to concentrate on excavating specific farms, churches, and graveyards. That year, while digging slowly through the frozen ground of a churchyard at the extreme south end of the East settlement, the Danish archeologist Paul Nørlund, made a most important discovery: opening some graves, he unearthed a collection of astonishingly well-preserved ordinary clothing. Made of the Greenland homespun celebrated in the Middle Ages, the apparel is the only major collection in existence of the everyday medieval dress typical of northern Europe.

[25] The fine garments of medieval nobility and clergymen, well preserved by subsequent generations, are familiar to us. But here, at the end of the earth, the "Ultima Thule" of ancient times, was a glimpse of the less familiar raiment of ordinary men and women: dresses, cloaks, and liripipe hoods. In their cut and styling, these clothes followed the fashions of Europe even up to the end of the fifteenth century, long after our last written news from Greenland.

[26] Near the churchyard where Nørlund made his find stood a Norse farm mentioned frequently in the sagas as an important trading post and the first port of call for ships that had successfully made the long journey from Scandinavia to Greenland. We can only surmise that ships continued to arrive in the fjords of Julianehaab even as late as the year 1500 and that trading continued. The population of the East settlement, decimated as it may have been, must have remained sufficiently vigorous to keep up with the latest fashion trends of eastern Europe. Over and above the struggle for survival, there must have been the continuing desire to impress their few neighbors.

[27] In later years, Nørlund went on to excavate the site of the cathedral, which was 88½ feet long and 52½ feet wide, and the bishop's domicile at Gardar, which was 164 feet long and contained a banquet hall large enough to serve several hundred guests. The site also included numerous smaller buildings for the storage of tithes and taxes, in the form of wool, furs, and walrus teeth, as well as barns that housed as many as 100 cows. The farm of Eric the Red at Brattahlid was excavated by Nørlund in 1932. Like the other buildings of Viking settlements, Eric's farmstead was designed to meet the practical needs of climate and occupation.

[28] Subsequent excavations made by the Danish National Museum at the East settlement as well as at the site of the West settlement to the north, established a special style of Greenland construction. Farm-

steads consisted of fifteen to twenty rooms with humans and their cows, horses, sheep, and pigs living together under one roof. Building materials were turf, which is exceptionally compact in northern latitudes, and stone boulders set into the ground to lend stability and support. Low, turf-covered roofs spanned the rooms, sloping gradually to three- to four-foot-thick turf walls calculated to keep the quarters warm. Dwellings had long fireplaces and often included pantries and bathhouses. These farms, shaped by wind and weather like the landscape itself, must have looked from a distance like insignificant hummocks under the towering mountains, with only an occasional wisp of smoke rising above the rooftops to suggest the human habitation within. On the inside, these houses must have been as cosy, snug, and busy as a hive. Even in wintertime, on at least one occasion following a wedding, the sagas tell us that at Eric the Red's farm "there was much chess playing, and story telling, and many other entertainments that enrich a household." And there were "great discussions" about going in search of Vinland "where, it was said, there was excellent land to be had."

[29] Then in the fall of 1961, a visitor from Greenland brought to my office at the National Museum in Copenhagen a round parcel wrapped in pink tissue paper and announced that it contained the skull of Eric the Red. Workmen digging the foundation of a hostel for school children from outlying sheep farms had unearthed the skull at a village on the site where Brattahlid had once stood. It had first been thought to be the skull of a sheep, but examination proved it was human and Norse; could it be that of Eric the Red?

[30] The possibility that I held Eric the Red's skull in my hand, and that other archeological treasures might also lie buried where it had been found, was enough to send me quickly to the site of Brattahlid for a firsthand look. When I got there and peered into the hostel foundations dug by the local workmen, I could see the dark contours of several graves. In the low sunlight, shadows also revealed the faint traces of the walls of a small building. The larger ruins of Eric's farm had already been uncovered a mere 300 yards away on lower ground. This newly uncovered small building, I thought, was most like Thjodhild's church—the first church built in the New World. Extensive excavations undertaken in the following summers by Knud Krogh, an architect, confirmed its identity. Probably dating back to the end of the year 1000, the church was of modest proportions: 11½ feet long and 6½ feet wide. Not more than twenty worshipers pressed closely together could have stood at one time under its roof. Like other buildings of the Viking settlements, this church had a thick turf roof and walls; it also had one wooden gable facing west.

[31] Surrounding the church was a graveyard from which the skeletons of 144 men, women, and children were excavated. These remains came from the earliest generations of Greenland Norse, for sometime during the eleventh century, a larger stone church with its own graveyard had been built directly in front of the Brattahlid farmhouses,

and Thjodhild's church fell into disuse. Judging by the skeletons' measurements, which match those of contemporary Scandinavians, these Vikings had powerful musculature and were a tall, strong people. We do not, however, know their individual identities. In the early days of Christianity in Greenland, the church banned the pagan custom of burying grave goods with the dead, but gravestones had not yet come into use. The skeletons therefore remain anonymous.

[32] *Eric the Red's Saga* ends with the story of the long voyage to Vinland by Thorfinn Karlsefni, an Icelander who had married the widow of one of Eric's sons. For three years Thorfinn led a party of 160 in exploring the new land discovered a few years before by Leif the Lucky. Many of the men took their wives and all kinds of livestock with them, "for it was their intention to colonize the country, if they could do so." Thorfinn's wife, who accompanied him, bore him a son in Vinland. During their explorations, some of the would-be colonists were killed in encounters with Indians. Perhaps fearing more attacks, the survivors abandoned the project and returned to Greenland.

[33] We do not know where all these early American explorers were buried but some of them ended up in the anonymous graves next to Thjodhild's church. And even if the skull that came to the Danish National Museum wrapped in pink tissue paper is not that of Eric the Red, it could well be that of one of the first Europeans to tread the North American Continent about five hundred years before Columbus made his historic landfall.

Questions on Meaning

1 Prepare an outline for a short paper or for a class discussion concerning the occupation of Greenland from the ninth to the fifteenth centuries. Include the following information: reasons the colonists first settled there; adaptations the original colonists and their descendents made to the environment that made it possible for them to endure under adverse conditions; cultural changes that occurred during these centuries; and possible reasons for the eventual deterioration of the Greenland settlements.

2 Comment on the methods that historians and other specialists have used to find out what they now know about the Greenland settlements. To what extent are they dependent on inferences from folk tales? To what extent is there scientific corroboration of the material in these tales?

3 Evaluate the author's treatment of his material. Has he convinced you that he is dealing with historical facts rather than promoting a pet theory about the settlement of Greenland?

THE LOST VIKINGS OF GREENLAND

Questions on Style and Structure

1 What is the basic purpose of the first three paragraphs? Before reading the essay, did you know much more about the Vikings than is contained in these initial paragraphs?

2 Does this essay have a thesis statement? If so, where is it?

3 Describe the basic structure of this essay. Into how many sections does it fall? Paragraph 23 begins with this statement: "Some aspects of Norse life in Greenland can be clarified by archeological finds, which supplement the written records." In what way is that sentence a clue to the organization of the essay? Are there other ways in which the material could be organized?

4 Select five paragraphs at random and test them for unity. Is each of these paragraphs devoted to a single main idea?

5 Examine the following sentence from paragraph 16: "Olaf destroyed the pagan temples, forbade the practice of sacrifices, forced his subjects to be baptized, and if they resisted, put them to death." Why is that version superior to the following: Olaf destroyed the pagan temples, forced his subjects to be baptized and put them to death if they resisted, and forbade the practice of sacrifices.

Exploring Words

1 *unsavory.* How many definitions for *unsavory* are there in your dictionary? Which one comes closest to Meldgaard's use?

2 *fjords.* What alternate spelling does your dictionary cite? Does it distinguish a *fjord* from a firth? Which American state is noted for its *fjords*?

3 *reconnoitered.* After checking your dictionary for the meaning(s) of this word, use it in a sentence of your own.

4 *ecclesiastical.* Could this word be used with reference to non-Christian religions (say, Buddhism)? Why or why not?

Suggestions for Writing

1 Write a brief history of the community you live in or of another community you know well. Use any of these sources that are available to you: early newspapers, recollections of old-timers, books, magazine articles, your own memories.

2 As Meldgaard does in showing that there is another side to the Vikings than the popular picture of them as ruthless barbarians, show how a group of people has been unfairly stereotyped. You do not have to deal with ethnic or national groups. You might, for example, treat such groups as police officers, tax collectors, or fraternity members.

Lonely Lives under the Big Sky
WILLIAM A. DOUGLASS

Getting Started

With Ideas

You will probably increase your understanding and appreciation of this article by taking a few minutes to look up some information about the Basque people and the land they come from before you begin. An article in an encyclopedia or a similar reference work will provide you with basic information about these people and will identify their homeland sufficiently so that you can find it on a map.

With Words

1 endemic (4)—from the Greek word meaning "dwelling in a place."
2 nascent (5)—from the Latin word meaning "to be born."
3 itinerant (6)—what do you do when you plan the *itinerary* of a trip?
4 tutelage (15)—the context and your recollection of the way this word was used in "An Exaltation of Larks" (p. 133) will prove helpful.
5 meticulously (24)—the context will be helpful here.
6 urbanite (29)—associate this word with *urban* and *suburbanite*.

[1] The Basque sheepherder of the American West has become a romanticized figure in popular literature. For those whose lives are dominated by urban pressures and ills, his life-style holds a primitivistic attraction; the thought of a solitary existence played out against spectacular mountain scenery lends itself to escapist dreams.

[2] This mystique has developed through a one-sided view of the Basque sheepherder's life-style. Along with the beauty of his environment, the freedom from the irritations of urban life, and the seemingly uncomplicated task of caring for a band of sheep, there is also the necessity of enduring months of boredom and loneliness. In the American West, sheep raising is characterized by transhumance. Under this system, sheep bands are summered in the remote high-mountain country and wintered in the low, arid, and sparsely populated valleys. Twice a year the sheep

Reprinted, with permission, from *Natural History* Magazine, March, 1973. Copyright © The American Museum of Natural History, 1973.

traverse as much as several hundred miles between these ranges. Today some outfits truck their animals, but many still trail them, and in this instance the herders cover the entire distance on foot and horseback.

[3] Constantly exposed to the physical elements, the herder must possess considerable self-reliance and endurance. As guardian of the sheep band, he is responsible for an asset worth many thousands of dollars. On the open range the sheep band is exposed to such predators as coyotes, lynx, and occasionally, mountain lions and bears, and the herder must be continually alert. There is also the danger of poisoning from toxic plants and bad water. Disease can strike, or a part of the band may wander off during a blizzard or when trailing through rugged country. At the same time, the herder lives in almost unbroken social isolation, and the nature of the occupation practically rules out the intimacies of family life.

[4] Because labor shortages have always been endemic to this low-status, low-paying industry, the willingness of Basques to migrate from Spain and France and enter the occupation continues to be a major factor in the sheep industry's growth. Speaking a language that cannot be shown definitively to share common roots with any other human tongue, the Basques are regarded as the mystery people of Europe, an image that is heightened by imprecise knowledge of their origins.

[5] Basque involvement in the open-range sheep industry dates from the days of the 1849 California gold rush. There were several hundred Basques in the ranks of the fortune seekers; many came directly from Argentina and Uruguay, where thousands of Basque immigrants had been livestockmen during the first half of the nineteenth century. In the 1850s and 1860s many of the Basque gold prospectors, notably those who had formerly lived in South America, left the mining camps and entered the nascent sheep and cattle industries of southern and central California.

[6] By the 1880s the Basques had established a reputation as the finest sheepmen in the American West, and by the first decade of the twentieth century a few Basques had become prominent sheep ranchers with impressive herds and private landholdings. Others worked as herders and were the preferred employees in Basque and non-Basque sheep outfits alike, often replacing other immigrant or American Indian sheepherders. And finally, the Basques were the most prominent ethnic group in the ranks of the itinerant sheep outfits, which were referred to by their detractors as "tramp bands."

[7] The itinerant sheep outfit was a one- or two-man operation requiring minimal capitalization. The shepherd-owner simply acquired about a thousand sheep, a pack animal, a tent, bedroll, and grubstake, then moved about the public lands searching for available pasturage. Most of the range was under federal ownership and as a part of the public domain, was legally open to all on a first-come basis. The legalities of the matter notwithstanding, competition for public pasturage and water among the itinerants and the settled cattle and sheep ranchers was at times fierce. On occasion, competition turned into conflict, and the result-

ing confrontations provided copy to the newspapers, litigation to the courts, and substance to the sheepman versus cattleman legend.

[8] That Basques were the most numerous element in the ranks of the itinerant sheepmen exacerbated the situation. Each year thousands of Basque males, for the most part young and single, emigrated from Europe to replace those who had returned or who had purchased their own bands. Most entered the West with the intention of returning to the Old World after acquiring substantial capital. Few were willing to remain sheepherders for long, but rather, expected to become sheep owners as quickly as possible. With little interest in a future in this country, the budding Basque sheep entrepreneur was loath to invest in land; instead he sought to increase the size of his band. As he did so, he required additional herders and camp tenders and would send to Europe for kinsmen or fellow villagers. Frequently, the newcomers would take part of their wages in ewes, running their own animals alongside those of their kinsman-employer. They usually did this for three or four years, until they had sufficient animals to form an independent band. At this point the sheepherder would "hive off" his new outfit, striking out in search of fresh pasturage.

[9] Since the owner of the parent outfit more often than not planned to return eventually to the Basque country, he was more interested in the short-term fluctuations of the lamb and wool markets than in the long-range prospects of the American sheep industry. He might therefore assist many kinsmen and fellow ethnics to become itinerant operators without giving much thought to the consequences of overgrazing.

[10] As a result, American ranchers held a dim view of Basques. The ubiquitous Basque itinerants were depicted as foreign usurpers of American resources, opportunists who bled the economy of the American West of wealth that was sorely needed for local development. Their presence inflamed passions and stimulated anti-Basque sentiments, rhetoric, and eventually, legislation.

[11] In the 1890s and early 1900s competition with the itinerants prompted many western ranchers to join eastern conservationists in supporting legislation to create the national forest system. The system controlled access of livestock to the summer ranges in the newly established national forests of the high-mountain country. Significantly, grazing applications were reviewed by local boards of settled ranchers who made both ownership of private land and United States citizenship conditions for approval. In 1934 the Taylor Grazing Act brought most of the remaining public domain under grazing regulations. This legislation specifically excluded both the landless and aliens from use of the range. Furthermore, passage of a series of restrictive immigration laws in the 1920s led to the National Origins Quota System; by 1924, the legal entry of Spanish citizens had been reduced to just 131 persons annually. The era of the itinerant sheepman was over.

[12] During the Second World War, abundant job opportunities and military service further reduced the number of American herders,

while at the same time meat and wool were crucial to the economy and war effort. In response, the Department of Immigration allowed several contingents of Basques to enter the country on a temporary basis, and Congress passed an unusual series of bills known as the Sheepherder Laws. Introduced by western senators and representatives, these laws conferred permanent residency upon Basques who had entered the United States illegally—usually by jumping ship in New York, Galveston, or San Francisco—and had then made their way to the sheep areas, where they were welcomed by the desperate ranchers. Once out on the range with the sheep, they were hidden from the authorities. Between 1942 and 1961, 383 men had their status legalized under the Sheepherder Laws.

[13] The piecemeal approach of the Sheepherder Laws, however, failed to alleviate the growing labor crisis. In 1950 western legislators led by Senator McCarran of Nevada, himself an ex-sheepman, sponsored legislation to exempt the Basque sheepherders from the Spanish quota. Consequently, the initial legislation permitted 250 herders to enter the United States and the numbers were increased in subsequent years. The Western Range Association has since imported thousands of herders from Spain and presently recruits between 300 and 400 annually. These men sign three-year contracts, during which time they are required to work for sheep ranchers, but upon termination of the contract they are eligible to apply for permanent-resident status. Once this is obtained, the herder is free to work at any occupation he chooses and may remain in the United States indefinitely.

[14] Because for more than a century Basques have been closely identified with herding, it has been assumed—for the most part, erroneously—that they have an extensive Old World background in the handling of sheep, and that they possess an exceptional psychological tolerance for solitude. This latter point merits further consideration.

[15] Today the contract herder travels by jet from Europe to the western United States. In many cases, 48 hours after he has taken leave of his family, he is out on the range under the tutelage of an experienced herder. Once he learns the trade, he is given charge of his own dogs and sheep band.

[16] During the lambing and shearing season of late spring and the period of shipping in the early fall, the bands of a particular outfit are concentrated and the herders enjoy each other's company for several weeks. Some may travel to a distant town to enjoy a few days of relaxation in a Basque hotel or to attend a Basque festival. Most, however, are herding for the single purpose of saving almost every cent they earn. Consequently, they may even forego the two weeks of vacation due them under their contract simply to avoid the temptations of towns. Many herders return to Europe after three years with several thousand dollars, no knowledge of English, and almost no experience other than that gained in the sheep camps.

[17] When trailing and when on the winter range, the herder is likely to have the daily companionship of at least one other man. Once the previous year's lambs are shipped off for butchering, two bands can be combined into one for the winter. In many outfits the two herders will spend the winter together, with one acting as the other's camp tender.

[18] When the bands are on the high summer range, however, the herder's physical and social isolation is almost complete. Each band occupies its own large tract—enough pasturage to support a thousand ewes and their lambs for an entire summer. This means that there are likely to be several miles of rugged mountain country separating one herder from another. During a period of four or five months, the herder's only direct human contact is with the camp tender.

[19] The camp tender, operating out of a base camp and supplied from the main camp, delivers goods on muleback to the three or four herders who are his responsibility. Frequently, the herders are a half day's journey away, which means that the camp tender requires a day to service each. Since he also spends a day preparing and baking large loaves of "sheepherders' bread," he is likely to visit each herder only about once every five days. The distances are great, so the camp tender's visit with the herder is likely to be short, usually only an hour or two. But these visits can be highly charged. The shrewd camp tender treats his herders to a good deal of horseplay, jokes of a sexual nature, and consciously animated conversation. The only other visitors are occasional backpackers who happen along. Actually most herders try to avoid them; the Basque's lack of familiarity with the English language and American culture makes such encounters awkward at best.

[20] Such, then, is the sheepherder's solitude today. When conversing among themselves, the men express greater concern for the problems of boredom and keeping their sanity than for the physical difficulties of life on the open range. Memories of the mental anguish of the first few months are particularly vivid. Some men recount that they cried themselves to sleep at night, and that during the long hours of the day, their minds were hyperactive, running over their lives in Europe, causing both a keen nostalgia for home and revival of long-forgotten unpleasant incidents, which were then worried over anew. At some point, however, the herder becomes inured to his circumstances and learns to tailor his mental activity to the demands of his situation.

[21] There is always the danger, of course, that a man will manage his solitude only too well. The herders have a vocabulary of madness in which the individual who has slipped over the edge is graphically referred to as having been "sagebrushed" or "sheeped." Fear of these derangements is not unfounded. In earlier periods of western history there were frequent newspaper reports of the detention or institutionalization of a "crazy Basco sheepherder." When, in 1907, the Basques of Boise, Idaho, founded a mutual aid society, formal provisions were made to assist the mentally unbalanced to return to their families in Spain and France.

[22] Similarly, there were frequent accounts in the early western newspapers of Basque herders committing suicide. Even now, in the Spanish Basque country, the villagers recognize that returned herders have undergone a personality change. They view them as being highly introverted and having a penchant for seeking out the company of other ex-herders. Many never resume normal social intercourse, while others require several months before they begin to converse freely.

[23] While the personalities of most herders are affected by their experiences, in the majority of cases the change is not so extreme as to call their sanity into question. The herders do cope with boredom and solitude in a variety of ways. The question becomes: how does man, the social animal par excellence, maintain his sense of humanity, his concept of self, in a state of almost total social isolation? The Basque sheepherder takes three measures: he humanizes the natural environment, personalizes his dealings with his animal charges, and resorts to stimuli from the outside world, such as radios.

[24] Summer herding is characterized more by boredom than by hard physical labor. While the herder must check the band occasionally to see that it remains within the confines of a particular day's grazing area, he is otherwise free to while away his time. Fishing, reading, napping, and puttering around the camp occupy many of his hours. Some men develop special interests, such as whittling or playing a musical instrument. It is said that one herder spent his free time turning over rocks, squashing the insects that he found, and then meticulously recording his kills in a notebook.

[25] There are two particular ways in which the majority of herders use their spare moments, while at the same time placing a human mark upon the natural environment. Over the years, many of the rocky, treeless, windswept ridges of the high country have acquired the appearance of ancient cemeteries. As far as the eye can see there are piles of carefully arranged stones, called *arri mutillak*, or "stone boys." Some of these are as tall as a man, mute monuments to the boredom of hundreds of Basque sheepherders.

[26] Wherever there is water in the mountains, aspen groves, the favored campsites of the sheepherders, are sure to grow. Over the decades, Basques have transformed such groves into veritable galleries of tree carvings. The technique involves serrating the bark of young saplings with the blade of a penknife. As the tree matures, the scars widen, bringing out the designer's intent. Basque tree carvings on some of the largest trunks date from the end of the last century.

[27] The themes of the carvings are many, although the majority are a simple "Kilroy was here" documentation of the carver's name and the date. The messages on some trees, however, are considerably more profound. One trunk discloses verses about the author's joy at the prospect of returning to his homeland; another comments upon the difficulties of the herder's life. Sexual ditties are common, while statements like *Viva Navarra*, "Long Live Navarre," and *Gora Euzkadi Azkatuta*, "Long Live the

Free Basque Country," reflect Old World regional loyalties or commitment to the modern Basque nationalist movement. Finally there are trees adorned with drawings, some amateurish and others highly skilled, whose subject matter ranges from pornography to abstract design.

[28] Few herders camp in an aspen grove without examining the tree carvings left by earlier herders, and they rarely move on without leaving their own mark on the youngest saplings. Thus, in the midst of his personal loneliness the herder has a sense of being in communication with both past and future generations of sheepherders.

[29] For lack of immediate human communication, the herder often personalizes his relations with his animals (jokes about sheepherders notwithstanding, cases of sodomy are extremely rare) and develops a keen sense of companionship with them that is very different from the affection an urbanite feels for his pets. He does not talk at or to his dogs, pack animals, and sheep, but rather with them. Rarely does he give them direct orders; instead he verbalizes his thoughts as if engaged in a dialogue. Shouting across a canyon at an errant band, he asks, "Where do you think you are going? You know that you should bed down along the creek." I have witnessed herders holding lengthy conversations with their dogs in which they explained the plan for the day.

[30] In the sheep outfit there is a necessary working relationship among men, dogs, pack animals, and sheep, the success of which depends upon the cooperation of all. It may take years for a herder to develop the proper mutual understanding with his dogs that makes man and canine a finely honed team capable of caring for the sheep with the greatest possible efficiency. To a lesser degree, the same is true of the relationship between the herder and his mount and pack animals. The herder likewise comes to recognize many of the sheep as individuals, each with its peculiar temperament and problems. Similarly, the band as a whole is seen as having its own characteristics to which the herder must adapt his herding practices. A winning combination of herder, dogs, pack animals, and band is not achieved overnight, nor should it be modified lightly. Herders have quit their employers when told they would be given different dogs or a different band of sheep.

[31] The sheepherder's physical isolation and lack of English largely preclude his participation in the wider society of the American West. Frequently, his only link with the outside world is his camp tender who brings not only his supplies but also reading matter and his correspondence from Europe. Most of the herders are poorly educated and are not accustomed to letter writing or extensive reading. It is common for a herder to go for months without writing his family, and some older herders have stopped corresponding altogether. Most herders have three or four books: Basque-language verse is popular, as are cheap editions of Spanish-language novels. The latter rotate among the herders. A very popular publication is the *Boletín del Banco de Vizcaya,* a newspaper published expressly for Basque herders by a banking concern in the Basque country.

It features information about European Basque sporting events, as well as detailed news of the villages from which the majority of herders are recruited. The herder may also acquire a few American magazines, more for their pictures than their text. Not surprisingly, *Playboy* is a likely choice.

[32] The herder's daily link with the outside world is his transistor radio. But again, his listening habits underscore his indifference to American life. The transistors are usually powerful enough to pull in Spanish-language radio broadcasts from Los Angeles and northern Mexico. Many listen to the daily Spanish-language newscast from Washington, D.C., but the most popular programs are the Sunday afternoon Basque-language broadcasts that originate on the local stations of Boise, Idaho; Elko, Nevada; and Buffalo, Wyoming.

[33] Basques who go to the West to herd sheep do not bring to the occupation either a specialized European background in sheepherding or a unique psychological capacity for social isolation. Rather, despite the romanticism surrounding them, they show a pronounced determination to undergo temporary physical and mental privation as an investment in a secure economic future. It is not that Basques suffer less than others in the solitude of mountains and desert; it is simply that they are more willing to endure the privations.

Questions on Meaning

1 Like other selections in this book, this essay begins with a statement of popular belief about a topic and then proceeds to show the inaccuracy of this belief. What information does Douglass provide to support his thesis that the life of a Basque sheepherder is not as romantic as it is generally thought to be?

2 Explain in some detail each of the three methods the author says Basque sheepherders use to adjust to their solitary existence.

3 Summarize Douglass's explanation of why so many sheepherders in this country are Basques.

Questions on Style and Structure

1 What does the introduction of this selection have in common with the introduction to "The Lost Vikings of Greenland"?

2 Note the unity of paragraphs 3 and 21. Then examine paragraphs 8, 16, and 24. Are they equally unified? Why or why not?

3 At the end of paragraph 7 is the sentence "On occasion, competition turned into conflict, and the resulting confrontations provided copy to the newspapers, litigation to the courts, and substance to the sheepman versus cattleman legend." Would the three phrases be as effective in any other order?

ESSAYS CHIEFLY INFORMATIVE

How about the order of the three phrases at the end of paragraph 16: "Many herders return to Europe after three years with several thousand dollars, no knowledge of English, and almost no experience other than that gained in the sheep camps"?

4 This sentence appears in paragraph 23: "While the personalities of most herders are affected by their experiences, in the majority of cases the change is not so extreme as to call their sanity into question." Compare the structure and effect of this sentence with those of the following two versions. Which version is better? Why?

 a While in the majority of cases the change is not so extreme as to call their sanity into question, the personalities of most herders are affected by their experiences.

 b The personalities of most herders are affected by their experiences; in the majority of cases the change is not so extreme as to call their sanity into question.

5 What device does Douglass use to make paragraph 29 coherent?

6 Which of the techniques discussed in the Introduction to Paragraph and Sentence Structure does Douglass employ to conclude his essay? Is this technique effectively handled?

Exploring Words

1 *endemic.* Check the several definitions of *endemic* your dictionary lists for this word. Does any one of these meanings exactly fit Douglass's use? If not, how do you account for his choice of the word?

2 *nascent.* Consult your dictionary to find at least three other words that have the same Latin root as *nascent.*

3 *itinerant.* Think of at least two kinds of *itinerant* employment besides sheepherding.

4 *tutelage.* Under whose *tutelage* have you learned the most?

5 *meticulously.* What are some tasks that you or someone you know well usually performs *meticulously*?

6 *urbanite.* The root of this word lends itself especially well to use with combining forms. You are surely familiar with *suburban,* and you may know that some sociologists have used the word *exurban* to refer to people who live in areas that are farther from cities than the sections that are called *suburbs.* One could coin the expressions *nonurban* and *antiurban.* What would these expressions mean?

Suggestions for Writing

1 Describe a way of life you feel is not sufficiently understood. This could be the life of a worker whose occupation you know more about than most peo-

ple do, or it could be the life style of someone who is considered outside the American "mainstream"—perhaps a self-styled "hippie," a natural-foods enthusiast, or a transcontinental hitchhiker. It could even be a "mainstream" but relatively unusual way of life, such as that of a middle-aged college student, an only child, or a female gas station attendant. Be sure to define your key terms or make their meanings entirely clear through the contexts in which you use them. As Douglass does, begin with the popular conception and then show its inaccuracies.

2 Would you agree that boredom is a prevalent American problem today? If so, what are some of the signs you have observed, and what are your thoughts about the causes?

A Noiseless Flash
JOHN HERSEY

Getting Started

With Ideas

This selection is the first chapter of *Hiroshima,* an account of the effect of the United States' 1945 atom-bombing of a Japanese city on six of its inhabitants. As you read through this work, it will be a good idea to keep in mind one key statement you will find in the introduction: "They [the six survivors treated here] still wonder why they lived when so many others died. Each of them counts many small items of chance or volition—a step taken in time, a decision to go indoors, catching one streetcar instead of the next—that spared him."

With Words

1 philanthropies (4)—from the Greek *phil,* meaning "love," and *anthropos,* meaning "mankind."
2 incendiary (11)—related to the Latin word meaning "to burn."
3 pommelled (14)—more often spelled *pummeled.*
4 hedonistic (15)—from the Latin word for "pleasure."
5 convivial (16)—from the Latin word for "banquet," which in turn is based on the Latin word meaning "to live."
6 xenophobic (19)—from the Greek word *xen,* meaning "foreigner," and *phobia,* meaning "fear" (*xen* is pronounced like the initial sound of *Xerox*).

[1] At exactly fifteen minutes past eight in the morning, on August 6, 1945, Japanese time, at the moment when the atomic bomb flashed above Hiroshima, Miss Toshiko Sasaki, a clerk in the personnel department of the East Asia Tin Works, had just sat down at her place in the plant office and was turning her head to speak to the girl at the next desk. At that same moment, Dr. Masakazu Fujii was settling down cross-legged to read the Osaka *Asahi* on the porch of his private hospital, overhanging one of the seven deltaic rivers which divide Hiroshima; Mrs. Hatsuyo Nakamura, a tailor's widow, stood by the window of her kitchen, watching a neighbor tearing down his house because it lay in the path of an air-raid-defense fire lane; Father Wilhelm Kleinsorge, a German priest of the Society of Jesus, reclined in his underwear on a cot on the top floor

From *Hiroshima* by John Hersey. Copyright 1946 and renewed 1974 by John Hersey. Reprinted by permission of Alfred A. Knopf, Inc. Originally appeared in *The New Yorker.*

of his order's three-story mission house, reading a Jesuit magazine, *Stimmen der Zeit;* Dr. Terufumi Sasaki, a young member of the surgical staff of the city's large, modern Red Cross Hospital, walked along one of the hospital corridors with a blood specimen for a Wassermann test in his hand; and the Reverend Mr. Kiyoshi Tanimoto, pastor of the Hiroshima Methodist Church, paused at the door of a rich man's house in Koi, the city's western suburb, and prepared to unload a handcart full of things he had evacuated from town in fear of the massive B-29 raid which everyone expected Hiroshima to suffer. A hundred thousand people were killed by the atomic bomb, and these six were among the survivors. They still wonder why they lived when so many others died. Each of them counts many small items of chance or volition—a step taken in time, a decision to go indoors, catching one streetcar instead of the next—that spared him. And now each knows that in the act of survival he lived a dozen lives and saw more death than he ever thought he would see. At the time, none of them knew anything.

[2] The Reverend Mr. Tanimoto got up at five o'clock that morning. He was alone in the parsonage, because for some time his wife had been commuting with their year-old baby to spend nights with a friend in Ushida, a suburb to the north. Of all the important cities of Japan, only two, Kyoto and Hiroshima, had not been visited in strength by *B-san,* or Mr. B, as the Japanese, with a mixture of respect and unhappy familiarity, called the B-29; and Mr. Tanimoto, like all his neighbors and friends, was almost sick with anxiety. He had heard uncomfortably detailed accounts of mass raids on Kure, Iwakuni, Tokuyama, and other nearby towns; he was sure Hiroshima's turn would come soon. He had slept badly the night before, because there had been several air-raid warnings. Hiroshima had been getting such warnings almost every night for weeks, for at that time the B-29s were using Lake Biwa, northeast of Hiroshima, as a rendezvous point, and no matter what city the Americans planned to hit, the Superfortresses streamed in over the coast near Hiroshima. The frequency of the warnings and the continued abstinence of Mr. B with respect to Hiroshima had made its citizens jittery; a rumor was going around that the Americans were saving something special for the city.

[3] Mr. Tanimoto is a small man, quick to talk, laugh, and cry. He wears his black hair parted in the middle and rather long; the prominence of the frontal bones just above his eyebrows and the smallness of his mustache, mouth, and chin give him a strange, old-young look, boyish and yet wise, weak and yet fiery. He moves nervously and fast, but with a restraint which suggests that he is a cautious, thoughtful man. He showed, indeed, just those qualities in the uneasy days before the bomb fell. Besides having his wife spend the nights in Ushida, Mr. Tanimoto had been carrying all the portable things from his church, in the close-packed residential district called Nagaragawa, to a house that belonged to a rayon manufacturer in Koi, two miles from the center of town. The rayon man, a Mr. Matsui, had

opened his then unoccupied estate to a large number of his friends and acquaintances, so that they might evacuate whatever they wished to a safe distance from the probable target area. Mr. Tanimoto had had no difficulty in moving chairs, hymnals, Bibles, altar gear, and church records by pushcart himself, but the organ console and an upright piano required some aid. A friend of his named Matsuo had, the day before, helped him get the piano out to Koi; in return, he had promised this day to assist Mr. Matsuo in hauling out a daughter's belongings. That is why he had risen so early.

[4] Mr. Tanimoto cooked his own breakfast. He felt awfully tired. The effort of moving the piano the day before, a sleepless night, weeks of worry and unbalanced diet, the cares of his parish—all combined to make him feel hardly adequate to the new day's work. There was another thing, too: Mr. Tanimoto had studied theology at Emory College, in Atlanta, Georgia; he had graduated in 1940; he spoke excellent English; he dressed in American clothes; he had corresponded with many American friends right up to the time the war began; and among a people obsessed with a fear of being spied upon—perhaps almost obsessed himself—he found himself growing increasingly uneasy. The police had questioned him several times, and just a few days before, he had heard that an influential acquaintance, a Mr. Tanaka, a retired officer of the Toyo Kisen Kaisha steamship line, an anti-Christian, a man famous in Hiroshima for his showy philanthropies and notorious for his personal tyrannies, had been telling people that Tanimoto should not be trusted. In compensation, to show himself publicly a good Japanese, Mr. Tanimoto had taken on the chairmanship of his local *tonarigumi*, or Neighborhood Association, and to his other duties and concerns this position had added the business of organizing air-raid defense for about twenty families.

[5] Before six o'clock that morning, Mr. Tanimoto started for Mr. Matsuo's house. There he found that their burden was to be a *tansu*, a large Japanese cabinet, full of clothing and household goods. The two men set out. The morning was perfectly clear and so warm that the day promised to be uncomfortable. A few minutes after they started, the air-raid siren went off—a minute-long blast that warned of approaching planes but indicated to the people of Hiroshima only a slight degree of danger, since it sounded every morning at this time, when an American weather plane came over. The two men pulled and pushed the handcart through the city streets. Hiroshima was a fan-shaped city, lying mostly on the six islands formed by the seven estuarial rivers that branch out from the Ota River; its main commercial and residential districts, covering about four square miles in the center of the city, contained three-quarters of its population, which had been reduced by several evacuation programs from a wartime peak of 380,000 to about 245,000. Factories and other residential districts, or suburbs, lay compactly around the edges of the city. To the south were the docks, an airport, and the island-studded Inland Sea. A rim of mountains run around the other three sides of the delta. Mr. Tanimoto and Mr. Matsuo took their way through the shopping center, already full of people,

and across two of the rivers to the sloping streets of Koi, and up them to the outskirts and foothills. As they started up a valley away from the tight-ranked houses, the all-clear sounded. (The Japanese radar operators, detecting only three planes, supposed that they comprised a reconnaissance.) Pushing the handcart up to the rayon man's house was tiring, and the men, after they had maneuvered their load into the driveway and to the front steps, paused to rest awhile. They stood with a wing of the house between them and the city. Like most homes in this part of Japan, the house consisted of a wooden frame and wooden walls supporting a heavy tile roof. Its front hall, packed with rolls of bedding and clothing, looked like a cool cave full of fat cushions. Opposite the house, to the right of the front door, there was a large, finicky rock garden. There was no sound of planes. The morning was still; the place was cool and pleasant.

[6] Then a tremendous flash of light cut across the sky. Mr. Tanimoto has a distinct recollection that it travelled from east to west, from the city toward the hills. It seemed a sheet of sun. Both he and Mr. Matsuo reacted in terror—and both had time to react (for they were 3,500 yards, or two miles, from the center of the explosion). Mr. Matsuo dashed up the front steps into the house and dived among the bedrolls and buried himself there. Mr. Tanimoto took four or five steps and threw himself between two big rocks in the garden. He bellied up very hard against one of them. As his face was against the stone, he did not see what happened. He felt a sudden pressure, and then splinters and pieces of board and fragments of tile fell on him. He heard no roar. (Almost no one in Hiroshima recalls hearing any noise of the bomb. But a fisherman in his sampan on the Inland Sea near Tsuzu, the man with whom Mr. Tanimoto's mother-in-law and sister-in-law were living, saw the flash and heard a tremendous explosion; he was nearly twenty miles from Hiroshima, but the thunder was greater than when the B-29s hit Iwakuni, only five miles away.)

[7] When he dared, Mr. Tanimoto raised his head and saw that the rayon man's house had collapsed. He thought a bomb had fallen directly on it. Such clouds of dust had risen that there was a sort of twilight around. In panic, not thinking for the moment of Mr. Matsuo under the ruins, he dashed out into the street. He noticed as he ran that the concrete wall of the estate had fallen over—toward the house rather than away from it. In the street, the first thing he saw was a squad of soldiers who had been burrowing into the hillside opposite, making one of the thousands of dugouts in which the Japanese apparently intended to resist invasion, hill by hill, life for life; the soldiers were coming out of the hole, where they should have been safe, and blood was running from their heads, chests, and backs. They were silent and dazed.

[8] Under what seemed to be a local dust cloud, the day grew darker and darker.

[9] At nearly midnight, the night before the bomb was dropped, an announcer on the city's radio station said that about two hundred B-29s

were approaching southern Honshu and advised the population of Hiroshima to evacuate to their designated "safe areas." Mrs. Hatsuyo Nakamura, the tailor's widow, who lived in the section called Nobori-cho and who had long had a habit of doing as she was told, got her three children—a ten-year-old boy, Toshio, an eight-year-old girl, Yaeko, and a five-year-old girl, Myeko—out of bed and dressed them and walked with them to the military area known as the East Parade Ground, on the northeast edge of the city. There she unrolled some mats and the children lay down on them. They slept until about two, when they were awakened by the roar of the planes going over Hiroshima.

[10] As soon as the planes had passed, Mrs. Nakamura started back with her children. They reached home a little after two-thirty and she immediately turned on the radio, which, to her distress, was just then broadcasting a fresh warning. When she looked at the children and saw how tired they were, and when she thought of the number of trips they had made in past weeks, all to no purpose, to the East Parade Ground, she decided that in spite of the instructions on the radio, she simply could not face starting out all over again. She put the children in their bedrolls on the floor, lay down herself at three o'clock, and fell asleep at once, so soundly that when planes passed over later, she did not waken to their sound.

[11] The siren jarred her awake at about seven. She arose, dressed quickly, and hurried to the house of Mr. Nakamoto, the head of her Neighborhood Association, and asked him what she should do. He said that she should remain at home unless an urgent warning—a series of intermittent blasts of the siren—was sounded. She returned home, lit the stove in the kitchen, set some rice to cook, and sat down to read that morning's Hiroshima *Chugoku*. To her relief, the all-clear sounded at eight o'clock. She heard the children stirring, so she went and gave each of them a handful of peanuts and told them to stay on their bedrolls, because they were tired from the night's walk. She had hoped that they would go back to sleep, but the man in the house directly to the south began to make a terrible hullabaloo of hammering, wedging, ripping, and splitting. The prefectural government, convinced, as everyone in Hiroshima was, that the city would be attacked soon, had begun to press with threats and warnings for the completion of wide fire lanes, which, it was hoped, might act in conjunction with the rivers to localize any fires started by an incendiary raid; and the neighbor was reluctantly sacrificing his home to the city's safety. Just the day before, the prefecture had ordered all able-bodied girls from the secondary schools to spend a few days helping to clear these lanes, and they started work soon after the all-clear sounded.

[12] Mrs. Nakamura went back to the kitchen, looked at the rice, and began watching the man next door. At first, she was annoyed with him for making so much noise, but then she was moved almost to tears by pity. Her emotion was specifically directed toward her neighbor, tearing down his home, board by board, at a time when there was so much un-

avoidable destruction, but undoubtedly she also felt a generalized, community pity, to say nothing of self-pity. She had not had an easy time. Her husband, Isawa, had gone into the Army just after Myeko was born, and she had heard nothing from or of him for a long time, until, on March 5, 1942, she received a seven-word telegram: "Isawa died an honorable death at Singapore." She learned later that he had died on February 15th, the day Singapore fell, and that he had been a corporal. Isawa had been a not particularly prosperous tailor, and his only capital was a Sankoku sewing machine. After his death, when his allotments stopped coming, Mrs. Nakamura got out the machine and began to take in piecework herself, and since then had supported the children, but poorly, by sewing.

[13] As Mrs. Nakamura stood watching her neighbor, everything flashed whiter than any white she had ever seen. She did not notice what happened to the man next door; the reflex of a mother set her in motion toward her children. She had taken a single step (the house was 1,350 yards, or three-quarters of a mile, from the center of the explosion) when something picked her up and she seemed to fly into the next room over the raised sleeping platform, pursued by parts of her house.

[14] Timbers fell around her as she landed, and a shower of tiles pommelled her; everything became dark, for she was buried. The debris did not cover her deeply. She rose up and freed herself. She heard a child cry, "Mother, help me!," and saw her youngest—Myeko, the five-year-old—buried up to her breast and unable to move. As Mrs. Nakamura started frantically to claw her way toward the baby, she could see or hear nothing of her other children.

[15] In the days right before the bombing, Dr. Masakazu Fujii, being prosperous, hedonistic, and at the time not too busy, had been allowing himself the luxury of sleeping until nine or nine-thirty, but fortunately he had to get up early the morning the bomb was dropped to see a house guest off on a train. He rose at six, and half an hour later walked with his friend to the station, not far away, across two of the rivers. He was back home by seven, just as the siren sounded its sustained warning. He ate breakfast and then, because the morning was already hot, undressed down to his underwear and went out on the porch to read the paper. This porch—in fact, the whole building—was curiously constructed. Dr. Fujii was the proprietor of a peculiarly Japanese institution: a private, single-doctor hospital. This building, perched beside and over the water of the Kyo River, and next to the bridge of the same name, contained thirty rooms for thirty patients and their kinfolk—for, according to Japanese custom, when a person falls sick and goes to a hospital, one or more members of his family go and live there with him, to cook for him, bathe, massage, and read to him, and to offer incessant familial sympathy, without which a Japanese patient would be miserable indeed. Dr. Fujii had no beds—only straw mats—for his patients. He did, however, have all sorts of modern equipment: an X-ray machine, diathermy apparatus, and a fine tiled labo-

ratory. The structure rested two-thirds on the land, one-third on piles over the tidal waters of the Kyo. This overhang, the part of the building where Dr. Fujii lived, was queer-looking, but it was cool in summer and from the porch, which faced away from the center of the city, the prospect of the river, with pleasure boats drifting up and down it, was always refreshing. Dr. Fujii had occasionally had anxious moments when the Ota and its mouth branches rose to flood, but the piling was apparently firm enough and the house had always held.

[16] Dr. Fujii had been relatively idle for about a month because in July, as the number of untouched cities in Japan dwindled and as Hiroshima seemed more and more inevitably a target, he began turning patients away, on the ground that in case of a fire raid he would not be able to evacuate them. Now he had only two patients left—a woman from Yano, injured in the shoulder, and a young man of twenty-five recovering from burns he had suffered when the steel factory near Hiroshima in which he worked had been hit. Dr. Fujii had six nurses to tend his patients. His wife and children were safe; his wife and one son were living outside Osaka, and another son and two daughters were in the country on Kyushu. A niece was living with him, and a maid and a manservant. He had little to do and did not mind, for he had saved some money. At fifty, he was healthy, convivial, and calm, and he was pleased to pass the evenings drinking whiskey with friends, always sensibly and for the sake of conversation. Before the war, he had affected brands imported from Scotland and America; now he was perfectly satisfied with the best Japanese brand, Suntory.

[17] Dr. Fujii sat down cross-legged in his underwear on the spotless matting of the porch, put on his glasses, and started reading the Osaka *Asahi*. He liked to read the Osaka news because his wife was there. He saw the flash. To him—faced away from the center and looking at his paper—it seemed a brilliant yellow. Startled, he began to rise to his feet. In that moment (he was 1,550 yards from the center), the hospital leaned behind his rising and, with a terrible ripping noise, toppled into the river. The Doctor, still in the act of getting to his feet, was thrown forward and around and over; he was buffeted and gripped; he lost track of everything, because things were so speeded up; he felt the water.

[18] Dr. Fujii hardly had time to think that he was dying before he realized that he was alive, squeezed tightly by two long timbers in a V across his chest, like a morsel suspended between two huge chopsticks—held upright, so that he could not move, with his head miraculously above water and his torso and legs in it. The remains of his hospital were all around him in a mad assortment of splintered lumber and materials for the relief of pain. His left shoulder hurt terribly. His glasses were gone.

[19] Father Wilhelm Kleinsorge, of the Society of Jesus, was, on the morning of the explosion, in rather frail condition. The Japanese wartime diet had not sustained him, and he felt the strain of being a foreigner

in an increasingly xenophobic Japan; even a German, since the defeat of the Fatherland, was unpopular. Father Kleinsorge had, at thirty-eight, the look of a boy growing too fast—thin in the face, with a prominent Adam's apple, a hollow chest, dangling hands, big feet. He walked clumsily, leaning forward a little. He was tired all the time. To make matters worse, he had suffered for two days, along with Father Cieslik, a fellow-priest, from a rather painful and urgent diarrhea, which they blamed on the beans and black ration bread they were obliged to eat. Two other priests then living in the mission compound, which was in the Nobori-cho section—Father Superior LaSalle and Father Schiffer—had happily escaped this affliction.

[20] Father Kleinsorge woke up about six the morning the bomb was dropped, and half an hour later—he was a bit tardy because of his sickness—he began to read Mass in the mission chapel, a small Japanese-style wooden building which was without pews, since its worshippers knelt on the usual Japanese matted floor, facing an altar graced with splendid silks, brass, silver, and heavy embroideries. This morning, a Monday, the only worshippers were Mr. Takemoto, a theological student living in the mission house; Mr. Fukai, the secretary of the diocese; Mrs. Murata, the mission's devoutly Christian housekeeper; and his fellow-priests. After Mass, while Father Kleinsorge was reading the Prayers of Thanksgiving, the siren sounded. He stopped the service and the missionaries retired across the compound to the bigger building. There, in his room on the ground floor, to the right of the front door, Father Kleinsorge changed into a military uniform which he had acquired when he was teaching at the Rokko Middle School in Kobe and which he wore during air-raid alerts.

[21] After an alarm, Father Kleinsorge always went out and scanned the sky, and in this instance, when he stepped outside, he was glad to see only the single weather plane that flew over Hiroshima each day about this time. Satisfied that nothing would happen, he went in and breakfasted with the other Fathers on substitute coffee and ration bread, which, under the circumstances, was especially repugnant to him. The Fathers sat and talked awhile, until, at eight, they heard the all-clear. They went then to various parts of the building. Father Schiffer retired to his room to do some writing. Father Cieslik sat in his room in a straight chair with a pillow over his stomach to ease his pain, and read. Father Superior LaSalle stood at the window of his room, thinking. Father Kleinsorge went up to a room on the third floor, took off all his clothes except his underwear, and stretched out on his right side on a cot and began reading his *Stimmen der Zeit*.

[22] After the terrible flash—which, Father Kleinsorge later realized, reminded him of something he had read as a boy about a large meteor colliding with the earth—he had time (since he was 1,400 yards from the center) for one thought: A bomb has fallen directly on us. Then, for a few seconds or minutes, he went out of his mind.

[23] Father Kleinsorge never knew how he got out of the house.

The next things he was conscious of were that he was wandering around in the mission's vegetable garden in his underwear, bleeding slightly from small cuts along his left flank; that all the buildings round about had fallen down except the Jesuits' mission house, which had long before been braced and double-braced by a priest named Gropper, who was terrified of earthquakes; that the day had turned dark; and that Murata-*san*, the housekeeper, was nearby, crying over and over, "*Shu Jesusu, awaremi tamai!* Our Lord Jesus, have pity on us!"

[24] On the train on the way into Hiroshima from the country, where he lived with his mother, Dr. Terufumi Sasaki, the Red Cross Hospital surgeon, thought over an unpleasant nightmare he had had the night before. His mother's home was in Mukaihara, thirty miles from the city, and it took him two hours by train and tram to reach the hospital. He had slept uneasily all night and had wakened an hour earlier than usual, and, feeling sluggish and slightly feverish, had debated whether to go the hospital at all; his sense of duty finally forced him to go, and he had started out on an earlier train than he took most mornings. The dream had particularly frightened him because it was so closely associated, on the surface at least, with a disturbing actuality. He was only twenty-five years old and had just completed his training at the Eastern Medical University, in Tsingtao, China. He was something of an idealist and was much distressed by the inadequacy of medical facilities in the country town where his mother lived. Quite on his own, and without a permit, he had begun visiting a few sick people out there in the evenings, after his eight hours at the hospital and four hours' commuting. He had recently learned that the penalty for practicing without a permit was severe; a fellow-doctor whom he had asked about it had given him a serious scolding. Nevertheless, he had continued to practice. In his dream, he had been at the bedside of a country patient when the police and the doctor he had consulted burst into the room, seized him, dragged him outside, and beat him up cruelly. On the train, he just about decided to give up the work in Mukaihara, since he felt it would be impossible to get a permit, because the authorities would hold that it would conflict with his duties at the Red Cross Hospital.

[25] At the terminus, he caught a streetcar at once. (He later calculated that if he had taken his customary train that morning, and if he had had to wait a few minutes for the streetcar, as often happened, he would have been close to the center at the time of the explosion and would surely have perished.) He arrived at the hospital at seven-forty and reported to the chief surgeon. A few minutes later, he went to a room on the first floor and drew blood from the arm of a man in order to perform a Wassermann test. The laboratory containing the incubators for the test was on the third floor. With the blood specimen in his left hand, walking in a kind of distraction he had felt all morning, probably because of the dream and his restless night, he started along the main corridor on his way toward the stairs. He was one step beyond an open window when the light of the

bomb was reflected, like a gigantic photographic flash, in the corridor. He ducked down on one knee and said to himself, as only a Japanese would, "Sasaki, *gambare!* Be brave!" Just then (the building was 1,650 yards from the center), the blast ripped through the hospital. The glasses he was wearing flew off his face; the bottle of blood crashed against one wall; his Japanese slippers zipped out from under his feet—but otherwise, thanks to where he stood, he was untouched.

[26] Dr. Sasaki shouted the name of the chief surgeon and rushed around to the man's office and found him terribly cut by glass. The hospital was in horrible confusion: heavy partitions and ceilings had fallen on patients, beds had overturned, windows had blown in and cut people, blood was spattered on the walls and floors, instruments were everywhere, many of the patients were running about screaming, many more lay dead. (A colleague working in the laboratory to which Dr. Sasaki had been walking was dead; Dr. Sasaki's patient, whom he had just left and who a few moments before had been dreadfully afraid of syphilis, was also dead.) Dr. Sasaki found himself the only doctor in the hospital who was unhurt.

[27] Dr. Sasaki, who believed that the enemy had hit only the building he was in, got bandages and began to bind the wounds of those inside the hospital; while outside, all over Hiroshima, maimed and dying citizens turned their unsteady steps toward the Red Cross Hospital to begin an invasion that was to make Dr. Sasaki forget his private nightmare for a long, long time.

[28] Miss Toshiko Sasaki, the East Asia Tin Works clerk, who is not related to Dr. Sasaki, got up at three o'clock in the morning on the day the bomb fell. There was extra housework to do. Her eleven-month-old brother, Akio, had come down the day before with a serious stomach upset; her mother had taken him to the Tamura Pediatric Hospital and was staying there with him. Miss Sasaki, who was about twenty, had to cook breakfast for her father, a brother, a sister, and herself, and—since the hospital, because of the war, was unable to provide food—to prepare a whole day's meals for her mother and the baby, in time for her father, who worked in a factory making rubber earplugs for artillery crews, to take the food by on his way to the plant. When she had finished and had cleaned and put away the cooking things, it was nearly seven. The family lived in Koi, and she had a forty-five-minute trip to the tin works, in the section of town called Kannonmachi. She was in charge of the personnel records in the factory. She left Koi at seven, and as soon as she reached the plant, she went with some of the other girls from the personnel department to the factory auditorium. A prominent local Navy man, a former employee, had committed suicide the day before by throwing himself under a train—a death considered honorable enough to warrant a memorial service, which was to be held at the tin works at ten o'clock that morning. In the large hall, Miss Sasaki and the others made suitable preparations for the meeting. This work took about twenty minutes.

[29] Miss Sasaki went back to her office and sat down at her desk. She was quite far from the windows, which were off to her left, and behind her were a couple of tall bookcases containing all the books of the factory library, which the personnel department had organized. She settled herself at her desk, put some things in a drawer, and shifted papers. She thought that before she began to make entries in her lists of new employees, discharges, and departures for the Army, she would chat for a moment with the girl at her right. Just as she turned her head away from the windows, the room was filled with a blinding light. She was paralyzed by fear, fixed still in her chair for a long moment (the plant was 1,600 yards from the center).

[30] Everything fell, and Miss Sasaki lost consciousness. The ceiling dropped suddenly and the wooden floor above collapsed in splinters and the people up there came down and the roof above them gave way; but principally and first of all, the bookcases right behind her swooped forward and the contents threw her down, with her left leg horribly twisted and breaking underneath her. There, in the tin factory, in the first moment of the atomic age, a human being was crushed by books.

Questions on Meaning

1 Twists of fate are mentioned in the final paragraphs of some of the sections treating the experiences of particular Hiroshima residents. Look for these twists in the endings of the sections about the following people:

   a Rev. Tanimoto (Note what happens to the soldiers working near his friend's house.)

   b Dr. Fujii (What falls on him?)

   c Dr. Sasaki (Consider, especially, the fate of the people he finds dead around him.)

   d Miss Sasaki (Note how she is injured.)

   Why do you think Hersey mentions each of the above details? What point is he able to make through this collection of ironies?

2 Some readers of the book from which this chapter is taken have said that Hersey narrates the activities of six representative inhabitants of Hiroshima on that fateful day. On the basis of your knowledge of life in a large Japanese city in 1945 (you probably know something about the religions and the industries of Japan, for example), in what ways do you think Hersey's choice of people is representative, and in what ways do you think it is not? Why do you suppose the author chose these six people to write about?

3 *Hiroshima* has been widely acclaimed for its objective treatment of its subjects. Do you agree with that assessment? Does Hersey, in his handling of details, reveal any attitude toward the six people whose lives he chronicles?

Questions on Style and Structure

1 Study very carefully the way in which Hersey concludes the separate accounts of the six people. Which conclusion do you find most effective? Why do you suppose he ends paragraph 18 with the sentence "His glasses were gone"?

2 The language of this selection can be said to be understated. Compare, for example, the two sentences following (the first is Hersey's). Which do you prefer? Why?

   a She heard a child cry, "Mother, help me!," and saw her youngest —Myeko, the five-year-old—buried up to her breast and unable to move. (paragraph 14)

   b She heard her terrified child scream, "Mother, help me!," and saw the heart-rending sight of her youngest—Myeko, who was only five years old—helplessly buried up to her breast and struggling vainly to free herself.

3 Hersey recounts the activities of the six residents of Hiroshima in great detail. For example, we learn that Dr. Fujii drank Suntory whiskey, that Dr. Sasaki was carrying the blood specimen in his left hand, that "Father Kleinsorge went up to a room on the third floor, took off all his clothes except his underwear, and stretched out on his right side on a cot and began reading his *Stimmen der Zeit.*" What do such details add to Hersey's narrative?

4 In his first paragraph, Hersey introduces the six main characters in this order: Miss Sasaki, Dr. Fujii, Mrs. Nakamura, Father Kleinsorge, Dr. Sasaki, the Reverend Mr. Tanimoto; in the remainder of the chapter, however, he does not follow this order. Do you consider this "inconsistency" a defect?

5 Is the last paragraph an adequate conclusion? Should the author have concluded with a more general paragraph (he does, after all, introduce the chapter with a paragraph that encompasses all six people)? Study, in particular, the last sentence of the paragraph. Is Hersey attempting to convey a "message"?

6 Note how many times the conjunction *and* is used in the last paragraph. What is the effect of this repeated use?

7 Compare the following pairs of sentences (the first of each pair is Hersey's). Which version do you find more effective? Why?

   a Under what seemed to be a local dust cloud, the day grew darker and darker. (paragraph 8)

   The day grew darker and darker under what seemed to be a local dust cloud.

   b The next things he was conscious of were that he was wandering around in the mission's vegetable garden in his underwear, bleeding slightly from small cuts along his left flank; that all the buildings round about had fallen down except the Jesuits' mission house, which had long before been braced and double-braced by a priest named Gropper, who was terrified of earthquakes; that the day had turned dark; and that Murata-*san*, the housekeeper, was nearby, crying over and over, *"Shu Jesusu, awaremi tamai!* Our Lord Jesus, have pity on us!" (paragraph 23)

The next things he was conscious of were that he was wandering around in the mission's vegetable garden in his underwear, bleeding slightly from small cuts along his left flank; that the day had turned dark; that Murata-*san*, the housekeeper, was nearby, crying over and over, *"Shu Jesusu, awaremi tamai!* Our Lord Jesus, have pity on us!" and that all the buildings round about had fallen down except the Jesuits' mission house, which had long before been braced and double-braced by a priest named Gropper, who was terrified of earthquakes.

There, in the tin factory, in the first moment of the atomic age, a human being was crushed by books. (paragraph 30)

A human being was crushed by books there, in the tin factory, in the first moment of the atomic age.

Exploring Words

1 *philanthropies.* Your dictionary probably lists more than one meaning for *philanthropy.* Which one applies to Hersey's use of the word?

2 *incendiary.* What relationship do you find between the words *incendiary, incense* (the noun), and *incense* (the verb—as in "His actions *incensed* me.")?

3 *pommelled.* Does your dictionary provide a synonym for *pommelled* that could be substituted for the word as it is used in this sentence? Why do you suppose Hersey chose to use *pommelled* here?

4 *hedonistic.* Think of or find in your dictionary a word that is more or less an antonym of *hedonistic.*

5 *convivial.* Write a sentence that fits your dictionary's definition of *convivial.*

6 *xenophobic.* There are very few words in English beginning with *x,* and almost all of those that exist are from Greek roots. Find in your dictionary two Greek roots starting with *x,* each of which is used at the beginnings of several English words. List the words you find that are based upon each of these roots, and be sure you understand the relationship between them.

Suggestions for Writing

1 Write about a disaster you or someone you know narrowly escaped. You will probably be able to work in some ironic touches.

2 Chronicle a particularly momentous day in your life. As Hersey does, you should let the significance of each event grow out of carefully chosen details and words rather than through explicit statements (for example, "It was very important to me because. . .").

The Sunless Sea
RACHEL CARSON

Getting Started

With Ideas

Before you read this selection, ask yourself what colors and sounds (if any) and what kinds of life you would expect to find if you were somehow able to travel down to the deepest reaches of the sea. Then read biologist Carson's account of conditions in the ocean depths, noting whether she corroborates your impressions or proves them false. Note, also, her uses of language, observing how she unfolds the mysteries of the sea in a style that is both poetic and scientific.

With Words

1. coveted (7)—from the Latin word meaning "desire." Surely you remember the Tenth Commandment.
2. aggregations (24)—from the Latin root meaning "to add to a flock."
3. predatory (25)—related to *prey* and to *predator*. (See "The Intellectual and Emotional World of the Cockroach" p. 179.)
4. foragings (25)—from an old Germanic word meaning "food" or "fodder."
5. ichthyologists (28)—from the Greek word meaning "fish."
6. abyssal (30)—pronounced a-bi'-sul. Think of the word *abyss*.
7. luminescence (38)—related to the Latin word *lux,* meaning "light."
8. anachronisms (52)—from a Greek prefix meaning "up," "back," or "again" and the Greek root *chron-,* meaning "time." Think of *chronology*. What other words do you know that are from *chron-?*

> Where great whales come sailing by,
> sail and sail, with unshut eye.
> —Matthew Arnold

[1] Between the sunlit surface waters of the open sea and the hidden hills and valleys of the ocean floor lies the least-known region of the sea. These deep, dark waters, with all their mysteries and their unsolved problems, cover a very considerable part of the earth. The whole world ocean extends over about three-fourths of the surface of the globe. If we subtract the shallow areas of the continental shelves and the scattered

From *The Sea Around Us* by Rachel L. Carson. Copyright © 1950, 1951, 1961 by Rachel L. Carson. Reprinted by permission of Oxford University Press, Inc.

banks and shoals, where at least the pale ghost of sunlight moves over the underlying bottom, there still remains about half the earth that is covered by miles-deep, lightless water, that has been dark since the world began.

[2] This region has withheld its secrets more obstinately than any other. Man, with all his ingenuity, has been able to venture only to its threshold. Wearing a diving helmet, he can walk on the ocean floor about 10 fathoms down. He can descend to an extreme limit of about 500 feet in a complete diving suit, so heavily armored that movement is almost impossible, carrying with him a constant supply of oxygen. Only two men in all the history of the world have had the experience of descending, alive, beyond the range of visible light. These men are William Beebe and Otis Barton. In the bathysphere, they reached a depth of 3028 feet in the open ocean off Bermuda, in the year 1934. Barton alone, in a steel sphere known as the benthoscope, descended to the great depth of 4500 feet off California, in the summer of 1949.

[3] Although only a fortunate few can ever visit the deep sea, the precise instruments of the oceanographer, recording light penetration, pressure, salinity, and temperature, have given us the materials with which to reconstruct in imagination these eerie, forbidding regions. Unlike the surface waters, which are sensitive to every gust of wind, which know day and night, respond to the pull of sun and moon, and change as the seasons change, the deep waters are a place where change comes slowly, if at all. Down beyond the reach of the sun's rays, there is no alternation of light and darkness. There is rather an endless night, as old as the sea itself. For most of its creatures, groping their way endlessly through its black waters, it must be a place of hunger, where food is scarce and hard to find, a shelterless place where there is no sanctuary from ever-present enemies, where one can only move on and on, from birth to death, through the darkness, confined as in a prison to his own particular layer of the sea.

[4] They used to say that nothing could live in the deep sea. It was a belief that must have been easy to accept, for without proof to the contrary, how could anyone conceive of life in such a place?

[5] A century ago the British biologist Edward Forbes wrote: "As we descend deeper and deeper into this region, the inhabitants become more and more modified, and fewer and fewer, indicating our approach to an abyss where life is either extinguished, or exhibits but a few sparks to mark its lingering presence." Yet Forbes urged further exploration of "this vast deep-sea region" to settle forever the question of the existence of life at great depths.

[6] Even then, the evidence was accumulating. Sir John Ross, during his exploration of the arctic seas in 1818, had brought up from a depth of 1000 fathoms mud in which there were worms, "thus proving there was animal life in the bed of the ocean notwithstanding the darkness, stillness, silence, and immense pressure produced by more than a mile of superincumbent water."

[7] Then from the surveying ship *Bulldog*, examining a proposed

northern route for a cable from Faroe to Labrador in 1860, came another report. The *Bulldog*'s sounding line, which at one place had been allowed to lie for some time on the bottom at a depth of 1260 fathoms, came up with 13 starfish clinging to it. Through these starfish, the ship's naturalist wrote, "the deep has sent forth the long coveted message." But not all the zoologists of the day were prepared to accept the message. Some doubters asserted that the starfish had "convulsively embraced" the line somewhere on the way back to the surface.

[8] In the same year, 1860, a cable in the Mediterranean was raised for repairs from a depth of 1200 fathoms. It was found to be heavily encrusted with corals and other sessile animals that had attached themselves at an early stage of development and grown to maturity over a period of months or years. There was not the slightest chance that they had become entangled in the cable as it was being raised to the surface.

[9] Then the *Challenger,* the first ship ever equipped for oceanographic exploration, set out from England in the year 1872 and traced a course around the globe. From bottoms lying under miles of water, from silent deeps carpeted with red clay ooze, and from all the lightless intermediate depths, net-haul after net-haul of strange and fantastic creatures came up and were spilled out on the decks. Poring over the weird beings thus brought up for the first time into the light of day, beings no man had ever seen before, the *Challenger* scientists realized that life existed even on the deepest floor of the abyss.

[10] The recent discovery that a living cloud of some unknown creatures is spread over much of the ocean at a depth of several hundred fathoms below the surface is the most exciting thing that has been learned about the ocean for many years.

[11] When, during the first quarter of the twentieth century, echo sounding was developed to allow ships while under way to record the depth of the bottom, probably no one suspected that it would also provide a means of learning something about deep-sea life. But operators of the new instruments soon discovered that the sound waves, directed downward from the ship like a beam of light, were reflected back from any solid object they met. Answering echoes were returned from intermediate depths, presumably from schools of fish, whales, or submarines; then a second echo was received from the bottom.

[12] These facts were so well established by the late 1930's that fishermen had begun to talk about using their fathometers to search for schools of herring. Then the war brought the whole subject under strict security regulations, and little more was heard about it. In 1946, however, the United States Navy issued a significant bulletin. It was reported that several scientists, working with sonic equipment in deep water off the California coast, had discovered a widespread "layer" of some sort, which gave back an answering echo to the sound waves. This reflecting layer, seemingly suspended between the surface and the floor of the Pacific, was found over an area 300 miles wide. It lay from 1000 to 1500 feet below the

surface. The discovery was made by three scientists, C. F. Eyring, R. J. Christensen, and R. W. Raitt, aboard the U.S.S. *Jasper* in 1942, and for a time this mysterious phenomenon, of wholly unknown nature, was called the ECR layer. Then in 1945 Martin W. Johnson, marine biologist of the Scripps Institution of Oceanography, made a further discovery which gave the first clue to the nature of the layer. Working aboard the vessel *E. W. Scripps,* Johnson found that whatever sent back the echoes moved upward and downward in rhythmic fashion, being found near the surface at night, in deep water during the day. This discovery disposed of speculations that the reflections came from something inanimate, perhaps a mere physical discontinuity in the water, and showed that the layer is composed of living creatures capable of controlled movement.

[13] From this time on, discoveries about the sea's "phantom bottom" came rapidly. With widespread use of echo-sounding instruments, it has become clear that the phenomenon is not something peculiar to the coast of California alone. It occurs almost universally in the deep ocean basins—drifting by day at a depth of several hundred fathoms, at night rising to the surface, and again, before sunrise, sinking into the depths.

[14] On the passage of the U.S.S. *Henderson* from San Diego to the Antarctic in 1947, the reflecting layer was detected during the greater part of each day, at depths varying from 150 to 450 fathoms, and on a later run from San Diego to Yokosuka, Japan, the *Henderson*'s fathometer again recorded the layer every day, suggesting that it exists almost continuously across the Pacific.

[15] During July and August 1947, the U.S.S. *Nereus* made a continuous fathogram from Pearl Harbor to the Arctic and found the scattering layer over all deep waters along this course. It did not develop, however, in the shallow Bering and Chuckchee seas. Sometimes in the morning, the *Nereus* fathogram showed two layers, responding in different ways to the growing illumination of the water; both descended into deep water, but there was an interval of twenty minutes between the two descents.

[16] Despite attempts to sample it or photograph it, no one is sure what the layer is, although the discovery may be made any day. There are three principal theories, each of which has its group of supporters. According to these theories, the sea's phantom bottom may consist of small planktonic shrimps, of fishes, or of squids.

[17] As for the plankton theory, one of the most convincing arguments is the well-known fact that many plankton creatures make regular vertical migrations of hundreds of feet, rising toward the surface at night, sinking down below the zone of light penetration very early in the morning. This is, of course, exactly the behavior of the scattering layer. Whatever composes it is apparently strongly repelled by sunlight. The creatures of the layer seem almost to be held prisoner at the end—or beyond the end—of the sun's rays throughout the hours of daylight, waiting only for the welcome return of darkness to hurry upward into the surface waters.

But what is the power that repels; and what the attraction that draws them surfaceward once the inhibiting force is removed? Is it comparative safety from enemies that makes them seek darkness? Is it more abundant food near the surface that lures them back under cover of night?

[18] Those who say that fish are the reflectors of the sound waves usually account for the vertical migrations of the layer by suggesting that the fish are feeding on planktonic shrimp and are following their food. They believe that the air bladder of a fish is, of all structures concerned, most likely from its construction to return a strong echo. There is one outstanding difficulty in the way of accepting this theory: we have no other evidence that concentrations of fish are universally present in the oceans. In fact, almost everything else we know suggests that the really dense populations of fish live over the continental shelves or in certain very definitely determined zones of the open ocean where food is particularly abundant. If the reflecting layer is eventually proved to be composed of fish, the prevailing views of fish distribution will have to be radically revised.

[19] The most startling theory (and the one that seems to have the fewest supporters) is that the layer consists of concentrations of squid, "hovering below the illuminated zone of the sea and awaiting the arrival of darkness in which to resume their raids into the plankton-rich surface waters." Proponents of this theory argue that squid are abundant enough, and of wide enough distribution, to give the echoes that have been picked up almost everywhere from the equator to the two poles. Squid are known to be the sole food of the sperm whale, found in the open oceans in all temperate and tropical waters. They also form the exclusive diet of the bottle-nosed whale and are eaten extensively by most other toothed whales, by seals, and by many sea birds. All these facts argue that they must be prodigiously abundant.

[20] It is true that men who have worked close to the sea surface at night have received vivid impressions of the abundance and activity of squids in the surface waters in darkness. Long ago Johan Hjort wrote:

> One night we were hauling long lines on the Faroe slope, working with an electric lamp hanging over the side in order to see the line, when like lightning flashes one squid after another shot towards the light . . . In October 1902 we were one night steaming outside the slopes of the coast banks of Norway, and for many miles we could see the squids moving in the surface waters like luminous bubbles, resembling large milky white electric lamps being constantly lit and extinguished.

[21] Thor Heyerdahl reports that at night his raft was literally bombarded by squids; and Richard Fleming says that in his oceanographic work off the coast of Panama it was common to see immense schools of squid gathering at the surface at night and leaping upward toward the lights that were used by the men to operate their instruments. But equally

spectacular surface displays of shrimp have been seen, and most people find it difficult to believe in the ocean-wide abundance of squid.

[22] Deep-water photography holds much promise for the solution of the mystery of the phantom bottom. There are technical difficulties, such as the problem of holding a camera still as it swings at the end of a long cable, twisting and turning, suspended from a ship which itself moves with the sea. Some of the pictures so taken look as though the photographer has pointed his camera at a starry sky and swung it in an arc as he exposed the film. Yet the Norwegian biologist Gunnar Rollefson had an encouraging experience in correlating photography with echograms. On the research ship *Johan Hjort* off the Lofoten Islands, he persistently got reflection of sound from schools of fish in 20 to 30 fathoms. A specially constructed camera was lowered to the depth indicated by the echogram. When developed, the film showed moving shapes of fish at a distance, and a large and clearly recognizable cod appeared in the beam of light and hovered in front of the lens.

[23] Direct sampling of the layer is the logical means of discovering its identity, but the problem is to develop large nets that can be operated rapidly enough to capture swift-moving animals. Scientists at Woods Hole, Massachusetts, have towed ordinary plankton nets in the layer and have found that euphausiid shrimps, glassworms, and other deep-water plankton are concentrated there; but there is still a possibility that the layer itself may actually be made up of larger forms feeding on the shrimps—too large or swift to be taken in the presently used nets. New nets may give the answer. Television is another possibility.

[24] Shadowy and indefinite though they be, these recent indications of an abundant life at mid-depths agree with the reports of the only observers who have actually visited comparable depths and brought back eyewitness accounts of what they saw. William Beebe's impressions from the bathysphere were of a life far more abundant and varied than he had been prepared to find, although, over a period of six years, he had made many hundreds of net-hauls in the same area. More than a quarter of a mile down, he reported aggregations of living things "as thick as I have ever seen them." At half a mile—the deepest descent of the bathysphere—Dr. Beebe recalled that "there was no instant when a mist of plankton . . . was not swirling in the path of the beam."

[25] The existence of an abundant deep-sea fauna was discovered, probably millions of years ago, by certain whales and also, it now appears, by seals. The ancestors of all whales, we know by fossil remains, were land mammals. They must have been predatory beasts, if we are to judge by their powerful jaws and teeth. Perhaps in their foragings about the deltas of great rivers or around the edges of shallow seas, they discovered the abundance of fish and other marine life and over the centuries formed the habit of following them farther and farther into the sea. Little by little their bodies took on a form more suitable for aquatic life; their hind limbs were reduced to rudiments, which may be discovered in a modern whale by dis-

section, and the forelimbs were modified into organs for steering and balancing.

[26] Eventually the whales, as though to divide the sea's food resources among them, became separated into three groups: the plankton-eaters, the fish-eaters, and the squid-eaters. The plankton-eating whales can exist only where there are dense masses of small shrimp or copepods to supply their enormous food requirements. This limits them, except for scattered areas, to arctic and antarctic waters and the high temperate latitudes. Fish-eating whales may find food over a somewhat wider range of ocean, but they are restricted to places where there are enormous populations of schooling fish. The blue water of the tropics and of the open ocean basins offers little to either of these groups. But that immense, square-headed, formidably toothed whale known as the cachalot or sperm whale discovered long ago what men have known for only a short time—that hundreds of fathoms below the almost untenanted surface waters of these regions there is an abundant animal life. The sperm whale has taken these deep waters for his hunting grounds; his quarry is the deep-water population of squids, including the giant squid Architeuthis, which lives pelagically at depths of 1500 feet or more. The head of the sperm whale is often marked with long stripes, which consist of a great number of circular scars made by the suckers of the squid. From this evidence we can imagine the battles that go on, in the darkness of the deep water, between these two huge creatures—the sperm whale with its 70-ton bulk, the squid with a body as long as 30 feet, and writhing, grasping arms extending the total length of the animal to perhaps 50 feet.

[27] The greatest depth at which the giant squid lives is not definitely known, but there is one instructive piece of evidence about the depth to which sperm whales descend, presumably in search of the squids. In April 1932, the cable repair ship *All America* was investigating an apparent break in the submarine cable between Balboa in the Canal Zone and Esmeraldas, Ecuador. The cable was brought to the surface off the coast of Colombia. Entangled in it was a dead 45-foot male sperm whale. The submarine cable was twisted around the lower jaw and was wrapped around one flipper, the body, and the caudal flukes. The cable was raised from a depth of 540 fathoms, or 3240 feet.

[28] Some of the seals also appear to have discovered the hidden food reserves of the deep ocean. It has long been something of a mystery where, and on what, the northern fur seals of the eastern Pacific feed during the winter, which they spend off the coast of North America from California to Alaska. There is no evidence that they are feeding to any great extent on sardines, mackerel, or other commercially important fishes. Presumably four million seals could not compete with commercial fishermen for the same species without the fact being known. But there is some evidence on the diet of the fur seals, and it is highly significant. Their stomachs have yielded the bones of a species of fish that has never been seen alive. Indeed, not even its remains have been found anywhere except in

the stomachs of seals. Ichthyologists say that this "seal fish" belongs to a group that typically inhabits very deep water, off the edge of the continental shelf.

[29] How either whales or seals endure the tremendous pressure changes involved in dives of several hundred fathoms is not definitely known. They are warm-blooded mammals like ourselves. Caisson disease, which is caused by the rapid accumulation of nitrogen bubbles in the blood with sudden release of pressure, kills human divers if they are brought up rapidly from depths of 200 feet or so. Yet, according to the testimony of whalers, a baleen whale, when harpooned, can dive straight down to a depth of half a mile, as measured by the amount of line carried out. From these depths, where it has sustained a pressure of half a ton on every inch of body, it returns almost immediately to the surface. The most plausible explanation is that, unlike the diver, who has air pumped to him while he is under water, the whale has in its body only the limited supply it carries down, and does not have enough nitrogen in its blood to do serious harm. The plain truth is, however, that we really do not know, since it is obviously impossible to confine a living whale and experiment on it, and almost as difficult to dissect a dead one satisfactorily.

[30] At first thought it seems a paradox that creatures of such great fragility as the glass sponge and the jellyfish can live under the conditions of immense pressure that prevail in deep water. For creatures at home in the deep sea, however, the saving fact is that the pressure inside their tissues is the same as that without, and, as long as this balance is preserved, they are no more inconvenienced by a pressure of a ton or so than we are by ordinary atmospheric pressure. And most abyssal creatures, it must be remembered, live out their whole lives in a comparatively restricted zone, and are never required to adjust themselves to extreme changes of pressure.

[31] But of course there are exceptions, and the real miracle of sea life in relation to great pressure is not the animal that lives its whole life on the bottom, bearing a pressure of perhaps five or six tons, but those that regularly move up and down through hundreds or thousands of feet of vertical change. The small shrimps and other planktonic creatures that descend into deep water during the day are examples. Fish that possess air bladders, on the other hand, are vitally affected by abrupt changes of pressure, as anyone knows who has seen a trawler's net raised from a hundred fathoms. Apart from the accident of being captured in a net and hauled up through waters of rapidly diminishing pressures, fish may sometimes wander out of the zone to which they are adjusted and find themselves unable to return. Perhaps in their pursuit of food they roam upward to the ceiling of the zone that is theirs, and beyond whose invisible boundary they may not stray without meeting alien and inhospitable conditions. Moving from layer to layer of drifting plankton as they feed, they may pass beyond the boundary. In the lessened pressure of these upper waters the gas enclosed within the air bladder expands. The fish becomes lighter and

more buoyant. Perhaps he tries to fight his way down again, opposing the upward lift with all the power of his muscles. If he does not succeed, he "falls" to the surface, injured and dying, for the abrupt release of pressure from without causes distension and rupture of the tissues.

[32] The compression of the sea under its own weight is relatively slight, and there is no basis for the old and picturesque belief that, at the deeper levels, the water resists the downward passage of objects from the surface. According to this belief, sinking ships, the bodies of drowned men, and presumably the bodies of the larger sea animals not consumed above by hungry scavengers, never reach the bottom, but come to rest at some level determined by the relation of their own weight to the compression of the water, there to drift forever. The fact is that anything will continue to sink as long as its specific gravity is greater than that of the surrounding water, and all large bodies descend, in a matter of a few days, to the ocean floor. As mute testimony to this fact, we bring up from the deepest ocean basins the teeth of sharks and the hard ear bones of whales.

[33] Nevertheless the weight of sea water—the pressing down of miles of water upon all the underlying layers—does have a certain effect upon the water itself. If this downward compression could suddenly be relaxed by some miraculous suspension of natural laws, the sea level would rise about 93 feet all over the world. This would shift the Atlantic coastline of the United States westward a hundred miles or more and alter other familiar geographic outlines all over the world.

[34] Immense pressure, then, is one of the governing conditions of life in the deep sea; darkness is another. The unrelieved darkness of the deep waters has produced weird and incredible modifications of the abyssal fauna. It is a blackness so divorced from the world of the sunlight that probably only the few men who have seen it with their own eyes can visualize it. We know that light fades out rapidly with descent below the surface. The red rays are gone at the end of the first 200 or 300 feet, and with them all the orange and yellow warmth of the sun. Then the greens fade out, and at 1000 feet only a deep, dark, brilliant blue is left. In very clear waters the violet rays of the spectrum may penetrate another thousand feet. Beyond this is only the blackness of the deep sea.

[35] In a curious way, the colors of marine animals tend to be related to the zone in which they live. Fishes of the surface waters, like the mackerel and herring, often are blue or green; so are the floats of the Portuguese men-of-war and the azure-tinted wings of the swimming snails. Down below the diatom meadows and the drifting sargassum weed, where the water becomes ever more deeply, brilliantly blue, many creatures are crystal clear. Their glassy, ghostly forms blend with their surroundings and make it easier for them to elude the ever-present, ever-hungry enemy. Such are the transparent hordes of the arrowworms or glassworms, the comb jellies, and the larvae of many fishes.

[36] At a thousand feet, and on down to the very end of the sun's rays, silvery fishes are common, and many others are red, drab brown, or

black. Pteropods are a dark violet. Arrowworms, whose relatives in the upper layers are colorless, are here a deep red. Jellyfish medusae, which above would be transparent, at a depth of 1000 feet are a deep brown.

[37] At depths greater than 1500 feet, all the fishes are black, deep violet, or brown, but the prawns wear amazing hues of red, scarlet, and purple. Why, no one can say. Since all the red rays are strained out of the water far above this depth, the scarlet raiment of these creatures can only look black to their neighbors.

[38] The deep sea has its stars, and perhaps here and there an eerie and transient equivalent of moonlight, for the mysterious phenomenon of luminescence is displayed by perhaps half of all the fishes that live in dimly lit or darkened waters, and by many of the lower forms as well. Many fishes carry luminous torches that can be turned on or off at will, presumably helping them find or pursue their prey. Others have rows of lights over their bodies, in patterns that vary from species to species and may be a sort of recognition mark or badge by which the bearer can be known as friend or enemy. The deep-sea squid ejects a spurt of fluid that becomes a luminous cloud, the counterpart of the 'ink' of his shallow-water relative.

[39] Down the reach of even the longest and strongest of the sun's rays, the eyes of fishes become enlarged, as though to make the most of any chance illumination of whatever sort, or they may become telescopic, large of lens, and protruding. In deep-sea fishes, hunting in dark waters, the eyes tend to lose the "cones" or color-perceiving cells of the retina, and to increase the "rods," which perceive dim light. Exactly the same modification is seen on land among the strictly nocturnal prowlers which, like abyssal fish, never see the sunlight.

[40] In their world of darkness, it would seem likely that some of the animals might have become blind, as has happened to some cave fauna. So, indeed, many of them have, compensating for the lack of eyes with marvelously developed feelers and long, slender fins and processes with which they grope their way, like so many blind men with canes, their whole knowledge of friends, enemies, or food coming to them through the sense of touch.

[41] The last traces of plant life are left behind in the thin upper layer of water, for no plant can live below about 600 feet even in very clear water, and few find enough sunlight for their food-manufacturing activities below 200 feet. Since no animal can make its own food, the creatures of the deeper waters live a strange, almost parasitic existence of utter dependence on the upper layers. These hungry carnivores prey fiercely and relentlessly upon each other, yet the whole community is ultimately dependent upon the slow rain of descending food particles from above. The components of this never-ending rain are the dead and dying plants and animals from the surface, or from one of the intermediate layers. For each of the horizontal zones or communities of the sea that lie, in tier after tier, between the surface and the sea bottom, the food supply is different and in

general poorer than for the layer above. There is a hint of the fierce and uncompromising competition for food in the saber-toothed jaws of some of the small, dragonlike fishes of the deeper waters, in the immense mouths and in the elastic and distensible bodies that make it possible for a fish to swallow another several times its size, enjoying swift repletion after a long fast.

[42] Pressure, darkness, and—we should have added only a few years ago—silence, are the conditions of life in the deep sea. But we know now that the conception of the sea as a silent place is wholly false. Wide experience with hydrophones and other listening devices for the detection of submarines has proved that, around the shore lines of much of the world, there is an extraordinary uproar produced by fishes, shrimps, porpoises, and probably other forms not yet identified. There has been little investigation as yet of sound in the deep, offshore areas, but when the crew of the *Atlantis* lowered a hydrophone into deep water off Bermuda, they recorded strange mewing sounds, shrieks, and ghostly moans, the sources of which have not been traced. But fish of shallower zones have been captured and confined in aquaria, where their voices have been recorded for comparison with sounds heard at sea, and in many cases satisfactory identification can be made.

[43] During the Second World War the hydrophone network set up by the United States Navy to protect the entrance to Chesapeake Bay was temporarily made useless when, in the spring of 1942, the speakers at the surface began to give forth, every evening, a sound described as being like "a pneumatic drill tearing up pavement." The extraneous noises that came over the hydrophones completely masked the sounds of the passage of ships. Eventually it was discovered that the sounds were the voices of fish known as croakers, which in the spring move into Chesapeake Bay from their offshore wintering grounds. As soon as the noise had been identified and analyzed, it was possible to screen it out with an electric filter, so that once more only the sounds of ships came through the speakers.

[44] Later in the same year, a chorus of croakers was discovered off the pier of the Scripps Institution at La Jolla. Every year from May until late September the evening chorus begins about sunset, and "increases gradually to a steady uproar of harsh froggy croaks, with a background of soft drumming. This continues unabated for two to three hours and finally tapers off to individual outbursts at rare intervals." Several species of croakers isolated in aquaria gave sounds similar to the "froggy croaks," but the authors of the soft background drumming—presumably another species of croaker—have not yet been discovered.

[45] One of the most extraordinarily widespread sounds of the undersea is the crackling, sizzling sound, like dry twigs burning or fat frying, heard near beds of the snapping shrimp. This is a small, round shrimp, about half an inch in diameter, with one very large claw which it uses to stun its prey. The shrimp are forever clicking the two joints of this claw together, and it is the thousands of clicks that collectively produce the

noise known as shrimp crackle. No one had any idea the little snapping shrimps were so abundant or so widely distributed until their signals began to be picked up on hydrophones. They have been heard all over a broad band that extends around the world, between latitudes 35° N and 35° S, (for example, from Cape Hatteras to Buenos Aires) in ocean waters less than 30 fathoms deep.

[46] Mammals as well as fishes and crustaceans contribute to the undersea chorus. Biologists listening through a hydrophone in an estuary of the St. Lawrence River heard "high-pitched resonant whistles and squeals, varied with the ticking and clucking sounds slightly reminiscent of a string orchestra tuning up, as well as mewing and occasional chirps." This remarkable medley of sounds was heard only while schools of the white porpoise were seen passing up or down the river, and so was assumed to be produced by them.

[47] The mysteriousness, the eerieness, the ancient unchangingness of the great depths have led many people to suppose that some very old forms of life—some "living fossils"—may be lurking undiscovered in the deep ocean. Some such hope may have been in the minds of the *Challenger* scientists. The forms they brought up in their nets were weird enough, and most of them had never before been seen by man. But basically they were modern types. There was nothing like the trilobites of Cambrian time or the sea scorpions of the Silurian, nothing reminiscent of the great marine reptiles that invaded the sea in the Mesozoic. Instead, there were modern fishes, squids, and shrimps, strangely and grotesquely modified, to be sure, for life in the difficult deep-sea world, but clearly types that have developed in rather recent geologic time.

[48] Far from being the original home of life, the deep sea has probably been inhabited for a relatively short time. While life was developing and flourishing in the surface waters, along the shores, and perhaps in the rivers and swamps, two immense regions of the earth still forbade invasion by living things. These were the continents and the abyss. As we have seen, the immense difficulties of surviving on land were first overcome by colonists from the sea about 300 million years ago. The abyss, with its unending darkness, its crushing pressures, its glacial cold, presented even more formidable difficulties. Probably the successful invasion of this region—at least by higher forms of life—occurred somewhat later.

[49] Yet in recent years there have been one or two significant happenings that have kept alive the hope that the deep sea may, after all, conceal strange links with the past. In December 1938, off the southeast tip of Africa, an amazing fish was caught alive in a trawl—a fish that was supposed to have been dead for at least 60 million years! This is to say, the last known fossil remains of its kind date from the Cretaceous, and no living example had been recognized in historic time until this lucky net-haul.

[50] The fishermen who brought it up in their trawl from a depth of only 40 fathoms realized that this five-foot, bright blue fish with its large head and strangely shaped scales, fins, and tail, was different from any-

thing they had ever caught before, and on their return to port they took it to the nearest museum. This single specimen of Latimeria, as the fish was christened, is so far the only one that has been captured, and it seems a reasonable guess that it may inhabit depths below those ordinarily fished, and that the South African specimen was a stray from its usual habitat.

[51] Occasionally a very primitive type of shark, known from its puckered gills as a "frillshark," is taken in waters between a quarter of a mile and half a mile down. Most of these have been caught in Norwegian and Japanese waters—there are only about 50 preserved in the museums of Europe and America—but recently one was captured off Santa Barbara, California. The frillshark has many anatomical features similar to those of the ancient sharks that lived 25 to 30 million years ago. It has too many gills and too few dorsal fins for a modern shark, and its teeth, like those of fossil sharks, are three-pronged and briarlike. Some ichthyologists regard it as a relic derived from very ancient shark ancestors that have died out in the upper waters but, through this single species, are still carrying on their struggle for earthly survival, in the quiet of the deep sea.

[52] Possibly there are other such anachronisms lurking down in these regions of which we know so little, but they are likely to be few and scattered. The terms of existence in these deep waters are far too uncompromising to support life unless that life is plastic, molding itself constantly to the harsh conditions, seizing every advantage that makes possible the survival of living protoplasm in a world only a little less hostile than the black reaches of interplanetary space.

Questions on Meaning

1 Comment on the appropriateness of the title. Does this selection, which is a chapter from Carson's book *The Sea Around Us,* cover only conditions in that portion of the sea that the sun's rays never reach? If not, why do you think the author chose this title?

2 Outline the selection, using the topics you looked for as you read—the colors, sounds, and creatures of the deep sea—for some of your headings. Should these topics all be major headings? (That is, should they all be marked by Roman numerals?) What other divisions of the work should be major headings? In your outline, be sure to include the evidence Carson uses to support her generalizations as subheadings to your major headings.

3 Which of the three theories that have been offered to explain the sea's "phantom bottom" do you think Carson believes is the least probable explanation? How did you reach this conclusion? Note carefully the language she employs in discussing this matter. How does she manage to keep the same tone that she has used in discussing other, less controversial, developments in marine biology?

ESSAYS CHIEFLY INFORMATIVE

Questions on Style and Structure

1 Which of the introductory techniques described in the Introduction to Paragraph and Sentence Structure does Carson employ?

2 Paragraph 3 contains this sentence: "Unlike the surface waters, which are sensitive to every gust of wind, which know day and night, respond to the pull of sun and moon, and change as the seasons change, the deep waters are a place where change comes slowly, if at all." And paragraph 9 contains this sentence: "From bottoms lying under miles of water, from silent deeps carpeted with red clay ooze, and from all the lightless intermediate depths, net-haul after net-haul of strange and fantastic creatures came up and were spilled out on the decks." How does Carson's arrangement of the clauses of both sentences make the sentences emphatic? Would the sentences be as effective or emphatic if they were arranged in another way?

3 Carson's subject matter is scientific. How frequently does she employ scientific terminology? Do such words and phrases as *eerie* (paragraph 3) and *weird beings* (paragraph 9) have a place in "scientific" writing?

4 In what specific way does paragraph 16 indicate a shift in the principle of organization of the essay? According to what principle have most of the preceding paragraphs been ordered? According to what principle are the next few paragraphs ordered?

5 You will note that the author is careful to unify her paragraphs. Examine, for example, paragraphs 17, 18, and 19. Around what main idea is each unified? How about paragraphs 22, 23, and 24?

6 Carson uses two common words in unusual ways in the following sentences:

a If he does not succeed, he *"falls"* to the surface, injured and dying, for the abrupt release of pressure from without causes distention and rupture of the tissues. (paragraph 31)

b These hungry carnivores prey fiercely and relentlessly upon each other, yet the whole community is ultimately dependent upon the slow *rain* of descending food particles from above. (paragraph 41)

How effectively are these words used? Would the sentences have been just as effective if Carson had used a more scientific terminology?

Exploring Words

1 *coveted.* Which of the meanings your dictionary lists for *covet* applies to Carson's use of the word?

2 *aggregations.* What relationship do you find between this word and *gregarious,* which you studied in "Going Home Again: The New American Scholarship Boy" (p. 116)?

3 *predatory.* Which one of the several dictionary definitions best fits Carson's use of this word?

4 *foragings.* You will not find *foraging* in your dictionary because it is a noun form built from a verb (that is, it is a gerund). Note that your dictionary lists several verb meanings of *forage.* To which of these is the word *foragings* related?

5 *ichthyologists.* How many other *-ologist* words can you think of that pertain to the study of different kinds of animal life?

6 *abyssal.* A more common word than *abyssal* is *abysmal.* Consult your dictionary for the difference between the two words, and then use *abysmal* in a sentence of your own.

7 *luminescence.* The suffix as well as the root of this word is frequently used in English words. What other nouns can you think of that end in *-escence?* What is the adjective form of each of these words?

8 *anachronisms.* Shakespeare's play *Julius Caesar* contains an *anachronism,* the striking of a clock (there were no clocks in Julius Caesar's day). Explain the relationship between Carson's use of the word and its use in the preceding sentence.

Suggestions for Writing

1 Critics have often commented on the precision and the vividness of Rachel Carson's descriptions of sea life; in this chapter, paragraphs 34 and 37 are especially good examples of her descriptive technique. Read these paragraphs again with particular attention to the author's uses of language. Then observe carefully for a few minutes or more a small segment of the natural world—perhaps the way hummingbirds flit about the coralbell plants in your own back yard or the way spiders spin their webs on your campus grounds—and write a description of the scene, striving for the accuracy, the clarity, and the power Carson's descriptive writing achieves.

2 Carson's treatment of the possible causes of the "phantom bottom" of the sea is a complex one that required considerable research. In a somewhat different vein, write a cause-and-effect paper based on personal experience or reflection. For example, you might treat the causes of friction between parents and teenagers, the reasons college students smoke, or the roots of apathy on your campus.

The Automobile Revolution
FREDERICK LEWIS ALLEN

Getting Started

With Ideas

The title of this essay suggests that the writer is concerned either with radical changes made *in* the automobile or with such changes in society brought about *by* the automobile. Note that the first sentence shows you which of these two possible directions Allen is taking and leads into the general idea about automobiles and change that the rest of the article develops. In fact, later in the introduction (as in most of the selections in this section and the next) there is one sentence that directly states at least a large part of that general idea. Mark that thesis sentence when you come to it.

With Words:

1 profusion (2)—from the Latin root for "poured forth." Have you ever heard the phrase *"profuse* apologies"?
2 obstreperous (3)—your mother may have called you *obstreperous* when you were a child. Such a usage is common. However, note that Allen's use is different because he applies the word to a nonhuman thing.
3 pathology (3)—from the Greek root meaning "suffering." The context should also be helpful.
4 vexatious (3)—one of the meanings of the Latin root is "annoy."
5 antidote (11)—this word frequently appears on the labels of poisons.
6 blighted (15)—you have probably heard this word used to describe what sometimes happens to plants. That association would be helpful in understanding Allen's figurative use of this word.

[1] In the year 1906 Woodrow Wilson, who was then president of Princeton University, said: "Nothing has spread socialistic feeling in this country more than the automobile," and added that it offered "a picture of the arrogance of wealth." Less than twenty years later, two women of Muncie, Indiana, both of whom were managing on small incomes, spoke their minds to investigators gathering facts for that admirable sociological study of an American community, *Middletown.* Said one, who was the

"The Automobile Revolution" in *The Big Change* by Frederick Lewis Allen. Copyright, 1952 by Frederick Lewis Allen. Reprinted by permission of Harper & Row, Publishers, Inc.

mother of nine children, "We'd rather do without clothes than give up the car." Said the other, "I'll go without food before I'll see us give up the car." And elsewhere another housewife, in answer to a comment on the fact that her family owned a car but no bathtub, uttered a fitting theme song for the automobile revolution. "Why," said she, "you can't go to town in a bathtub!"

[2] This change in the status of the automobile from a luxury for the few to a necessity for the many—a change which, as we shall see, progressively transformed American communities and daily living habits and ideas throughout the half century—did not come about abruptly. It could not. For it depended upon three things. First, a reliable, manageable, and not too expensive car. Second, good roads. And third, garages and filling stations in profusion. And all these three requirements had to come slowly, by degrees, each reinforcing the others; a man who had tried to operate a filling station beside a dusty rural road in 1906 would have speedily gone bankrupt. But it was during the nineteen-twenties that the impact of the change was felt most sharply from year to year.

[3] When Woodrow Wilson spoke in 1906, and for years thereafter, the automobile had been a high-hung, noisy vehicle which couldn't quite make up its mind that it was not an obstreperous variety of carriage. It was so unreliable in its performance, so likely to be beset by tire blowouts, spark-plug trouble, carburetor trouble, defects in the transmission, and other assorted ailments, that a justly popular song of the time celebrated the troubles of the owner who "had to get under, get out and get under." The country doctors who in increasing numbers were coming to use the little brass-nosed Fords of the day had to be students of mechanical as well as human pathology. Each car had a toolbox on the running board, and tourists were accustomed to carrying with them blowout patches, French chalk, and a variety of tire irons against that awful moment when a tire would pop, miles from any help. One had to crank the engine by hand—a difficult and sometimes dangerous business. All cars except the limousines of the wealthy were open, with vertical windshields which gave so little protection against wind and dust to those in the back seat that dusters and even goggles were widely worn; and a gust of rain would necessitate a frantic raising of the folding top and a vexatious fitting and buttoning of the side curtains.

[4] Roads were mostly dusty or muddy, with no through routes. Even as late as 1921 there was no such thing as an officially numbered highway. In that year the *Automobile Blue Book* warned those who proposed to drive from Richford, Vermont, to Montreal: "Chains on all four wheels absolutely essential in wet weather." And it advised tourists in general that "where mountain roads, sandy stretches, and muddy places are to be met with, a shovel with a collapsible handle" might prove very useful. At the time when Wilson spoke, panicky horses were still a hazard for the driver in remote districts, and speed limits set by farmer-minded local officials were sometimes low indeed: my personal memory tells me—

unbelievably but I think reliably— that in tranquil Holderness, New Hampshire, the original legal limit was six miles an hour.

[5] Ford's energetic driving down of prices helped to make the automobile more popular, but equally responsible were a series of vital improvements: the invention of an effective self-starter, first designed by Charles F. Kettering and installed in the Cadillac in 1912; the coming, within the next two or three years, of the demountable rim and the cord tire; but above all, the introduction of the closed car. As late as 1916 only 2 per cent of the cars manufactured in the United States were closed; by 1926, 72 per cent of them were.

[6] What had happened was that manufacturers had learned to build closed cars that were not hideously expensive, that did not rattle themselves to pieces, and that could be painted with a fast-drying but durable paint; and that meanwhile the car-buying public had discovered with delight that a closed car was something quite different from the old "horseless carriage." It was a power-driven room on wheels—storm-proof, lockable, parkable all day and all night in all weathers. In it you could succumb to speed fever without being battered by the wind. You could close its windows against dust or rain. You could use it to fetch home the groceries, to drive to the golf club or the railroad station, to cool off on hot evenings, to reach a job many miles distant and otherwise inaccessible, to take the family out for a day's drive or a week-end excursion, to pay an impromptu visit to friends forty or fifty miles away, or, as innumerable young couples were not slow to learn, to engage in private intimacies. One of the cornerstones of American morality had been the difficulty of finding a suitable locale for misconduct; now this cornerstone was crumbling. And if the car was also a frequent source of family friction ("No, Junior, you are *not* taking it tonight"), as well as a destroyer of pedestrianism, a weakener of the churchgoing habit, a promoter of envy, a lethal weapon when driven by heedless, drunken, or irresponsible people, and a formidable convenience for criminals seeking a safe getaway, it was nonetheless indispensable.

[7] Furthermore, a car was now less expensive to maintain than in the days when the cost of successive repairs might mount up to a formidable sum each year. And it could be bought on easy payments. The installment selling of cars, virtually unknown before World War I, spread so rapidly that by 1925 over three-quarters of all cars, new and old, were being sold this way.

[8] Over these same years more and more roads had been paved, as public officials discovered that appropriations for highway surfacing were no longer considered mere favors to the rich; and the garages and filling stations had multiplied.

[9] The result of all these developments was a headlong rush to buy cars on the part of innumerable people to whom the idea of becoming automobile owners would have seemed fantastic only a few years before.

In 1915 there were less than 2½ million cars registered in the United States. By 1920 there were over 9 million; by 1925, nearly 20 million; by 1930, over 26½ million.

[10] So it was that the years between 1918 and 1930 introduced to America a long series of novelties which are now such familiar features of the American scene that one might think we had always had them: automatic traffic lights, concrete roads with banked curves, six-lane boulevards, one-way streets, officially numbered highways, tourist homes, and tourist cabins; and lined the edges of the major thoroughfares with that garish jumble of roadside services and businesses that Benton Mackaye and Lewis Mumford called "road town"—roadside diners, hot-dog stands, peanut stands, fruit and vegetable stalls, filling station after filling station, and used-car lots.

[11] Meanwhile an antidote to the increasing snarl and confusion and frustration of traffic through the built-up areas of the East was already in preparation. For a generation the officials of Westchester County, New York, had been disturbed by the polluted condition of the little Bronx River and by its tendency to flood, and had been planning to restrict and control its flow while making it the chief attraction of a long strip of parkway— which almost incidentally would contain a through automobile road. When this road was opened to the public in 1925, motorists and traffic commissions and regional planners happily saw in it the answer to their prayers: an ample highway, with traffic lanes separated at intervals, uncluttered by local traffic, winding through a landscape undefaced by commerce. On such a highway one could make time most agreeably. Other parkways, wider and straighter, were thereupon built, both in Westchester County and elsewhere; existing through highways were rebuilt to by-pass towns along their way; so that by August, 1931, Mackaye and Mumford, writing in *Harper's,* could announce that it had at last been recognized that the automobile was less like a family carriage than like a family locomotive, and also could look forward prophetically to a now-familiar scene. The time would come, they predicted, when a motorist with a long drive before him would ease into the fast traffic on a "townless highway" and presently would be spinning along "with less anxiety and more safety at 60 miles an hour than he used to have in the old road-town confusion at 25." When that day came, they said, the automobile would have become "an honor to our mechanical civilization and not a reproach to it."

[12] In 1931 those days had not yet arrived. There was still no Merritt Parkway, no Pennsylvania Turnpike; there were no butterfly intersections; there was no such majestic combination of separate lanes of traffic as would be seen by the mid-century at Cahuenga Pass in Los Angeles, where no less than fourteen lanes were to run side by side. Already motor busses had arrived in quantity, but the progressive ripping up of trolley tracks had only begun. Already motor trucks were taking freight business away from the railroads, but there was still no such vast and humming all-

night traffic of trucks, truck tractors, and semi-trailers between our great cities as later years were to bring. And that perfect symbol of our national mobility, the residential trailer, was only just appearing: the first trailer had been built in 1929 by a bacteriologist, for vacation use, but these houses on wheels were not to arrive in force until the mid-thirties. Yet already the pattern of the automobile age had been set.

II

[13] No such startling change in the habits of a people could have taken place without having far-reaching social effects. Let us glance at a few of them.

[14] 1. It developed the motorized suburb. Where a suburb had previously been accessible by railroad, but had been limited in size because of the difficulty of reaching the station from any place more than a mile or so away from it, it grew with startling speed, as real-estate subdividers bought up big tracts of property and laid out Woodmere Road and Edgemont Drive and Lakeside Terrace, suitable for English-cottage-type or Spanish-villa-type or New-England-saltbox-type (or, later, ranch-type) houses with attached garages; where the children would have the benefit of light and air and play space, and their parents would have the benefit of constant battles over the policies of the local school board; where the wife would gulp down her coffee at 7:52 to drive her husband to the 8:03 train before driving her children to school and doing the family errands.

[15] In a suburb which had previously been inaccessible by railroad the same phenomenon took place with only a slight variation: the earner of the family drove all the way from his almost-rural cottage to his place of work—and worried about the parking problem in the city. The number of Americans whose heart and treasure were twenty miles apart, as Agnes Rogers has put it, was vastly increased. And as more and more people whose living was dependent upon work at the center of the city fled to the leafy outskirts, urban planners began to be concerned about the blighted areas around the center of the city, where land values were falling and a general deterioration was manifest.

[16] 2. The coming of the automobile age brought other changes too. It caused a widespread shift of business, and of economic and social importance, from the railroad town to the off-the-railroad one; from the farm that was four miles from a railroad station but had poor soil to the fertile farm that was twenty or fifty miles from rail; and from the center of the small city to its outskirts.

[17] The hotel on Main Street, that had formerly been the one and only place for the traveling salesman to stop, lost business to the tourist camp on Highway 84. In due course this tourist camp was transformed into a new kind of roadside hotel, which offered overnight privacy—and sometimes luxury—without having to carry the economic load of high land value and of maintaining a restaurant and other public rooms. The shops along Main Street lost business to the new Sears Roebuck store at the

edge of town, with its ample parking lot. City department stores, becoming painfully aware of their dwindling appeal to commuters, opened suburban branches to catch the out-of-town trade. And by the mid-century, shopping centers were beginning to be developed out in the open countryside, where the prime essential of parking space would be abundant.

[18] The big summer hotel lost business, as the automobile opened up to a vast number of people the opportunity either to range from motel to motel or to have their own summer cottages, to which they could travel not only for the summer, but even for occasional week ends at other times in the year, by wedging the family into a car that bulged with people, suitcases, and assorted duffle. In resort after resort a pattern of change was repeated: the big hotel on the point, or at the beach, or on the hilltop was torn down, while the number of cottages in the neighborhood of its site doubled, tripled, quadrupled; and meanwhile the Friday afternoon traffic out of the city to various points, beaches, and hilltops became denser and denser. The trunk manufacturers lost business to the suitcase manufacturers, and the express companies languished.

[19] During the single decade of the nineteen-twenties, railroad passenger traffic was almost cut in half; only commuter traffic held up. (In the outskirts of New York, the next two decades were to witness a decline even in railroad commuter traffic, as the new parkways, bridges, and tunnels into Manhattan swelled the number of commuters by bus and by private car.)

[20] 3. The automobile age brought a parking problem that was forever being solved and then unsolving itself again. During the early nineteen-twenties the commuters who left their cars at the suburban railroad station at first parked them at the edge of the station drive; then they needed a special parking lot, and pretty soon an extended parking lot, and in due course a still bigger one—and the larger the lot grew, the more people wanted to use it. New boulevards, widened roads, and parkways relieved the bottlenecks at the approaches to the big cities—and invited more and more cars to enter. At the end of the half century the question, "Where do I park?" was as annoyingly insistent as it had been at any time since the arrival of the automobile.

[21] 4. The new dispensation brought sudden death. During the nineteen-twenties the number of people slaughtered annually by cars in the United States climbed from a little less than 15,000 in 1922 to over 32,000 in 1930; eighteen years later, in 1948, it stood at almost exactly the 1930 figure. As cars had become more powerful, and roads had become more persuasively straight and smooth, and speeds had increased, the shocking death toll each week end had led to the more cautious licensing of drivers and inspection of cars, to the multiplication of warning signs along the roadsides, and to the study of the causes and cures of death on the highway by such organizations as the National Safety Council and the Automotive Safety Council. But meanwhile youngsters had learned to play "chicken," and hot-rod enthusiasts had taken to the road; and many older

drivers, after a few drinks, found it easy to persuade themselves that they should overtake and pass that damned old creeping car at the crest of a hill, and even the most sedate motorist sometimes fell asleep at the wheel—and now the accidents that took place, while less frequent, were more lethal. So that at the turn of the half century one could still predict with reasonable certainty that a holiday week end would bring several hundred men, women, and children to an abrupt and gory end.

[22] 5. Along with the telephone, the radio, and the other agencies of communication, the automobile revolution ended the isolation of the farmer. In 1900 Ray Stannard Baker, describing a wave of prosperity among the farmers of the Midwest, had said that when a farmer did well, the first thing he did was to paint the barn; the second was to add a porch to his house; the third was to buy a piano; and the fourth was to send his children to college. By the mid-twenties the purchase of a car was likely to come even before the painting of the barn—and a new piano was a rarity. The widening use of the tractor was enlarging farms; and with the aid of the profusion of scientific information which was made available through the publications and county agents of the Department of Agriculture, the farmer was becoming less and less a laborer by hand, using rule-of-thumb methods, and more and more a businessman of the soil, an operator of machines, and a technologist. No longer, now, when he visited town, was he a rube, a hayseed, whose wife and daughters looked hick in calico. By 1939 the Sears Roebuck catalogue was listing dresses "inspired by Schiaparelli," and in 1940 it solemnly announced that "The traditional lapse between the acceptance of new fashions . . . in metropolitan centers and on farms apparently no longer exists."

[23] 6. The automobile broadened geographical horizons, especially for people who had hitherto considered themselves too poor to travel. One could still find, here and there, men and women who had never ventured farther from home than the county seat, but their number was dwindling fast. For now the family who had always stayed at home on their day off could drive to the lakes or the shore, and on their vacation could range widely over the land, see new things, engage in new sports, meet new people. Even their daily radius of activity lengthened startlingly: by the nineteen-forties it might be a matter of routine for a rural family to drive ten or fifteen miles to do their shopping, twenty or thirty to see the movies, fifty to visit a doctor or dentist.

[24] Furthermore, the automobile weakened the roots which held a family to one spot. Always a mobile people by comparison with the peoples of Europe, now Americans followed the economic tides more readily than ever before, moving by automobile—and before long by trailer—wherever there might be a call for construction workers, or fruit pickers, or airplane mechanics. Sober intellectuals were wont to deplore the growing American restlessness and to praise the man who was rooted to the land where he and his forefathers had been born and bred; but the automobile

suited the American genius. For that genius was not static but venturesome; Americans felt that a rolling stone gathers experience, adventure, sophistication, and—with luck—new and possibly fruitful opportunities.

[25] 7. The automobile revolution engendered personal pride. When I say this I am not thinking of the envy-in-reverse of the man or woman who revels in having a finer model of car than the neighbors can afford, but of something less readily defined but no less real. Someone has said that the Asiatic, long accustomed to humiliation at the hands of the lordly white European, will endure it no longer after he has once sat at the controls of a tractor or a bulldozer. Similarly the American who has been humbled by poverty, or by his insignificance in the business order, or by his racial status, or by any other circumstance that might demean him in his own eyes, gains a sense of authority when he slides behind the wheel of an automobile and it leaps forward at his bidding, ready to take him wherever he may personally please. If he drives a bus or a huge truck trailer his state is all the more kingly, for he feels himself responsible for the wielding of a sizable concentration of force.

[26] This effect of the automobile revolution was especially noticeable in the South, where one began to hear whites complaining about "uppity niggers" on the highways, where there was no Jim Crow. But the new sense of pride was dispersed far more widely than that; in some degree it affected almost everyone on the road. In 1950 the civilian labor force of the United States was estimated to number a little less than 59 million men and women; in the same year the number of drivers in the United States was estimated to be a little larger: 59,300,000. More than one driver for every jobholder! Never before in human history, perhaps, had any such proportion of the nationals of any land known the lifting of the spirit that the free exercise of power can bring.

Questions on Meaning

1 Having read the entire essay, do you think that the author's use of the word *revolution* in his title is appropriate? Before you answer this question, check the several meanings for the word listed in your dictionary. Then refer to specific information in the article to justify your answer.

2 Examine the list of social effects of the automobile with which Allen concludes this selection. Why do you think he uses the order he has chosen, ending with the point he lists as number 7?

3 This selection is from a book published in 1957. Do you think that Allen's treatment of this segment of American history would have been any different if he had written the book in the mid-1970s?

ESSAYS CHIEFLY INFORMATIVE

Questions on Style and Structure

1 Allen begins the first paragraph with a series of quotations. How effective are they in arousing your interest? Would the paragraph be as effective had the final quotation appeared elsewhere? Note the transitional devices that he used to stitch the quotations together.

2 A distinctive feature of the author's style is his fondness for parallel structure. Here is an example:

It caused a widespread shift of business, and of economic and social importance, *from* the railroad town *to* the off-the-railroad one; *from* the farm that was four miles from a railroad station but had poor soil *to* the fertile farm that was twenty or fifty miles from rail; and *from* the center of the small city *to* its outskirts. (paragraph 16)

What other examples of parallel sentence elements or parallel sentences can you find?

3 Allen's sentences are often worthy of study because they are structured for variety and emphasis. Why are the following sentences particularly effective? (Review the relevant section of the Introduction to Paragraph and Sentence Structure.)

a And if the car was also a frequent source of family friction ("No, Junior, you are *not* taking it tonight"), as well as a destroyer of pedestrianism, a weakener of the churchgoing habit, a promoter of envy, a lethal weapon when driven by heedless, drunken, or irresponsible people, and a formidable convenience for criminals seeking a safe getaway, it was nonetheless indispensable. (paragraph 6)

b For now the family who had always stayed at home on their day off could drive to the lakes or the shore, and on their vacation could range widely over the land, see new things, engage in new sports, meet new people. (paragraph 23)

What other sentences that are striking in their emphasis can you find?

4 The selection is divided into two basic sections. How do the two sections differ?

5 We have seen other authors use pronouns to achieve coherence. Can you locate passages that Allen makes coherent through the use of pronouns? (Review the Introduction to Paragraph and Sentence Structure if necessary.)

6 Paragraph 12 is a good example of a coherent paragraph. What devices for coherence does the author use there?

7 Is the concluding paragraph adequate? Does Allen need a more comprehensive conclusion?

Exploring Words

1 *profusion*. After checking your dictionary, use *profusion* appropriately in a sentence of your own.

2 *obstreperous*. The use of *obstreperous* is not limited to children and automobiles. When was the last time you behaved *obstreperously*?

3 *pathology*. Does your dictionary indicate that this word can be used with reference to nonliving things? What are *pathological* liars, and what are *pathological* drunkards?

4 *vexatious*. Name several things that you would describe as *vexatious*.

5 *antidote*. Note that Allen's use of this word is metaphorical. Construct a sentence of your own, using the word similarly. Then use the word *poison* metaphorically.

6 *blighted*. Can you think of other words dealing with plants that are used metaphorically (as *branch* is used in "a branch of mathematics")?

Suggestions for Writing

1 In what ways would your life be different if you did not have an automobile in a world in which automobiles existed or if you lived in a world in which they did not exist?

2 What do you think is the future of the automobile in America?

3 Analyze the effects of another modern invention on American life.

ESSAYS CHIEFLY PERSUASIVE

The Sloburbs
JOSEPH WOOD KRUTCH

Getting Started

With Ideas

What do you suppose Krutch's subject in this essay will be? What attitude or point of view does his title suggest? What tone does it lead you to expect?

With Words

1 paradoxes (1)—some theologians and philosophers assert that the existence of evil in a world governed by a beneficent deity is a *paradox*. See also Rothenberg's use of *paradox* in "Peaceful Coexistence with Rattlesnakes" (p. 41) and Rodriguez's use of *paradoxically* in "Going Home Again: The New American Scholarship Boy" (p. 116).
2 frowzier (5)—a form of *frowzy*. The context will be helpful here.
3 agglomeration (6)—from the Latin word meaning "to heap up." Think of *conglomerate*.
4 quasi-organic (7)—the prefix *quasi-* means "seemingly."
5 superfluities (9)—pronounced su-per-flu'-i-ties. Related to *superfluous* (pronounced su-per'-flu-us).
6 antithesis (10)—see "My Wood" (p. 50).
7 analogous (14)—related to *analogy*. See "The Spider and the Wasp" (p. 141).

[1] At Los Angeles we were told that the San Francisco Airport was fogged in, and we were given a choice. We could go to a hotel for the night and hope that the weather would clear or we could resign ourselves to a nine-hour bus ride. I chose the bus while reflecting sourly on the paradoxes of today's travel. A few months before I had come to San Francisco from Tokyo in exactly the same time it would take me to get there from Los Angeles. But one compensation—if you can call it that—did develop. I got the most extensive view I have ever had of what is now commonly called the sloburbs. Also, the fullest realization of their horror.

[2] Nowhere are they worse than in the Los Angeles area and nowhere are they more extensive. For several hours the same dismal scenes changed so little that it was hard to believe one was moving at all. Gas station, motel, car lot, bar, hamburger stand; then gas station, motel,

Reprinted by permission of William Morrow & Co., Inc. from *And Even If You Do* by Joseph Wood Krutch. Copyright © 1965 by Joseph Wood Krutch.

car lot, bar and hamburger stand again—all bathed in the hellish glow of neon. Daylight would have made everything look shabbier but not more attractive.

[3] Los Angeles can, of course, be accused of no more than a bad eminence. Nearly all American towns, even quite small ones, present a more or less extensive version of the same picture. The newer and the faster growing the community the more it intends to be a sloburb and nothing else, and sloburbs are so much alike that if you were carried into one blindfolded you would often find it impossible to say not only where you were, but even whether you were north or south or east or west.

[4] Tucson, where I now live, is no exception. In fact, it is rather worse than many because so much of its explosive growth is recent and takes the form of rapidly spreading sloburbs. They have not yet reached the area where I live but they are creeping towards it, and as I drove home the other day through spreading ugliness I was again amazed that this sort of anti-city could be so characterless. Everything looks improvised, random, unrelated to everything else, as though it had no memory of yesterday and no expectation of tomorrow.

[5] Nor is this true only of the motel, bar, hamburger-stand complex. It is almost equally so of a new kind of "business district," which is less a district than a ribbon of commercial establishments growing longer and longer as "downtown" shrinks or stagnates. Here the repetitive succession is not unlike that of the only slightly frowzier parade of eateries, drinkeries and sleeperies. The supermarkets (one every few hundred yards) are the most imposing of the commercial establishments. Between them come drugstores (which sell more toys, sporting equipment and sandwiches than they do drugs), dime stores, TV repair shops and auto supply emporia in a sort of procession which is repeated as soon as the repertory has completed itself.

[6] Yet this is far from being a depressed area. It is actually a very prosperous one and real-estate prices skyrocket in what is only a little better than a sort of shantytown. Poverty, I reminded myself, creates slums and slums can be even uglier. But I wondered if ever before in history a prosperous people had consented to live in communities so devoid of every grace and dignity, so slum-like in everything except the money they represent. They are something new and almost uniquely unattractive—neither country nor village nor town nor city—just an agglomeration without plan, without any sense of unity or direction, as though even offices and shops were thought of as disposable, like nearly everything else in our civilization, and therefore not worth considering from any standpoint except the make-do of the moment.

[7] A real metropolis has a quasi-organic unity. There is a nerve center more or less elaborate which includes whatever public buildings, theaters, auditoriums and major commercial emporia the community can support. From the impressiveness of this nerve center one can judge

pretty accurately just to what degree it is a metropolis rather than a town or a village. Its suburbs and even its slums are related to the whole. But a large sloburb like that which surrounds and all but engulfs Los Angeles differs from that of the village on the highway in nothing except area. You could cut a piece of it and set the piece down anywhere and you could not tell that it had grown up around Los Angeles, rather than where you found it. A suburb implies a city to which it is attached but what we are increasingly developing are huge agglomerations which cannot be called suburbs because there is no urbs to own them.

[8] Why, then, have the sloburbs become the most characteristic aspect of modern America? Why are they the only real urban development new to our time, as much our special contribution to the look and feel of our environment as the skyscraper was that of the first half of the century?

[9] If you accept the now usual assumption that whatever we do or are is the necessary result of "evolving technology," then the answer is easy. Technological progress has made the population explosion supportable and necessitated rapid growth. The automobile has made us mobile, and prosperity has not only created the demand for the superfluities to which two-thirds of the enterprises in the sloburbs cater but also encouraged the tendency to regard everything, including architecture, as disposable. Stores, office buildings and even churches will be "turned in" for new ones in a year or two. That is progress.

[10] If on the other hand you believe that evolving technology is only half the story, that human beings are capable of resisting as well as of yielding to pressures, then the question why we have consented to the sloburbs remains; why we are to all appearances so contented with them. Remember that sloburbs are the product of wealth and abundance. The motel-café regions cater to those who have much leisure; the merchandising sloburbs depend at least as much upon what might be called luxury goods as they do upon necessities. Why is there so little luxurious, or even decently dignified, about the buildings which house them, the merchandising methods they employ? Why should an abundant society be content to accept communities so obviously the antithesis of that "graceful living" which the service magazines talk about and declare to be nowadays open to all?

[11] Some of the frequent answers to that question also are easy: Americans have no taste, no sense of dignity, no ability to discriminate between the informality to which they are committed and the slovenliness of the sloburbs. Their civic pride does not extend beyond pride in increasing size and that prosperity which means that most of its citizens are making money building sloburbs or operating them. Given the primary fact of profit, nothing else is very important. Certainly aesthetic considerations are not. Arizona, for instance, tempts the tourist with the pretense that its proudest boast is its natural beauty. But it really prefers billboards, as is

evidenced by the fact that it recently again rejected the offer of the national government to grant a bonus if it would keep the main highways clear of them.

[12] These also are, of course, familiar charges and not without an element of truth. But they are not quite the whole story, not quite fair. The typical American is not indifferent to everything except profit. He is merely indifferent to some of the things which others consider important. He has, for example, an enormous faith in schooling—which he assumes to be the same thing as education. In Tucson, for example, by far the most imposing buildings are the absurdly elaborate schools, which the same citizens who prefer billboards to scenic grandeur, seem willing to support through very high taxes. The consensus seems to be essentially this: It is just that citizens should be taxed heavily and also expected to contribute generously. But they should never, under any circumstances, be prevented from making a profit. Hospitals also seem to be among the non-profit institutions to which citizens point with pride. But they are unwilling to do anything to slow the spread of sloburbs. The zoning regulations are a farce. If an area is zoned for residents only, that usually means that no business can be established there until somebody wants to establish one—at which time the zoning is promptly changed. Order, dignity, grace and beauty are things that are simply not worth paying even a small price for. Schooling, recreation and health should be supported. But the other parts of, and provisions for, the good life are not the community's business. Perhaps this tolerance is part of the kindly slovenliness in manners and morals to which we seem more and more inclined. But it is enough to permit the development of communities which it is impossible to imagine an earlier generation submitting to without protest.

[13] Some years ago I decided that for me the city was paying diminishing returns and I moved away from it. This was a choice I have never regretted but it was related to my time of life as well as to certain aspects of my temperament. It did not mean that I had no regard for cities and what they have contributed to civilization. But the sloburbs have none of the advantages of country, village or genuine city life. They do not, like real cities, provide a sufficiently large minority of citizens of intellectual and artistic taste to support cultural institutions proportionate to the size of their populations. Neither do they provide that "life of the streets" which is another of the chief attractions offered by a real city. Anywhere in a sloburb one may buy gasoline, cocktails, beer and hamburgers. But one cannot go window-shopping or indulge in any of the other activities which in New York or San Francisco draw strollers down the streets of the urban core. Neither, of course, can one breathe fresh air or enjoy the beauties of nature. One can only breathe gas fumes and revel in the glow of neon. Of all the places into which one's lot may be cast; few—not even those minimum-security prisons called garden apartments of the sort I pass on my

way once or twice a year from Manhattan to Kennedy—strike me as more dismal.

[14] Thinking of a real city as something analogous to a living creature where highly differentiated organs are all related to, and coordinated by, a central nervous system, I found myself wondering to just what sort of creature an individual sloburb might be compared. Most of even the so-called primitive organisms are wholes in the sense that the parts are related to one another and cannot exist except in connection with some center. You can't, in most cases, just break off a section and expect it to survive. Neither can most of such simple organisms grow indefinitely without any natural boundaries or shape. Hence, if a sloburb is analogous to any living thing it must be, I think, to one of the myxomycetes or slime molds. These remarkable blobs found especially in damp, rotting logs have no shape, no characteristic size and no community center. They consist of an agglomeration of one-celled individuals without a trace of the differentiation characteristic of even the more primitive multi-cellular organisms. You may break one blob into a hundred pieces and each will prosper as satisfactorily as it did when it was part of a larger blob. Put the pieces into contact again and they will merge much as the sloburbs spreading out from two communities merge when they meet. And given favorable conditions, the size of the blob grows and grows without there being any theoretical reason why it should not ultimately cover the earth. Such an eventuality might make a good horror movie. But no better than one that showed the whole face of America covered ultimately by one vast sloburb.

Questions on Meaning

1 According to Krutch, how do "sloburbs" differ from suburbs and from cities?

2 What, exactly, does Krutch find most distasteful about "sloburbs"?

3 Why does he pay so much attention to the "sloburbs" surrounding Los Angeles?

4 How does he account for contemporary America's tolerance of these places?

Questions on Style and Structure

1 The title of this piece reveals the author's fondness for word-play. Where in the essay does he reveal this love?

2 Which of the techniques discussed in the Introduction to Paragraph and Sentence Structure does Krutch employ to introduce this essay?

ESSAYS CHIEFLY PERSUASIVE

3 Where in paragraph 1 does Krutch state his thesis? What is it?

4 Study very carefully the first sentence in each paragraph after paragraph 1, and underline the words or phrases that provide transitions from preceding paragraphs.

5 What is the function of paragraph 11? Of paragraph 12?

6 How would you characterize the tone of this essay? Would it be accurate, for example, to say that Krutch is angry or harsh in his critique of "sloburbs"?

7 Why may the following sentences be considered emphatic?

  a Nowhere are they worse than in the Los Angeles area and nowhere else are they more extensive. (paragraph 2)
  b Poverty, I reminded myself, creates slums and slums can be even uglier. (paragraph 6)
  c These remarkable blobs found especially in damp, rotting logs have no shape, no characteristic size and no community center. (paragraph 14)

8 Paragraph 14 contains a good example of how a writer develops his point through an analogy. How appropriate and effective is Krutch's analogy? Can you think of another analogy that would be appropriate here?

Exploring Words

1 *paradoxes.* In what sense was the situation in which Krutch found himself in Los Angeles a *paradoxical* one? Compare Krutch's use of *paradox* with Rothenberg's in "Peaceful Coexistence with Rattlesnakes" (p. 41).

2 *frowzier.* Your dictionary probably lists two quite different meanings for *frowzy.* Which one applies to Krutch's use of the word? How do you explain the development of two such different senses for the same word?

3 *agglomeration.* Which one of your dictionary's listed meanings for *agglomeration* applies to Krutch's use? Why do you suppose Krutch uses the word so many times in this essay? (It is in paragraphs 6, 7, and 14.)

4 *quasi-organic.* Quasi- is a prefix that is used in a few established English words, but it appears more frequently in coined expressions, like Krutch's *quasi-organic.* What words beginning with *quasi-* does your dictionary contain? What expressions beginning with *quasi-* can you coin that you think you might have occasion to use sometime?

5 *superfluities.* Check your dictionary's treatment of this word, note Krutch's use of it, and then make a list of some of the things your neighbors and friends buy in "sloburb" shopping centers that you consider *superfluities.*

6 *antithesis.* In what ways does Krutch find the sloburbs to be the *antithesis* of "graceful living"?

7 *analogous.* Write a sentence using *analogous* appropriately, keeping in mind your dictionary's definition and Krutch's use of the word.

Suggestions for Writing

1 Write a thoughtful (but not necessarily negative) comment on the provisions your home town (or a community you know well) makes for what you consider "the good life" for its citizens. Would you like to bring your children up in the same place or the same kind of place that you grew up in? Why? Was it a "sloburb"? (If it was what Krutch would call a "sloburb," perhaps you can show another side to life there from the one Krutch shows.)

2 Analyze any facet of contemporary American life that you find disturbing.

The Civil Rights Movement: What Good Was It?
ALICE WALKER

Getting Started

With Ideas

Alice Walker was a recent college graduate when she wrote this essay, which won a prize in a 1967 Phi Beta Kappa-sponsored contest for young American writers. To understand and appreciate this work fully, you should—as much as possible—take yourself back to the America of the late 1960s. You may remember this period dimly as a time of "hippie" and "flower child" activity, campus rebellions (chiefly associated with the Vietnam War), and civil rights demonstrations. Note that Walker draws some contrasts between the attitudes of the "hippies" of the period and those of the civil rights workers with whom she was associated.

With Words

1 pensive (9)—from the Middle English word meaning "to think" and the Latin word meaning "to weigh, ponder, or consider."
2 innuendo (11)—from the Latin word meaning "to hint."
3 urbane (11)—associate it with *urban,* but also note the meaning the context suggests. See also *urbanite* in "Lonely Lives under the Sky" (p. 198).
4 vicarious (11)—one kind of *vicarious* pleasure is the kind you get when you lose yourself in a good movie or book. But note that Walker uses the word in a somewhat different sense here.
5 ignominiously (13)—*ignominious* is often used in the phrase *"ignominious* defeat." See also "The Eye of a Deer" (p. 17).
6 nihilists (18)—from the Latin word meaning "nothing." Think of *nil* and *annihilate.*
7 paternalists (23)—from the Latin word for "father."

[1] Someone said recently to an old black lady from Mississippi, whose legs had been badly mangled by local police who arrested her for "disturbing the peace," that the civil rights movement was dead, and

Reprinted from *The American Scholar*, Volume 36, Number 4, Autumn, 1967. Copyright © 1967 by the United Chapters of Phi Beta Kappa. By permission of the publishers.

THE CIVIL RIGHTS MOVEMENT: WHAT GOOD WAS IT?

asked, since it was dead, what she thought about it. The old lady replied, hobbling out of his presence on her cane, that the civil rights movement was like herself, "if it's dead, it shore ain't ready to lay down!"

[2] This old lady is a legendary freedom fighter in her small town in the Delta. She has been severely mistreated for insisting on her rights as an American citizen. She has been beaten for singing movement songs, placed in solitary confinement in prisons for talking about freedom, and placed on bread and water for praying aloud to God for her jailers' deliverance. For such a woman the civil rights movement will never be over as long as her skin is black. It also will never be over for twenty million others with the same "affliction," for whom the movement can never "lay down," no matter how it is killed by the press and made dead and buried by the white American public. As long as one black American survives, the struggle for equality with other Americans must also survive. This is a debt we owe to those blameless hostages we leave to the future, our children.

[3] Still, white liberals and deserting civil rights sponsors are quick to justify their disaffection from the movement by claiming that it is all over. "And since it is over," they will ask, "would someone kindly tell me what has been gained by it?" They then list statistics supposedly showing how much more advanced segregation is now than ten years ago—in schools, housing, jobs. They point to a gain in conservative politicians during the last few years. They speak of ghetto riots and of the recent survey that shows that most policemen are admittedly too anti-Negro to do their jobs in ghetto areas fairly and effectively. They speak of every area that has been touched by the civil rights movement as somehow or other going to pieces.

[4] They rarely talk, however, about human attitudes among Negroes that have undergone terrific changes just during the past seven to ten years (not to mention all those years when there was a movement and only the Negroes knew about it). They seldom speak of changes in personal lives because of the influence of people in the movement. They see general failure and few, if any, individual gains.

[5] They do not understand what it is that keeps the movement from "laying down" and Negroes from reverting to their former *silent* second-class status. They have apparently never stopped to wonder why it is always the white man—on his radio and in his newspaper and on his television—who says that the movement is dead. If a Negro were audacious enough to make such a claim, his fellows might hanker to see him shot. The movement is dead to the white man because it no longer interests him. And it no longer interests him because he can afford to be uninterested: he does not have to live by it, with it, or for it, as Negroes must. He can take a rest from the news of beatings, killings and arrests that reach him from North and South—if his skin is white. Negroes cannot now and will never be able to take a rest from the injustices that plague them for they—not the white man—are the target.

[6] Perhaps it is naïve to be thankful that the movement "saved" a

large number of individuals and gave them something to live for, even if it did not provide them with everything they wanted. (Materially, it provided them with precious little that they wanted.) When a movement awakens people to the possibilities of life, it seems unfair to frustrate them by then denying what they had thought was offered. But what was offered? What was promised? What was it all about? What good did it do? Would it have been better, as some have suggested, to leave the Negro people as they were, unawakened, unallied with one another, unhopeful about what to expect for their children in some future world?

[7] I do not think so. If knowledge of my condition is all the freedom I get from a "freedom movement," it is better than unawareness, forgottenness and hopelessness, the existence that is like the existence of a beast. Man only truly lives by knowing, otherwise he simply performs, copying the daily habits of others, but conceiving nothing of his creative possibilities as a man, and accepting someone else's superiority and his own misery.

[8] When we are children, growing up in our parents' care, we await the spark from the outside world. Sometimes our parents provide it—if we are lucky—sometimes it comes from another source far from home. We sit, paralyzed, surrounded by our anxiety and dread, hoping we will not have to grow up into the narrow world and ways we see about us. We are hungry for a life that turns us on; we yearn for a knowledge of living that will save us from our innocuous lives that resemble death. We look for signs in every strange event; we search for heroes in every unknown face.

[9] It was just six years ago that I began to be alive. I had, of course, been living before—for I am now twenty-three—but I did not really know it. And I did not know it because nobody told me that I—a pensive, yearning, typical high-school senior, but Negro—existed in the minds of others as I existed in my own. Until that time my mind was locked apart from the outer contours and complexion of my body as if it and the body were strangers. The mind possessed both thought and spirit—I wanted to be an author or a scientist—which the color of the body denied. I had never seen myself and existed as a statistic exists, or as a phantom. In the white world I walked, less real to them than a shadow; and being young and well-hidden among the slums, among people who also did not exist—either in books or in films or in the government of their own lives—I waited to be called to life. And, by a miracle, I was called.

[10] There was a commotion in our house that night in 1960. We had managed to buy our first television set. It was battered and overpriced, but my mother had gotten used to watching the afternoon soap operas at the house where she worked as maid, and nothing could satisfy her on days when she did not work but a continuation of her "stories." So she pinched pennies and bought a set.

[11] I remained listless throughout her "stories," tales of pregnancy, abortion, hypocrisy, infidelity and alcoholism. All these men and

women were white and lived in houses with servants, long staircases that they floated down, patios where liquor was served four times a day to "relax" them. But my mother, with her swollen feet eased out of her shoes, her heavy body relaxed in our only comfortable chair, watched each movement of the smartly coiffed women, heard each word, pounced upon each innuendo and inflection, and for the duration of these "stories" she saw herself as one of them. She placed herself in every scene she saw, with her braided hair turned blonde, her two hundred pounds compressed into a sleek size seven dress, her rough dark skin smooth and *white*. Her husband became dark and handsome, talented, witty, urbane, charming. And when she turned to look at my father sitting near her in his sweat shirt with his smelly feet raised on the bed to "air," there was always a tragic look of surprise on her face. Then she would sigh and go out to the kitchen looking lost and unsure of herself. My mother, a truly great woman—who raised eight children of her own and half a dozen of the neighbors' without a single complaint—was convinced that she did not exist compared to "them." She subordinated her soul to theirs and became a faithful and timid supporter of the "Beautiful White People." Once she asked me, in a moment of vicarious pride and despair, if I didn't think that "they" were "jest naturally smarter, prettier, better." My mother asked this; a woman who never got rid of any of her children, never cheated on my father, was never a hypocrite if she could help it, and never even tasted liquor. She could not even bring herself to blame "them" for making her believe what they wanted her to believe: that if she did not look like them, think like them, be sophisticated and corrupt-for-comfort's-sake like them, she was a nobody. Black was not a color on my mother, it was a shield that made her invisible. The heart that beat out its life in the great shadow cast by the American white people never knew that it was really "good."

[12] Of course, the people who wrote the soap opera scripts always made the Negro maids in them steadfast, trusty and wise in a home-remedial sort of way; but my mother, a maid for nearly forty years, never once identified herself with the scarcely glimpsed black servant's face beneath the ruffled cap. Like everyone else, in her daydreams at least, she thought she was free.

[13] Six years ago, after half-heartedly watching my mother's soap operas and wondering whether there wasn't something more to be asked of life, the civil rights movement came into my life. Like a good omen for the future, the face of Dr. Martin Luther King, Jr., was the first black face I saw on our new television screen. And, as in a fairy tale, my soul was stirred by the meaning for me of his mission—at the time he was being rather ignominiously dumped into a police van for having led a protest march in Alabama—and I fell in love with the sober and determined face of the movement. The singing of "We Shall Overcome"—that song betrayed by nonbelievers in it—rang for the first time in my ears. The influence that my mother's soap operas might have had on me became impossible. The life of Dr. King, seeming bigger and more miraculous than

the man himself, because of all he had done and suffered, offered a pattern of strength and sincerity I felt I could trust. He had suffered much because of his simple belief in nonviolence, love and brotherhood. Perhaps the majority of men could not be reached through these beliefs, but because Dr. King kept trying to reach them in spite of danger to himself and his family, I saw in him the hero for whom I had waited so long.

[14] What Dr. King promised was not a ranch-style house and an acre of manicured lawn for every black man, but jail and finally freedom. He did not promise two cars for every family, but the courage one day for all families everywhere to walk without shame and unafraid on their own feet. He did not say that one day it will be us chasing perspective buyers out of our prosperous well-kept neighborhoods, or in other ways exhibiting our snobbery and ignorance as all other ethnic groups before us have done; what he said was that we had a right to live anywhere in this country we chose, and a right to a meaningful well-paying job to provide us with the upkeep of our homes. He did not say we had to become carbon copies of the white American middle-class; but he did say we had the right to become whatever we wanted to become.

[15] Because of the movement, because of an awakened faith in the newness and imagination of the human spirit, because of "black and white together"—for the first time in our history in some human relationship on and off TV—because of the beatings, the arrests, the hell of battle during the past years, I have fought harder for my life and for a chance to be myself, to be something more than a shadow or a number, than I have ever done before in my life. Before there had seemed to be no real reason for struggling beyond the effort for daily bread. Now there was a chance at that other that Jesus meant when He said we could not live by bread alone.

[16] I have fought and kicked and fasted and prayed and cursed and cried myself to the point of existing. It has been like being born again, literally. Just "knowing" has meant everything to me. Knowing has pushed me out into the world, into college, into places, into people.

[17] Part of what existence means to me is knowing the difference between what I am now and what I was then. It is being capable of looking after myself intellectually as well as financially. It is being able to tell when I am being wronged and by whom. It means being awake to protect myself and the ones I love. It means being a part of the world community, and being *alert* to which part it is that I have joined, and knowing how to change to another part if that part does not suit me. To know is to exist; to exist is to be involved, to move about, to see the world with my own eyes. This, at least, the movement has given me.

[18] The hippies and other nihilists would have me believe that it is all the same whether the people in Mississippi have a movement behind them or not. Once they have their rights, they say, they will run all over themselves trying to be just like everybody else. They will be well-fed, complacent about things of the spirit, emotionless, and without that marvelous humanity and "soul" that the movement has seen them practice

time and time again. What has the movement done, they ask, with the few people it has supposedly helped? Got them white-collar jobs, moved them into standardized ranch houses in white neighborhoods, given them intellectual accents to go with their nondescript gray flannel suits? "What are these people now?" they ask. And then they answer themselves, "Nothings!"

[19] I would find this reasoning—which I have heard many, many times, from hippies and nonhippies alike—amusing, if I did not also consider it serious. For I think it is a delusion, a copout, an excuse to disassociate themselves from a world in which they feel too little has been changed or gained. The real question, however, it appears to me, is not whether poor people will adopt the middle-class mentality once they are well-fed, rather, it is whether they will ever be well-fed enough to be able to choose whatever mentality they think will suit them. The lack of a movement did not keep my mother from *wishing* herself bourgeois in her daydreams.

[20] There is widespread starvation in Mississippi. In my own state of Georgia there are more hungry families than Lester Maddox would like to admit—or even see fed. I went to school with children who ate red dirt. The movement has prodded and pushed some liberal senators into pressuring the government for food so that the hungry may eat. Food stamps that were two dollars and out of the reach of many families not long ago have been reduced to fifty cents. The price is still out of the reach of some families, and the government, it seems to a lot of people, could spare enough free food to feed its own people. It angers people in the movement that it does not; they point to the billions in wheat we send free each year to countries abroad. Their government's slowness while people are hungry, its unwillingness to believe that there are Americans starving, its stingy cutting of the price of food stamps, make many civil rights workers throw up their hands in disgust. But they do not give up. They do not withdraw into the world of psychedelia. They apply what pressure they can to make the government give away food to hungry people. They do not plan so far ahead in their disillusionment with society that they can see these starving families buying identical ranch-style houses and sending their snobbish children to Bryn Mawr and Yale. They take first things first and try to get them fed.

[21] They do not consider it their business, in any case, to say what kind of life the people they help must lead. How one lives is, after all, one of the rights left to the individual—when and if he has opportunity to choose. It is not the prerogative of the middle class to determine what is worthy of aspiration.

[22] There is also every possibility that the middle-class people of tomorrow will turn out ever so much better than those of today. I even know some middle-class people of today who are not *all* bad. Often, thank God, what monkey sees, monkey *avoids* doing at all costs. So it may be, concerning what is deepest in him, with the Negro.

[23] I think there are so few Negro hippies today because middle-

class Negroes, although well-fed, are not careless. They are required by the treacherous world they live in to be clearly aware of whoever or whatever might be trying to do them in. They are middle-class in money and position, but they cannot afford to be middle-class in complacency. They distrust the hippie movement because they know that it can do nothing for Negroes as a group but "love" them, which is what all paternalists claim to do. And since the only way Negroes can survive (which they cannot do, unfortunately, on love alone) is with the support of the group, they are wisely wary and stay away.

[24] A white writer tried recently to explain that the reason for the relatively few Negro hippies is that Negroes have built up a "super-cool" that cracks under LSD and makes them have a "bad trip." What this writer doesn't guess at is that Negroes are needing drugs less than ever these days for any kind of trip. While the hippies are "tripping," Negroes are going after power, which is so much more important to their survival and their children's survival than LSD and pot.

[25] Everyone would be surprised if the Israelis ignored the Arabs and took up "tripping" and pot smoking. In this country we are the Israelis. Everybody who can do so would like to forget this, of course. But for us to forget it for a minute would be fatal. "We Shall Overcome" is just a song to most Americans, *but we must do it*. Or die.

[26] What good was the civil rights movement? If it had just given this country Dr. King, a leader of conscience for once in our lifetime, it would have been enough. If it had just taken black eyes off white television stories, it would have been enough. If it had fed one starving child, it would have been enough.

[27] If the civil rights movement is "dead," and if it gave us nothing else, it gave us each other forever. It gave some of us bread, some of us shelter, some of us knowledge and pride, all of us comfort. It gave us our children, our husbands, our brothers, our fathers, as men reborn and with a purpose for living. It broke the pattern of black servitude in this country. It shattered the phony "promise" of white soap operas that sucked away so many pitiful lives. It gave us history and men far greater than Presidents. It gave us heroes, selfless men of courage and strength, for our little boys to follow. It gave us hope for tomorrow. It called us to life.

[28] Because we live, it can never die.

Questions on Meaning

1 What are the principal reasons Walker gives for believing that the civil rights movement is not dead?

2 Explain the criticism Walker thinks "hippies and other nihilists" have made of "the movement." How does she answer this criticism?

THE CIVIL RIGHTS MOVEMENT: WHAT GOOD WAS IT?

3 In what way does the author's treatment of her mother's interest in TV soap operas contribute to the development of her thesis?
4 What do the following quotations mean?

   a Until that time [when she was introduced to the civil rights movement] my mind was locked apart from the outer contours and complexion of my body. . . . (paragraph 9)
   b I had never seen myself and existed as a statistic exists, or as a phantom. (paragraph 9)
   c Black was not a color on my mother, it was a shield that made her invisible. (paragraph 11)

Questions on Style and Structure

1 Which of the introductory techniques discussed in the Introduction to Paragraph and Sentence Structure does Walker use?
2 You will note that coherence in paragraph 3 is achieved primarily through the use of the pronoun *they.* What other paragraphs are similarly made coherent through the consistent use of a pronoun?
3 You will also note that paragraph 26 is made coherent through the use of parallel sentences. In what other paragraphs is this device employed?
4 How unified are Walker's paragraphs? Does she usually begin with topic sentences?
5 Note the manner in which the author stitches paragraphs together. What are the transitional markers between paragraphs?
6 How effective is Walker's conclusion?

Exploring Words

1 *pensive.* Pensive is often used with the word *mood.* What kinds of experiences put you in a *pensive* mood?
2 *innuendo.* Check the synonyms your dictionary lists for *innuendo.* Why do you think Walker chose this word instead of one of its synonyms?
3 *urbane.* Look up your dictionary's definition of *urbane.* What relationship in meaning do you find between this word and *urban?*
4 *vicarious.* Which one of the several meanings your dictionary gives for *vicarious* applies to Walker's use of the word?
5 *ignominiously.* Compare Walker's use of *ignominiously* with Dolph's use in "The Eye of a Deer" (p. 17). In what ways are the contexts similar?
6 *nihilists.* Check the dictionary's definition of *nihilist.* Why do you suppose Walker considers the people she calls "hippies" to be *nihilists?*

7 *paternalists*. Check your dictionary's definition of this word, and then explain in your own words what Walker means when she says that all *paternalists* "do nothing for Negroes as a group but [claim to] 'love' them."

Suggestions for Writing

1 Justify your participation in any "movement." The term need not apply to an organized movement but could describe any purposeful activity in which a significant number of people have participated.
2 Walker says that discovering Martin Luther King, Jr., and his ideals was a significant influence on her development. What similar influence has helped to shape your life?

Getting at the Truth
MARCHETTE CHUTE

Getting Started

With Ideas

The author of this essay is a biographer who specializes in the Elizabethan age. In this selection, she develops a theory about "truth," one that biographers can use in testing the accuracy of their interpretation of historical "facts" (and one which you, incidentally, can probably use in much of your college work—especially in preparing research papers). As you read, pay particular attention to the way she defines *truth* in the first paragraph. Also, note the metaphor she introduces in that paragraph to explain the complexity of the problem; much of the rest of the essay develops the comparison established by that metaphor.

You will find that Chute's essay on a rather complex subject is written in unusually straightforward and simple language. For this reason, the Getting Started With Words and the Exploring Words sections are omitted here.

[1] This is a rather presumptuous title for a biographer to use, since truth is a very large word. In the sense that it means the reality about a human being it is probably impossible for a biographer to achieve. In the sense that it means a reasonable presentation of all the available facts it is more nearly possible, but even this limited goal is harder to reach than it appears to be. A biographer needs to be both humble and cautious when he remembers the nature of the material he is working with, for a historical fact is rather like the flamingo that Alice in Wonderland tried to use as a croquet mallet. As soon as she got its neck nicely straightened out and was ready to hit the ball, it would turn and look at her with a puzzled expression, and any biographer knows that what is called a "fact" has a way of doing the same.

[2] Here is a small example. When I was writing my forthcoming biography, "Ben Jonson of Westminster," I wanted to give a paragraph or two to Sir Philip Sidney, who had a great influence on Jonson. No one thinks of Sidney without thinking of chivalry, and to underline the point I intended to use a story that Sir Fulke Greville told of him. Sidney died of gangrene, from a musket shot that shattered his thigh, and Greville says

---

"Getting at the Truth" appeared in *Saturday Review*, September 19, 1953. Copyright 1953 by *Saturday Review*. Reprinted by permission of *Saturday Review*.

that Sidney failed to put on his leg armor while preparing for battle because the marshal of the camp was not wearing leg armor and Sidney was unwilling to do anything that would give him a special advantage.

[3] The story is so characteristic both of Sidney himself and of the misplaced high-mindedness of late Renaissance chivalry that I wanted to use it, and since Sir Fulke Greville was one of Sidney's closest friends the information seemed to be reliable enough. But it is always well to check each piece of information as thoroughly as possible and so I consulted another account of Sidney written by a contemporary, this time a doctor who knew the family fairly well. The doctor, Thomas Moffet, mentioned the episode but he said that Sidney left off his leg armor because he was in a hurry.

[4] The information was beginning to twist in my hand and could no longer be trusted. So I consulted still another contemporary who had mentioned the episode, to see which of the two he agreed with. This was Sir John Smythe, a military expert who brought out his book a few years after Sidney's death. Sir John was an old-fashioned conservative who advocated the use of heavy armor even on horseback, and he deplored the current craze for leaving off leg protection, "the imitating of which . . . cost that noble and worthy gentleman Sir Philip Sidney his life."

[5] So here I was with three entirely different reasons why Sidney left off his leg armor, all advanced by careful writers who were contemporaries of his. The flamingo had a legitimate reason for looking around with a puzzled expression.

[6] The only thing to do in a case like this is to examine the point of view of the three men who are supplying the conflicting evidence. Sir Fulke Greville was trying to prove a thesis: that his beloved friend had an extremely chivalric nature. Sir John Smythe also was trying to prove a thesis: that the advocates of light arming followed a theory that could lead to disaster. Only the doctor, Thomas Moffet, was not trying to prove a thesis. He was not using his own explanation to reinforce some point he wanted to make. He did not want anything except to set down on paper what he believed to be the facts; and since we do not have Sidney's own explanation of why he did not put on leg armor, the chances are that Dr. Moffet is the safest man to trust.

[7] For Moffet was without desire. Nothing can so quickly blur and distort the facts as desire—the wish to use the facts for some purpose of your own—and nothing can so surely destroy the truth. As soon as the witness wants to prove something he is no longer impartial and his evidence is no longer to be trusted.

[8] The only safe way to study contemporary testimony is to bear constantly in mind this possibility of prejudice and to put almost as much attention on the writer himself as on what he has written. For instance, Sir Anthony Weldon's description of the Court of King James is lively enough and often used as source material; but a note from the publisher admits

that the pamphlet was issued as a warning to anyone who wished to "side with this bloody house" of Stuart. The publisher, at any rate, did not consider Weldon an impartial witness. At about the same time Arthur Wilson published his history of Great Britain, which contained an irresistibly vivid account of the agonized death of the Countess of Somerset. Wilson sounds reasonably impartial; but his patron was the Earl of Essex, who had good reason to hate that particular countess, and there is evidence that he invented the whole scene to gratify his patron.

[9] Sometimes a writer will contradict what he has already written, and in that case the only thing to do is to investigate what has changed his point of view. For instance, in 1608 Captain John Smith issued a description of his capture by Powhatan, and he made it clear that the Indian chief had treated him with unwavering courtesy and hospitality. In 1624 the story was repeated in Smith's "General History of Virginia," but the writer's circumstances had changed. Smith needed money, "having a prince's mind imprisoned in a poor man's purse," and he wanted the book to be profitable. Powhatan's daughter, the princess Pocahontas, had recently been in the news, for her visit to England had aroused a great deal of interest among the sort of people that Smith hoped would buy his book. So Smith supplied a new version of the story, in which the once-hospitable Powhatan would have permitted the hero's brains to be dashed out if Pocahontas had not saved his life. It was the second story that achieved fame, and of course it may have been true. But it is impossible to trust it because the desire of the writer is so obviously involved; as Smith said in his prospectus, he needed money and hoped that the book would give "satisfaction."

[10] It might seem that there was an easy way for a biographer to avoid the use of this kind of prejudiced testimony. All he has to do is to construct his biography from evidence that cannot be tampered with—from parish records, legal documents, bills, accounts, court records, and so on. Out of these solid gray blocks of impersonal evidence it should surely be possible to construct a road that will lead straight to the truth and that will never bend itself to the misleading curve of personal desire.

[11] This might be so if the only problem involved were the reliability of the material. But there is another kind of desire that is much more subtle, much more pervasive, and much more dangerous than the occasional distortions of fact that contemporary writers may have permitted themselves to make; and this kind of desire can destroy the truth of a biography even if every individual fact in it is as solid and as uncompromising as rock. Even if the road is built of the best and most reliable materials it can still curve away from the truth because of this other desire that threatens it: the desire of the biographer himself.

[12] A biographer is not a court record or a legal document. He is a human being, writing about another human being, and his own temperament, his own point of view, and his own frame of reference are unconsciously imposed upon the man he is writing about. Even if the biographer

is free from Captain Smith's temptation—the need for making money—and wants to write nothing but the literal truth, he is still handicapped by the fact that there is no such thing as a completely objective human being.

[13] An illustration of what can happen if the point of view is sufficiently strong is the curious conclusion that the nineteenth-century biographers reached about William Shakespeare. Shakespeare joined a company of London actors in 1594, was listed as an actor in 1598 and 1603, and was still listed as one of the "men actors" in the company in 1609. Shortly before he joined this company Shakespeare dedicated two narrative poems to the Earl of Southampton, and several years after Shakespeare died his collected plays were dedicated to the Earl of Pembroke. This was his only relationship with either of the two noblemen, and there is nothing to connect him with them during the fifteen years in which he belonged to the same acting company and during which he wrote nearly all his plays.

[14] But here the desire of the biographers entered in. They had been reared in the strict code of nineteenth-century gentility and they accepted two ideas without question. One was that there are few things more important than an English lord; the other was that there are few things less important than a mere actor. They already knew the undeniable fact that Shakespeare was one of the greatest men who ever lived; and while they could not go quite so far as to claim him as an actual member of the nobility, it was clear to them that he must have been the treasured friend of both the Earl of Southampton and the Earl of Pembroke and that he must have written his plays either while basking in their exalted company or while he was roaming the green countryside by the waters of the river Avon. (It is another basic conviction of the English gentleman that there is nothing so inspiring as nature.) The notion that Shakespeare had spent all these years as the working member of a company of London actors was so abhorrent that it was never seriously considered. It could not be so; therefore it was not.

[15] These biographers did their work well. When New South Wales built its beautiful memorial library to Shakespeare, it was the coat of arms of the Earl of Southampton that alternated with that of royalty in dignified splendor over the bookshelves. Shakespeare had been re-created in the image of desire, and desire will always ignore whatever is not relevant to its purpose. Because the English gentlemen did not like Shakespeare's background it was explained away as though it had never existed, and Shakespeare ceased to be an actor because so lowly a trade was not suited to so great a man.

[16] All this is not to say that a biography should be lacking in a point of view. If it does not have a point of view it will be nothing more than a kind of expanded article for an encyclopedia—a string of facts arranged in chronological order with no claim to being a real biography at all. A biography must have a point of view and it must have a frame of ref-

erence. But it should be a point of view and a frame of reference implicit in the material itself and not imposed upon it.

[17] It might seem that the ideal biographical system, if it could be achieved, would be to go through the years of research without feeling any kind of emotion. The biographer would be a kind of fact-finding machine and then suddenly, after his years of research, a kind of total vision would fall upon him and he would transcribe it in his best and most persuasive English for a waiting public. But research is fortunately not done by machinery, nor are visions likely to descend in that helpful manner. They are the product not only of many facts but also of much thinking, and it is only when the biographer begins to get emotional in his thinking that he ought to beware.

[18] It is easy enough to make good resolutions in advance, but a biographer cannot altogether control his sense of excitement when the climax of his years of research draws near and he begins to see the pieces fall into place. Almost without his volition, A, B, and D fit together and start to form a pattern, and it is almost impossible for the biographer not to start searching for C. Something turns up that looks remarkably like C, and with a little trimming of the edges and the ignoring of one very slight discrepancy it will fill the place allotted for C magnificently.

[19] It is at this point that the biographer ought to take a deep breath and sit on his hands until he has had time to calm down. He has no real, fundamental reason to believe that his discovery is C, except for the fact that he wants it to be. He is like a man looking for a missing piece in a difficult jigsaw puzzle, who has found one so nearly the right shape that he cannot resist the desire to jam it into place.

[20] If the biographer had refused to be tempted by his supposed discovery of C and had gone on with his research, he might have found not only the connecting, illuminating fact he needed but much more besides. He is not going to look for it now. Desire has blocked the way. And by so much his biography will fall short of what might have been the truth.

[21] It would not be accurate to say that a biographer should be wholly lacking in desire. Curiosity is a form of desire. So is the final wish to get the material down on paper in a form that will be fair to the reader's interest and worthy of the subject. But a subconscious desire to push the facts around is one of the most dangerous things a biographer can encounter, and all the more dangerous because it is so difficult to know when he is encountering it.

[22] The reason Alice had so much trouble with her flamingo is that the average flamingo does not wish to be used as a croquet mallet. It has other purposes in view. The same thing is true of a fact, which can be just as self-willed as a flamingo and has its own kind of stubborn integrity. To try to force a series of facts into a previously desired arrangement is a form of misuse to which no self-respecting fact will willingly submit itself. The best and only way to treat it is to leave it alone and be willing to follow where it leads, rather than to press your own wishes upon it.

[23] To put the whole thing into a single sentence: you will never succeed in getting at the truth if you think you know, ahead of time, what the truth ought to be.

Questions on Meaning

1 According to Chute, what kind of "desire" should a biographer guard against? What kinds of "desire" should be considered legitimate, even helpful?

2 In your own words, distinguish between the two kinds of "truth" Chute mentions. Which of the two does the tests she recommends for biographers lead to?

3 What is the thesis of the essay? Where is it stated explicitly?

Questions on Style and Structure

1 How effective is the reference in the first paragraph to the flamingo in Lewis Carroll's work? Where else in the essay does the author refer to the flamingo?

2 Chute uses the same technique to achieve emphasis in each of the following sentences. What is this technique?

   a Nothing can so quickly blur and distort the facts as desire—the wish to use the facts for some purpose of your own—and nothing can so surely destroy the truth. (paragraph 7)

   b As soon as the witness wants to prove something he is no longer impartial and his evidence is no longer to be trusted. (paragraph 7)

   c But there is another kind of desire that is much more subtle, much more pervasive, and much more dangerous than the occasional distortions of fact that contemporary writers may have permitted themselves to make. . . . (paragraph 11)

   d He is a human being, writing about another human being, and his own temperament, his own point of view, and his own frame of reference are unconsciously imposed upon the man he is writing about. (paragraph 12)

3 Paragraph 9 is a carefully unified paragraph from the opening sentence (which serves as a topic statement) to the final sentence. Which other paragraphs do you find striking for their unity? Are there any paragraphs that could be combined?

4 Chute, like McGinley, uses figurative language in her writing. How are the following passages particularly appropriate and effective?

a Out of these solid gray blocks of impersonal evidence it should surely be possible to construct a road that will lead straight to the truth and that will never bend itself to the misleading curve of personal desire. (paragraph 10)

b ... and this kind of desire can destroy the truth of a biography even if every individual fact in it is as solid and uncompromising as rock. (paragraph 11)

c He is like a man looking for a missing piece in a difficult jigsaw puzzle, who has found one so nearly the right shape that he cannot resist the desire to jam it into place. (paragraph 19)

5 What device does the author use to make paragraph 19 coherent? In which other paragraphs does she use the same device?

6 What technique does Chute use to conclude the essay? Should she have combined the last two paragraphs?

Suggestions for Writing

1 Write a paper explaining difficulties you have had "getting at the truth" about something. How "flamingo-like" were the facts? What methods did you use in interpreting them? How satisfied were you with the results?

2 Read several newspaper or magazine accounts of the same event or incident. Then, in an essay, explain any differences you find. Pay particular attention to the reporter's choice of words. Do any of the accounts use words that reveal bias or that could create bias?

The Language of Statesmen
LOUIS J. HALLE

Getting Started

With Ideas

Although the words *statesman* and *politician* could be used to refer to the same person, most people associate different qualities with the two terms. In what sense might the language of someone you refer to as a "statesman" be different from that of a person you describe as a "politician"? As you read Halle's essay, consider whether his concept of a "statesman" is similar to your own, and note what he says characterizes the language of this kind of political leader.

With Words

1 prosaic (1)—associate it with *prose*.
2 incantation (4)—this word, which is derived from the Latin word for "sing," is related to *chant* and *enchant*.
3 magnanimous (11)—from the Latin words for "great" and for "spirit."
4 aboriginal (13)—from the Latin word meaning "from the beginning."
5 epitomized (13)—associate this word, which is from the Greek word meaning "to cut short," with *epitome*.

[1] If we have in our minds a sharper distinction between poetry and prose than exists in fact, it is because we are misled by the difference between the appearance on paper of what is presented as the one and what as the other. At its best, prose has always verged on poetry, and in our own day especially, what is presented as poetry may be utterly prosaic. A composition that appears as prose may, in fact, represent poetry better than another that appears as poetry. No one questions that the following is poetry, although cast in the typographic form of prose:

> Yea, though I walk through the valley of the shadow of death, I will fear no evil: for thou art with me; thy rod and thy staff they comfort me. . . .

"The Language of Statesmen" appeared in *Saturday Review,* October 16, 1971. Copyright 1971 by *Saturday Review*. Reprinted by permission of *Saturday Review*.

THE LANGUAGE OF STATESMEN

If, then, we rid our minds of a categorical distinction based on superficial form only, we are in a position to resolve a common paradox pertaining to the language of statesmanship.

[2] Lincoln's Gettysburg Address is not notable for the substance of what is said in it, which is commonplace. Why, then, should it rank among the greatest utterances of statesmanship? Why, should it remain unforgettable when utterances of other American Presidents, far richer in content, have been quickly forgotten? The answer is that, like the Twenty-third Psalm, it is a poem.

[3] To appreciate this, one must read the Address aloud, even if soundlessly, as an actor reads Shakespeare to himself. The Twenty-third Psalm and the Gettysburg Address are poems not so much on account of any images they contain as on account of their music: their rhythms, their beat, the echo of their phrases, the symmetry of passages that rise, each from the level of its beginning only to return to it again, as a passage in music takes flight from the keynote only to conclude, like a bird, by coming to rest on it again.

[4] The theme of the Address is dedication, the dedication of a national cemetery, and the word "dedicate" is repeated like an incantation, gaining in power and meaning at each repetition.

[5] "The world will little note nor long remember what we say here, but it can never forget what they did here." This has equilibrium as well as rhythm, for it is statement and response.

[6] The large rhythm of the phrases in the Twenty-third Psalm tends to be triple:

> He maketh me to lie down in green pastures.
> He leadeth me beside the still waters.
> He restoreth my soul.

And again:

> Thou preparest a table before me in the presence of mine enemies.
> Thou anointest my head with oil.
> My cup runneth over.

The second set of diminishing phrases echoes the first. In the Gettysburg Address the rhythm is primarily duple, secondarily triple, the two rhythms setting each other off, as in so much of Bach's music.

[7] Certainly Lincoln was not consciously practicing the principles of poetics when he composed what he referred to as "a few appropriate remarks." Presumably, because his mind had been formed so largely on the King James Bible, his language fell into certain rhythms naturally. So one who does nothing but read sonnets will at last find himself speaking, naturally and unconsciously, in iambic pentameters.

[8] Evidence of this tendency can be found in Lincoln's private letters, which have, in greater or lesser degree, the same elements of poetry as his public utterances. His letter of August 22, 1862, to Horace

Greeley is an example. After its opening statement ("I have just read yours of the 19th, addressed to myself through the New York 'Tribune.' "), it goes on:

> If there be in it any statements or assumptions of fact which I may know to be erroneous, I do not, now and here, controvert them. If there be in it any inferences which I may believe to be falsely drawn, I do not, now and here, argue against them. If there be perceptible in it an impatient and dictatorial tone, I waive it in deference to an old friend whose heart I have always supposed to be right.

The rest of the letter (which at one point falls into a rhyme in keeping with the context) has the same rhythmical quality, the same beat. The style was the man, and therefore it was consistent throughout his writings.

[9] Here is Walter Pater's famous description of Leonardo's *Mona Lisa:*

> She is older than the rocks among which she sits; like the vampire, she has been dead many times, and learned the secrets of the grave; and has been a diver in deep seas, and keeps their fallen day about her; and trafficked for strange webs with Eastern merchants: and, as Leda, was the mother of Helen of Troy, and, as Saint Anne, the mother of Mary; and all this has been to her but as the sound of lyres and flutes, and lives only in the delicacy with which it has moulded the changing lineaments, and tinged the eyelids and the hands.

William Butler Yeats, in his *Oxford Book of Modern Verse,* presents this as a poem, having broken it up into lines of varying length for the purpose.

[10] The question arises whether the elements of poetry to which I have drawn attention have any fundamental importance, whether they are more than the mere ornamentation of language, the serious purpose of which is not to produce pleasant sounds but to say something.

[11] Would it not be extraordinary if the judgment of the centuries on what constituted great utterance had consistently gone to mere ornament? Would it not be extraordinary if this judgment were wrong in preferring the Gettysburg Address, as empty of substance as it is, to the forgotten address of February 22, 1947, in which Secretary of State Marshall, aware that the United States faced one of the greatest crises in world history, summoned the American people to adopt a higher standpoint and a more magnanimous attitude than in the past, and on that basis at last to shoulder their worldwide responsibilities—but summoned them to do this in language that would hardly have served for an argument in favor of raising the postman's salary? Surely such judgment is not wrong, and poetry is not something that is merely added to the substance of language like the icing on a cake.

[12] Having argued that what passes for prose may be poetry, I

am tempted to make the further argument that language itself is poetry. At least there is a sense in which it is. Again I go to music for an analogy. The difference between noise, on the one hand, and musical tone, on the other, is that the former represents chaos and the latter order. Noise represents chaos because there is no regularity in the frequency of its vibrations, while musical tone represents order because its vibrations are rhythmical, occurring at fixed intervals. Language is logic, and logic, too, represents order as opposed to chaos. So language as logic is related to sound as music. Each is confined by rule, whether the rule of fixed intervals or the rule of logical sequence.

[13] My premise is that all mankind in its present condition, its evolution uncompleted, is suspended between the aboriginal chaos, above which it has risen some way, and a higher order of which it still perceives only glimmers. Each one of us, at least with part of his being, aspires to the higher order and is drawn to it. Therefore, when we organize ourselves into societies, it is not only for the sake of greater physical security and economic advantage; it is also for the sake of realizing a nobler life than is possible for wild animals rooting in the woods. The Athenians of the fifth century B.C. did not give their devotion to Athens merely because it sheltered them behind a stone wall and allowed them to make a living. They did so as well—indeed they did so primarily—because it represented the order epitomized in the Parthenon, in the statues of Phidias, and in the religious dramas performed at the foot of the Acropolis. Certainly the patriotism that caused Americans to break with the England of George III was based on the vision of a higher life that seemed already on the way to realization in our new national society.

[14] If this is so, the political leadership is failing in its role if it confines itself to the problems of physical security and the economy. Abraham Lincoln, even while exercising the leadership of one side in a civil war that was being fought with savage partisanship, rose above the partisanship to the vision of a national union, embracing both sides alike, that had to redeem a sordid past, the guilt of which both shared, and thereby to attain a state of grace. All this he made explicit, while the war was still being fought, in the poem that we know as his Second Inaugural Address. With little change, parts of it might be included among the Psalms.

[15] In the present stage of our development, I say, we men are uneasily suspended between a sordid chaos and the sublime order of which we have intimations. It is the function of poets—as of painters, sculptors, and musicians—to catch these intimations and enshrine them for us in the forms of language or of the graphic arts. This is also the function of political leadership at the highest level, a function that can be discharged only in what an early poet called "wingéd words."

[16] The elements of a higher order, enshrined in language by our greatest leaders, are not represented only by such attitudes as those of compassion and magnanimity that we may think of as constituting the content of the Second Inaugural Address. They are also represented by the

rhythmic forms into which inspired language falls, by the shapes its phrases take, and by the harmony of its sounds. At the highest level, then, as perhaps at the lowest too, thought and language are inseparable. The greatest political leadership has always expressed itself in poetry—under whatever guise. That is why the Gettysburg Address, while saying so little, still says so much.

Questions on Meaning

1 Look up the words *statesman* and *politician* in your dictionary. You will probably find more than one meaning listed for each word. Does any one of the meanings listed for *statesman* apply especially to Halle's use of the word or to the associations you have with it?

2 What false distinction does Halle think most people make between poetry and prose? In what sense does he consider the language of statesmen poetic? In what sense does he find all language poetic?

3 What does Halle say people are looking for when they band together in societies? What, then, is the primary responsibility of a political leader? How can the use of appropriate language by a "statesman" help him fulfill this responsibility?

4 In your own words, what is the main idea of the essay?

Questions on Style and Structure

1 What is the purpose of the introductory paragraph? Which statement comes closest to being a thesis statement?

2 In paragraph 8, Halle quotes from Lincoln's letter to Horace Greeley and discusses its "rhythmical quality" and "beat." Another way of describing those sentences is to call them "parallel." Where does Halle himself use such sentences?

3 The author tries to distinguish between "poetic" utterances and "prosaic" language. Here is an excerpt from John F. Kennedy's address to the United Nations on September 25, 1961:

Never have the nations of the world had so much to lose or so much to gain. Together we shall save our planet or together we shall perish in its flames. Save it we can, and save it we must, and then shall we earn the eternal thanks of mankind and, as peacemakers, the eternal blessing of God.

Would you characterize this passage as "poetic" or "prosaic"? If it is "poetic," what are the elements that make it so?

4 Some of Halle's sentences are complex in their structure. Study the example below, and comment on its effectiveness:

Abraham Lincoln, even while exercising the leadership of one side in a civil war that was being fought with savage partisanship, rose above the partisanship to the vision of a national union, embracing both sides alike, that had to redeem a sordid past, the guilt of which both shared, and thereby to attain a state of grace. (paragraph 14)

Should the sentence be divided into shorter ones? Why or why not?

5 The following sentence, which Halle quotes from the Gettysburg Address, can be labeled a balanced sentence:

The world will little note nor long remember what we say here, but it can never forget what they did here.

Note that Lincoln contrasts two ideas in similar grammatical constructions, just as Alexander Pope does in his famous "To err is human, to forgive, divine." Compose a few balanced sentences of your own.

6 Compare the following pairs of sentences (the first version of each is Halle's). Which version in each pair do you prefer? Why?

a The answer is that, like the Twenty-third Psalm, it is a poem. (paragraph 2)

The answer is that it is a poem like the Twenty-third Psalm.

b Evidence of this tendency can be found in Lincoln's private letters, which have, in greater or lesser degree, the same elements of poetry as his public utterances. (paragraph 8)

Evidence of this tendency can be found in Lincoln's private letters, which have the same elements of poetry as his public utterances, in greater or lesser degree.

c Each one of us, at least with part of his being, aspires to the higher order and is drawn to it. (paragraph 13)

Each one of us aspires to the higher order and is drawn to it, at least with part of his being.

7 How effectively does the author conclude his essay?

Exploring Words

1 *prosaic.* Which one of the definitions listed in your dictionary applies to Halle's use of this word? Try writing a sentence using the word in another sense.

2 *incantation.* Again, you will probably find more than one meaning listed in your dictionary. Does Halle's usage fit any of these meanings, or is he using the word in a metaphorical sense that your dictionary does not include?

3 *magnanimous.* What is the most recent *magnanimous* act you have observed, read about, or engaged in?

4 *aboriginal.* After consulting your dictionary, write a sentence explaining the relationship of *aboriginal* to *aborigine* (you have probably heard that word used in reference to certain people living in Australia).

ESSAYS CHIEFLY PERSUASIVE

5 *epitomized.* Write a sentence using *epitome* in one of the senses that your dictionary mentions for this word.

Suggestions for Writing

1 Halle concludes his essay by saying that "the Gettysburg Address, while saying so little, still says so much." Reprinted here is the complete address. Illustrate what Halle means by presenting a close analysis of its stylistic elements. Be sure to read it aloud before you begin writing your first draft.

Four score and seven years ago our fathers brought forth on this continent, a new nation, conceived in Liberty, and dedicated to the proposition that all men are created equal.

Now we are engaged in a great Civil War, testing whether that nation, or any nation so conceived and so dedicated, can long endure. We are met on a great battlefield of that war. We have come to dedicate a portion of that field, as a final resting place for those who here gave their lives that that nation might live. It is altogether fitting and proper that we should do this.

But, in a larger sense, we cannot dedicate—we cannot consecrate—we cannot hallow—this ground. The brave men, living and dead, who struggled here, have consecrated it far above our poor power to add or detract. The world will little note, nor long remember what we say here, but it can never forget what they did here. It is for us the living, rather, to be dedicated here to the unfinished work which they who fought here have thus far so nobly advanced. It is rather for us to be here dedicated to the great task remaining before us—that from these honored dead we take increased devotion to that cause for which they gave the last full measure of devotion—that we here highly resolve that these dead shall not have died in vain—that this nation, under God, shall have a new birth of freedom—and that government of the people, by the people, for the people, shall not perish from the earth.

2 Write a political speech on a specific issue, using the most statesmanlike language you can command.

From
The American Way of Death
JESSICA MITFORD

Getting Started

With Ideas

Beginning with a quotation you may recognize as Biblical, Jessica Mitford establishes both her topic and her point of view toward that topic in the first paragraph of this selection (which is the first chapter of a full-length book). Moreover, in the first two paragraphs, she uses language that prepares the reader for a tone of caustic criticism throughout the work. What words do you find in these paragraphs that establish that tone?

With Words

1 macabre (3)—from the French word meaning "a dance of death."
2 dramaturgic (10)—associate it with *drama*.
3 euphemisms (11)—when you come to this word in Mitford's essay, remember the occupational *euphemisms* you explored in "The Dog Census" (p. 20).
4 ostentatious (16)—the context will help you determine the meaning of this word.

> How long, I would ask, are we to be subjected to the tyranny of custom and undertakers? Truly, it is all vanity and vexation of spirit—a mere mockery of woe, costly to all, far, far beyond its value; and ruinous to many; hateful, and an abomination to all; yet submitted to by all, because none have the moral courage to speak against it and act in defiance of it.
> —Lord Essex

[1] O death, where is thy sting? O grave, where is thy victory? Where, indeed. Many a badly stung survivor, faced with the aftermath of some relative's funeral, has ruefully concluded that the victory has been

Copyright © 1963, by Jessica Mitford. Reprinted by permission of Simon & Schuster, Inc.

won hands down by a funeral establishment—in disastrously unequal battle.

[2] Much has been written of late about the affluent society in which we live, and much fun poked at some of the irrational "status symbols" set out like golden snares to trap the unwary consumer at every turn. Until recently, little has been said about the most irrational and weirdest of the lot, lying in ambush for all of us at the end of the road—the modern American funeral.

[3] If the Dismal Traders (as an eighteenth-century English writer calls them) have traditionally been cast in a comic role in literature, a universally recognized symbol of humor from Shakespeare to Dickens to Evelyn Waugh, they have successfully turned the tables in recent years to perpetrate a huge, macabre and expensive practical joke on the American public. It is not consciously conceived of as a joke, of course; on the contrary, it is hedged with admirably contrived rationalizations.

[4] Gradually, almost imperceptibly, over the years the funeral men have constructed their own grotesque cloud-cuckooland where the trappings of Gracious Living are transformed, as in a nightmare, into the trappings of Gracious Dying. The same familiar Madison Avenue language, with its peculiar adjectival range designed to anesthetize sales resistance to all sorts of products, has seeped into the funeral industry in a new and bizarre guise. The emphasis is on the same desirable qualities that we have all been schooled to look for in our daily search for excellence: comfort, durability, beauty, craftsmanship. The attuned ear will recognize too the convincing quasi-scientific language, so reassuring even if unintelligible.

[5] So that this too, too solid flesh might not melt, we are offered "solid copper—a quality casket which offers superb value to the client seeking long-lasting protection," or "the Colonial Classic Beauty—18 gauge lead coated steel, seamless top, lap-jointed welded body construction." Some are equipped with foam rubber, some with innerspring mattresses. Elgin offers "the revolutionary 'Perfect-Posture' bed." Not every casket need have a silver lining, for one may choose between "more than 60 color matched shades, magnificent and unique masterpieces" by the Cheney casket-lining people. Shrouds no longer exist. Instead, you may patronize a grave-wear couturière who promises "handmade original fashions—styles from the best in life for the last memory—dresses, men's suits, negligees, accessories." For the final, perfect grooming: "Nature-Glo—the ultimate in cosmetic embalming." And, where have we heard that phrase "peace of mind protection" before? No matter. In funeral advertising, it is applied to the Wilbert Burial Vault, with its ⅜-inch precast asphalt inner liner plus extra-thick, reinforced concrete—all this "guaranteed by Good Housekeeping." Here again the Cadillac, status symbol par excellence, appears in all its gleaming glory, this time transformed into a pastel-colored funeral hearse.

[6] You, the potential customer for all this luxury, are unlikely to read the lyrical descriptions quoted above, for they are culled from *Mortuary Management* and *Casket and Sunnyside*, two of the industry's eleven trade magazines. For you there are ads in your daily newspaper, generally found on the obituary page, stressing dignity, refinement, high-caliber professional service and that intangible quality, *sincerity*. The trade advertisements are, however, instructive, because they furnish an important clue to the frame of mind into which the funeral industry has hypnotized itself.

[7] A new mythology, essential to the twentieth-century American funeral rite, has grown up—or rather has been built up step by step—to justify the peculiar customs surrounding the disposal of our dead. And, just as the witch doctor must be convinced of his own infallibility in order to maintain a hold over his clientele, so the funeral industry has had to "sell itself" on its articles of faith in the course of passing them along to the public.

[8] The first of these is the tenet that today's funeral procedures are founded in "American tradition." The story comes to mind of a sign on the freshly sown lawn of a brand-new Midwest college: "There is a tradition on this campus that students never walk on this strip of grass. This tradition goes into effect next Tuesday." The most cursory look at American funerals of past times will establish the parallel. Simplicity to the point of starkness, the plain pine box, the laying out of the dead by friends and family who also bore the coffin to the grave—these were the hallmarks of the traditional funeral until the end of the nineteenth century.

[9] Secondly, there is the myth that the American public is only being given what it wants—an opportunity to keep up with the Joneses to the end. "In keeping with our high standard of living, there should be an equally high standard of dying," says the past president of the Funeral Directors of San Francisco. "The cost of a funeral varies according to individual taste and the niceties of living the family has been accustomed to." Actually, choice doesn't enter the picture for the average individual, faced, generally for the first time, with the necessity of buying a product of which he is totally ignorant, at a moment when he is least in a position to quibble. In point of fact the cost of a funeral almost always varies, not "according to individual taste" but according to what the traffic will bear.

[10] Thirdly, there is an assortment of myths based on half-digested psychiatric theories. The importance of the "memory picture" is stressed—meaning the last glimpse of the deceased in open casket, done up with the latest in embalming techniques and finished off with a dusting of makeup. A newer one, impressively authentic-sounding, is the need for "grief therapy," which is beginning to go over big in mortuary circles. A historian of American funeral directing hints at the grief-therapist idea when speaking of the new role of the undertaker—"the dramaturgic role, in which the undertaker becomes a stage manager to create an appropriate atmosphere and to move the funeral party through a drama in which social

relationships are stressed and an emotional catharsis or release is provided through ceremony."

[11] Lastly, a whole new terminology, as ornately shoddy as the satin rayon casket liner, has been invented by the funeral industry to replace the direct and serviceable vocabulary of former times. Undertaker has been supplanted by "funeral director" or "mortician." (Even the classified section of the telephone directory gives recognition to this; in its pages you will find "Undertakers—see Funeral Directors.") Coffins are "caskets"; hearses are "coaches," or "professional cars"; flowers are "floral tributes"; corpses generally are "loved ones," but mortuary etiquette dictates that a specific corpse be referred to by name only—as, "Mr. Jones"; cremated ashes are "cremains." Euphemisms such as "slumber room," "reposing room," and "calcination—the *kindlier* heat" abound in the funeral business.

[12] If the undertaker is the stage manager of the fabulous production that is the modern American funeral, the stellar role is reserved for the occupant of the open casket. The decor, the stagehands, the supporting cast are all arranged for the most advantageous display of the deceased, without which the rest of the paraphernalia would lose its point—*Hamlet* without the Prince of Denmark. It is to this end that a fantastic array of costly merchandise and services is pyramided to dazzle the mourners and facilitate the plunder of the next of kin.

[13] Grief therapy, anyone? But it's going to come high. According to the funeral industry's own figures, the *average* undertaker's bill in 1961 was $708 for casket and "services," to which must be added the cost of a burial vault, flowers, clothing, clergy and musician's honorarium, and cemetery charges. When these costs are added to the undertaker's bill, the total average cost for an adult's funeral is, as we shall see, closer to $1,450.

[14] The question naturally arises, *is* this what most people want for themselves and their families? For several reasons, this has been a hard one to answer until recently. It is a subject seldom discussed. Those who have never had to arrange for a funeral frequently shy away from its implications, preferring to take comfort in the thought that sufficient unto the day is the evil thereof. Those who have acquired personal and painful knowledge of the subject would often rather forget about it. Pioneering "Funeral Societies" or "Memorial Associations," dedicated to the principle of dignified funerals at reasonable cost, have existed in a number of communities throughout the country, but their membership has been limited for the most part to the more sophisticated element in the population—university people, liberal intellectuals—and those who, like doctors and lawyers, come up against problems in arranging funerals for their clients.

[15] Some indication of the pent-up resentment felt by vast numbers of people against the funeral interests was furnished by the astonishing response to an article by Roul Tunley, titled "Can You Afford to

Die?" in *The Saturday Evening Post* of June 17, 1961. As though a dike had burst, letters poured in from every part of the country to the *Post*, to the funeral societies, to local newspapers. They came from clergymen, professional people, old-age pensioners, trade unionists. Three months after the article appeared, an estimated six thousand had taken pen in hand to comment on some phase of the high cost of dying. Many recounted their own bitter experiences at the hands of funeral directors; hundreds asked for advice on how to establish a consumer organization in communities where none exists; others sought information about pre-need plans. The membership of the funeral societies skyrocketed. The funeral industry, finding itself in the glare of public spotlight, has begun to engage in serious debate about its own future course—as well it might.

[16] Is the funeral inflation bubble ripe for bursting? A few years ago, the United States public suddenly rebelled against the trend in the auto industry towards ever more showy cars, with their ostentatious and nonfunctional fins, and a demand was created for compact cars patterned after European models. The all-powerful auto industry, accustomed to *telling* the customer what sort of car he wanted, was suddenly forced to *listen* for a change. Overnight, the little cars became for millions a new kind of status symbol. Could it be that the same cycle is working itself out in the attitude towards the final return of dust to dust, that the American public is becoming sickened by ever more ornate and costly funerals, and that a status symbol of the future may indeed be the simplest kind of "funeral without fins"?

Questions on Meaning

1 In paragraph 11, Mitford speaks of a "whole new terminology" that funeral industry people have recently developed. What purposes does this new terminology serve? In what ways do the new terms she mentions differ from their earlier counterparts?

2 What differences does Mitford point out between the tone of advertisements in funeral industry trade magazines and that of advertisements intended for the general public? How does she account for these differences?

3 According to Mitford, what basic American attitudes or drives are funeral people taking advantage of?

4 What does Mitford think is the fundamental "funeral problem" in the United States today? What does she suggest will probably be the ultimate solution to the problem?

5 Are questions 1 through 4 of this section answered explicitly or by implication in the selection?

ESSAYS CHIEFLY PERSUASIVE

Questions on Style and Structure

1 Analyze carefully the tone that Mitford achieves throughout this essay, noting especially the following words and phrases: "Where, indeed" (paragraph 1); "cloud-cuckooland" (paragraph 4); "couturière" (paragraph 5); "lyrical" (paragraph 6); "done up" (paragraph 10); "finished off" (paragraph 10); "go over big" (paragraph 10); "Grief therapy, anyone?" (paragraph 13); "to come high" (paragraph 13). Why is Mitford's tone appropriate to her purpose? How do her tone and purpose differ from those of Krutch in "The Sloburbs" (p. 249)?

2 The following passages allude to the Bible and Shakespeare's *Hamlet*. Look up these passages, and study the contexts in which they appear. How effectively does Mitford handle these allusions?

O Death, where is thy sting? O grave, where is thy victory? (paragraph 1) [1 Cor. 15:55]

So that this too, too solid flesh might not melt. . . ." (paragraph 5) [The line in this Shakespearean play reads "Oh that this too, too solid flesh would melt." *Hamlet,* act 1, sc. 2, line 129]

". . . sufficient unto the day is the evil thereof." (paragraph 14) [Matt. 6:34]

3 In paragraph 12, why is the author's use of such words as *stagehands* and her reference to *Hamlet* justified?

4 In paragraph 11, Mitford satirizes the euphemisms that have "been invented by the funeral industry to replace the direct and serviceable vocabulary of former times." Later, in paragraph 15, she uses the phrase "pre-need plans." Would you consider the phrase another euphemism?

5 Did you find the concluding paragraph of this selection effective? Why is "funeral without fins" an effective or ineffective phrase?

Exploring Words

1 *macabre.* You will probably find synonyms for *macabre* listed in your dictionary. Why do you suppose Mitford chose *macabre* for her sentence instead of one of those synonyms?

2 *dramaturgic.* In what other occupations (besides the theater) do people assume *dramaturgic* roles?

3 *euphemisms.* Mitford implies that undertakers use *euphemisms* for several reasons. What are they?

4 *ostentatious.* After consulting your dictionary, write a sentence using *ostentatious* appropriately.

FROM *THE AMERICAN WAY OF DEATH*

Suggestions for Writing

1 Try writing a satirical criticism of a practice you think is both foolish and wrong. Be sure that your tone is consistent throughout (although you need not be humorous in every paragraph any more than Mitford is) and that you establish your purpose early in the paper.

2 Or you may be in the mood for serious reflection on the subject of this piece—death. You could, for example, express your thoughts about facing your own death or that of someone close to you, or you could describe the kind of funeral and funeral-related activities you would prefer for yourself or for someone you love.

3 Discuss a little-known industry or activity about which you have some knowledge.

4 Analyze any other symbol-laden ritual in America (for example, weddings).

Why the Devil Don't You Teach Freshmen to Write?
EDWIN R. CLAPP

Getting Started

With Ideas

Has anyone ever asked you why you can't write or implied that you can't? Both professional educators and concerned observers of the educational scene are asking the question Professor Clapp raises here. In fact, some are saying the problem he addresses has reached the proportions of a national scandal. Before you read the article, think a bit about your own experiences with writing. What was emphasized in your precollege composition instruction? What attitudes have college instructors in courses other than composition taken toward your writing? You will find that Clapp is concerned with these matters as well as with the problem of what should be done in freshman composition classes. See if your own experiences support what he says.

With Words

1 calumny (3)—from the Latin word meaning "to deceive."
2 inextricably (5)—the root of this word means "stricken" (a form of *strike*), and you already know the prefixes *in-* and *ex-*.
3 anomalies (7)—the context will be helpful here.
4 taxonomy (8)—from the Greek root *tax,* meaning "arrangement."
5 dichotomy (11)—the Greek prefix *dich-* means "in two" or "apart," and the Greek word *temnein* means "to cut."
6 heterogeneous (12)—the Greek prefix *hetere-* (or *hetero-*) means "different."
7 panacea (14)—from the Greek prefix meaning "all" and a Greek word meaning "to heal."
8 platitudinous (16)—a *platitude* is a saying that has become an "old chestnut."
9 utopian (16)—the source of this word is the title of a sixteenth-century prose narrative by Thomas More, a work that described an imaginary and ideal country.

"Why the Devil Don't You Teach Freshmen to Write?" appeared in *Saturday Review,* February 20, 1965. Copyright 1965 by *Saturday Review.* Reprinted by permission of *Saturday Review.*

10. microcosm, macrocosm (18)—from Greek prefixes meaning "small" and "large" and a Greek word meaning "world." (You probably also know the English word *cosmos*.)

---

[1] Despite all the outcry and accusation in recent years, despite the growing mass and competence of professional assaults upon the problem, it seems that Johnny still "can't write." One reason is, I think, a misunderstanding, both lay and learned, of what writing means. When the man next to me in the Chicago plane discovers that I teach English, he mumbles something about watching his grammar. When Dr. Stackblower, associate professor of anthropology, bears down on me roaring, "Why the devil don't you teach the freshmen to write?" I know that he has just read some paper rich in orthographical mayhem. If Johnny makes a gross blunder in usage or spelling, both businessman and academic are shocked by his "English." But if Johnny scrambles the logic of his argument, or drifts into irrelevance, or dishes out bland generalizations innocent of support, or winds up in Timbuktu when he set out for Oshkosh—the man in the plane (or the street) is unlikely to be aware of error. And if Dr. Stackblower is, he will charge it to incompetence in anthropology. That "English" is implicated never crosses either of their minds.

[2] I think we need to be clearer about what writing involves, what we want of Johnny, and what in practice we are willing to do to get it. Though "Johnny" may stand for any of his avatars from the elementary to the graduate school, let our Johnny be a college undergraduate, while "we" are all those charged with his education. In this context, let us look at him and at writing and at ourselves.

[3] Writing has two dimensions: literacy and competence. Literacy involves what is often called "correctness" or "mechanics"—the ability to spell, to punctuate, to follow accepted conventions of grammar and usage, to employ everyday words in their common meanings. Such ability is certainly necessary. Writing in which it is lacking is at best irritating and distracting, at worst incomprehensible. As a description of writing, however, literacy is incomplete, external, and negative; it represents the capacity not to make mistakes. But it is an easy definition. The capacity it represents is clearly visible within the framework of the sentence. It lends itself to measure. Misspellings and grammatical errors can be counted. Tests based upon them can be devised and used as indices of verbal skill. Spelling above all—both to Professor Stackblower and the man in the plane for Chicago—is the great sign and symbol of the command of language. Be thou as chaste as ice, as pure as snow—and misspell "cat"—thou shalt not escape calumny. By and large the great world, lay and learned, equates "good English" with literacy, and particularly with spelling.

[4] In contrast with literacy, competence means the ability to control language as the vehicle of thought and feeling, to recognize a subject and its boundaries, to order and support ideas, to conduct an argument or define a quality, to distinguish what is relevant from what is not, to express with precision differences of mood and force and meaning. Usually it is consistent with and inclusive of literacy as a substructure above and beyond which it grows, but this is not always true. Otherwise competent writers may, for instance, spell badly. Competence is manifested in the substance, organization, and texture of discourse in its larger units as well as in the sentence. Subtler and more complex than literacy, it is not hard to recognize but does not lend itself to counting. And when recognized, competence may by its very nature be thought of less as mastery of expression than as an aspect of the thing expressed. Thus it may go undervalued or even unnoted when Johnny's writing is assessed. And yet, competence—far more than literacy—is the true goal, both for Johnny and for all of us.

[5] If we fret over Johnny's English, we must be clear what we are asking of him. We have confused literacy and competence, as definitions of ability and as desired ends. We have demanded literacy, when we *ought* to demand competence—not as a flat alternative, which it is not, but as an ability of greater value that in the fullness of its attainment will bring literacy with it, if only as a kind of by-product. Spelling we must make a special case. It is as much a matter of social decorum as an essential of communication; and when a genuine problem, it must be attacked as a distinctive one, often in terms of both psychology and language. (I hope not to be misunderstood; I want Johnny to spell. But spelling has come to occupy a place in the public mind out of all proportion to its significance, and thus to obscure more important issues.) We can have more of competence and literacy (*and* better spelling) than we now have; we can have it tomorrow in the college and the day after in the schools, but only at the price of looking harder at ourselves as well as at Johnny. We shall need more dollars in some places, and—as competence in writing is inextricably involved with competence in reading, and this with thought—perhaps more sweat and tears. But to begin with, more light.

[6] *Why* is the ability to write well seemingly attained so seldom, so incompletely, and with such difficulty? A full answer would require a book. It would involve the nature of language and our understanding of language, the character of American society and education, and the whole fabric of the modern world—all interwoven and all changing. I can attempt here only a sketch of some chapters.

[7] First, Johnny's failures are sometimes more apparent than real; or, more accurately, they are of differing orders of magnitude. Demanding literacy as we do, we may overlook genuine if partial competence. I have struggled with more than one Johnny whose knowledge and insight

were matched by his command of expression in everything save spelling, but whose feats in this department so occupied the foreground of attention as to obscure his real merits. Professor Stackblower naturally writes him down as another example of the inadequacies of the English Department. But to make due allowance for such anomalies is no more than to nibble off an edge of the problem.

[8] Second, the teaching of "English," particularly but not only in the elementary and secondary school, has often meant a formally conceived literacy of labels and categories abstracted from the communicative and expressive functions of language, a literacy operating with equally external tools and devices—rote memory, workbooks, rigid and sometimes quite wrong grammatical dicta divorced from the plain facts of usage, the taxonomy of discourse. There is no doubt an element of necessity in all this. Much remains to be learned about the teaching of the language skills. But much is a product of confused aims, ignorance, and acceptance of the easy way, and for this the institution that educates the teacher bears a substantial responsibility.

[9] Third, in the schools the basic relationships (differences as well as similarities) between spoken and written language, reading and writing, bread-and-butter prose and imaginative literature, and their implications for teaching have remained relatively undeveloped. In particular, the coupled reading and writing of expository prose, the prose of thought, seems to have been neglected; and this coupling is crucial for competence. There are all sorts of reasons: the overloaded teacher struggling with too many and too large classes (one place where more dollars are needed), the resultant impossibility of an adequate amount of critical attention to an adequate amount of student writing, the nice questions of the kinds of reading appropriate to the several stages of Johnny's development and of how best to explore with him the processes of the mind expressed in an ordered world of prose—plus the brute fact that thought is hard.

[10] Fourth, the universality of English as the language of all the disciplines has had mixed consequences for the teaching and learning of reading and writing. Successful expression everywhere involves the same elements: precision, clarity, order, relevance. But this very commonalty, this fact that he takes the vehicle of language for granted, gives the teacher of biology or history or economics an option between meaningful exploitation of reading and writing in *his* area and buck passing, between opportunity and escape. He may consider English, construed as literacy, strictly the business of the English teacher, and ignore the shared world of competence. With honorable exceptions, lip service, if that, has for the most part been given the idea that every teacher has a responsibility for how his students write; and the idea that he has a vested interest, let alone a responsibility, in how they read has not even been suggested—even though to distinguish reading and writing from thinking and knowing is almost an exercise in tautology. Nor does this situation represent merely

inertia or indifference, or one more expression of that academic tribalism to which the departmentalization of learning gives rise—though all these may contribute.

[11] A fifth consideration, closely related to the last but more basic, is the nature of language itself. If "all art constantly aspires to the condition of music," because in music content and form are one, in language the separation of the thing said from the way of saying, the what from the how, is in some partial and superficial sense possible. Thus "English" comes to be considered the garment of thought, discrete from the substance, which alone is biology or history or economics. One can detach the conventions, the mechanics, the "rules" of punctuation, grammar, usage (and of course spelling!) from fact and idea, keep the latter for oneself and relegate the former to the exclusive custody of the English teacher, who thus becomes essentially a glorified proofreader. This is no fancy. I have been approached more than once by a professor of, let us say, engineering, who wanted me to find him a colleague to attend to the English of a report writing course while *his* staff took care of the engineering. Now, it is certainly true that the instructor in English is not *per se* qualified in engineering. It is just as true that the engineer really qualified as engineer ought also to be qualified in the world of discourse that engineering shares. We have returned to, perhaps in part accounted for, the dichotomy between literacy and competence. If the teacher of whatever subject thinks of English as only literacy, incidental or alien to the subject itself, the student is to be forgiven if *he* comes to regard English as a garb to be put on primarily or exclusively for the eccentrics who teach it. And his indignation is to be understood, if not pardoned, when he is confronted by the instructor in biology or history or economics or engineering who insists that thought and expression are facets of the same thing and that the student is accountable to him for both. Fortunately, this instructor is as little a figure of fiction as Professor Stackblower; unfortunately, there are not so many of him.

[12] A last reason for Johnny's parlous condition is that in school and out "good English," whether construed as literacy or competence, is in our time and society an artefact and a minority attainment. Very likely *good* English or French or Greek has always been a mark of education. For language itself is speech and usage, but popular and educated speech and usage are not identical, and *written* language (that which is read and composed to be read) is not identical with either, although closer to and largely governed by the standards of the latter. We expect educated speech to be in appropriate ways literate; we expect educated writing to be competent as well. We Americans are a democratic and heterogeneous society, divided by region and sometimes by origin; mobile, often in a significant sense homeless; quite variously schooled; instructed to a degree by sound and picture (as in popular conversation, radio, television); often lacking in bookish background and tradition; in tastes and ideals much drawn to the immediate and physical, the practical and technological. Should we be

surprised that in such a context literacy in terms of upper-middle-class usage (not to mention competence in a form of discourse reaching toward art) is imperfectly attained by our young through the limited process of formal education? If this sketch gives something like a true picture of the reasons why "English" is the way it is, what is to be done about Johnny?

[13] Education, like politics, is an art of the possible. The beginning of wisdom is, in the cant phrase, to "take the student where he is." Where is Johnny? He is, you will recall, a college undergraduate, let's say a freshman. He has typically been exposed to a number of years of drill founded on a traditional and dubious grammar; he has done some writing of quite variable amount and character; he has read a few standard works of literature and probably a slender but startling miscellany of contemporary fare; he doesn't know how to pursue an idea through a piece of prose that has one; he concocts what *he* considers English for his English teacher and is shocked if anybody else expects this odd behavior of him; and, as there is no guarantee that he spells correctly, Professor Stackblower is quite likely to be displeased with him. He has grown up believing that English means literacy because this is what he has been taught, and if it hasn't taken very well he is rather apologetic about it. Probably nobody has had time, strength, or inclination to help him very far toward competence. But, perhaps just because he is now eighteen or thereabouts, he can be helped toward competence and, if necessary, literacy into the bargain.

[14] The initial help must come from the English Department. "Freshman composition" has, of course, been taught in a fantastic variety of ways, and I have no pet formula to peddle, certainly no panacea. The essentials are, negatively, not to rehash the conventions of grammar again *seriatim et ad nauseam;* positively, to read a certain amount of serious well-fabricated exposition in order to discover the subject, its parts, their ordonnance and function—in short what it says and how and why; and to do some writing of the same kind and in the same spirit. Johnny is to discover, if he hasn't, that reading, writing, and thinking are a kind of three-wheeler which will take him down a number of roads. *En route,* he is firmly reminded that literacy is expected of him (spelling, too). He may find the going tough, but all the roads will take him toward competence, whatever incidental signs they bear. They are long roads, and he may not get all the way.

[15] He will not—any more often than he does now—unless what happens to him in his English class is reinforced by what happens to him elsewhere. Johnny must come to believe that how he writes matters, not just to his English instructor, but to everybody else. He *won't* believe this unless in the first place he writes—instead of filling in boxes in multiple-choice tests. He won't, unless in the second place his instructor in history or biology or economics also believes it, and shows Johnny that he does. Even Professor Stackblower, if he would trouble only to circle Johnny's misspellings in a paper or two and give Johnny to understand that his

grades have taken a shocking turn for the worse because of them, might be surprised by Johnny's improvement. I have seen it happen. Strangely enough, this simple step does not always occur to Stackblower.

[16] To some it will seem platitudinous, and to others (especially battle-hardened academicians) utopian, to propose that college faculties take reasonable responsibility for whatever standards of literacy and/or competence they profess. The grounds for misgiving were succinctly put by the dean of a school of business administration who had requested the English Department to provide additional discipline in writing for his students. When I asked why his faculty shouldn't undertake this task themselves, he lowered his voice and said, "Frankly, I don't think they know enough—and besides, it's too hard work!" It may well be that Professor Kitzhaber is right in doubting (in his useful little book *Themes, Theories, and Therapy*) that any general and sustained faculty acceptance of "reasonable responsibility" is forthcoming. If so, in my opinion Johnny will stay where he is.

[17] But mine is a genuinely modest proposal. By "reasonable responsibility" I mean that when in any course in any department student writing is demanded, the judgment of this writing should be consistent with accepted institutional standards applicable to the occasion, and that this judgment should be reflected in grades. I don't ask that all members of a faculty set themselves up as grammarians or rhetoricians, or that as readers they devote the time and energy to style and structure one expects of the instructor in English. I ask that the faculty member who professes to be scandalized by misspelling and other gross errors at the level of literacy make known his displeasure in terms Johnny will understand. Neither great *expertise* nor effort would be required merely to check these off, particularly if some institution-wide code were adopted. As to competence, it is this that the faculty member who is baffled and offended by vagueness, confusion, and general impenetrability is seeking, although he may not consciously set out to demand clarity, order, or even evidence. One recalls the astonished delight with which M. Jourdain discovered that he was talking prose. I wish my colleagues to become aware that prose on the level of competence, the prose of written discourse, is what they really want of students. I think that they can get it, or get more of it than they have. Johnny is capable of writing better than he does—on demand. Such a demand would be far more potent than any addition to the standard formal requirements in English.

[18] We have been talking about Johnny—and Joanne—simply as undergraduates. They may be destined for business, or the professions, or government service, or housewifery. If they come, however painfully, to understand that "English" means something more and other than literacy, this is a gain not only today for them as individuals and for the microcosm of the college, but also tomorrow for their children and the macrocosm of society and the schools. Faculty responsibility means much more than merely pacifying Professor Stackblower.

[19] But to say "tomorrow" brings us back to my colleagues in English. If Johnny and Joanne are headed for careers as *English* teachers, they ought to be better equipped than their predecessors. I have been saying that undergraduate Johnny, whether in spite of or because of his experience in the schools, can be got to write. His teachers can be educated to do more for him, to help him further and earlier up the ladder of literacy and competency. I can attempt no blueprint here, but let my colleagues read and take to themselves Dr. Conant's description of typical faculty attitudes in *The Education of American Teachers*. We in college English need to accept responsibility for educating the public-school teacher, as we do the graduate student. We need to make a larger place in our curricula for language and writing alongside literature (which is what everbody, including me, yearns to teach). If we can—and I think we can—get Johnny to put whatever brains he has into learning *really* to read and *really* to write, we shall have done our whole duty as teachers of English, including our duty to literature. Perhaps it is the first duty of all teachers.

Questions on Meaning

1 In your own words, explain the two "dimensions" of writing Clapp speaks of.
2 Clapp insists that the two kinds of writing skills are interdependent. Explain his point.
3 In what ways are college students' writing problems the result of a general misunderstanding of the relationship between the two kinds of skills?
4 What is the principal suggestion the author makes for solving the college writing problem? Do you agree with his solution?

Questions on Style and Structure

1 Paragraph 1 is a well-developed paragraph. How successful is it in arousing your interest? Notice the manner in which the author provides transitions from sentence to sentence.
2 This is a carefully organized essay. If you were to make an outline of it, what would your main headings and their order be?
3 In paragraph 5, Clapp achieves coherence partly through the use of the pronoun *we*. Can you find another paragraph that is made coherent through the consistent use of a pronoun?
4 Some of Clapp's sentences are stylistically interesting. For example, the first sentence could have been written: "It seems that Johnny still 'can't write' despite all the outcry and accusation in recent years, despite the growing mass and competence of professional assaults upon the problem." Which

version do you prefer? Why? Try your hand at rewriting a few of the author's sentences. Then see which version you prefer.
5. The author sometimes judiciously repeats words for emphasis, as he does in this sentence from paragraph 6: "*Why* is the ability to write well seemingly attained *so* seldom, *so* incompletely, and with such difficulty?" Can you find other examples of such repetition?

Exploring Words

1. *calumny.* Although your dictionary may give some synonyms for this word, probably none would fit into Clapp's sentence as well as *calumny.* How do you explain the appropriateness of *calumny* in that context?
2. *inextricably. Inextricably* is often used with a word like *intertwined, interwoven,* or *involved.* With what has your life recently become *inextricably* intertwined, interwoven, or involved?
3. *anomalies.* After checking your dictionary's definition of the word, try filling in the blanks in the sentence "Of all the ——s in the ——, he (or she) is the greatest *anomaly.*"
4. *taxonomy.* Check your dictionary's definition of *taxonomy.* Does Clapp's use fit either of the definitions given or is he using the term metaphorically?
5. *dichotomy.* Find another word in your dictionary ending in *-otomy* that has a meaning similar to that of *dichotomy.*
6. *heterogeneous.* Many people confuse the terms *heterogeneous* and *homogeneous.* Look up both words, and then write a sentence using each word.
7. *panacea.* Clapp speaks of *panaceas* for teaching freshman composition. What are some other problems for which *panaceas* are sometimes offered?
8. *platitudinous.* What are some *platitudes* that you heard frequently while growing up? (One might have been "Early to bed and early to rise makes a man healthy, wealthy, and wise.")
9. *utopian.* Does your dictionary's definition of this word suggest that it would ordinarily be used positively or negatively? Which connotations does Clapp's usage provide? Considering the source of the word, why do you think it has taken on the connotations that it has?
10. *microcosm* and *macrocosm.* After consulting your dictionary, explain Clapp's use of these terms. What is the meaning of the sentence in which they are used?

Suggestions for Writing

1. In paragraph 13, Clapp briefly describes the kind of experience Johnny had in English classes before he came to college. Write an essay in which you explain what kind of training you yourself had.

2 Write a sample letter to your high school principal suggesting ways in which the English program at your former school could be improved to prepare students for college more effectively.

3 Compare your senior English class with your freshman composition class. You could deal with such matters as approach, standards, textbooks, and assignments.

Daniel Webster
JOHN F. KENNEDY

Getting Started

With Ideas

This selection is a chapter from John F. Kennedy's *Profiles in Courage*. If you have read any portions of this book, read reviews of it, or seen it dramatized on television, you probably know that it is a collection of biographical sketches of American statesmen who, in Kennedy's judgment, demonstrated courage by placing their consciences and convictions above political expediency and personal ambitions. The picture Kennedy gives here of Daniel Webster is a complex one. To be sure you understand it, it will be a good idea to remember any impressions you have gotten of Webster from previous reading (you may, for instance, know Stephen Vincent Benét's story *The Devil and Daniel Webster*). Then note as you read whether these impressions are confirmed or contradicted by Kennedy's account of Webster's last years in the American political scene.

With Words

1 peroration (5)—you can tell it has something to do with a formal speech. See if the context does not suggest a more specific meaning.
2 amorphous (7)—from the Greek prefix *a-*, meaning "without," and the Greek root *morph,* meaning "form."
3 culpable (18)—from the Latin word *culpa,* meaning "fault." Perhaps you have heard *culpable* used in reference to insurance matters or automobile accidents. And if you are familiar with the Catholic church practice of confession, you may know the phrase *mea culpa.*
4 intransigence (29)—the context will probably give you an understanding of at least a very general meaning for this word, especially if you remember that *in* means "not" and *trans* means "across."

". . . Not as a Massachusetts Man . . . But as an American . . ."

[1] The blizzardy night of January 21, 1850, was no night in Washington for an ailing old man to be out. But wheezing and coughing

". . . not as a Massachusetts man but as an American . . ." Daniel Webster in *Profiles in Courage* by John F. Kennedy. Copyright © 1955 by John F. Kennedy. By permission of Harper & Row, Publishers, Inc.

fitfully, Henry Clay made his way through the snowdrifts to the home of Daniel Webster. He had a plan—a plan to save the Union—and he knew he must have the support of the North's most renowned orator and statesman. He knew that he had no time to lose, for that very afternoon President Taylor, in a message to Congress asking California's admission as a free state, had only thrown fuel on the raging fire that threatened to consume the Union. Why had the President failed to mention New Mexico, asked the North? What about the Fugitive Slave Law being enforced, said the South? What about the District of Columbia slave trade, Utah, Texas boundaries? Tempers mounted, plots unfolded, disunity was abroad in the land.

[2] But Henry Clay had a plan—a plan for another Great Compromise to preserve the nation. For an hour he outlined its contents to Daniel Webster in the warmth of the latter's comfortable home, and together they talked of saving the Union. Few meetings in American history have ever been so productive or so ironic in their consequences. For the Compromise of 1850 added to Henry Clay's garlands as the great Pacificator; but Daniel Webster's support which insured its success resulted in his political crucifixion, and, for half a century or more, his historical condemnation.

[3] The man upon whom Henry Clay called that wintry night was one of the most extraordinary figures in American political history. Daniel Webster is familiar to many of us today as the battler for Jabez Stone's soul against the devil in Stephen Vincent Benét's story. But in his own lifetime, he had many battles against the devil for his own soul—and some he lost. Webster, wrote one of his intimate friends, was "a compound of strength and weakness, dust and divinity," or in Emerson's words "a great man with a small ambition."

[4] There could be no mistaking he was a great man—he looked like one, talked like one, was treated like one and insisted he was one. With all his faults and failings, Daniel Webster was undoubtedly the most talented figure in our Congressional history: not in his ability to win men to a cause—he was no match in that with Henry Clay; not in his ability to hammer out a philosophy of government—Calhoun outshone him there; but in his ability to make alive and supreme the latent sense of oneness, of Union, that all Americans felt but which few could express.

[5] But how Daniel Webster could express it! How he could express almost any sentiments! Ever since his first speech in Congress—attacking the War of 1812—had riveted the attention of the House of Representatives as no freshman had ever held it before, he was the outstanding orator of his day—indeed, of all time—in Congress, before hushed throngs in Massachusetts and as an advocate before the Supreme Court. Stern Chief Justice Marshall was said to have been visibly moved by Webster's famous defense in the Dartmouth College case—"It is, sir, as I have said, a small college—and yet there are those who love it." After his oration on the two hundredth founding of Plymouth Colony, a young Harvard scholar wrote:

> I was never so excited by public speaking before in my life. Three or four times I thought my temple would burst with the rush of blood.... I was beside myself and I am still so.

And the peroration of his reply to Senator Hayne of South Carolina, when secession had threatened twenty years earlier, was a national rallying cry memorized by every schoolboy—"Liberty and Union, now and forever, one and inseparable!"

[6] A very slow speaker, hardly averaging a hundred words a minute, Webster combined the musical charm of his deep organ-like voice, a vivid imagination, an ability to crush his opponents with a barrage of facts, a confident and deliberate manner of speaking and a striking appearance to make his orations a magnet that drew crowds hurrying to the Senate chamber. He prepared his speeches with the utmost care, but seldom wrote them out in a prepared text. It has been said that he could think out a speech sentence by sentence, correct the sentences in his mind without the use of a pencil and then deliver it exactly as he thought it out.

[7] Certainly that striking appearance was half the secret of his power, and convinced all who looked upon his face that he was one born to rule men. Although less than six feet tall, Webster's slender frame when contrasted with the magnificent sweep of his shoulders gave him a theatrical but formidable presence. But it was his extraordinary head that contemporaries found so memorable, with the features Carlyle described for all to remember: "The tanned complexion, the amorphous crag-like face; the dull black eyes under the precipice of brows, like dull anthracite furnaces needing only to be blown; the mastiff mouth accurately closed." One contemporary called Webster "a living lie, because no man on earth could be so great as he looked."

[8] And Daniel Webster was not as great as he looked. The flaw in the granite was the failure of his moral senses to develop as acutely as his other faculties. He could see nothing improper in writing to the President of the Bank of the United States—at the very time when the Senate was engaged in debate over a renewal of the Bank's charter—noting that "my retainer has not been received or refreshed as usual." But Webster accepted favors not as gifts but as services which he believed were rightly due him. When he tried to resign from the Senate in 1836 to recoup speculative losses through his law practice, his Massachusetts businessmen friends joined to pay his debts to retain him in office. Even at his deathbed, legend tells us, there was a knock at his door, and a large roll of bills was thrust in by an old gentleman, who said that "At such a time as this, there should be no shortage of money in the house."

[9] Webster took it all and more. What is difficult to comprehend is that he saw no wrong in it—morally or otherwise. He probably believed that he was greatly underpaid, and it never occurred to him that by his own free choice he had sold his services and his talents, however extraordinary they might have been, to the people of the United States, and no one else, when he drew his salary as United States Senator. But Webster's

support of the business interests of New England was not the result of the money he obtained, but of his personal convictions. Money meant little to him except as a means to gratify his peculiar tastes. He never accumulated a fortune. He never was out of debt. And he never was troubled by his debtor status. Sometimes he paid, and he always did so when it was convenient, but as Gerald W. Johnson says, "Unfortunately he sometimes paid in the wrong coin—not in legal tender—but in the confidence that the people reposed in him."

[10] But whatever his faults, Daniel Webster remained the greatest orator of his day, the leading member of the American Bar, one of the most renowned leaders of the Whig party, and the only Senator capable of checking Calhoun. And thus Henry Clay knew he must enlist these extraordinary talents on behalf of his Great Compromise. Time and events proved he was right.

[11] As the God-like Daniel listened in thoughtful silence, the sickly Clay unfolded his last great effort to hold the Union together. Its key features were five in number: (1) California was to be admitted as a free (nonslaveholding) state; (2) New Mexico and Utah were to be organized as territories without legislation either for or against slavery, thus running directly contrary to the hotly debated Wilmot Proviso which was intended to prohibit slavery in the new territories; (3) Texas was to be compensated for some territory to be ceded to New Mexico; (4) the slave trade would be abolished in the District of Columbia; and (5) a more stringent and enforceable Fugitive Slave Law was to be enacted to guarantee return to their masters of runaway slaves captured in Northern states. The Compromise would be condemned by the Southern extremists as appeasement, chiefly on its first and fourth provisions; and by the Northern abolitionists as 90 per cent concessions to the South with a meaningless 10 per cent sop thrown to the North, particularly because of the second and fifth provisions. Few Northerners could stomach any strengthening of the Fugitive Slave Act, the most bitterly hated measure—and until Prohibition, the most flagrantly disobeyed—ever passed by Congress. Massachusetts had even enacted a law making it a crime for anyone to enforce the provisions of the Act in that state!

[12] How could Henry Clay then hope to win approval to such a plan from Daniel Webster of Massachusetts? Was he not specifically on record as a consistent foe of slavery and a supporter of the Wilmot Proviso? Had he not told the Senate in the Oregon Debate:

> I shall oppose all slavery extension and all increase of slave representation in all places, at all times, under all circumstances, even against all inducements, against all supposed limitation of great interests, against all combinations, against all compromises.

That very week he had written a friend: "From my earliest youth, I have regarded slavery as a great moral and political evil. . . . You need not fear that I shall vote for any compromise or do anything inconsistent with the past."

[13] But Daniel Webster feared that civil violence "would only rivet the chains of slavery the more strongly." And the preservation of the Union was far dearer to his heart than his opposition to slavery.

[14] And thus on that fateful January night, Daniel Webster promised Henry Clay his conditional support, and took inventory of the crisis about him. At first he shared the views of those critics and historians who scoffed at the possibility of secession in 1850. But as he talked with Southern leaders and observed "the condition of the country, I thought the inevitable consequences of leaving the existing controversies unadjusted would be Civil War." "I am nearly broken down with labor and anxiety," he wrote his son. "I know not how to meet the present emergency, or with what weapons to beat down the Northern and Southern follies now raging in equal extremes. . . . I have poor spirits and little courage."

[15] Two groups were threatening in 1850 to break away from the United States of America. In New England, Garrison was publicly proclaiming, "I am an Abolitionist and, therefore, for the dissolution of the Union." And a mass meeting of Northern abolitionists declared that "the Constitution is a covenant with death and an agreement with hell." In the South, Calhoun was writing to a friend in February of 1850, "Disunion is the only alternative that is left for us." And in his last great address to the Senate, read for him on March 4, only a few short weeks before his death, while he sat by too feeble to speak, he declared, "The South will be forced to choose between abolition and secession."

[16] A preliminary convention of Southerners, also instigated by Calhoun, urged a full-scale convention of the South at Nashville for June of that fateful year to popularize the idea of dissolution.

[17] The time was ripe for secession, and few were prepared to speak for union. Even Alexander Stephens of Georgia, anxious to preserve the Union, wrote friends in the South who were sympathetic with his views that "the feeling among the Southern members for a dissolution of the Union . . . is becoming much more general. Men are now beginning to talk of it seriously who twelve months ago hardly permitted themselves to think of it. . . . the crisis is not far ahead. . . . A dismemberment of this Republic I now consider inevitable." During the critical month preceding Webster's speech, six Southern states, each to secede ten years later, approved the aims of the Nashville Convention and appointed delegates. Horace Greeley wrote on February 23:

> There are sixty members of Congress who this day desire and are plotting to effect the idea of a dissolution of the Union. We have no doubt the Nashville Convention will be held and that the leading purpose of its authors is the separation of the slave states . . . with the formation of an independent confederacy.

Such was the perilous state of the nation in the early months of 1850.

[18] By the end of February, the Senator from Massachusetts had

determined upon his course. Only the Clay Compromise, Daniel Webster decided, could avert secession and civil war; and he wrote a friend that he planned "to make an honest truth-telling speech and a Union speech, and discharge a clear conscience." As he set to work preparing his notes, he received abundant warning of the attacks his message would provoke. His constituents and Massachusetts newspapers admonished him strongly not to waver in his consistent anti-slavery stand, and many urged him to employ still tougher tones against the South. But the Senator from Massachusetts had made up his mind, as he told his friends on March 6, "to push my skiff from the shore alone." He would act according to the creed with which he had challenged the Senate several years earlier:

> Inconsistencies of opinion arising from changes of circumstances are often justifiable. But there is one sort of inconsistency that is culpable: it is the inconsistency between a man's conviction and his vote, between his conscience and his conduct. No man shall ever charge me with an inconsistency of that kind.

[19] And so came the 7th of March, 1850, the only day in history which would become the title of a speech delivered on the Senate floor. No one recalls today—no one even recalled in 1851—the formal title Webster gave his address, for it had become the "Seventh of March" speech as much as Independence Day is known as the Fourth of July.

[20] Realizing after months of insomnia that this might be the last great effort his health would permit, Webster stimulated his strength for the speech by oxide of arsenic and other drugs, and devoted the morning to polishing up his notes. He was excitedly interrupted by the Sergeant at Arms, who told him that even then—two hours before the Senate was to meet—the chamber, the galleries, the anterooms and even the corridors of the Capitol were filled with those who had been traveling for days from all parts of the nation to hear Daniel Webster. Many foreign diplomats and most of the House of Representatives were among those vying for standing room. As the Senate met, members could scarcely walk to their seats through the crowd of spectators and temporary seats made of public documents stacked on top of each other. Most Senators gave up their seats to ladies, and stood in the aisles awaiting Webster's opening blast.

[21] As the Vice President's gavel commenced the session, Senator Walker of Wisconsin, who held the floor to finish a speech begun the day before, told the Chair that "this vast audience has not come to hear me, and there is but one man who can assemble such an audience. They expect to hear him, and I feel it is my duty, as it is my pleasure, to give the floor to the Senator from Massachusetts."

[22] The crowd fell silent as Daniel Webster rose slowly to his feet, all the impressive powers of his extraordinary physical appearance—the great, dark, brooding eyes, the wonderfully bronzed complexion, the majestic domed forehead—commanding the same awe they had commanded for more than thirty years. Garbed in his familiar blue tailed

coat with brass buttons, and a buff waistcoat and breeches, he deliberately paused a moment as he gazed about at the greatest assemblage of Senators ever to gather in that chamber—Clay, Benton, Houston, Jefferson Davis, Hale, Bell, Cass, Seward, Chase, Stephen A. Douglas and others. But one face was missing—that of the ailing John C. Calhoun.

[23] All eyes were fixed on the speaker; no spectator save his own son knew what he would say. "I have never before," wrote a newspaper correspondent, "witnessed an occasion on which there was deeper feeling enlisted or more universal anxiety to catch the most distinct echo of the speaker's voice."

[24] In his moments of magnificent inspiration, as Emerson once described him, Webster was truly "the great cannon loaded to the lips." Summoning for the last time that spell-binding oratorical ability, he abandoned his previous opposition to slavery in the territories, abandoned his constituents' abhorrence of the Fugitive Slave Law, abandoned his own place in the history and hearts of his countrymen and abandoned his last chance for the goal that had eluded him for over twenty years—the Presidency. Daniel Webster preferred to risk his career and his reputation rather than risk the Union.

[25] "Mr. President," he began, "I wish to speak today, not as a Massachusetts man, nor as a Northern man, but as an American and a Member of the Senate of the United States. . . . I speak today for the preservation of the Union. Hear me for my cause."

[26] He had spoken but for a short time when the gaunt, bent form of Calhoun, wrapped in a black cloak, was dramatically assisted into his seat, where he sat trembling, scarcely able to move, and unnoticed by the speaker. After several expressions of regret by Webster that illness prevented the distinguished Senator from South Carolina from being present, Calhoun struggled up, grasping the arms of his chair, and in a clear and ghostly voice proudly announced, "The Senator from South Carolina *is* in his seat." Webster was touched, and with tears in his eyes he extended a bow toward Calhoun, who sank back exhausted and feeble, eyeing the Massachusetts orator with a sphinx-like expression which disclosed no hint of either approval or disapproval.

[27] For three hours and eleven minutes, with only a few references to his extensive notes, Daniel Webster pleaded the Union's cause. Relating the grievances of each side, he asked for conciliation and understanding in the name of patriotism. The Senate's main concern, he insisted, was neither to promote slavery nor to abolish it, but to preserve the United States of America. And with telling logic and remarkable foresight he bitterly attacked the idea of "peaceable secession":

> Sir, your eyes and mine are never destined to see that miracle. The dismemberment of this vast country without convulsion! Who is so foolish . . . as to expect to see any such thing? . . . Instead of speaking of the possibility or utility of secession, in-

stead of dwelling in those caverns of darkness, . . . let us enjoy the fresh air of liberty and union. . . . Let us make our generation one of the strongest and brightest links in that golden chain which is destined, I fondly believe, to grapple the people of all the states to this Constitution for ages to come.

[28] There was no applause. Buzzing and astonished whispering, yes, but no applause. Perhaps his hearers were too intent—or too astonished. A reporter rushed to the telegraph office. "Mr. Webster has assumed a great responsibility," he wired his paper, "and whether he succeeds or fails, the courage with which he has come forth at least entitles him to the respect of the country."

[29] Daniel Webster did succeed. Even though his speech was repudiated by many in the North, the very fact that one who represented such a belligerent constituency would appeal for understanding in the name of unity and patriotism was recognized in Washington and throughout the South as a *bona fide* assurance of Southern rights. Despite Calhoun's own intransigence, his Charleston *Mercury* praised Webster's address as "noble in language, generous and conciliatory in tone. Mr. Calhoun's clear and powerful exposition would have had something of a decisive effect if it had not been so soon followed by Mr. Webster's masterly playing." And the New Orleans *Picayune* hailed Webster for "the moral courage to do what he believes to be just in itself and necessary for the peace and safety of the country."

[30] And so the danger of immediate secession and bloodshed passed. As Senator Winthrop remarked, Webster's speech had "disarmed and quieted the South [and] knocked the Nashville Convention into a cocked hat." The *Journal of Commerce* was to remark in later months that "Webster did more than any other man in the whole country, and at a greater hazard of personal popularity, to stem and roll back the torrent of sectionalism which in 1850 threatened to overthrow the pillars of the Constitution and the Union."

[31] Some historians—particularly those who wrote in the latter half of the nineteenth century under the influence of the moral earnestness of Webster's articulate Abolitionist foes—do not agree with Allan Nevins, Henry Steele Commager, Gerald Johnson and others who have praised the Seventh of March speech as "the highest statesmanship . . . Webster's last great service to the nation." Many deny that secession would have occurred in 1850 without such compromises; and others maintain that subsequent events proved eventual secession was inevitable regardless of what compromises were made. But still others insist that delaying war for ten years narrowed the issues between North and South and in the long run helped preserve the Union. The spirit of conciliation in Webster's speech gave the North the righteous feeling that it had made every attempt to treat the South with fairness, and the defenders of the Union were thus united more strongly against what they felt to be South-

ern violations of those compromises ten years later. Even from the military point of view of the North, postponement of the battle for ten years enabled the Northern states to increase tremendously their lead in popularity, voting power, production and railroads.

[32] Undoubtedly this was understood by many of Webster's supporters, including the business and professional men of Massachusetts who helped distribute hundreds of thousands of copies of the Seventh of March speech throughout the country. It was understood by Daniel Webster, who dedicated the printed copies to the people of Massachusetts with these words: "Necessity compels me to speak true rather than pleasing things. . . . I should indeed like to please you; but I prefer to save you, whatever be your attitude toward me."

[33] But it was not understood by the Abolitionists and Free Soilers of 1850. Few politicians have had the distinction of being scourged by such talented constituents. The Rev. Theodore Parker, heedless of the dangers of secession, who had boasted of harboring a fugitive slave in his cellar and writing his sermons with a sword over his ink stand and a pistol in his desk "loaded and ready for defense," denounced Webster in merciless fashion from his pulpit, an attack he would continue even after Webster's death: "No living man has done so much," he cried, "to debauch the conscience of the nation. . . . I know of no deed in American history done by a son of New England to which I can compare this, but the act of Benedict Arnold." "Webster," said Horace Mann, "is a fallen star! Lucifer descending from Heaven!" Longfellow asked the world: "Is it possible? Is this the Titan who hurled mountains at Hayne years ago?" And Emerson proclaimed that "Every drop of blood in that man's veins has eyes that look downward. . . . Webster's absence of moral faculty is degrading to the country." To William Cullen Bryant, Webster was "a man who has deserted the cause which he lately defended, and deserted it under circumstances which force upon him the imputation of a sordid motive." And to James Russell Lowell he was "the most meanly and foolishly treacherous man I ever heard of."

[34] Charles Sumner, who would be elevated to the Senate upon his departure, enrolled the name of Webster on "the dark list of apostates. Mr. Webster's elaborate treason has done more than anything else to break down the North." Senator William H. Seward, the brilliant "Conscience" Whig, called Webster a "traitor to the cause of freedom." A mass meeting in Faneuil Hall condemned the speech as "unworthy of a wise statesman and a good man," and resolved that "Constitution or no Constitution, law or no law, we will not allow a fugitive slave to be taken from the state of Massachusetts." As the Massachusetts Legislature enacted further resolutions wholly contrary to the spirit of the Seventh of March speech, one member called Webster "a recreant son of Massachusetts who misrepresents her in the Senate"; and another stated that "Daniel Webster will be a fortunate man if God, in his sparing mercy, shall preserve his life long enough for him to repent of this act and efface this stain on his name."

[35] The Boston *Courier* pronounced that it was "unable to find that any Northern Whig member of Congress concurs with Mr. Webster"; and his old defender, the Boston *Atlas,* stated, "His sentiments are not our sentiments nor we venture to say of the Whigs of New England." The New York *Tribune* considered it "unequal to the occasion and unworthy of its author"; the New York *Evening Post* spoke in terms of a "traitorous retreat . . . a man who deserted the cause which he lately defended"; and the Abolitionist press called it "the scarlet infamy of Daniel Webster. . . . An indescribably base and wicked speech."

[36] Edmund Quincy spoke bitterly of the "ineffable meanness of the lion turned spaniel in his fawnings on the masters whose hands he was licking for the sake of the dirty puddings they might have to toss to him." And finally, the name of Daniel Webster was humiliated for all time in the literature of our land by the cutting words of the usually gentle John Greenleaf Whittier in his immortal poem "Ichabod":

> So fallen! so lost! the light withdrawn
>   Which once he wore!
> The glory from his gray hairs gone
>   Forevermore! . . .
>
> Of all we loved and honored, naught
>   Save power remains;
> A fallen angel's pride of thought,
>   Still strong in chains. . . .
>
> Then pay the reverence of old days
>   To his dead fame;
> Walk backward, with averted gaze,
>   And hide the shame!

[37] Years afterward Whittier was to recall that he penned this acid verse "in one of the saddest moments of my life." And for Daniel Webster, the arrogant, scornful giant of the ages who believed himself above political rancor, Whittier's attack was especially bitter. To some extent he had attempted to shrug off his attackers, stating that he had expected to be libeled and abused, particularly by the Abolitionists and intellectuals who had previously scorned him, much as George Washington and others before him had been abused. To those who urged a prompt reply, he merely related the story of the old deacon in a similar predicament who told his friends, "I always make it a rule never to clean up the path until the snow is done falling."

[38] But he was saddened by the failure of a single other New England Whig to rise to his defense, and he remarked that he was

> engaged in a controversy in which I have neither a leader nor a follower from among my own immediate friends. . . . I am tired of standing up here, almost alone from Massachusetts, contending for practical measures absolutely essential to the good of the

country. . . . For five months . . . no one of my colleagues manifested the slightest concurrence in my statements. . . . Since the 7th of March there has not been an hour in which I have not felt a crushing weight of anxiety. I have sat down to no breakfast or dinner to which I have brought an unconcerned and easy mind.

[39] But, although he sought to explain his objectives and reassure his friends of his continued opposition to slavery, he nevertheless insisted he would

stand on the principle of my speech to the end. . . . If necessary I will take the stump in every village in New England. . . . What is to come of the present commotion in men's minds I cannot foresee; but my own convictions of duty are fixed and strong, and I shall continue to follow those convictions without faltering. . . . In highly excited times it is far easier to fan and feed the flames of discord, than to subdue them; and he who counsels moderation is in danger of being regarded as failing in his duty to his party.

[40] And the following year, despite his seventy years, Webster went on extended speaking tours defending his position: "If the chances had been one in a thousand that Civil War would be the result, I should still have felt that thousandth chance should be guarded against by any reasonable sacrifice." When his efforts—and those of Clay, Douglas and others—on behalf of compromise were ultimately successful, he noted sarcastically that many of his colleagues were now saying "They always meant to stand by the Union to the last."

[41] But Daniel Webster was doomed to disappointment in his hopes that this latent support might again enable him to seek the Presidency. For his speech had so thoroughly destroyed those prospects that the recurring popularity of his position could not possibly satisfy the great masses of voters in New England and the North. He could not receive the Presidential nomination he had so long desired; but neither could he ever put to rest the assertion, which was not only expressed by his contemporary critics but subsequently by several nineteenth-century historians, that his real objective in the Seventh of March speech was a bid for Southern support for the Presidency.

[42] But this "profound selfishness," which Emerson was so certain the speech represented, could not have entered into Daniel Webster's motivations. "Had he been bidding for the Presidency," as Professor Nevins points out, "he would have trimmed his phrases and inserted weasel-words upon New Mexico and the fugitive slaves. The first precaution of any aspirant for the Presidency is to make sure of his own state and section; and Webster knew that his speech would send echoes of denunci-

ation leaping from Mount Mansfield to Monamoy Light." Moreover, Webster was sufficiently acute politically to know that a divided party such as his would turn away from politically controversial figures and move to an uncommitted neutral individual, a principle consistently applied to this day. And the 1852 Whig Convention followed exactly this course. After the procompromise vote had been divided for fifty-two ballots between Webster and President Fillmore, the convention turned to the popular General Winfield Scott. Not a single Southern Whig supported Webster. And when the Boston Whigs urged that the party platform take credit for the Clay Compromise, of which, they said, "Daniel Webster, with the concurrence of Henry Clay and other profound statesmen, was the author," Senator Corwin of Ohio was reported to have commented sarcastically, "And I, with the concurrence of Moses and some extra help, wrote the Ten Commandments."

[43] So Daniel Webster, who neither could have intended his speech as an improvement of his political popularity nor permitted his ambitions to weaken his plea for the Union, died a disappointed and discouraged death in 1852, his eyes fixed on the flag flying from the mast of the sailboat he had anchored in view of his bedroom window. But to the very end he was true to character, asking on his deathbed, "Wife, children, doctor, I trust on this occasion I have said nothing unworthy of Daniel Webster." And to the end he had been true to the Union, and to his greatest act of courageous principle; for in his last words to the Senate, Webster had written his own epitaph:

> I shall stand by the Union . . . with absolute disregard of personal consequences. What are personal consequences . . . in comparison with the good or evil which may befall a great country in a crisis like this? . . . Let the consequences be what they will, I am careless. No man can suffer too much, and no man can fall too soon, if he suffer or if he fall in defense of the liberties and Constitution of his country.

Questions on Meaning

1 Kennedy mentions several negative impressions of Webster's character and accomplishments. One of these views he specifically indicates that he shares. Which is it? Do you think Kennedy agrees with any of the other negative views he mentions? If not, why does he pay so much attention to them?

2 In paragraph 29, Kennedy points out several diverse interpretations of the significance of Webster's "Seventh of March" speech. What are these interpretations? Which one does Kennedy favor? How do you know?

3 See how many of the provisions of the Clay-Webster compromise you can remember without checking back. Which two were particularly disturbing to most of Webster's Massachusetts constituents?

4 According to Kennedy, why did Webster agree to Clay's plan? Does Kennedy convince you that he was true to his most basic principles in doing so?

5 What description does Kennedy give of the state of the union in 1850?

6 Briefly, explain the main idea of the article.

7 Do you feel that this selection has been placed on the proper side of the line that this book draws between works that are "chiefly informative" and those that are "chiefly persuasive"? Why?

Questions on Style and Structure

1 A sentence in which contrasting ideas are expressed in parallel or balanced syntactic patterns is said to contain antithesis. The following example from Kennedy's Inaugural Address is a good example of antithesis: "And so, my fellow Americans, ask not what your country can do for you; ask what you can do for your country." Can you find examples of such antithesis in this selection? Clue: such sentences often contain the "not . . . but . . ." pattern, as in the opening sentence of the Inaugural Address: "We observe today *not* a victory of party *but* a celebration of freedom, symbolizing an end as well as a beginning, signifying renewal as well as change." Construct three antithetical sentences of your own.

2 How effectively does Kennedy provide coherence between paragraphs? For example, are paragraphs 1 through 5 stitched together well?

3 Is the division between paragraphs 15 and 16 warranted? Why do you suppose Kennedy separated paragraphs 34 and 35, 35 and 36, and 36 and 37?

4 Writers sometimes conclude essays with a quotation. How effective is Kennedy's conclusion?

Exploring Words

1 *peroration.* Look up the dictionary definition. What portion of Webster's speech is Kennedy referring to in this passage?

2 *amorphous.* Write a sentence using the word in a way that is consistent with a definition you find in your dictionary and with Carlyle's use of the word.

3 *culpable.* Actually, Webster's use of *culpable* is a bit inaccurate, at least according to modern usage. After checking your dictionary's definition of the word, comment on the appropriateness of the phrase "one sort of inconsistency that is *culpable.*"

4 *intransigence.* Which of the synonyms or explanations of the meaning of *intransigence* given in your dictionary is especially appropriate for Kennedy's use of the word?

DANIEL WEBSTER

Suggestions for Writing

1 Write a profile of someone you know well—a friend, a teacher, or a family member, for example—emphasizing one quality that you are aware of but that not everyone in this person's circle understands or appreciates. You will probably want to focus on one limited portion of your subject's life, as Kennedy does.

2 Daniel Webster, according to this account by Kennedy, made a difficult decision only after considerable soul-searching. You have probably had to make some difficult decisions in your life. Write an essay in which you explore one of these decisions. What conflicts did you face? How did you finally resolve the dilemma? What were the consequences?

3 Kennedy's *Profiles in Courage* attempts to define and illustrate one kind of courage—political courage. Write an essay in which you define and exemplify different kinds of courage.

Letter from Birmingham Jail
MARTIN LUTHER KING, JR.

Getting Started

With Ideas

In this essay in letter form, King responds eloquently to a letter from a group of southern clergymen who had written to him criticizing some of the activities Alice Walker praises in her selection (p. 256). As you read the essay, be sure you understand: (1) what, exactly, King and his followers had been doing in Alabama that brought about their jail sentences; (2) what objections to their activities were raised by the clergymen who wrote to Dr. King (some of these objections you will need to understand by inference; King does not state all of them directly); and (3) what answer King gives to each criticism offered. Also, you should note the work's outstanding stylistic features. Many of the writing techniques you have found in earlier selections in this book are used with particular vigor here. In fact, this essay, along with King's famous "I Have a Dream" speech, is generally recognized as one of the strongest pieces of persuasive writing to come out of twentieth-century America.

With Words

1. harried (14)—you may have seen or heard this word used as an adjective (for example, "He looks *harried*"), but note that King uses it as a verb. You will find the context helpful here, too.
2. paternalistically (23)—from the Latin word for "father." See *paternalists* in "The Civil Rights Movement: What Good Was It?" (p. 256).
3. precipitated (25)—from the Latin word meaning "headlong." Associating it with *precipice* may be helpful.
4. complacency (27)—from the Latin word meaning "to be very pleasing."

"Letter from Birmingham Jail"—April 16, 1963—in *Why We Can't Wait* by Martin Luther King, Jr. Copyright © 1963 by Martin Luther King, Jr. By permission of Harper & Row, Publishers, Inc.

Author's Note: This response to a published statement by eight fellow clergymen from Alabama (Bishop C. C. J. Carpenter, Bishop Joseph A. Durick, Rabbi Hilton L. Grafman, Bishop Paul Hardin, Bishop Holan B. Harmon, the Reverend George M. Murray, the Reverend Edward V. Ramage and the Reverend Earl Stallings) was composed under somewhat constricting circumstances. Begun on the margins of the newspaper in which the statement appeared while I was in jail, the letter was continued on scraps of writing paper supplied by a friendly Negro trusty, and concluded on a pad my attorneys were eventually permitted to leave me. Although the text remains in substance unaltered, I have indulged in the author's prerogative of polishing it for publication.

LETTER FROM BIRMINGHAM JAIL

April 16, 1963

My Dear Fellow Clergymen:

[1] While confined here in the Birmingham city jail, I came across your recent statement calling my present activities "unwise and untimely." Seldom do I pause to answer criticism of my work and ideas. If I sought to answer all the criticisms that cross my desk, my secretaries would have little time for anything other than such correspondence in the course of the day, and I would have no time for constructive work. But since I feel that you are men of genuine good will and that your criticisms are sincerely set forth, I want to try to answer your statement in what I hope will be patient and reasonable terms.

[2] I think I should indicate why I am here in Birmingham, since you have been influenced by the view which argues against "outsiders coming in." I have the honor of serving as president of the Southern Christian Leadership Conference, an organization operating in every southern state, with headquarters in Atlanta, Georgia. We have some eighty-five affiliated organizations across the South, and one of them is the Alabama Christian Movement for Human Rights. Frequently we share staff, educational and financial resources with our affiliates. Several months ago the affiliate here in Birmingham asked us to be on call to engage in a nonviolent direct-action program if such were deemed necessary. We readily consented, and when the hour came we lived up to our promise. So I, along with several members of my staff, am here because I was invited here. I am here because I have organizational ties here.

[3] But more basically, I am in Birmingham because injustice is here. Just as the prophets of the eighth century B.C. left their villages and carried their "thus saith the Lord" far beyond the boundaries of their home towns, and just as the Apostle Paul left his village of Tarsus and carried the gospel of Jesus Christ to the far corners of the Greco-Roman world, so am I compelled to carry the gospel of freedom beyond my own home town. Like Paul, I must constantly respond to the Macedonian call for aid.

[4] Moreover, I am cognizant of the interrelatedness of all communities and states. I cannot sit idly by in Atlanta and not be concerned about what happens in Birmingham. Injustice anywhere is a threat to justice everywhere. We are caught in an inescapable network of mutuality, tied in a single garment of destiny. Whatever affects one directly, affects all indirectly. Never again can we afford to live with the narrow, provincial "outside agitator" idea. Anyone who lives inside the United States can never be considered an outsider anywhere within its bounds.

[5] You deplore the demonstrations taking place in Birmingham. But your statement, I am sorry to say, fails to express a similar concern for the conditions that brought about the demonstrations. I am sure that none of you would want to rest content with the superficial kind of social analysis that deals merely with effects and does not grapple with underlying causes. It is unfortunate that demonstrations are taking place in Bir-

mingham, but it is even more unfortunate that the city's white power structure left the Negro community with no alternative.

[6] In any nonviolent campaign there are four basic steps: collection of the facts to determine whether injustices exist; negotiation; self-purification; and direct action. We have gone through all these steps in Birmingham. There can be no gainsaying the fact that racial injustice engulfs this community. Birmingham is probably the most thoroughly segregated city in the United States. Its ugly record of brutality is widely known. Negroes have experienced grossly unjust treatment in the courts. There have been more unsolved bombings of Negro homes and churches in Birmingham than in any other city in the nation. These are the hard, brutal facts of the case. On the basis of these conditions, Negro leaders sought to negotiate with the city fathers. But the latter consistently refused to engage in good-faith negotiation.

[7] Then, last September, came the opportunity to talk with leaders of Birmingham's economic community. In the course of the negotiations, certain promises were made by the merchants—for example, to remove the stores' humiliating racial signs. On the basis of these promises, the Reverend Fred Shuttlesworth and the leaders of the Alabama Christian Movement for Human Rights agreed to a moratorium on all demonstrations. As the weeks and months went by, we realized that we were the victims of a broken promise. A few signs, briefly removed, returned; the others remained.

[8] As in so many past experiences, our hopes had been blasted, and the shadow of deep disappointment settled upon us. We had no alternative except to prepare for direct action, whereby we would present our very bodies as a means of laying our case before the conscience of the local and the national community. Mindful of the difficulties involved, we decided to undertake a process of self-purification. We began a series of workshops on nonviolence, and we repeatedly asked ourselves: "Are you able to accept blows without retaliating?" "Are you able to endure the ordeal of jail?" We decided to schedule our direct-action program for the Easter season, realizing that except for Christmas, this is the main shopping period of the year. Knowing that a strong economic-withdrawal program would be the by-product of direct action, we felt that this would be the best time to bring pressure to bear on the merchants for the needed change.

[9] Then it occurred to us that Birmingham's mayoral election was coming up in March, and we speedily decided to postpone action until after election day. When we discovered that the Commissioner of Public Safety, Eugene "Bull" Connor, had piled up enough votes to be in the run-off, we decided again to postpone action until the day after the run-off so that the demonstrations could not be used to cloud the issues. Like many others, we waited to see Mr. Connor defeated, and to this end we endured postponement after postponement. Having aided in this community need, we felt that our direct-action program could be delayed no longer.

[10] You may well ask: "Why direct action? Why sit-ins, marches and so forth? Isn't negotiation a better path?" You are quite right in calling for negotiation. Indeed, this is the very purpose of direct action. Nonviolent direct action seeks to create such a crisis and foster such a tension that a community which has constantly refused to negotiate is forced to confront the issue. It seeks so to dramatize the issue that it can no longer be ignored. My citing the creation of tension as part of the work of the nonviolent-resister may sound rather shocking. But I must confess that I am not afraid of the word "tension." I have earnestly opposed violent tension, but there is a type of constructive, nonviolent tension which is necessary for growth. Just as Socrates felt that it was necessary to create a tension in the mind so that individuals could rise from the bondage of myths and half-truths to the unfettered realm of creative analysis and objective appraisal, so must we see the need for nonviolent gadflies to create the kind of tension in society that will help men rise from the dark depths of prejudice and racism to the majestic heights of understanding and brotherhood.

[11] The purpose of our direct-action program is to create a situation so crisis-packed that it will inevitably open the door to negotiation. I therefore concur with you in your call for negotiation. Too long has our beloved Southland been bogged down in a tragic effort to live in monologue rather than dialogue.

[12] One of the basic points in your statement is that the action that I and my associates have taken in Birmingham is untimely. Some have asked: "Why didn't you give the new city administration time to act?" The only answer that I can give to this query is that the new Birmingham administration must be prodded about as much as the outgoing one, before it will act. We are sadly mistaken if we feel that the election of Albert Boutwell as mayor will bring the millennium to Birmingham. While Mr. Boutwell is a much more gentle person than Mr. Connor, they are both segregationists, dedicated to maintenance of the status quo. I have hope that Mr. Boutwell will be reasonable enough to see the futility of massive resistance to desegregation. But he will not see this without pressure from devotees of civil rights. My friends, I must say to you that we have not made a single gain in civil rights without determined legal and nonviolent pressure. Lamentably, it is an historical fact that privileged groups seldom give up their privileges voluntarily. Individuals may see the moral light and voluntarily give up their unjust posture; but, as Reinhold Niebuhr has reminded us, groups tend to be more immoral than individuals.

[13] We know through painful experience that freedom is never voluntarily given by the oppressor; it must be demanded by the oppressed. Frankly, I have yet to engage in a direct-action campaign that was "well timed" in the view of those who have not suffered unduly from the disease of segregation. For years now I have heard the word "Wait!" It rings in the ear of every Negro with piercing familiarity. This "Wait" has almost always meant "Never." We must come to see, with one of our distinguished jurists, that "justice too long delayed is justice denied."

[14] We have waited for more than 340 years for our constitutional and God-given rights. The nations of Asia and Africa are moving with jetlike speed toward gaining political independence, but we still creep at horse-and-buggy pace toward gaining a cup of coffee at a lunch counter. Perhaps it is easy for those who have never felt the stinging darts of segregation to say, "Wait." But when you have seen vicious mobs lynch your mothers and fathers at will and drown your sisters and brothers at whim; when you have seen hate-filled policemen curse, kick and even kill your black brothers and sisters; when you see the vast majority of your twenty million Negro brothers smothering in an airtight cage of poverty in the midst of an affluent society; when you suddenly find your tongue twisted and your speech stammering as you seek to explain to your six-year-old daughter why she can't go to the public amusement park that has just been advertised on television, and see tears welling up in her eyes when she is told that Funtown is closed to colored children, and see ominous clouds of inferiority beginning to form in her little mental sky, and see her beginning to distort her personality by developing an unconscious bitterness toward white people; when you have to concoct an answer for a five-year-old son who is asking: "Daddy, why do white people treat colored people so mean?"; when you take a cross-country drive and find it necessary to sleep night after night in the uncomfortable corners of your automobile because no motel will accept you; when you are humiliated day in and day out by nagging signs reading "white" and "colored"; when your first name becomes "nigger," your middle name becomes "boy" (however old you are) and your last name becomes "John," and your wife and mother are never given the respected title "Mrs."; when you are harried by day and haunted by night by the fact that you are a Negro, living constantly at tiptoe stance, never quite knowing what to expect next, and are plagued with inner fears and outer resentments; when you are forever fighting a degenerating sense of "nobodiness"—then you will understand why we find it difficult to wait. There comes a time when the cup of endurance runs over, and men are no longer willing to be plunged into the abyss of despair. I hope, sirs, you can understand our legitimate and unavoidable impatience.

[15] You express a great deal of anxiety over our willingness to break laws. This is certainly a legitimate concern. Since we so diligently urge people to obey the Supreme Court's decision of 1954 outlawing segregation in the public schools, at first glance it may seem rather paradoxical for us consciously to break laws. One may well ask: "How can you advocate breaking some laws and obeying others?" The answer lies in the fact that there are two types of laws: just and unjust. I would be the first to advocate obeying just laws. One has not only a legal but a moral responsibility to obey just laws. Conversely, one has a moral responsibility to disobey unjust laws. I would agree with St. Augustine that "an unjust law is no law at all."

[16] Now, what is the difference between the two? How does one determine whether a law is just or unjust? A just law is a man-made code that squares with the moral law or the law of God. An unjust law is a code that is out of harmony with the moral law. To put it in the terms of St. Thomas Aquinas: An unjust law is a human law that is not rooted in eternal law and natural law. Any law that uplifts human personality is just. Any law that degrades human personality is unjust. All segregation statutes are unjust because segregation distorts the soul and damages the personality. It gives the segregator a false sense of superiority and the segregated a false sense of inferiority. Segregation, to use the terminology of the Jewish philosopher Martin Buber, substitutes an "I—it" relationship for an "I—thou" relationship and ends up relegating persons to the status of things. Hence segregation is not only politically, economically and sociologically unsound, it is morally wrong and sinful. Paul Tillich has said that sin is separation. Is not segregation an existential expression of man's tragic separation, his awful estrangement, his terrible sinfulness? Thus it is that I can urge men to obey the 1954 decision of the Supreme Court, for it is morally right; and I can urge them to disobey segregation ordinances, for they are morally wrong.

[17] Let us consider a more concrete example of just and unjust laws. An unjust law is a code that a numerical or power majority group compels a minority group to obey but does not make binding on itself. This is *difference* made legal. By the same token, a just law is a code that a majority compels a minority to follow and that it is willing to follow itself. This is *sameness* made legal.

[18] Let me give another explanation. A law is unjust if it is inflicted on a minority that, as a result of being denied the right to vote, had no part in enacting or devising the law. Who can say that the legislature of Alabama which set up that state's segregation laws was democratically elected? Throughout Alabama all sorts of devious methods are used to prevent Negroes from becoming registered voters, and there are some counties in which, even though Negroes constitute a majority of the population, not a single Negro is registered. Can any law enacted under such circumstances be considered democratically structured?

[19] Sometimes a law is just on its face and unjust in its application. For instance, I have been arrested on a charge of parading without a permit. Now, there is nothing wrong in having an ordinance which requires a permit for a parade. But such an ordinance becomes unjust when it is used to maintain segregation and to deny citizens the First-Amendment privilege of peaceful assembly and protest.

[20] I hope you are able to see the distinction I am trying to point out. In no sense do I advocate evading or defying the law, as would the rabid segregationist. That would lead to anarchy. One who breaks an unjust law must do so openly, lovingly, and with a willingness to accept the penalty. I submit that an individual who breaks a law that conscience tells

him is unjust, and who willingly accepts the penalty of imprisonment in order to arouse the conscience of the community over its injustice, is in reality expressing the highest respect for law.

[21] Of course, there is nothing new about this kind of civil disobedience. It was evidenced sublimely in the refusal of Shadrach, Meshach and Abednego to obey the laws of Nebuchadnezzar, on the ground that a higher moral law was at stake. It was practiced superbly by the early Christians, who were willing to face hungry lions and the excruciating pain of chopping blocks rather than submit to certain unjust laws of the Roman Empire. To a degree, academic freedom is a reality today because Socrates practiced civil disobedience. In our own nation, the Boston Tea Party represented a massive act of civil disobedience.

[22] We should never forget that everything Adolf Hitler did in Germany was "legal" and everything the Hungarian freedom fighters did in Hungary was "illegal." It was "illegal" to aid and comfort a Jew in Hitler's Germany. Even so, I am sure that, had I lived in Germany at the time, I would have aided and comforted my Jewish brothers. If today I lived in a Communist country where certain principles dear to the Christian faith are suppressed, I would openly advocate disobeying that country's antireligious laws.

[23] I must make two honest confessions to you, my Christian and Jewish brothers. First, I must confess that over the past few years I have been gravely disappointed with the white moderate. I have almost reached the regrettable conclusion that the Negro's great stumbling block in his stride toward freedom is not the White Citizen's Counciler or the Ku Klux Klanner, but the white moderate, who is more devoted to "order" than to justice; who prefers a negative peace which is the absence of tension to a positive peace which is the presence of justice; who constantly says: "I agree with you in the goal you seek, but I cannot agree with your methods of direct action"; who paternalistically believes he can set the timetable for another man's freedom; who lives by a mythical concept of time and who constantly advises the Negro to wait for a "more convenient season." Shallow understanding from people of good will is more frustrating than absolute misunderstanding from people of ill will. Lukewarm acceptance is much more bewildering than outright rejection.

[24] I had hoped that the white moderate would understand that law and order exist for the purpose of establishing justice and that when they fail in this purpose they become the dangerously structured dams that block the flow of social progress. I had hoped that the white moderate would understand that the present tension in the South is a necessary phase of the transition from an obnoxious negative peace, in which the Negro passively accepted his unjust plight, to a substantive and positive peace, in which all men will respect the dignity and worth of human personality. Actually, we who engage in nonviolent direct action are not the creators of tension. We merely bring to the surface the hidden tension that is already alive. We bring it out in the open, where it can be seen and dealt

with. Like a boil that can never be cured so long as it is covered up but must be opened with all its ugliness to the natural medicines of air and light, injustice must be exposed, with all the tension its exposure creates, to the light of human conscience and the air of national opinion before it can be cured.

[25] In your statement you assert that our actions, even though peaceful, must be condemned because they precipitate violence. But is this a logical assertion? Isn't this like condemning a robbed man because his possession of money precipitated the evil act of robbery? Isn't this like condemning Socrates because his unswerving commitment to truth and his philosophical inquiries precipitated the act by the misguided populace in which they made him drink hemlock? Isn't this like condemning Jesus because his unique God-consciousness and never-ceasing devotion to God's will precipitated the evil act of crucifixion? We must come to see that, as the federal courts have consistently affirmed, it is wrong to urge an individual to cease his efforts to gain his basic constitutional rights because the quest may precipitate violence. Society must protect the robbed and punish the robber.

[26] I had also hoped that the white moderate would reject the myth concerning time in relation to the struggle for freedom. I have just received a letter from a white brother in Texas. He writes: "All Christians know that the colored people will receive equal rights eventually, but it is possible that you are in too great a religious hurry. It has taken Christianity almost two thousand years to accomplish what it has. The teachings of Christ take time to come to earth." Such an attitude stems from a tragic misconception of time, from the strangely irrational notion that there is something in the very flow of time that will inevitably cure all ills. Actually, time itself is neutral; it can be used either destructively or constructively. More and more I feel that the people of ill will have used time much more effectively than have the people of good will. We will have to repent in this generation not merely for the hateful words and actions of the bad people but for the appalling silence of the good people. Human progress never rolls in on wheels of inevitability; it comes through the tireless efforts of men willing to be co-workers with God, and without this hard work, time itself becomes an ally of the forces of social stagnation. We must use time creatively, in the knowledge that the time is always ripe to do right. Now is the time to make real the promise of democracy and transform our pending national elegy into a creative psalm of brotherhood. Now is the time to lift our national policy from the quicksand of racial injustice to the solid rock of human dignity.

[27] You speak of our activity in Birmingham as extreme. At first I was rather disappointed that fellow clergymen would see my nonviolent efforts as those of an extremist. I began thinking about the fact that I stand in the middle of two opposing forces in the Negro community. One is a force of complacency, made up in part of Negroes who, as a result of long years of oppression, are so drained of self-respect and a sense of "some-

bodiness" that they have adjusted to segregation; and in part of a few middle-class Negroes who, because of a degree of academic and economic security and because in some ways they profit by segregation, have become insensitive to the problems of the masses. The other force is one of bitterness and hatred, and it comes perilously close to advocating violence. It is expressed in the various black nationalist groups that are springing up across the nation, the largest and best-known being Elijah Muhammad's Muslim movement. Nourished by the Negro's frustration over the continued existence of racial discrimination, this movement is made up of people who have lost faith in America, who have absolutely repudiated Christianity, and who have concluded that the white man is an incorrigible "devil."

[28] I have tried to stand between these two forces, saying that we need emulate neither the "do-nothingism" of the complacent nor the hatred and despair of the black nationalist. For there is the more excellent way of love and nonviolent protest. I am grateful to God that, through the influence of the Negro church, the way of nonviolence became an integral part of our struggle.

[29] If this philosophy had not emerged, by now many streets of the South would, I am convinced, be flowing with blood. And I am further convinced that if our white brothers dismiss as "rabble-rousers" and "outside agitators" those of us who employ nonviolent direct action, and if they refuse to support our nonviolent efforts, millions of Negroes will, out of frustration and despair, seek solace and security in black-nationalist ideologies—a development that would inevitably lead to a frightening racial nightmare.

[30] Oppressed people cannot remain oppressed forever. The yearning for freedom eventually manifests itself, and that is what has happened to the American Negro. Something within has reminded him of his birthright of freedom, and something without has reminded him that it can be gained. Consciously or unconsciously, he has been caught up by the *Zeitgeist,* and with his black brothers of Africa and his brown and yellow brothers of Asia, South America and the Caribbean, the United States Negro is moving with a sense of great urgency toward the promised land of racial justice. If one recognizes this vital urge that has engulfed the Negro community, one should readily understand why public demonstrations are taking place. The Negro has many pent-up resentments and latent frustrations, and he must release them. So let him march; let him make prayer pilgrimages to the city hall; let him go on freedom rides—and try to understand why he must do so. If his repressed emotions are not released in nonviolent ways, they will seek expression through violence; this is not a threat but a fact of history. So I have not said to my people: "Get rid of your discontent." Rather, I have tried to say that this normal and healthy discontent can be channeled into the creative outlet of nonviolent direct action. And now this approach is being termed extremist.

[31] But though I was initially disappointed at being categorized as an extremist, as I continued to think about the matter I gradually

gained a measure of satisfaction from the label. Was not Jesus an extremist for love: "Love your enemies, bless them that curse you, do good to them that hate you, and pray for them which despitefully use you, and persecute you." Was not Amos an extremist for justice: "Let justice roll down like waters and righteousness like an ever-flowing stream." Was not Paul an extremist for the Christian gospel: "I bear in my body the marks of the Lord Jesus." Was not Martin Luther an extremist: "Here I stand; I cannot do otherwise, so help me God." And John Bunyan: "I will stay in jail to the end of my days before I make a butchery of my conscience." And Abraham Lincoln: "This nation cannot survive half slave and half free." And Thomas Jefferson: "We hold these truths to be self-evident, that all men are created equal . . ." So the question is not whether we will be extremists, but what kind of extremists we will be. Will we be extremists for hate or for love? Will we be extremists for the preservation of injustice or for the extension of justice? In that dramatic scene on Calvary's hill three men were crucified. We must never forget that all three were crucified for the same crime—the crime of extremism. Two were extremists for immorality, and thus fell below their environment. The other, Jesus Christ, was an extremist for love, truth and goodness, and thereby rose above his environment. Perhaps the South, the nation and the world are in dire need of creative extremists.

[32] I had hoped that the white moderate would see this need. Perhaps I was too optimistic; perhaps I expected too much. I suppose I should have realized that few members of the oppressor race can understand the deep groans and passionate yearnings of the oppressed race, and still fewer have the vision to see that injustice must be rooted out by strong, persistent and determined action. I am thankful, however, that some of our white brothers in the South have grasped the meaning of this social revolution and committed themselves to it. They are still all too few in quantity, but they are big in quality. Some—such as Ralph McGill, Lillian Smith, Harry Golden, James McBride Dabbs, Ann Braden and Sarah Patton Boyle—have written about our struggle in eloquent and prophetic terms. Others have marched with us down nameless streets of the South. They have languished in filthy, roach-infested jails, suffering the abuse and brutality of policemen who view them as "dirty nigger-lovers." Unlike so many of their moderate brothers and sisters, they have recognized the urgency of the moment and sensed the need for powerful "action" antidotes to combat the disease of segregation.

[33] Let me take note of my other major disappointment. I have been so greatly disappointed with the white church and its leadership. Of course, there are some notable exceptions. I am not unmindful of the fact that each of you has taken some significant stands on this issue. I commend you, Reverend Stallings, for your Christian stand on this past Sunday, in welcoming Negroes to your worship service on a nonsegregated basis. I commend the Catholic leaders of this state for integrating Spring Hill College several years ago.

[34] But despite these notable exceptions, I must honestly reiterate that I have been disappointed with the church. I do not say this as one of those negative critics who can always find something wrong with the church. I say this as a minister of the gospel, who loves the church; who was nurtured in its bosom; who has been sustained by its spiritual blessings and who will remain true to it as long as the cord of life shall lengthen.

[35] When I was suddenly catapulted into the leadership of the bus protest in Montgomery, Alabama, a few years ago, I felt we would be supported by the white church. I felt that the white ministers, priests and rabbis of the South would be among our strongest allies. Instead, some have been outright opponents, refusing to understand the freedom movement and misrepresenting its leaders; all too many others have been more cautious than courageous and have remained silent behind the anesthetizing security of stained-glass windows.

[36] In spite of my shattered dreams, I came to Birmingham with the hope that the white religious leadership of this community would see the justice of our cause and, with deep moral concern, would serve as the channel through which our just grievances could reach the power structure. I had hoped that each of you would understand. But again I have been disappointed.

[37] I have heard numerous southern religious leaders admonish their worshipers to comply with a desegregation decision because it is the law, but I have longed to hear white ministers declare: "Follow this decree because integration is morally right and because the Negro is your brother." In the midst of blatant injustices inflicted upon the Negro, I have watched white churchmen stand on the sideline and mouth pious irrelevancies and sanctimonious trivialities. In the midst of a mighty struggle to rid our nation of racial and economic injustice, I have heard many ministers say: "Those are social issues, with which the gospel has no real concern." And I have watched many churches commit themselves to a completely otherworldly religion which makes a strange, un-Biblical distinction between body and soul, between the sacred and the secular.

[38] I have traveled the length and breadth of Alabama, Mississippi and all the other southern states. On sweltering summer days and crisp autumn mornings I have looked at the South's beautiful churches with their lofty spires pointing heavenward. I have beheld the impressive outlines of her massive religious-education buildings. Over and over I have found myself asking: "What kind of people worship here? Who is their God? Where were their voices when the lips of Governor Barnett dripped with words of interposition and nullification? Where were they when Governor Wallace gave a clarion call for defiance and hatred? Where were their voices of support when bruised and weary Negro men and women decided to rise from the dark dungeons of complacency to the bright hills of creative protest?"

[39] Yes, these questions are still in my mind. In deep disappointment I have wept over the laxity of the church. But be assured that my

tears have been tears of love. There can be no deep disappointment where there is not deep love. Yes, I love the church. How could I do otherwise? I am in the rather unique position of being the son, the grandson and the great-grandson of preachers. Yes, I see the church as the body of Christ. But, oh! How we have blemished and scarred that body through social neglect and through fear of being nonconformists.

[40] There was a time when the church was very powerful—in the time when the early Christians rejoiced at being deemed worthy to suffer for what they believed. In those days the church was not merely a thermometer that recorded the ideas and principles of popular opinion; it was a thermostat that transformed the mores of society. Whenever the early Christians entered a town, the people in power became disturbed and immediately sought to convict the Christians for being "disturbers of the peace" and "outside agitators." But the Christians pressed on, in the conviction that they were "a colony of heaven," called to obey God rather than man. Small in number, they were big in commitment. They were too God-intoxicated to be "astronomically intimidated." By their effort and example they brought an end to such ancient evils as infanticide and gladiatorial contests.

[41] Things are different now. So often the contemporary church is a weak, ineffectual voice with an uncertain sound. So often it is an arch-defender of the status quo. Far from being disturbed by the presence of the church, the power structure of the average community is consoled by the church's silent—and often even vocal—sanction of things as they are.

[42] But the judgment of God is upon the church as never before. If today's church does not recapture the sacrificial spirit of the early church, it will lose its authenticity, forfeit the loyalty of millions, and be dismissed as an irrelevant social club with no meaning for the twentieth century. Every day I meet young people whose disappointment with the church has turned into outright disgust.

[43] Perhaps I have once again been too optimistic. Is organized religion too inextricably bound to the status quo to save our nation and the world? Perhaps I must turn my faith to the inner spiritual church, the church within the church, as the true *ekklesia* and the hope of the world. But again I am thankful to God that some noble souls from the ranks of organized religion have broken loose from the paralyzing chains of conformity and joined us as active partners in the struggle for freedom. They have left their secure congregations and walked the streets of Albany, Georgia, with us. They have gone down the highways of the South on tortuous rides for freedom. Yes, they have gone to jail with us. Some have been dismissed from their churches, have lost the support of their bishops and fellow ministers. But they have acted in the faith that right defeated is stronger than evil triumphant. Their witness has been the spiritual salt that has preserved the true meaning of the gospel in these troubled times. They have carved a tunnel of hope through the dark mountain of disappointment.

[44] I hope the church as a whole will meet the challenge of this

decisive hour. But even if the church does not come to the aid of justice, I have no despair about the future. I have no fear about the outcome of our struggle in Birmingham, even if our motives are at present misunderstood. We will reach the goal of freedom in Birmingham and all over the nation, because the goal of America is freedom. Abused and scorned though we may be, our destiny is tied up with America's destiny. Before the pilgrims landed at Plymouth, we were here. Before the pen of Jefferson etched the majestic words of the Declaration of Independence across the pages of history, we were here. For more than two centuries our forebears labored in this country without wages; they made cotton king; they built the homes of their masters while suffering gross injustice and shameful humiliation—and yet out of a bottomless vitality they continued to thrive and develop. If the inexpressible cruelties of slavery could not stop us, the opposition we now face will surely fail. We will win our freedom because the sacred heritage of our nation and the eternal will of God are embodied in our echoing demands.

[45] Before closing I feel impelled to mention one other point in your statement that has troubled me profoundly. You warmly commended the Birmingham police force for keeping "order" and "preventing violence." I doubt that you would have so warmly commended the police force if you had seen its dogs sinking their teeth into unarmed, nonviolent Negroes. I doubt that you would so quickly commend the policemen if you were to observe their ugly and inhumane treatment of Negroes here in the city jail; if you were to watch them push and curse old Negro women and young Negro girls; if you were to see them slap and kick old Negro men and young boys; if you were to observe them, as they did on two occasions, refuse to give us food because we wanted to sing our grace together. I cannot join you in your praise of the Birmingham police department.

[46] It is true that the police have exercised a degree of discipline in handling the demonstrators. In this sense they have conducted themselves rather "nonviolently" in public. But for what purpose? To preserve the evil system of segregation. Over the past few years I have consistently preached that nonviolence demands that the means we use must be as pure as the ends we seek. I have tried to make clear that it is wrong to use immoral means to attain moral ends. But now I must affirm that it is just as wrong, or perhaps even more so, to use moral means to preserve immoral ends. Perhaps Mr. Connor and his policemen have been rather nonviolent in public, as was Chief Pritchett in Albany, Georgia, but they have used the moral means of nonviolence to maintain the immoral end of racial injustice. As T. S. Eliot has said: "The last temptation is the greatest treason: To do the right deed for the wrong reason."

[47] I wish you had commended the Negro sit-inners and demonstrators of Birmingham for their sublime courage, their willingness to suffer and their amazing discipline in the midst of great provocation. One day the South will recognize its real heroes. They will be the James Merediths, with the noble sense of purpose that enables them to face jeering and hos-

tile mobs, and with the agonizing loneliness that characterizes the life of the pioneer. They will be old, oppressed, battered Negro women, symbolized in a seventy-two-year-old woman in Montgomery, Alabama, who rose up with a sense of dignity and with her people decided not to ride segregated buses, and who responded with ungrammatical profundity to one who inquired about her weariness: "My feets is tired, but my soul is at rest." They will be the young high school and college students, the young ministers of the gospel and a host of their elders, courageously and nonviolently sitting in at lunch counters and willingly going to jail for conscience' sake. One day the South will know that when these disinherited children of God sat down at lunch counters, they were in reality standing up for what is best in the American dream and for the most sacred values in our Judaeo-Christian heritage, thereby bringing our nation back to those great wells of democracy which were dug deep by the founding fathers in their formulation of the Constitution and the Declaration of Independence.

[48] Never before have I written so long a letter. I'm afraid it is much too long to take your precious time. I can assure you that it would have been much shorter if I had been writing from a comfortable desk, but what else can one do when he is alone in a narrow jail cell, other than write long letters, think long thoughts and pray long prayers?

[49] If I have said anything in this letter that overstates the truth and indicates an unreasonable impatience, I beg you to forgive me. If I have said anything that understates the truth and indicates my having a patience that allows me to settle for anything less than brotherhood, I beg God to forgive me.

[50] I hope this letter finds you strong in the faith. I also hope that circumstances will soon make it possible for me to meet each of you, not as an integrationist or a civil-rights leader but as a fellow clergyman and a Christian brother. Let us all hope that the dark clouds of racial prejudice will soon pass away and the deep fog of misunderstanding will be lifted from our fear-drenched communities, and in some not too distant tomorrow the radiant stars of love and brotherhood will shine over our great nation with all their scintillating beauty.

Yours for the cause of Peace and Brotherhood,
Martin Luther King, Jr.

Questions on Meaning

1 What answers does King give to each criticism the clergymen raised? Divide a page into two columns, listing the objections in one column and King's responses in the other. Use your own language throughout. Which of King's arguments do you find most convincing? Why?

2 A key concept in this essay is the distinction King makes between just laws and unjust laws. Explain this distinction in your own words, being careful not to misrepresent the author.

3 How does King support the judgment that "One has a moral responsibility to disobey unjust laws"? Do you agree with his position?

Questions on Style and Structure

1 King was very fond of using parallel sentences. How many examples can you find? Which passages do you think are most effective?

2 There are numerous similes and metaphors in this letter. Underline as many as you can. Are they appropriate and fresh? Note in particular those that deal with height and depth and light and darkness.

3 In the first paragraph of the letter, King says that he will try to answer the statement of the Alabama clergymen in "patient and reasonable terms." Would you agree that his language is "patient and reasonable"?

4 The following passage from paragraph 24 presents an analogy:

> Actually, we who engage in nonviolent direct action are not the creators of tension. We merely bring to the surface the hidden tension that is already alive. We bring it out in the open, where it can be seen and dealt with. Like a boil that can never be cured so long as it is covered up but must be opened with all its ugliness to the natural medicines of air and light, injustice must be exposed, with all the tension its exposure creates, to the light of human conscience and the air of national opinion before it can be cured.

Locate other analogies. How appropriate and effective are they?

5 The fourth sentence of paragraph 14 is very long, containing many parallel elements and numerous concrete details. It is a *periodic* sentence. Should King have divided this sentence into briefer ones? Why?

6 There are many references to religious leaders (such as Martin Buber and Paul Tillich) and to Biblical history in this letter. How effective are they, and why do you suppose King used so many?

7 If you were to outline this letter, what would the major headings and their order be?

8 How effective is King's conclusion? Do you find the heavy use of figurative language effective?

Exploring Words

1 *harried.* Use both the adjective and the verb form of this word in sentences of your own.

2 *paternalistically.* One might expect a word derived from a source meaning "father" to have taken on positive connotations. Does your dictionary suggest that this word is generally used with positive or with negative connotations? Which connotation does it have in King's usage?

3 *precipitated.* Check your dictionary, and then determine the relationship of the words *precipice, precipitation,* and *precipitate.*

4 *complacency.* As King has used the word *complacency,* does it relate to the adjective *complacent* or the adjective *complaisant?*

Suggestions for Writing

1 Write a letter defending a position you have been criticized for holding or one you think the person you are writing to might not be predisposed to accept. For example, you might write a letter to your parents defending a change in major that will mean an additional year in college (at their expense). Or you might write a letter to an officer or member of an organization (a service club, a fraternity, a sorority, a church group) explaining why you cannot join or continue membership.

2 Discuss as eloquently as you can a strong conviction that you hold. Use parallel sentences and figurative language when appropriate.

3 Write an essay in which you explain some course of action that should be taken (for example, by your college or municipal government).

Why History
HENRY STEELE COMMAGER

Getting Started

With Ideas

When you begin reading an essay with a title that directly asks or clearly implies the question "Why?" it is a good idea to have a pencil in hand and to number in the margins the author's main points as you come across them. For this complex, but logically organized, essay, the method will work especially well. Here Henry Steele Commager—an eminent contemporary historian—presents his rationale for the teaching of history, answering the questions What history? and How should history be taught? as he treats the more basic question: Why teach history at all? Like many writers who carefully organize complex ideas, Commager provides conspicuous transitions between major divisions and frequently indicates his method of ordering by using expressions like "first" and "another reason." With pencil in hand, you can translate these markers into your own shorthand (for example, Reasons 1, 2, 3) and thereby make sure that you are following his thinking, at the same time forming an outline for later study.

With Words

1. Philistine (2)—the *Philistines* were the traditional enemies of the Israelites in the Old Testament. See if you can determine from the context what qualities we now associate with the word.
2. vindicates (2)—from the Latin word meaning "to lay claim to" or "avenge."
3. ostentatious (5)—whom do you know who dresses *ostentatiously* or who drives an *ostentatious* automobile? See also "The American Way of Death" (p. 279).
4. vicariously (8)—what experiences have you had only *vicariously*—for example, through reading about someone else's adventures? See also the way Walker used the word in "The Civil Rights Movement: What Good Was It?" (p. 256).
5. assiduous (21)—the context will help you determine the meaning of this word.
6. parochialism (28)—from the Latin word for "parish." You are probably familiar with the phrase *"parochial* school," but note that *parochialism* is here used in a metaphorical sense.
7. microcosms (40)—is your university or college a *microcosm* of the world outside?
8. exigency (40)—this word, which comes from the Latin word meaning "to demand," is pronounced ek'-si-jen-si.

"Why History" appeared in *American Education*, June 1965. Reprinted by permission of *American Education*.

9 amalgam (42)—relate the word to *amalgamation* and *Amalgamated* Steel, as you did in reading "The Silver Horn" (p. 91).

---

[1] We should begin, in all fairness, with the question: why teach history at all? What is the *use* of history?

[2] That sounds like a Philistine question, but it is not. The very fact that it comes up so frequently vindicates, in a sense, its relevance. Who, after all, asks what is the use of mathematics or biology or accounting?

[3] Let us admit at once that in a practical way history has no use. Let us concede that it is not good for anything that can be weighed or measured or counted, that can be *used* as chemistry or accounting can be used. It will not save us from repeating the errors of the past; it will not solve problems; it will not show us how to win wars or, more important, how to avoid them. It will not provide us with scientific explanations of depressions or keys to prosperity, with scientific guides to nominations and elections, with scientific controls over great questions of national policy. It will not contribute in any overt way to progress.

[4] But the same can be said, of course, for many other things which society values and which men cherish. What use, after all, is a Beethoven sonata, or a painting by Renoir, or a statue by Milles, or a sonnet by Wordsworth? What use, for that matter, are a great many quite mundane things which society takes for granted and on which it lavishes immense thought and effort: baseball, for example, or a rose garden?

[5] Happily a civilized society does not devote all of its thought and effort to things whose usefulness can be statistically demonstrated. There are other criteria than that of ostentatious usefulness and even other meanings of the term "useful" than those acknowledged by the Thomas Gradgrinds of this world.

[6] History is useful in the sense that art is useful—or music or poetry or flowers; perhaps even in the sense that religion and philosophy are useful. Like history, these do not provide certain answers to questions. If you study philosophy, even if you embrace religion, you are in a sense engaged in a gamble, but it is a gamble which all sensible men accept. It is one of those gambles which William James had in mind in that famous passage: "Suppose that the world's author put the case to you before creation, saying: 'I am going to make a world not certain to be saved, a world the perfection of which shall be conditional, merely, the condition being that each several agent does its own level best. I offer you the chance of taking part in such a world. Its safety, you see, is unwarranted. It is a real adventure, with real danger, yet it may win through. . . . Will you join the procession? Will you trust yourself and trust the other agents enough to face the risk?'"

[7] All of us, in a sense, accept this gamble. All of us, too, instinctively, accept the gamble submitted to us by the study of things which have no guaranteed use. For without these things life would be poorer and meaner; without them we should be denied those intellectual and moral experiences that give meaning and richness to life itself.

[8] Can we go beyond this? I think we can. If history does not have measurable use, it does have rewards and values: we may even call them pleasures. The first and perhaps the richest pleasure of history is that it adds new dimensions to life itself by enormously extending our perspective and enlarging our experience. It permits us to enter vicariously into the past, to project our vision back over thousands of years, and to enlarge it to embrace all the peoples of the earth.

[9] Through the pages of history we can hear Pericles deliver his Funeral Oration to the Athenians, trek with the Crusaders to the Holy Land, sail with Columbus past the gates of Hercules, share the life of Goethe at the little Court of Weimar, listen to the Lincoln-Douglas debates in little dusty prairie towns, and stand beside Winston Churchill as he rallies the people of Britain to their finest hour.

[10] History can supply us with all of those elements that Henry James thought most essential to the life of the mind: density, variety, intricacy, richness in the pattern of thought, and with it a "sense of the past."

[11] This immense enlargement of experience carries with it a second pleasure or reward, for it means that history provides us with great companions. This consideration is perhaps more familiar to adults who have learned how rare is contemporary greatness than to the young who may imagine that they will live on a stage crowded with heroic characters.

[12] Wherever the historian or biographer has been, he has given new depth and range to our associations. We have but to take the books down from the serried shelves to be admitted to the company and the confidence of Voltaire and Rousseau, Johnson and Boswell, Thomas Jefferson and George Washington, William James and Justice Holmes. We can, indeed, come to know these and other great men more intimately than their contemporaries knew them, for we can read their letters, journals, and diaries. All this is not merely one of the pleasures of history; it is one of the indispensable pleasures of life.

[13] The best thing we can do for young people is to keep constantly before their eyes the spectacle of greatness. History presents them with that spectacle, and it makes clear what are the attributes of greatness.

[14] A third and familiar pleasure of history is the experience of identifying the present with the past and thus adding a new dimension to places. It was Thomas Macaulay who observed, "the pleasure of history is analogous in many respects to that produced by foreign travel. The student is transported into a new state of society. . . . His mind is enlarged by contemplating the wide diversities of laws, of morals, and of manners."

[15] But history is far more rewarding than travel, for it enables the reader to travel not only in the dimension of space but in the dimension of time, to know not only contemporary England but Roman Britain, to wander with a good guide not only through modern Florence but through the Florence of Leonardo and Michelangelo. It enables us to see the present through the eyes of the past, to give a new dimension to whatever place we visit.

[16] Suppose we chose to introduce the young to the little town of Salem. It is a lovely town in its own right, its handsome old white frame houses still standing so staunchly along Chestnut and Federal Streets. As we look at it through the eyes of history we conjure up a straggling village, older even than Boston, ever busy with fishing and with theological disputes, and we remember that Roger Williams preached here and Mistress Anne Hutchinson too. We look at Gallows Hill and recall the dark story of Salem witchcraft, which haunted Nathaniel Hawthorne, who grew up here and whose spirit still broods over the town.

[17] We conjure up Salem at the turn of the century, when its proud captains sailed all the waters of the globe, when the flag of Salem was thought to be the flag of an independent nation, and when the spoils of the pepper trade and the China trade glittered in every drawing room. And we people its tree-lined streets with perhaps the most remarkable galaxy of talent and genius that one little American town ever boasted.

[18] There is another and perhaps a deeper value in history, for history is the memory of man, and it is therefore the way by which man knows himself. A people without history is like a man without memory: each generation would have to learn everything anew—make the same discoveries, invent the same tools and techniques, wrestle with the same problems, commit the same errors. And as the individual man can know himself only by knowing his own past, so mankind can know itself only through its past. As that remarkable Oxford philosopher-historian, Robin Collingwood, has said in answering the question, "What is history for?"

"My answer is that history is 'for' Human self-knowledge.

". . . Knowing yourself means knowing what you can do, and since nobody knows what he can do until he tries, the only clue to what man can do is what man has done. The value of history, then, is that it teaches us what man has done and thus what man is. (*The Idea of History,* p. 10)

[19] For well over two thousand years the study of history has been the interest, the passion, the delight, the consolation of the richest minds. From the days of Homer and Thucydides down to our own day philosophers and scholars have been zealous to record the deeds of the past and to praise famous men. Almost all of our greatest statesmen from Jefferson to Kennedy have been nursed on the study of history, almost all of our imaginative writers from Washington Irving and Nathaniel Hawthorne to William Faulkner and Robert Frost have immersed themselves in his-

tory. No subject except religion has won the allegiance of noble minds for as long a span of time as history has.

[20] If then we are justified in teaching history, what history should we teach?

[21] There is, after all, so much of it. The most assiduous scholars cannot master even a small part of it in a lifetime of study—cannot master the whole history of a single one of many nations, of a single one of many eras.

[22] Clearly then we must be highly selective. But we do not have any agreed-on standard for selection. We cannot say that we should teach the most important history or the most interesting history, for both of these terms are subjective. We cannot say that there is any one body of history that everyone must know, for this is palpably untrue. We cannot say, let us teach what we want to teach or teach what interests us most, for we have an obligation to our society and to the next generation. No, this question of what history to teach is a serious one.

[23] On the whole, however, we have greatly oversimplified the problem—we in America and schoolmen in every other country as well. For the answer is almost everywhere the same: teach the history of your own country, teach national history. The French take this for granted, the Germans, the Danes, the Mexicans, and so do we in America. With us the teaching of American history is almost a non-stop process: we teach it in elementary school and in the high school; then we teach it again in the college.

[24] The logic of teaching boys and girls national history is persuasive enough. One of the essential ingredients of nationalism is a common past, a common memory, a common heritage of tragedy and of glory—so all the historians of nationalism have asserted. If we are to have a nation we must, then, provide this ingredient.

[25] One of the essential ingredients of unity is a body of common denominators—a common body of references and allusions; common heroes, villains, poets, and storytellers; common symbols; common monuments—a flag, a ballad, a shrine, a song, a legend.

[26] And one of the essential ingredients of freedom and self-government—it was Jefferson who insisted on this—is a people trained to liberty through the study of history, trained to self-government through the study of democracy, trained by history to conduct themselves as freeborn Americans should.

[27] All of these arguments for the study of national history are persuasive. But they are not conclusive. There is something to be said on the other side as well.

[28] There is, for example, the consideration that we have, if anything, too much emphasis on nationalism and that we need to abate this emphasis, not to increase it. There is the consideration that one of the dangers to good citizenship is precisely parochialism: that a study of other peoples and other eras might make much wiser and better citizens. After

all, it is pointed out, the Founding Fathers were not trained on American history—there was none.

[29] There is the consideration that much of American history can be allowed to take care of itself; after all, youngsters are exposed to it ceaselessly—in newspapers and magazines, over the radio and on the television, in story books and picture books, in lectures and addresses, in a thousand allusions. How can anyone grow up in a country and not absorb its history? No, the school should be a kind of countervailing force, should give children what they will not in all likelihood get in later years: the history of other peoples and other times.

[30] For a large number of students there is still another consideration. At least half of those who finish secondary school will go on to college. The percentage will in all likelihood increase, and the day when 14 years of schooling will be taken for granted or required by law is not far distant. Almost all youngsters will therefore have a chance to study American history at a more mature age later on. Why not give them something different in high school or, if not something different, at least something more?

[31] But what? There is difficulty; although there is pretty general agreement on the importance of national history, there is no such agreement on the alternative.

[32] When we consider alternate or supplementary programs, two kinds of history commend themselves. One might be called traditional history—the study of those great epochs of the past or of those great nations that by common consent have contributed most to our own inheritance. Traditionally this has meant Greece and Rome, the Renaissance and the Age of Discovery, and—in the United States at least—the history of England.

[33] Now there is much to be said for introducing young people to one or all of these areas of history. This is one way of introducing them to civilization: this is one way of introducing them to their own inheritance. It is one way of recognizing and paying "our debt" to Greece and Rome, to the Renaissance, to what used to be called the "mother country." There are other arguments as well. It is the classical world and the Renaissance that by common consent are the glorious eras of Western history. It is England—or Britain—which has had far and away the strongest impact of all nations on the world in which we live.

[34] Because these eras of history have seemed fascinating they have attracted the best literature, and if youngsters are to be tempted into the study of history it will be through great literature—the great writers of these epochs, the great historians who have written about these epochs. What better introduction to history than Homer and Herodotus and Thucydides? What better introduction, at a later stage, than Gibbon and Mahaffey and Grote and Zimmern? Or, let students immerse themselves in the glorious story of Renaissance Florence; of Venice, that "eldest child of

liberty"; of Elizabethan England. These are the books that will open new worlds, that will inflame the imagination!

[35] But there is a second approach to history which clamors for consideration. That is the history of the very old and the very new nations.

[36] Here we are—say the champions of this new history—in the midst of a revolution. We have neglected and ignored two-thirds of the human race; we have neglected or ignored the history of Asia and of Africa and even of our neighbors south of the Rio Grande. Let us equip ourselves to understand this great revolution; let us welcome the scores of new nations in the globe, and the old ones too—like China and India. Let us expose the young to their history and their literature.

[37] No one, surely, can quarrel with this diagnosis. The prescription is another matter entirely. Can it be done, and done well, in the time available to the study of history in the secondary school?

[38] Is it possible for teachers, ill-trained as most of them are, to survey the "world, from China to Peru," in Dr. Johnson's phrase? Is it possible to find teaching materials for so complex a task? Is it possible to do justice—or to avoid injustice—to fifty or a hundred nations in the few months available? If teacher and student engage in a convulsive effort to learn something about China, India, Pakistan, Japan, the Arab world, Israel, the Congo, South Africa, and the twenty States of South America, will they achieve anything more than historical indigestion?

[39] In all fairness we must answer that we do not know. But so far this enterprise has not worked very well. Perhaps the British are more nearly right than some of our educators. The British approach to this problem of understanding scores of peoples and nations is not to study the history or the literature or the government of each. That, they think, is hopeless. It is rather to train those carefully selected young men who are to go out and deal with these countries in what might be called the fundamentals of history, of literature, and of politics.

[40] In the past these fundamentals were simple enough: in history it was Greece and Rome; in literature it was Greek and Latin; in politics it was Aristotle and perhaps John Locke and John Stuart Mill. These histories and these writers provided, so the British thought, microcosms of the world, and students thoroughly immersed in this study would be prepared for any exigency.

[41] During the nineteenth century that method worked pretty well. Perhaps it worked better than the very different American approach to the same problem.

[42] We come then to an even more difficult and controversial question: how should history be taught? There are only a limited number of ways in which to teach history in the elementary and secondary schools, and these are familiar enough. We can choose among them, or we can attempt a kind of amalgam of them.

[43] First, we can undertake to instruct the young in the "facts" of

history. Our instinct is to shy away from this method and this objective. This is a sound instinct, for we all recognize that the "facts" of history, far from being hard, are in fact elusive, inconclusive, and subjective. We all know that when we look at them closely they act like the Cheshire Cat—they disappear, all but the grin. Yet we should not repudiate this approach altogether.

[44] Something is to be said for having a knowledge of essential historical facts—facts of chronology, geography, and biography—just as something is to be said for having a firm grasp of the multiplication table or English grammar. No one supposes that knowing the multiplication table will enable the student to understand mathematics, or that knowing some of the rules of grammar will enable him to understand literature. But most of us would agree that without knowing these elementary things he can scarcely hope to understand more sophisticated relationships and ideas.

[45] But it will be said that the "facts" of history are readily available in textbooks or almanacs. So they are. But life goes easier if they are an instinctive part of what we carry about with us—for example, the words of the national anthem, the geography of streets of our home town, or the value of coins. Perhaps it is not really important to know that Arthur succeeded Garfield in the Presidency, but it simplifies matters if we can take for granted that all do know this.

[46] Second and more important is, of course, understanding. If understanding cannot operate without facts, facts are useless without understanding. We teach history so that our students may understand the past and the present. Increasingly we fob off the young with "problems" which are, as often as not, contrived and artificial.

[47] Increasingly we present history to them as a series of headaches—not the story of the Westward movement but the "problems of the frontier," not the winning of independence but the "problem of imperial organization," not the spectacle of social and humanitarian reform but the "problem of social reform." To ask young people to study the problem of the West without reading Parkman or the problem of the Civil War without reading Freeman's *Lee* or Benét's *John Brown's Body* is, in a sense, like asking them to read the Kinsey report before they have read any love poetry.

[48] Most of the historians who have achieved some kind of immortality have known this almost instinctively and have combined narrative and drama with analysis and interpretation. There are exceptions to be sure: Frederick W. Maitland, Lord Acton, or Ernest Cassirer come to mind. But no one would try to enlist the interest of high school students with these authors. Every child, however, can read Froissart or Shakespeare (Churchill said that he learned English history from Shakespeare), Macaulay or Parkman; let them do so. The Maitlands and the Cassirers will come later.

[49] What we will probably get is something of a combination of these various approaches to the teaching of history. We will continue to teach some agreed-on "facts," however dubious their philosophical foundations; we will introduce students to "problems," or they will force themselves upon the attention of the students. We will appeal, if we can, to the imagination. These are not and cannot be separate activities; they are as much part of the same process as reading notes, using the fingers, and understanding the score are part of playing the piano.

[50] But there is a chronological arrangement, one rooted perhaps in nature rather than in logic. It is this: first stir and enlist the imagination by telling a story; then concentrate on getting the sequence of "facts"—the chronology, the geography, and the like—under control; then turn to the problems.

[51] It is the imagination and the basis of facts that are most important for the purposes of teaching; the problems will, in a sense, take care of themselves. One of the difficulties of so much of the current emphasis on analysis—we call it the "problem" method—is that students are expected to analyze a complex body of data and draw conclusions from that analysis on the basis of the most meager and inconclusive information.

[52] This approach is supposed to be more "scientific" than narration, for example; but it is not one accepted by scientists. No student is expected to analyze problems in biology or physics or chemistry on the basis of a smattering of data. Solving "problems" on the basis of odds and ends of facts would never do for these scientific disciplines; there is no reason to suppose that it will work in history. Indeed this method of approach may do more harm than good, by inculcating slovenly habits of thinking upon the young.

[53] A third method of teaching is to excite interest in the spectacle of history and to stir the imagination. This is the old, the traditional approach to history, and not for children alone but for all those who inquired about the past. The first historians were storytellers—the writers of the Old Testament, Homer, Herodotus, Thucydides, and Plutarch—and so too most of their successors down through the centuries.

[54] Teaching is itself the imaginative communication between the old and the young, the imaginative transmission of knowledge and, it is hoped, of wisdom from generation to generation. Certainly history offers no exception to this general principle. Here, if anywhere, such imaginative communication should be encouraged. For no other subject, it is safe to say, can be relied upon more confidently to catch the imagination of the young. No other offers such continuous drama; no other presents such a spectacle of greatness. If there is any value in history, our first task must surely be to catch the interest of the young, to persuade them to read and to study history, to open ι p to them the inexhaustibly rich world of the past.

[55] One fair objection to so much of the history teaching of our

own time is that as it has grown more "scientific" it has grown less interesting to the average student; as it increases its appeal to scholars, it loses its appeals to those who are not scholars—that is, to the great mass of the people.

[56] Those who plan our curriculums and who teach seem sometimes to act as if high school were not only the last chance students would have at any subject but the only chance, the only agency of instruction. But should we not keep in mind that students do not study American history in a vacuum or in isolation? Most of them have studied it before, most of them, it is safe to say, will study it again. All of them are exposed to history in some form or other almost every day. They read history in their newspapers and magazines, they see it on television and on the films; they consider it in discussions of current affairs.

[57] Most of them will be tempted to the contemplation of American history the rest of their lives. They do not have to learn everything during these high school years, nor to solve all the problems. It is enough that they become familiar with the problems and with some of the ways of thinking about them. It is enough that they acquire a taste for the reading and study of history, a taste and a habit, so that they will turn to it again and again in the years ahead, not as a chore nor even as a duty—but as a delight.

Questions on Meaning

1. Convert your marginal notes into a topic outline of the essay. One of your major headings will probably be "Why History?" or something of the sort. How, then, can you explain Commager's title? Did he choose a title that applies only to one section of his essay? If so, why? Is there any part of the work in which he departs from a strictly ordered treatment of topics? If so, why does he do this?

2. Commager frequently goes to great lengths to avoid oversimplifying an issue or making unsupportable generalizations. For example, after summarizing the arguments for stressing American history in the history curriculum of American schools, he adds, "There is something to be said for the other side as well." Then he proceeds to give a number of reasons why he thinks the teaching of American history has been overemphasized in the schools of this country. Find other examples of this kind of qualification. Do you find this restrained, "middle-ground" approach effective or disturbing? Is this approach (which is really a kind of tone) consistent with his thesis?

3. What is the thesis of the article? Where is it stated most specifically?

4. How specific is Commager in his treatment of the *how* and the *what* of history teaching? For example, to what extent does he let you know what he would do if he were responsible for the history curriculum of a school district or a college? Is his degree of specificity on these matters appropriate, considering what his thesis is?

ESSAYS CHIEFLY PERSUASIVE

Questions on Style and Structure

1 Commager uses a fairly common technique to introduce his essay. What is it?

2 Paragraph 38 provides us with an excellent example of parallel sentences:

> Is it possible for teachers, ill-trained as most of them are, to survey the "world, from China to Peru," in Dr. Johnson's phrase? Is it possible to find teaching materials for so complex a task? Is it possible to do justice—or to avoid injustice—to fifty or a hundred nations in the few months available?

Are there other examples of parallel sentences in the selection?

3 The author is also fond of employing parallel elements within individual sentences. The following is an example of such a sentence:

> But history is far more rewarding than travel, for it enables the reader *to travel not only* in the dimension of space *but* in the dimension of time, *to know not only* contemporary England *but* Roman Britain, *to wander* with a good guide *not only* through modern Florence *but* through the Florence of Leonardo and Michelangelo. (paragraph 15)

Can you find several other examples of such parallelism? Try your hand at constructing a few such sentences yourself.

4 Paragraph 24 contains a sentence in which the author repeats an important word for emphasis: "One of the essential ingredients of nationalism is a common past, a common memory, a common heritage of tragedy and of glory—so all the historians of nationalism have asserted." Where else does Commager use this device?

5 The author is very skillful in structuring his sentences. Compare the following pairs of sentences (the first version is Commager's). Which version is superior?

   a But the same can be said, of course, for many other things which society values and which men cherish. (paragraph 4)

   But the same can be said for many other things which society values and which men cherish, of course.

   b All of us, in a sense, accept this gamble. (paragraph 7)

   All of us accept this gamble in a sense.

6 What is the function of paragraph 3, in which Commager makes a number of concessions?

Exploring Words

1 *Philistine.* After checking your dictionary and noting Commager's use of the word, think of someone you might describe as a *Philistine.* (What does your dictionary say about the matter of capitalizing this word?)

2 *vindicates.* Your dictionary probably lists several meanings for *vindicate.* Which one applies to Commager's use of the word? Try writing a sentence using the word in another sense. (For example, you might explain a situation in which you have been *vindicated.*)

3 *ostentatious.* What do you suppose the expression *"ostentatious* as a peacock" means?

4 *vicariously.* Commager says that history "permits us to enter *vicariously* into the past. . . ." What are some ways that you might enter *vicariously* into the future?

5 *assiduous.* Consult your dictionary, and then write a sentence describing yourself using either *assiduous* or *assiduously.*

6 *parochialism.* Check your dictionary's treatment of the metaphorical sense of *parochial.* (The noun form is derived from this metaphorical sense.) Then explain in your own words why the author considers *parochialism* "one of the dangers to good citizenship."

7 *microcosms.* Try using *microcosm* in a sentence of your own.

8 *exigency.* This word is often used to follow the word *any,* as it is in Commager's sentence. Why do you suppose this is so?

9 *amalgam.* What synonyms for this word does your dictionary provide? Which ones come closest to Commager's use of *amalgam?*

Suggestions for Writing

1 Write a defense of a subject in school or college that you have found most satisfying, addressing yourself to an audience of students who have tried to avoid this subject as long as possible or who succeeded in avoiding it altogether. For example, your topic might be "Why Advanced Composition?," "Why Calculus?," or "Why High School Auto Shop?"

2 Discuss those aspects of history that you wish you had learned more fully. Why do you feel they are important?

3 Using as your basis one issue of the daily newspaper, write a "social" history of your community for that particular day. In other words, explain what life was like for the "average" person.

Doctors, Dollars, and Dangerous Drugs
RUTH MULVEY HARMER

Getting Started

With Ideas

The title of this selection, the title of the book from which it is taken—*American Medical Avarice*—and the content of the first paragraph should prepare you for the argument that follows. After you have read Harmer's introduction, you will know by inference the general point she is making about "doctors, dollars, and dangerous drugs." (That is, you will if you think about the *contrast* implied by the structure and the wording of this paragraph.) Then, as you read the rest of the work, you can look for the specific information she provides to support this implied generalization.

With Words

1. nostrums (1)—the context will be helpful here.
2. incontrovertible (2)—associate it with *controversy,* and remember that *in* can mean *not.*
3. endemic (4)—the Latin word from which this word is derived means "the action of dwelling."
4. circumspection (7)—from the Latin prefix *circum-,* meaning "around," and the Latin word *specere,* meaning "to look."
5. pragmatically (24)—the source of this word is the same as that of the word *practical.*
6. jettisoning (30)—from the Old French word meaning "the action of throwing."
7. gratuities (36)—associate it with *gratuitous.*

---

[1] The notion is widespread that here in America, where things are *different,* drugs are safe. Surely, the drug industry can be relied on, that extension of all the Arrowsmiths who have toiled selflessly in their laboratories to defeat disease and hold back death. Surely, the government agencies are carrying out their mission of public protection. Surely, the AMA and its individual members, whose primary concern is the welfare of

From *American Medical Avarice* by Ruth Mulvey Harmer. Copyright © 1975 by Ruth Mulvey Harmer. Reprinted by permission of Abelard-Schuman, Publisher.

patients, would not allow us to be exposed to dangers and deceits. Had not the AMA been founded largely to protect Americans from being preyed upon by the makers of dangerous nostrums and useless quacksalver brews? Had not Sir William Osler spoken for the profession in 1902 when he branded the large pharmaceutical houses medicine's "insidious foe," which threatened to become "a huge parasite, eating the vitals of the body medical"?[1]

[2] The situation had not changed, however, as was made clear during the Senate hearings more than a decade ago. In response to a nationwide demand for "something" to protect the American people from the profit-hungry drug and medical industries, Senator Estes Kefauver submitted the bill S. 1522 to Congress. It seemed to most sophisticated persons just what the doctors should have ordered long ago. Not only would costs be reduced, but patients would finally have some real defense against dangerous drugs. New standards would be set to ensure the quality, purity, effectiveness, and safety of all drugs; the Department of Health, Education, and Welfare would have power to enforce them. It seemed impossible to believe that any responsible person or organization could oppose such vital safeguards. HEW testified on its behalf; so did the Department of Justice, the Patent Office, the National Consumers League, the AFL-CIO, health-insurance groups, organizations of retired persons, many private physicians of distinguished reputation. Dr. A. Dale Console, former medical director of the Squibb drug corporation, appealed for enactment of the bill. Even the board chairman of the PMA, president of Eli Lilly, expressed approval of a large portion of it. Was it possible that the AMA . . . ? It was, indeed. In the face of incontrovertible evidence, over the opposition of its own Council on Drugs, with total disregard for public interest, the American Medical Association announced its implacable opposition to everything in the bill.[2]

[3] In the decade that followed, the consequences of AMA opposition have been spelled out in considerable magnitude.

[4] Iatrogenic diseases, which are induced in a patient by a physician's treatment and particularly by drug therapy, have become both endemic and epidemic. By 1965, at least 1,500,000 hospital admissions a year were held due to adverse drug reactions; and those reactions were of such severity that the hospital stay of those patients was about 40 percent greater than the average stay of all patients.[3] No improvement occurred during the next decade. In mid-1974, Dr. Milton Silverman, research pharmacologist at the University of California, and Dr. Philip R. Lee,

---

[1] Herman M. and Anne R. Somers, *Doctors, Patients, and Health Insurance* (Washington, D.C.: The Brookings Institution, 1961), pp. 103–04.

[2] For brief accounts, see Estes Kefauver and Irene Till, *In a Few Hands* (New York: Pantheon Books, 1965), and Richard Harris, *The Real Voice* (New York: Macmillan, 1963).

[3] Donald C. Brodie, *Drug Utilization and Drug Utilization Review and Control* (Rockville, Md.: DHEW Publication No. (HSM) 72-3002, 1970), pp. 1–2.

former U.S. assistant secretary for health and scientific affairs, estimated that "unnecessary and irrational" use of prescription drugs is killing at least 100,000 Americans a year and making millions sick.[4] The researchers pointed out that the number of fatalities is actually much higher—between 130,000 and 140,000; however, they said, about 20 percent of those can be considered unpredictable, "acts of God," involving terminal illnesses or emergencies in which doctors use drug combinations they would not use if it were not a life and death matter.[5]

[5] Their estimate is—despite AMA and pharmaceutical industry protests—conservative since they included only those hospitalized. "We know nothing of those who are sick at home, or even die at home," Dr. Silverman pointed out; "Drug reaction is not a reportable disease." (Other researchers have pointed out that adverse drug reactions are frequently misdiagnosed as asthma, flu, infections, anemia, gastrointestinal, and kidney disorders.)

[6] Once in the hospital, for any reason, the chances of succumbing to drug therapy are also pretty high. This is not surprising because patients often receive between 10 and 20 different medications daily during their hospital stay. Also, the number of medications that are given in error is thought to be pretty high. In a study of 900 patients at the Johns Hopkins Hospital several years ago, Dr. L. E. Cluff and his associates found the incidence of adverse drug reactions to be 10.8 percent, excluding "mild gastrointestinal side effects."[6] (Johns Hopkins, it should be pointed out, is one of the country's outstanding hospitals.) Other studies are even grimmer. A Canadian research team detected adverse reactions to drugs in 15 percent of the patients they studied; when combined with "errors in the administration of drugs," the figure rose to 30 percent. Thus, three of every ten persons admitted to hospitals studied (the better hospitals) become victims of drug-induced diseases.[7] Those diseases prolong the hospitalization of some patients by an average stay of nine days. They also increase the costs to the patient. A study was made of the direct and indirect costs incurred by 41 patients admitted to a Midwestern university teaching hospital. Because of adverse drug reactions, researchers estimated them to be at least $116,835.[8] How to measure the emotional, physical, and psychological costs to the victim? How to calculate the suffering involved for the victims' families?

---

[4] Milton Silverman and Philip R. Lee, *Pills, Profits, and Politics* (Berkeley: University of California Press, 1974), p. 266.

[5] Harry Nelson, "Prescription Drug Abuse Kills 100,000 Yearly, Two Claim," *Los Angeles Times*, June 10, 1974.

[6] *Drug Utilization and Drug Utilization Review and Control,* pp. 24–25.

[7] B. C. Hoddinott, et al., "Drug Reactions and Errors in Administration on a Medical Ward," *Canadian Medical Association Journal,* 97 (1967), p. 1001.

[8] *Drug Utilization and Drug Utilization Review and Control,* p. 25.

[7] Rational persons do not quarrel with the idea that in order to achieve major gains it may be necessary to accept some losses. And no rational person would deny the major gains that have resulted from drugs developed during recent decades that have surely played an important role in the dramatic decline in death rates from some diseases since "wonder drug therapy" was introduced in the 1940s. However, as specialists have been pointing out, antibiotics produce allergic responses: some mild, some fatal. Some are inherently toxic, damaging ears, kidney, liver, and blood. Some cure one infection and provoke the development of another, which may be more dangerous. According to Dr. Louis Weinstein, chief of the infectious disease service of New England Medical Center Hospitals, they "must always" be used with circumspection and discrimination. They should be administered "only" in situations where they are known to be useful. "To do otherwise is to expose patients to the risk of reactions that may be more deadly than the infections from which they suffer." [9]

[8] In 1972 Dr. Harry E. Simmons, director of the Bureau of Drugs in the FDA, estimated before a Senate subcommittee that "superinfections" may be killing tens of thousands of persons yearly in this country. He indicated that each year as many as 300,000 cases of superinfections may be caused by antibiotic therapy that kills one set of microorganisms and allows another group to flourish.[10] Between 30 and 50 percent of the cases of superinfections are fatal. Evidence also was submitted to Senator Gaylord Nelson's subcommittee which showed the overuse and misuse of antibiotics. Researchers studying a 500-bed community hospital found that antibiotic therapy was justified in only 12.9 percent of the cases; it was "questionable" in 21.5 percent; and "irrational" in 65.6 percent.[11] Is this circumspection and discrimination?

[9] Of the 400,000,000 prescriptions for antibiotics written annually, many are for colds and minor viral infections, for which they are of not the slightest use. The same kind of casualness applies to other commonly prescribed medications, no less dangerous.

[10] For years, doctors and scientific researchers on both sides of the Atlantic have been issuing warning notes about the indiscriminate vaccination practices in this country. England and other countries abandoned compulsory vaccination some years ago. Not only was there a general news blackout in this country about the matter, but government agencies were used to prevent information from reaching the public. For example, after writing a book called *Polio Control* in 1946, Dr. Eleanor McBean of

[9] "Antibiotics: Curative Drugs," ed. by Samuel Proger, *The Medicated Society* (New York: Macmillan, 1968), pp. 85–89.

[10] "Deaths Laid to Needless Use of Antibiotics," *Los Angeles Times*, December 8, 1972.

[11] *Competitive Problems in the Drug Industry: Present Status of Competition in the Pharmaceutical Industry,* Hearings Before the Subcommittee on Monopoly, Select Committee on Small Business, Ninetieth Congress (Washington, D.C.: Government Printing Office, 1967), Part 3, p. 1039.

Los Angeles received a memorable reminder of the power of the medical establishment. Performing what she considered a public service in alerting people to the dangers of vaccines and making every effort to keep the book factual and legal, she had it checked twice before printing: with a lawyer and with officials at the Los Angeles Post Office. The Better Business Bureau, she reported, instructed newspapers not to sell advertising space. When the book continued to sell, the Post Office issued a fraud order against the book and her publishing company and refused mail delivery to her, entirely, as she pointed out recently, "without due process of law or proof of guilt." [12]

[11] To be opposed to indiscriminate vaccinations was equated with being against the public good. Between 14,000,000 and 17,000,000 smallpox vaccinations have been administered annually in the country, although there has not been one case of smallpox since 1949. Adverse reactions have ranged from minor ailments to fatal encephalitis. In 1968 alone, nine deaths were linked to smallpox vaccination.[13]

[12] In 1971, private warnings gave way to public concern after a research microbiologist in the Division of Biologics Standards reported that tests performed on vaccines against measles, mumps, and others that are commonly used "caused apprehensions of such grave nature that they might well serve as a basis for condemnation." [14] The U.S. Public Health Service followed up with a recommendation that states take action to halt or to curb vaccination programs.[15]

[13] Risks all out of proportion to possible benefits have been accepted by unsuspecting patients so that the drug industry and the medical establishment could pursue profits. Senator Kefauver cited MER/29 as "a classic" instance.[16] By the end of 1963, only three years after its introduction, the Richardson-Merrell corporation had been indicted by a grand jury for having falsified reports about the toxic effects of MER/29 to the government, and the company was a defendant in more than 400 damage suits brought by injured persons. One of the plaintiffs won a $675,000 judgment.[17] The drug had appeared on the market in the summer of 1960, glowingly advertised in the *JAMA* as "the first cholesterol-lowering agent to inhibit the formation of excess cholesterol within the body. . . . [The] absence of toxicity [has been] established by two years of clinical investigation." [18] Soon after, warnings of danger came: another company discovered that cataracts developed in rats and dogs treated with the drug;

---

[12] Eleanor McBean, Statement, September 20 1973. (Typewritten)

[13] *Con$umer New$week* (November 1, 1971), p. 4.

[14] *Congressional Record* (October 15, 1971), pp. S16293–99.

[15] *Con$umer New$week* (November 1, 1971), p. 4.

[16] Kefauver and Till, op. cit., p. 60.

[17] *San Francisco Examiner,* June 8, 1965.

[18] *JAMA* (June 25, 1960).

the Mayo Clinic reported in January 1961, that skin disorders and loss of hair were associated with use of the drug and in October gave extensive information on side effects, including the development of cataracts. Yet the ads continued to appear in the *JAMA*. In the November 4, 1961, issue, it was claimed: "After three years' clinical experience . . . after use in more than 300,000 patients, few toxic or serious side effects have been reported." [19] The drug was formally removed from the market a few months later. Two years after that, the company and three scientists pleaded *nolo contendere* to criminal charges of suppressing and altering test results.[20]

[14] Cortisone offers another striking example of the dangers of using a drug indiscriminately. Adrenal cortical hormones, cortisone, or corticosteroids can be valuable drugs to help patients suffering from Addison's or Cushing's diseases, in which there is an over- or under-production of hormones. However, as Col. Robert H. Moser of the U.S. Army Medical Corps pointed out recently, cortisone was introduced on the market with "fanfare." Newspapers carried "wild tales" of hospital patients who had been crippled with arthritis dancing in the corridors. In short order, doctors were enthusiastically writing prescriptions for the stuff for almost anyone with an ache or pain.[21] But the dangers the patients faced covered an almost incredible range. The symptoms of Cushing's disease are most obvious: moon face, fat on abdomen and hips, purple streaks due to stretching of the skin, growth of a soft tissue lump on the upper spine, acne, and wasting of the muscles of the extremities. Less obvious symptoms often became apparent. Adverse reactions ran the whole gamut of psychiatric disorders, ranging from the wildest elation to suicidal depression. Blood pressure increased. The normal production of protein tissue was interrupted. The healing of surgical wounds was impaired. Patients suffered from cataracts. They developed large ulcers of the stomach. Still later, more subtle dangers came to light. Patients taking the substances for arthritis, asthma, or nephrotic syndrome might develop an acute appendicitis or pneumonia which could easily go undetected for some time since the drugs masked normal signs of infection. At the same time, it was found that the corticosteroids could facilitate the spread and propagation of tuberculosis, blood stream bacterial infections, virus and fungus infections. Some patients who had received a high dosage of corticosteroids for a long time might suffer irreversible shock while undergoing surgery.

[15] It is not surprising that Dr. Moser warned his colleagues that:

> We must create an atmosphere of rational caution and critical evaluation, where each physician will pause before putting pen to prescription pad and ask himself, "Do I know enough about

---

[19] Kefauver and Till, op. cit., p. 63.

[20] Hubert H. Humphrey, "Myths About Federal Drug Policies," *New Republic* (May 16, 1964), p. 17.

[21] "Diseases Due to Drug Treatment," *The Medicated Society*, pp. 165–79.

this drug to prescribe it? Does the possible benefit I hope to derive from this drug outweigh its potential hazard?"[22]

[16] There is, sadly, no indication that physicians are likely to ask those uncomfortable questions as long as they continue to be propagandized by the drug industry.

[17] With the exception of Thalidomide, there exists no more revealing example of the madness of the policy of administering drugs recklessly than the use of chloramphenicol.

[18] During the 1940s, Parke Davis scientists discovered the substance in some Venezuelan soil samples of molds. It was found to be effective in treating Rocky Mountain spotted fever, scrub typhus, and several other diseases relatively rare in this country, but difficult to treat. Within a short time, researchers managed to synthesize it commercially at a low cost of less than 10 cents a capsule. The company named the antibiotic Chloromycetin, obtained a patent, and began production in the United States and Britain. Parke Davis was understandably confident it had struck gold. During 1949, its first year on the market, sales exceeded $9,000,000. A year later, they passed the $28,000,000 total; in 1951, they reached $52,000,000.

[19] Shortly after Chloromycetin was licensed, however, "unexpected" clinical reports began to associate it with aplastic anemia, a blood disease with a fatality rate of about 50 percent. The Food and Drug Administration and the AMA's Council on Drugs both investigated the drug and took action in June 1952. An editorial in the *JAMA* warned doctors about possible reactions, and the FDA refused to approve further shipments of the drug until a National Research Council committee submitted its findings. Two months later, it revealed that 177 of the 410 cases of serious blood disorders studied were "definitely known" to have been associated with Chloromycetin.[23] Parke Davis was ordered to change the drug's label to warn that the drug should not be used "indiscriminately or for minor infections." However, the opinion was that: "It should continue to be available for careful use by the medical profession in those serious and sometimes fatal diseases in which its use is necessary."[24] Those cases, as has been noted, are rare in this country.

[20] Sales plummeted. Parke Davis, which had soared to first place because of Chloromycetin, dropped to fifth place in sales in 1954. The sure cure for that, officials decided, was to pressure the company's 980 salesmen to persuade doctors that Chloromycetin was the safe answer for everything from acne to mild urinary infections. Memos and instructions from the president and sales director advised them to tell doctors that all was well, that the FDA had officially cleared the drug. Physicians

---

[22] Ibid., p. 179.

[23] ". . . *Particularly Chloromycetin*," Report by the California Senate Factfinding Committee on Public Health and Safety, January 1963.

[24] Ibid., p. 10.

looked at the ads, listened to the salesmen, and, despite continuing reports in medical journals, were persuaded. Among them was Dr. Albe M. Watkins, a general practitioner from southern California. In 1952, confident of its safety, he and a urologist had given the drug to his ten-year-old son James, who had suffered a urinary infection. Dr. Watkins first realized his son was in danger when the child kneeled on the living room floor to retrieve a toy that had fallen under a sofa. After he had stood up again, his knees were black and blue. The drug had presumably caused the depression of the production of platelets in the bone marrow. If the platelets are sufficiently decreased in number, bleeding may result. "From then on," Dr. Watkins said later, "there was no stopping the bleeding." After James's death, the Watkins family, the doctor, his wife (a graduate nurse), and two other sons, got in their car and headed east. His goal was to alert other doctors and government officials about the drug. Stopping at small towns and large, he called on other physicians to ask about their experiences with the drug. By the time he reached the Food and Drug Administration offices in Washington, he had recorded 294 other cases of adverse side effects and fatal reactions to the drug.[25]

[21] His efforts to have the drug restricted were supported by others, also profoundly concerned about the dangers, and sales began to plummet, down $15,000,000 by 1963.[26] In that year, a California State Senate Fact-finding Committee launched an investigation. (It had intended at first to look into the entire antibiotics matter, but pressures from the drug lobby forced the committee to retrench.) The hearings were called ". . . *Particularly Chloromycetin*," and the committee finally proposed that the use of the drug be limited to hospitals so that constant blood checks could be made on the patients.

[22] Among the procession of victims testifying in favor of the proposal was another southern California physician, another bereaved parent. Dr. Franklin Farman, a diplomate of the American Board of Urology, told the committee that his five-year-old daughter had also died in 1952 following the administration of Chloromycetin. "In my opinion," he said, "there is hardly one case or one sick person in this state today that of his own free will would choose to take Chloromycetin knowing the full risk he runs in its causing either temporary or permanent bone marrow depression."[27] Another witness was Edgar F. Elfstrom, a California newspaper publisher. His nineteen-year-old daughter had died several years before after having taken the drug for a sore throat and mild urinary infection. Still another man told the committee that his mother had also died of aplastic anemia after taking Chloromycetin, which her physician had prescribed for a cold.

[23] Parke Davis has been forced to defend itself against a number of victims. The first settlement was made in 1961 on behalf of a

---

[25] Bob Diebold, "Physician Urges Caution with Prescribed Drugs," *Los Angeles Times,* March 7, 1968.

[26] "The Peculiar Success of Chloromycetin," *Consumer Reports* (October 1970), p. 617.

[27] ". . . *Particularly Chloromycetin*," pp. 65–66.

woman whose doctor had prescribed Chloromycetin first for a sore gum and then for a bronchial infection. She died of the treatment. In making the judgment against the manufacturer, the court noted that Parke Davis had been "aware" that the warning label on the drug at the time it was prescribed was "ambiguous, inadequate and incomplete." [28] Twelve years later, the California State Supreme Court upheld a $400,000 award made by a lower court, agreeing with a jury finding that the drug firm "negligently failed to provide an adequate warning as to the dangers of Chloromycetin by so 'watering down' its warnings and so overpromoting the drug that members of the medical profession were caused to prescribe it when it was not justified." [29] Parke Davis has been successful using these measures and Chloromycetin has continued to sell well.

[24] During the Nelson subcommittee hearings in 1968, Dr. Henry Dowling singled out the drug as "perhaps the most flagrant example of bad therapeutic judgment" on the part of some doctors.[30] It was pointed out that between 90 and 99 percent of prescriptions handed to patients should never been written. The Food and Drug Commissioner had earlier confessed himself at his "wit's end" about the matter. "What it comes down to in bald terms is: What can be done to protect you from your doctors?" [31] Nothing, nothing at all. In 1970, an estimated 790,000 people in the United States were receiving the drug, sales topped $82,000,000, and new markets had been opened. The United States government was sending South Vietnam enough Chloromycetin to treat between 150,000 and 200,000 patients, *with no restrictions imposed on its use*. The government's position was summed up for reporters by Navy Captain J. William Cox, a physician who advises the Defense Medical Materials Board. Asserting that the South Vietnam rate of consumption of the drug "is not indicated by our standard or practice," he brushed off the drug shipments pragmatically: "But neither are leeches and lots of other things they use." [32]

[25] Parke Davis has been making enormous profits on foreign sales of Chloromycetin in a way scarcely calculated to win friends for this country when facts are known. The drug has been marketed in Italy with the inducement that it is "remarkably without secondary reaction." In Japan, Chloromycetin has been touted as "a remarkably ideal antibiotic which increases the resistive power of bodies under stress and accelerates

---

[28] "The Peculiar Success of Chloromycetin," *Consumer Reports* (October 1970), p. 618.

[29] "$400,000 Award Against Drug Firm Upheld," *Los Angeles Times*, March 15, 1973.

[30] *Advertising of Proprietary Medicines*, Hearings Before the Subcommittee on Monopoly of the Select Committee on Small Business, United States Senate, Ninety-Second Congress (Washington, D.C.: Government Printing Office, 1973), Part 3, p. 1142.

[31] "At Wit's End to Stop Misuse of Potent Antibiotic—Goddard," *Los Angeles Times*, March 1, 1968.

[32] "U.S. Admits Vietnam Gets Perilous Drug," *Los Angeles Times*, November 18, 1970.

the recuperative process."[33] In Mexico, where it is sold over the counter, a doctor recommended it several years ago to me and my husband as a cure for our child's sore throat. He was positive of that, even without examining her throat or making any kind of tests. When I told him what I had learned about the drug from the legislative investigation in California, he looked at me pityingly and shrugged: "Well, aspirin is dangerous, too."

[26] If the AMA had acted, who knows how many lives might have been spared, how much suffering averted. And the AMA could have acted, as its own Council on Drugs had urged. It could have insisted that the ads point out the dangers of the drug prominently as it did point out that the *only* disease for which it has continued to be a drug of choice is typhoid fever.

[27] That kind of service for both doctors and patients had been provided in 1905, when the AMA had set up its Council on Pharmacy and Chemistry to provide members with reliable information about the safety and value of drugs in order to defend doctors from "the bastard literature which floods the mail" and to "protect the public and the medical profession against fraud, undesirable secrecy, and objectionable advertising."

[28] Of paramount importance was the *New and Unofficial Remedies*, which the AMA began to publish in 1907. Every medication the Council considered might have merit was listed and described. In 1913 that was supplemented with a handbook, *Useful Drugs*, and in 1929, the Council adopted an insigne. Manufacturers whose drugs were approved received the AMA "Seal of Acceptance," which they were permitted to use on their packages and in their advertisements. No drug could be advertised which had not been evaluated by the Council and found acceptable.[34] The doctors relied on *Useful Drugs* and on the seal. A survey made by the AMA in 1953 showed that 71 percent of the physicians interviewed felt the seal had great value; more than half said they considered it more important than a company's reputation.[35]

[29] The drug industry was less than enthusiastic about the control measures the AMA was imposing. It found a way to counter them in the 1950s, when the AMA was seeking new sources of revenue to fight compulsory insurance programs. The business staff invited Ben Gaffin and Associates, Inc., to discover how the sale of advertising space in the *JAMA* and other AMA publications could be increased. That was quickly and conveniently determined: The drug industry would step up its advertising in return for a number of "policy changes."

[30] Changes included jettisoning the Seal of Acceptance and abandoning the publication of *Useful Drugs*. Instead, the drug industry would publish and distribute to doctors its own guide and index to pre-

---

[33] "The Peculiar Success of Chloromycetin," p. 618.

[34] Jeffrey Bishop, "Drug Evaluation Programs of the AMA, 1905–1966," *JAMA* (May 9, 1966), pp. 496–98.

[35] Richard Harris, op. cit., p. 126.

scriptions, the *Physician's Desk Reference*. Most doctors seemed unaware of the fact that it was an advertising tract. In it, all the material about every drug listed was prepared, edited, approved, and paid for by the manufacturer. As an indication of its objectivity and completeness, in the 1962 edition Parke Davis deleted from the Chloromycetin entry all references to hazards, and inserted a statement that doctors could get all necessary information from the package insert and from the salesmen.[36]

[31] In return, the drug industry advertised. And what advertising drug advertising is. Ethical drug ads are as weighted with the cant of quacks and hucksters as pitches can be. Medical journals, which should confine advertisers to facts and scientific information, carry the same emotional appeals that characterize the ads for over-the-counter drugs in slick magazines and on radio and TV. The old familiar ills of insomnia, tension, obesity, constipation, coughs and wheezes, aches and pains are garishly portrayed and prescribed for. Smiling beauties and high-powered athletes suggest that depression, whether caused by stacks of dirty dishes or driving in freeway traffic, can be overcome and that "the active girl can stay active every day of the month."

[32] Although the Kefauver-Harris drug law attempted to correct some of the advertising abuses by demanding that precautions and side effects be specified in detail, the advertising has found a way to overcome that important reform. For instance, in a recent full-page ad in full color for premarin, a hormone product, only one-fifteenth of the page is devoted to a cautionary note.[37] An ad for Haldol (haloperidol) that regularly appeared in the *JAMA* in 1972 is representative of the sales approach. The first page shows a framed picture of a smiling gray-haired woman. Above her head appears the quote: "We don't want to put Mother in a home, but . . ." The second page, in very large type, urges use of the drug "when disturbed behavior complicates caring for the elderly." On the third page, in small type, are warnings against the drug which is held useful in some cases of agitation and psychotic behavior. Mother might be better off in a home, judging from the fine print, although, of course, she might be dosed with it there. Adverse effects include: neuromuscular reactions, insomnia, restlessness, anxiety, euphoria, agitation, drowsiness, vertigo, seizures of an epileptic type, impaired heart, liver, skin, and blood, loss of appetite, nausea, dry mouth, blurred vision, and urinary retention.[38]

[33] Most distressing, perhaps, and certainly most popular are the ads for psychoactive drugs. The advertising in almost any medical journal being published offers clear explanation for America's having become "a nation of middle class junkies." Doctors have become drug pushers, writing nearly 100,000,000 prescriptions a year for uppers and downers and flattener-outers. Two of the most widely advertised tension relievers, Va-

---

[36] "The Peculiar Success of Chloromycetin," p. 618.

[37] *JAMA* (January 24, 1972).

[38] *JAMA* (June 26, 1972).

lium and Librium, were recently held so dangerous they were almost ordered off the market. For years, glowing ads had so deluded doctors and patients about their mildness and safety that they were widely prescribed for even the most minor display of tension.

[34] Responsible professionals have protested such advertising abuses to no avail. Dr. Robert Seidenberg, a practicing psychiatrist and clinical professor of psychiatry at the State University of New York, said of the *JAMA*'s ad policy: "Even *Good Housekeeping* and *Parents' Magazine* do better in protecting their reader-consumers. Is the AMA guilty of drug abuse?" [39]

[35] Censorship charges were also made before the subcommittee by Dr. Edward Pinckney, a former editor of the *JAMA*. He listed a whole series of false and misleading claims that were made in the *JAMA* ads in a single 1969 edition, including Serc, which the FDA had started withdrawal proceedings against one year earlier. He said that an editorial protesting such advertising that he had written for the *JAMA* had been rejected by an AMA official on the grounds that drug advertising was the journal's "principal source of revenue." [40]

[36] As dangerous as the education by media advertising can be, even more so is that provided doctors by mail and by the industry's 15,000 or so salesmen. In *The Doctors' Dilemma,* Dr. Louis Lasagna of Johns Hopkins, one of the most distinguished pharmacologists in the country, described the material sent out to doctors (whose names are on the lists that the AMA rents to the drug companies) as "a numbers racket, with its never-ending barrage of new products, confusing names, conflicting dosage schedules and indications, claims and counter claims." By 1969, the industry was spending at least $22,500,000 on direct-mail advertising to persuade doctors to write prescriptions for their brands.[41] The drug industry woos the men of medicine with inducements of all kinds: office equipment, "samples" (some of which are passed along to patients), golf needs, tickets, trips, food and drink. In order to influence doctors to prescribe their products, the drug industry has even invaded the medical schools. Among the gratuities provided students at most schools are textbooks and monographs, pocket notebooks and calendars, slide rules, black leather bags, with examining instruments, anatomical models. Additionally, it arranges trips to pharmaceutical plants and to scientific meetings, including board, room, and entertainment. Students are provided free drugs for themselves and their families; those with children are given baby food and other baby supplies.[42] The detail salesmen come to be their friends and benefactors.

[37] The huge sales of Chloromycetin certainly prove the almost

[39] *Advertising of Proprietary Medicines,* Part 2, p. 541.

[40] *Competitive Problems in the Drug Industry,* Part 14, p. 5727.

[41] Ibid., p. 5775.

[42] Ibid., pp. 5509–10.

incredible influence the salesmen exert over the prescription pads. The popularity of Merck Sharpe & Dohme's Indocin also proves that the salesmen are effective. An antiinflammatory drug used for some arthritic problems, Indocin was so briskly promoted that within two years it had become one of the 200 most-frequently prescribed agents in the country. Despite hazards associated with its use, including asthma, aplastic anemia, hepatitis, jaundice (including some fatal cases), ulcerations, and sometimes fatal hemorrhaging, the drug was being improperly prescribed for such conditions as minor sprains and bursitis. Distressingly, it was also given to children, with fatal results in some cases, despite specific cautions against it.[43] In response to an FDA order to correct the misrepresentations and misleading claims, Merck modified its ads and the package inserts to convey the warning that the drug "must be used cautiously, if at all, and with the expectation that serious side effects may occur." However, bulletins to salesmen instructed them to convince doctors that "therapy with Indocin is safer"—presumably, safer even than aspirin.

[38] To make sure that the story was told, financial encouragement was provided. "Now every extra bottle of 1,000 Indocin that you sell is worth an extra $2.80 in incentive payments. Go get it. Pile it on!!!" [44]

[39] Doctors did have some partial defense against that kind of "education." But the AMA had disarmed the Council on Drugs in order to oblige the drug makers and to stimulate their financial support.

[40] Several years ago, some insurgents in the AMA, particularly doctors working with the Council on Drugs, determined to launch a resistance movement—to revive the Seal of Acceptance and to provide doctors with a handbook of drug evaluations based on scientific evidence rather than the puffery that characterizes the *Physician's Desk Reference*.

[41] The story of the killing power of the drug industry, as told in 1973 by Dr. John Adriani, a former chairman of the AMA Council on Drugs, director of the Department of Anesthesia of Charity Hospital in New Orleans, and a university professor, makes instructive reading for all who object to American citizens being used as guinea pigs and as gulls to be exploited.[45] Dr. Adriani determined to administer some life-saving aid to the AMA before it deteriorated completely. The AMA's image in the 1960s was badly tarnished, and its membership was dropping seriously. Finally what he calls the "paid bureaucracy" at 535 North Dearborn Street in Chicago agreed, after the Kefauver hearings, to do something. Three million dollars were appropriated and a staff hired to prepare an official book on drug evaluations, a replacement for the drug industry's *Reference*.

---

[43] Ibid., Part 8, p. 3506.

[44] Ibid., p. 3508.

[45] Copies of the statements presented to the Nelson Senate subcommittee were provided me by Dr. Adriani, including the statement of February 6, 1973. In an accompanying letter, he described his grave concern about the "paid bureaucracy" in charge of AMA affairs and his desire to prevent the "further deterioration" of the organization.

However, when Dr. Adriani became chairman of the Council on Drugs in 1968, he found that the staff had written only one chapter of the proposed volume; it had managed to spend $2,000,000 in the process. Dr. Adriani had himself appointed chairman of a special ad hoc committee of three *volunteers*. He then enlisted the aid of other reputable specialists, and within a year the committee had prepared 89 of the 90 chapters.

[42] In January of 1971, just as the first edition of *AMA Drug Evaluations* was about to be sent to the bindery, the chairman of the AMA Board of Trustees, Dr. Max Parrott, told the Council: "We want to hold the book up for a couple of months." The reason? So that "our friends" the Pharmaceutical Manufacturers Association could see it. Over the Council's objection, page proofs were sent. They came back three months later, accompanied by "three or four crates full of changes [the PMA] wanted to make." The PMA generously volunteered to pay for all the "changes," which actually amounted to revising the whole book. The Council agreed to some minor changes, but stood fast on substantive points. It condemned a number of heavily advertised drug combinations as "irrational." And it offended the drug industry in other ways.

[43] *AMA Drug Evaluations* received excellent reviews when it appeared in 1971; doctors called it a "wonderful" prescribing manual since it categorized by disease rather than by drug; it specified the drug of first, second, and third choice; it recommended quantities for use; and it gave other vital information. Even so, Dr. Adriani and his colleagues were not satisfied. He noticed that without his consent or knowledge, the paid staff had made changes in ten of the chapters that he had written. Other unauthorized changes had also been made. Even before the book was circulated, he and Dr. Harry C. Shirkey, his successor as Council chairman, and Dr. Daniel L. Azarnoff voted to move ahead with a second edition.

[44] Others were upset with the manual for a different reason, not the least of which were officials of the PMA. They were in a position to make their displeasure felt and they did. As a result, drug advertising in the *JAMA* dropped sharply after Dr. Adriani and his colleagues took on the job of preparing the book. Between 1968 and 1972, the page count fell from 4227 to 2558. That made the Board of Trustees unhappy, too. The feeling was enhanced, Dr. Adriani believes, because the PMA president was such a "good friend of the Board of Trustees." C. Joseph Stetler, former AMA legal counsel, took on that job as successor to Dr. Austin Smith, who had become PMA president after a number of years as editor of the *JAMA*.

[45] In September 1972, a delegation of the Board of Trustees appeared before the Council and said that the statement "The Council does not recommend this drug" could not be used in the new edition. Dr. Adriani and his colleagues objected strenuously. Why not? The trustees answered with a lame explanation that the statement did not "mean" anything by itself. The Council countered with an offer to specify reasons. Un-

derstandably feeling trapped, the delegation agreed to "buy that." However, after leaving they apparently realized that they had left with a far worse bargain than they had originally gone to the Council for. The error was remedied a month later when the Board of Trustees summarily abolished the Council and thus halted all work on the new book.

[46] The AMA denied charges of a "sellout" made by Dr. Adriani, Dr. Shirkey, and other Council members. PMA President Stetler also denied that pressure had been applied on the editors to conform with the wishes of the drug manufacturers. But, to date no convincing reason has been given for the action; no convincing defense has been made to the charge that the AMA and the PMA were "in cahoots" against American patients.

[47] What can be done to halt the irrational and dangerous practices? The answer to that question is not easy, but a number of proposals that would be helpful were made to the Nelson subcommittee. For one thing, far more rigid restrictions should be placed on drug advertising; and the Federal Trade Commission and the Food and Drug Administration should be forced to move vigorously against makers of false and misleading claims. Disinterested experts like Dr. Adriani and his colleagues on the former AMA Council on Drugs, with the aid of other groups like the American Public Health Association, should be asked to prepare a compendium of prescription drugs. That committee should be charged with notifying physicians of adverse reactions. Drug dispensing should be monitored more carefully; recently hospitals have been employing pharmacists to improve drug-use practices. Computers should be used more widely, to store in memory banks and produce on demand the drug histories of patients.

[48] The formulary system, which has been used in hospitals in this country since 1816, should be put into practice generally. Under that, drugs are screened, approved, prescribed, and dispensed usually by generic names, and drug quality is maintained, drug costs and drug inventories are minimal, and patient welfare is the objective of the hospital. State, regional, and even national drug councils could monitor the prescribing habits of doctors through computer systems, and either caution doctors who prescribe improperly or have them prosecuted for going beyond reasonable bounds.

[49] Ultimately, of course, medical schools will have to do more to educate doctors more completely. Recently, Dr. Donald C. Brodie, associate dean of the School of Pharmacy at the University of California in San Francisco, demanded that an answer be provided to why the physician should be "the dupe of the detail man [salesman]." If a doctor cannot "hold his own" in a five-minute conference with a salesman, he said, "it is certainly an indictment of his profession and of the educational system that produced him." [46]

---

[46] *Drug Utilization and Drug Utilization Review and Control*, p. 29.

Questions on Meaning

1 What are the dangerous drugs Harmer treats in this selection? What is the most convincing evidence she gives of the danger of each?

2 What are the chief reasons, according to Harmer, that the drug problem she describes exists in the United States today?

3 What role has the AMA played in the conflict the author says has developed between drug companies and certain reform-minded doctors and legislators?

4 Do you find Harmer's argument convincing? Why or why not?

Questions on Style and Structure

1 In paragraph 1, the writer uses a device to achieve coherence that you have found authors using many times in the essays you have read. What is that device? Do you find it effective?

2 In the first paragraph, Harmer introduces a tone of sarcasm or irony: "Surely, the AMA and its individual members, whose primary concern is the welfare of patients, would not allow us to be exposed to dangers and deceits." Can you find other examples of this later tone in the work? Where?

3 In paragraph 2, the author employs a technique she comes back to several times later in the selection: the rhetorical question. Note that the first rhetorical question is incomplete. In what sense is this half-question consistent with the tone that has already been established? What other rhetorical question do you find? Why do you suppose this writer finds their use particularly appropriate to her purpose here?

4 Note the abundance of direct quotations in this work; in a majority of the paragraphs, there are quotations attributed to specific people. Why do you suppose that Harmer uses this technique so frequently—considerably more often than the writers of any other selection in this book? What do the quotations accomplish that is appropriate to the author's purpose?

5 In addition to the long direct quotations she frequently includes, Harmer often places single words and phrases in quotation marks when she is not quoting anyone. Note, for example, "something" in paragraph 2 and "wonder drug therapy" in paragraph 7. What effect does she accomplish by using this technique?

Exploring Words

1 *nostrums.* Consult your dictionary for the origin of this word. What relationship do you find between the meaning of the term as it is used today and the meaning of the Latin word from which it comes?

2 *incontrovertible. Incontrovertible* is often used with the word *evidence.* As you can tell by checking your dictionary for the present meaning and the

etymology of *incontrovertible,* it is a word writers use only when they are very sure of their facts. What are some words that might be used with *evidence* that would indicate varying degrees of uncertainty?

3 *endemic.* Use the word accurately in a sentence of your own.

4 *circumspection.* After checking the definition of *circumspection,* indicate what Harmer means when she says that recently developed drugs should be used "with *circumspection* and discrimination."

5 *pragmatically. Pragmatically,* the adverb form of *pragmatic,* has many different connotations. Consult your dictionary's treatment of both *pragmatic* and the base word, *pragmatism,* to determine which meaning comes closest to Harmer's use. If none comes very close (dictionaries differ considerably in the ways they treat the word), see if you can determine the connotations Harmer intends by relating *pragmatically* to its context.

6 *jettisoning.* Which of the meanings listed for *jettisoning* applies to Harmer's use of the word? Is her use here effective? Why? Would any of the words your dictionary lists as synonyms be as effective? Why or why not?

7 *gratuitous.* Like other words used in this selection, *gratuitous* is rich in connotations. Find a dictionary meaning that justifies Harmer's use of the word, and then explain her choice. Is her use a metaphorical extension of the meaning you found?

Suggestions for Writing

1 As Harmer does, write an attack on a group that you feel is in some way guilty of abuses—perhaps a professional group or perhaps one you have encountered in school or through an avocation. Be particularly careful to avoid unsupportable generalizations.

2 Criticize a practice in your school or community you feel is unfair. Again, be sure of your evidence and watch out for the inappropriate use of generalizations.

On Various Kinds of Thinking
JAMES HARVEY ROBINSON

Getting Started

With Ideas

As the title suggests, the author of this essay uses the organizational principle of *classification* to treat an especially abstract and complex subject. For this reason, you will find it helpful to read the work with a pencil in hand, as you did "Why History," noting in the margin the place where each category of thinking is introduced; you will find that the author provides a kind of running outline of the essay through numbered subheadings that mark its major divisions. Note, however, that he combines introductory and concluding paragraphs with these numbered divisions, breaking the convention of separating the introduction and conclusion of an essay from its body.

With Words

1. ignoble (7)—from the Latin prefix *in-*, meaning "not," and the word *noble*.
2. omnipotent (9)—the Latin prefix *omni-* means "all." This word is pronounced with the accent on the second syllable.
3. imputation (11)—from the Latin word meaning "to consider."
4. illicit (11)—this word is derived from the combination of *in-* (converted to *il-*) and the Latin word for "lawful."
5. onus (17)—the context will be helpful here.
6. abstruse (20)—from the Latin word meaning "to conceal."
7. gratuitous (20)—if someone says, "You may have it *gratis*," what does he or she mean?
8. pristine (24)—associate this word with *prior*, and note the context.
9. lethargic (35)—this word is from the Greek word meaning "forgetfulness," but the modern English term has considerably extended the meaning of the original Greek word.

> Good sense is, of all things among men, the most equally distributed; for everyone thinks himself so abundantly provided with it that those even who are the most difficult to satisfy in everything else do not usually desire a larger measure of this quality than they already possess.
>
> —Descartes.

"On Various Kinds of Thinking" ("The truest and most . . . seek further information before making it.") in *The Mind in the Making* by James Harvey Robinson. Copyright, 1921 by Harper & Row, Publishers, Inc. By permission of Harper & Row, Publishers, Inc.

We see man to-day, instead of the frank and courageous recognition of his status, the docile attention to his biological history, the determination to let nothing stand in the way of the security and permanence of his future, which alone can establish the safety and happiness of the race, substituting blind confidence in his destiny, unclouded faith in the essentially respectful attitude of the universe toward his moral code, and a belief no less firm that his traditions and laws and institutions necessarily contain permanent qualities of reality.

—William Trotter.

1. ON VARIOUS KINDS OF THINKING

[1] The truest and most profound observations on Intelligence have in the past been made by the poets and, in recent times, by story-writers. They have been keen observers and recorders and reckoned freely with the emotions and sentiments. Most philosophers, on the other hand, have exhibited a grotesque ignorance of man's life and have built up systems that are elaborate and imposing, but quite unrelated to actual human affairs. They have almost consistently neglected the actual process of thought and have set the mind off as something apart to be studied by itself. *But no such mind, exempt from bodily processes, animal impulses, savage traditions, infantile impressions, conventional reactions, and traditional knowledge, ever existed,* even in the case of the most abstract of metaphysicians. Kant entitled his great work *A Critique of Pure Reason*. But to the modern student of mind pure reason seems as mythical as the pure gold, transparent as glass, with which the celestial city is paved.

[2] Formerly philosophers thought of mind as having to do exclusively with conscious thought. It was that within man which perceived, remembered, judged, reasoned, understood, believed, willed. But of late it has been shown that we are unaware of a great part of what we perceive, remember, will, and infer; and that a great part of the thinking of which we are aware is determined by that of which we are not conscious. It has indeed been demonstrated that our unconscious psychic life far outruns our conscious. This seems perfectly natural to anyone who considers the following facts:

[3] The sharp distinction between the mind and the body is, as we shall find, a very ancient and spontaneous uncritical savage prepossession. What we think of as "mind" is so intimately associated with what we call "body" that we are coming to realize that the one cannot be understood without the other. Every thought reverberates through the body, and, on the other hand, alterations in our physical condition affect our whole attitude of mind. The insufficient elimination of the foul and decaying products of digestion may plunge us into deep melancholy, whereas a few whiffs of nitrous monoxide may exalt us to the seventh heaven of supernal

knowledge and godlike complacency. And *vice versa,* a sudden word or thought may cause our heart to jump, check our breathing, or make our knees as water. There is a whole new literature growing up which studies the effects of our bodily secretions and our muscular tensions and their relation to our emotions and our thinking.

[4] Then there are hidden impulses and desires and secret longings of which we can only with the greatest difficulty take account. They influence our conscious thought in the most bewildering fashion. Many of these unconscious influences appear to originate in our very early years. The older philosophers seem to have forgotten that even they were infants and children at their most impressionable age and never could by any possibility get over it.

[5] The term "unconscious," now so familiar to all readers of modern works on psychology, gives offense to some adherents of the past. There should, however, be no special mystery about it. It is not a new animistic abstraction, but simply a collective word to include all the physiological changes which escape our notice, all the forgotten experiences and impressions of the past which continue to influence our desires and reflections and conduct, even if we cannot remember them. What we can remember at any time is indeed an infinitesimal part of what has happened to us. We could not remember anything unless we forgot almost everything. As Bergson says, the brain is the organ of forgetfulness as well as of memory. Moreover, we tend, of course, to become oblivious to things to which we are thoroughly accustomed, for habit blinds us to their existence. So the forgotten and the habitual make up a great part of the so-called "unconscious."

[6] If we are ever to understand man, his conduct and reasoning, and if we aspire to learn to guide his life and his relations with his fellows more happily than heretofore, we cannot neglect the great discoveries briefly noted above. We must reconcile ourselves to novel and revolutionary conceptions of the mind, for it is clear that the older philosophers, whose works still determine our current views, had a very superficial notion of the subject with which they dealt. But for our purposes, with due regard to what has just been said and to much that has necessarily been left unsaid (and with the indulgence of those who will at first be inclined to dissent), *we shall consider mind chiefly as conscious knowledge and intelligence, as what we know and our attitude toward it—our disposition to increase our information, classify it, criticize it, and apply it.*

[7] We do not think enough about thinking, and much of our confusion is the result of current illusions in regard to it. Let us forget for the moment any impressions we may have derived from the philosophers, and see what seems to happen in ourselves. The first thing that we notice is that our thought moves with such incredible rapidity that it is almost impossible to arrest any specimen of it long enough to have a look at it. When we are offered a penny for our thoughts we always find that we have recently had so many things in mind that we can easily make a selection

which will not compromise us too nakedly. On inspection we shall find that even if we are not downright ashamed of a great part of our spontaneous thinking it is far too intimate, personal, ignoble or trivial to permit us to reveal more than a small part of it. I believe this must be true of everyone. We do not, of course, know what goes on in other people's heads. They tell us very little and we tell them very little. The spigot of speech, rarely fully opened, could never emit more than driblets of the ever renewed hogshead of thought—*noch grösser wie's Heidelberger Fass*. We find it hard to believe that other people's thoughts are as silly as our own, but they probably are.

[8] We all appear to ourselves to be thinking all the time during our waking hours, and most of us are aware that we go on thinking while we are asleep, even more foolishly than when awake. When uninterrupted by some practical issue we are engaged in what is now known as a *reverie*. This is our spontaneous and favorite kind of thinking. We allow our ideas to take their own course and this course is determined by our hopes and fears, our spontaneous desires, their fulfillment or frustration; by our likes and dislikes, our loves and hates and resentments. There is nothing else anything like so interesting to ourselves as ourselves. All thought that is not more or less laboriously controlled and directed will inevitably circle about the beloved Ego. It is amusing and pathetic to observe this tendency in ourselves and in others. We learn politely and generously to overlook this truth, but if we dare to think of it, it blazes forth like the noontide sun.

[9] The reverie or "free association of ideas" has of late become the subject of scientific research. While investigators are not yet agreed on the results, or at least on the proper interpretation to be given to them, there can be no doubt that our reveries form the chief index to our fundamental character. They are a reflection of our nature as modified by often hidden and forgotten experiences. We need not go into the matter further here, for it is only necessary to observe that the reverie is at all times a potent and in many cases an omnipotent rival to every other kind of thinking. It doubtless influences all our speculations in its persistent tendency to self-magnification and self-justification, which are its chief preoccupations, but it is the last thing to make directly or indirectly for honest increase of knowledge.[1] Philosophers usually talk as if such thinking did not exist or were in some way negligible. This is what makes their speculations so unreal and often worthless.

---

[1] The poet-clergyman, John Donne, who lived in the time of James I, has given a beautifully honest picture of the doings of a saint's mind: "I throw myself down in my chamber and call in and invite God and His angels thither, and when they are there I neglect God and His angels for the noise of a fly, for the rattling of a coach, for the whining of a door. I talk on in the same posture of praying, eyes lifted up, knees bowed down, as though I prayed to God, and if God or His angels should ask me when I thought last of God in that prayer I cannot tell. Sometimes I find that I had forgot what I was about, but when I began to forget it I cannot tell. A memory of yesterday's pleasures, a fear of to-morrow's dangers, a straw under my knee, a noise in mine ear, a light in mine eye, an anything, a nothing, a fancy, a chimera in my brain troubles me in my prayer."—Quoted by Robert Lynd. *The Art of Letters,* pp. 46–47.

[10] The reverie, as any of us can see for himself, is frequently broken and interrupted by the necessity of a second kind of thinking. We have to make practical decisions. Shall we write a letter or no? Shall we take the subway or a bus? Shall we have dinner at seven or half past? Shall we buy U. S. Rubber or a Liberty Bond? Decisions are easily distinguishable from the free flow of the reverie. Sometimes they demand a good deal of careful pondering and the recollection of pertinent facts; often, however, they are made impulsively. They are a more difficult and laborious thing than the reverie, and we resent having to "make up our mind" when we are tired, or absorbed in a congenial reverie. Weighing a decision, it should be noted, does not necessarily add anything to our knowledge, although we may, of course, seek further information before making it.

2. RATIONALIZING

[11] A third kind of thinking is stimulated when anyone questions our belief and opinions. We sometimes find ourselves changing our minds without any resistance or heavy emotion, but if we are told that we are wrong we resent the imputation and harden our hearts. We are incredibly heedless in the formation of our beliefs, but find ourselves filled with an illicit passion for them when anyone proposes to rob us of their companionship. It is obviously not the ideas themselves that are dear to us, but our self-esteem, which is threatened. We are by nature stubbornly pledged to defend our own from attack, whether it be our person, our family, our property, or our opinion. A United States Senator once remarked to a friend of mine that God Almighty could not make him change his mind on our Latin-American policy. We may surrender, but rarely confess ourselves vanquished. In the intellectual world at least peace is without victory.

[12] Few of us take the pains to study the origin of our cherished convictions; indeed, we have a natural repugnance to so doing. We like to continue to believe what we have been accustomed to accept as true, and the resentment aroused when doubt is cast upon any of our assumptions leads us to seek every manner of excuse for clinging to them. *The result is that most of our so-called reasoning consists in finding arguments for going on believing as we already do.*

[13] I remember years ago attending a public dinner to which the Governor of the state was bidden. The chairman explained that His Excellency could not be present for certain "good" reasons; what the "real" reasons were the presiding officer said he would leave us to conjecture. This distinction between "good" and "real" reasons is one of the most clarifying and essential in the whole realm of thought. We can readily give what seem to us "good" reasons for being a Catholic or a Mason, a Republican or a Democrat, an adherent or opponent of the League of Nations. But the "real" reasons are usually on quite a different plane. Of course the importance of this distinction is popularly, if somewhat obscurely, recog-

nized. The Baptist missionary is ready enough to see that the Buddhist is not such because his doctrines would bear careful inspection, but because he happened to be born in a Buddhist family in Tokio. But it would be treason to his faith to acknowledge that his own partiality for certain doctrines is due to the fact that his mother was a member of the First Baptist church of Oak Ridge. A savage can give all sorts of reasons for his belief that it is dangerous to step on a man's shadow, and a newspaper editor can advance plenty of arguments against the Bolsheviki. But neither of them may realize why he happens to be defending his particular opinion.

[14] The "real" reasons for our beliefs are concealed from ourselves as well as from others. As we grow up we simply adopt the ideas presented to us in regard to such matters as religion, family relations, property, business, our country, and the state. We unconsciously absorb them from our environment. They are persistently whispered in our ear by the group in which we happen to live. Moreover, as Mr. Trotter has pointed out, these judgments, being the product of suggestion and not of reasoning, have the quality of perfect obviousness, so that to question them

> . . . is to the believer to carry skepticism to an insane degree, and will be met by contempt, disapproval, or condemnation, according to the nature of the belief in question. When, therefore, we find ourselves entertaining an opinion about the basis of which there is a quality of feeling which tells us that to inquire into it would be absurd, obviously unnecessary, unprofitable, undesirable, bad form, or wicked, we may know that that opinion is a nonrational one, and probably, therefore, founded upon inadequate evidence.[2]

[15] Opinions, on the other hand, which are the result of experience or of honest reasoning do not have this quality of "primary certitude." I remember when as a youth I heard a group of business men discussing the question of the immortality of the soul, I was outraged by the sentiment of doubt expressed by one of the party. As I look back now I see that I had at the time no interest in the matter, and certainly no least argument to urge in favor of the belief in which I had been reared. But neither my personal indifference to the issue, nor the fact that I had previously given it no attention, served to prevent an angry resentment when I heard *my* ideas questioned.

[16] This spontaneous and loyal support of our preconceptions—this process of finding "good" reasons to justify our routine beliefs—is known to modern psychologists as "rationalizing"—clearly only a new name for a very ancient thing. Our "good" reasons ordinarily have no value in promoting honest enlightenment, because, no matter how solemnly

---

[2] *Instincts of the Herd,* p. 44.

they may be marshaled, they are at bottom the result of personal preference or prejudice, and not of an honest desire to seek or accept new knowledge.

[17] In our reveries we are frequently engaged in self-justification, for we cannot bear to think ourselves wrong, and yet have constant illustrations of our weaknesses and mistakes. So we spend much time finding fault with circumstances and the conduct of others, and shifting on to them with great ingenuity the onus of our own failures and disappointments. *Rationalizing is the self-exculpation which occurs when we feel ourselves, or our group, accused of misapprehension or error.*

[18] The little word *my* is the most important one in all human affairs, and properly to reckon with it is the beginning of wisdom. It has the same force whether it is *my* dinner, *my* dog, and *my* house, or *my* faith, *my* country, and *my* God. We not only resent the imputation that our watch is wrong, or our car shabby, but that our conception of the canals of Mars, of the pronunciation of "Epictetus," of the medicinal value of salicine, or the date of Sargon I, are subject to revision.

[19] Philosophers, scholars, and men of science exhibit a common sensitiveness in all decisions in which their *amour propre* is involved. Thousands of argumentative works have been written to vent a grudge. However stately their reasoning, it may be nothing but rationalizing, stimulated by the most commonplace of all motives. A history of philosophy and theology could be written in terms of grouches, wounded pride, and aversions, and it would be far more instructive than the usual treatments of these themes. Sometimes, under Providence, the lowly impulse of resentment leads to great achievements. Milton wrote his treatise on divorce as a result of his troubles with his seventeen-year-old wife, and when he was accused of being the leading spirit in a new sect, the Divorcers, he wrote his noble *Areopagitica* to prove his right to say what he thought fit, and incidentally to establish the advantage of a free press in the promotion of Truth.

[20] All mankind, high and low, thinks in all the ways which have been described. The reverie goes on all the time not only in the mind of the mill hand and the Broadway flapper, but equally in weighty judges and godly bishops. It has gone on in all the philosophers, scientists, poets, and theologians that have ever lived. Aristotle's most abstruse speculations were doubtless tempered by highly irrelevant reflections. He is reported to have had very thin legs and small eyes, for which he doubtless had to find excuses, and he was wont to indulge in very conspicuous dress and rings and was accustomed to arrange his hair carefully.[3] Diogenes the Cynic exhibited the impudence of a touchy soul. His tub was his distinction. Tennyson in beginning his "Maud" could not forget his chagrin over losing his patrimony years before as the result of an

---

[3] Diogenes Laertius, book v.

unhappy investment in the Patent Decorative Carving Company. These facts are not recalled here as a gratuitous disparagement of the truly great, but to insure a full realization of the tremendous competition which all really exacting thought has to face, even in the minds of the most highly endowed mortals.

[21] And now the astonishing and perturbing suspicion emerges that perhaps almost all that had passed for social science, political economy, politics, and ethics in the past may be brushed aside by future generations as mainly rationalizing. John Dewey has already reached this conclusion in regard to philosophy.[4] Veblen [5] and other writers have revealed the various unperceived presuppositions of the traditional political economy, and now comes an Italian sociologist, Vilfredo Pareto, who, in his huge treatise on general sociology, devotes hundreds of pages to substantiating a similar thesis affecting all the social sciences.[6] This conclusion may be ranked by students of a hundred years hence as one of the several great discoveries of our age. It is by no means fully worked out, and it is so opposed to nature that it will be very slowly accepted by the great mass of those who consider themselves thoughtful. As a historical student I am personally fully reconciled to this newer view. Indeed, it seems to me inevitable that just as the various sciences of nature were, before the opening of the seventeenth century, largely masses of rationalizations to suit the religious sentiments of the period, so the social sciences have continued even to our own day to be rationalizations of uncritically accepted beliefs and customs.

[22] *It will become apparent as we proceed that the fact that an idea is ancient and that it has been widely received is no argument in its favor, but should immediately suggest the necessity of carefully testing it as a probable instance of rationalization.*

3. HOW CREATIVE THOUGHT TRANSFORMS THE WORLD

[23] This brings us to another kind of thought which can easily be distinguished from the three kinds described above. It has not the usual qualities of the reverie, for it does not hover about our personal complacencies and humiliations. It is not made up of the homely decisions forced upon us by everyday needs, when we review our little stock of existing information, consult our conventional preferences and obligations, and

---

[4] *Reconstruction in Philosophy.*

[5] *The Place of Science in Modern Civilization.*

[6] *Traité de Sociologie Générale, passim.* The author's term *"derivations"* seems to be his precise way of expressing what we have called the "good" reasons, and his *"residus"* correspond to the "real" reasons. He well says, "*L'homme éprouve le besoin de raisonner, et en outre d'étendre un voile sur ses instincts et sur ses sentiments*"—hence, rationalization. (P. 788.) His aim is to reduce sociology to the "real" reasons. (P. 791.)

make a choice of action. It is not the defense of our own cherished beliefs and prejudices just because they are our own—mere plausible excuses for remaining of the same mind. On the contrary, it is that peculiar species of thought which leads us to *change* our mind.

[24] It is this kind of thought that has raised man from his pristine, subsavage ignorance and squalor to the degree of knowledge and comfort which he now possesses. On his capacity to continue and greatly extend this kind of thinking depends his chance of groping his way out of the plight in which the most highly civilized peoples of the world now find themselves. In the past this type of thinking has been called Reason. But so many misapprehensions have grown up around the word that some of us have become very suspicious of it. I suggest, therefore, that we substitute a recent name and speak of "creative thought" rather than of Reason. *For this kind of meditation begets knowledge, and knowledge is really creative inasmuch as it makes things look different from what they seemed before and may indeed work for their reconstruction.*

[25] In certain moods some of us realize that we are observing things or making reflections with a seeming disregard of our personal preoccupations. We are not preening or defending ourselves; we are not faced by the necessity of any practical decision, nor are we apologizing for believing this or that. We are just wondering and looking and mayhap seeing what we never perceived before.

[26] Curiosity is as clear and definite as any of our urges. We wonder what is in a sealed telegram or in a letter in which some one else is absorbed, or what is being said in the telephone booth or in low conversation. This inquisitiveness is vastly stimulated by jealousy, suspicion, or any hint that we ourselves are directly or indirectly involved. But there appears to be a fair amount of personal interest in other people's affairs even when they do not concern us except as a mystery to be unraveled or a tale to be told. The reports of a divorce suit will have "news value" for many weeks. They constitute a story, like a novel or play or moving picture. This is not an example of pure curiosity, however, since we readily identify ourselves with others, and their joys and despair then become our own.

[27] We also take note of, or "observe," as Sherlock Holmes says, things which have nothing to do with our personal interests and make no personal appeal either direct or by way of sympathy. This is what Veblen so well calls "idle curiosity." And it is usually idle enough. Some of us when we face the line of people opposite us in a subway train impulsively consider them in detail and engage in rapid inferences and form theories in regard to them. On entering a room there are those who will perceive at a glance the degree of preciousness of the rugs, the character of the pictures, and the personality revealed by the books. But there are many, it would seem, who are so absorbed in their personal reverie or in some definite purpose that they have no bright-eyed energy for idle curiosity. The tendency to miscellaneous observation we come by honestly enough, for we note it in many of our animal relatives.

[28] Veblen, however, uses the term "idle curiosity" somewhat ironically, as is his wont. It is idle only to those who fail to realize that it may be a very rare and indispensable thing from which almost all distinguished human achievement proceeds. Since it may lead to systematic examination and seeking for things hitherto undiscovered. For research is but diligent search which enjoys the high flavor of primitive hunting. Occasionally and fitfully idle curiosity thus leads to creative thought, which alters and broadens our own views and aspirations and may in turn, under highly favorable circumstances, affect the views and lives of others, even for generations to follow. An example or two will make this unique human process clear.

[29] Galileo was a thoughtful youth and doubtless carried on a rich and varied reverie. He had artistic ability and might have turned out to be a musician or painter. When he had dwelt among the monks at Valambrosa he had been tempted to lead the life of a religious. As a boy he busied himself with toy machines and he inherited a fondness for mathematics. All these facts are of record. We may safely assume also that, along with many other subjects of contemplation, the Pisan maidens found a vivid place in his thoughts.

[30] One day when seventeen years old he wandered into the cathedral of his native town. In the midst of his reverie he looked up at the lamps hanging by long chains from the high ceiling of the church. Then something very difficult to explain occurred. He found himself no longer thinking of the building, worshipers, or the services; of his artistic or religious interests; of his reluctance to become a physician as his father wished. He forgot the question of a career and even the *graziosissime donne*. As he watched the swinging lamps he was suddenly wondering if mayhap their oscillations, whether long or short, did not occupy the same time. Then he tested this hypothesis by counting his pulse, for that was the only timepiece he had with him.

[31] This observation, however remarkable in itself, was not enough to produce a really creative thought. Others may have noticed the same thing and yet nothing came of it. Most of our observations have no assignable results. Galileo may have seen that the warts on a peasant's face formed a perfect isosceles triangle, or he may have noticed with boyish glee that just as the officiating priest was uttering the solemn words, *ecce agnus Dei*, a fly lit on the end of his nose. To be really creative, ideas have to be worked up and then "put over," so that they become a part of man's social heritage. The highly accurate pendulum clock was one of the later results of Galileo's discovery. He himself was led to reconsider and successfully to refute the old notions of falling bodies. It remained for Newton to prove that the moon was falling, and presumably all the heavenly bodies. This quite upset all the consecrated views of the heavens as managed by angelic engineers. The universality of the laws of gravitation stimulated the attempt to seek other and equally important natural laws and cast

grave doubts on the miracles in which mankind had hitherto believed. In short, those who dared to include in their thought the discoveries of Galileo and his successors found themselves in a new earth surrounded by new heavens.

[32] On the 28th of October, 1831, three hundred and fifty years after Galileo had noticed the isochronous vibrations of the lamps, creative thought and its currency had so far increased that Faraday was wondering what would happen if he mounted a disk of copper between the poles of a horsehoe magnet. As the disk revolved an electric current was produced. This would doubtless have seemed the idlest kind of an experiment to the stanch business men of the time, who, it happened, were just then denouncing the child-labor bills in their anxiety to avail themselves to the full of the results of earlier idle curiosity. But should the dynamos and motors which have come into being as the outcome of Faraday's experiment be stopped this evening, the business man of to-day, agitated over labor troubles, might, as he trudged home past lines of "dead" cars, through dark streets to an unlighted house, engage in a little creative thought of his own and perceive that he and his laborers would have no modern factories and mines to quarrel about had it not been for the strange practical effects of the idle curiosity of scientists, inventors, and engineers.

[33] The examples of creative intelligence given above belong to the realm of modern scientific achievement, which furnishes the most striking instances of the effects of scrupulous, objective thinking. But there are, of course, other great realms in which the recording and embodiment of acute observation and insight have wrought themselves into the higher life of man. The great poets and dramatists and our modern storytellers have found themselves engaged in productive reveries, noting and artistically presenting their discoveries for the delight and instruction of those who have the ability to appreciate them.

[34] The process by which a fresh and original poem or drama comes into being is doubtless analogous to that which originates and elaborates so-called scientific discoveries; but there is clearly a temperamental difference. The genesis and advance of painting, sculpture, and music offer still other problems. We really as yet know shockingly little about these matters, and indeed very few people have the least curiosity about them.[7] Nevertheless, creative intelligence in its various forms and activities is what makes man. Were it not for its slow, painful, and constantly discouraged operations through the ages man would be no more than a

---

[7] Recently a re-examination of creative thought has begun as a result of new knowledge which discredits many of the notions formerly held about "reason." See, for example, *Creative Intelligence*, by a group of American philosophic thinkers; John Dewey, *Essays in Experimental Logic* (both pretty hard books); and Veblen, *The Place of Science in Modern Civilization*. Easier than these and very stimulating are Dewey, *Reconstruction in Philosophy*, and Woodworth, *Dynamic Psychology*.

species of primate living on seeds, fruit, roots, and uncooked flesh, and wandering naked through the woods and over the plains like a chimpanzee.

[35] The origin and progress and future promotion of civilization are ill understood and misconceived. These should be made the chief theme of education, but much hard work is necessary before we can reconstruct our ideas of man and his capacities and free ourselves from innumerable persistent misapprehensions. There have been obstructionists in all times, not merely the lethargic masses, but the moralists, the rationalizing theologians, and most of the philosophers, all busily if unconsciously engaged in ratifying existing ignorance and mistakes and discouraging creative thought. Naturally, those who reassure us seem worthy of honor and respect. Equally naturally those who puzzle us with disturbing criticisms and invite us to change our ways are objects of suspicion and readily discredited. Our personal discontent does not ordinarily extend to any critical questioning of the general situation in which we find ourselves. In every age the prevailing conditions of civilization have appeared quite natural and inevitable to those who grew up in them. The cow asks no questions as to how it happens to have a dry stall and a supply of hay. The kitten laps its warm milk from a china saucer, without knowing anything about porcelain; the dog nestles in the corner of a divan with no sense of obligation to the inventors of upholstery and the manufacturers of down pillows. So we humans accept our breakfasts, and our trains and telephones and orchestras and movies, our national Constitution, or moral code and standards of manners, with the simplicity and innocence of a pet rabbit. We have absolutely inexhaustible capacities for appropriating what others do for us with no thought for a "thank you." We do not feel called upon to make any least contribution to the merry game ourselves. Indeed, we are usually quite unaware that a game is being played at all.

[36] We have now examined the various classes of thinking which we can readily observe in ourselves and which we have plenty of reasons to believe go on, and always have been going on, in our fellow-men. We can sometimes get quite pure and sparkling examples of all four kinds, but commonly they are so confused and intermingled in our reverie as not to be readily distinguishable. The reverie is a reflection of our longings, exultations, and complacencies, our fears, suspicions, and disappointments. We are chiefly engaged in struggling to maintain our self-respect and in asserting that supremacy which we all crave and which seems to us our natural prerogative. It is not strange, but rather quite inevitable, that our beliefs about what is true and false, good and bad, right and wrong, should be mixed up with the reverie and be influenced by the same considerations which determine its character and course. We resent criticisms of our views exactly as we do of anything else connected with ourselves. Our

notions of life and its ideals seem to us to be *our own* and as such necessarily true and right, to be defended at all costs.

[37] *We very rarely consider, however, the process by which we gained our convictions.* If we did so, we could hardly fail to see that there was usually little ground for our confidence in them. Here and there, in this department of knowledge or that, some one of us might make a fair claim to have taken some trouble to get correct ideas of, let us say, the situation in Russia, the sources of our food supply, the origin of the Constitution, the revision of the tariff, the policy of the Holy Roman Apostolic Church, modern business organization, trade unions, birth control, socialism, the League of Nations, the excess-profits tax, preparedness, advertising in its social bearings; but only a very exceptional person would be entitled to opinions on all of even these few matters. And yet most of us have opinions on all these, and on many other questions of equal importance, of which we may know even less. We feel compelled, as self-respecting persons, to take sides when they come up for discussion. We even surprise ourselves by our omniscience. Without taking thought we see in a flash that it is most righteous and expedient to discourage birth control by legislative enactment, or that one who decrees intervention in Mexico is clearly wrong, or that big advertising is essential to big business and that big business is the pride of the land. As godlike beings why should we not rejoice in our omniscience?

[38] It is clear, in any case, that our convictions on important matters are not the result of knowledge or critical thought, nor, it may be added, are they often dictated by supposed self-interest. Most of them are *pure prejudices* in the proper sense of that word. We do not form them ourselves. They are the whisperings of "the voice of the herd." We have in the last analysis no responsibility for them and need assume none. They are not really our own ideas, but those of others no more well informed or inspired than ourselves, who have got them in the same careless and humiliating manner as we. It should be our pride to revise our ideas and not to adhere to what passes for respectable opinion, for such opinion can frequently be shown to be not respectable at all. We should, in view of the considerations that have been mentioned, resent our supine credulity. As an English writer has remarked:

[39] "If we feared the entertaining of an unverifiable opinion with the warmth with which we fear using the wrong implement at the dinner table, if the thought of holding a prejudice disgusted us as does a foul disease, then the dangers of man's suggestibility would be turned into advantages." [8]

[40] The purpose of this essay is to set forth briefly the way in which the notions of the herd have been accumulated. This seems to me the best, easiest, and least invidious educational device for cultivating a

---

[8] Trotter, *op. cit.*, p. 45. The first part of this little volume is excellent.

proper distrust for the older notions on which we still continue to rely.

[41] The "real" reasons, which explain how it is we happen to hold a particular belief, are chiefly historical. Our most important opinions—those, for example, having to do with traditional, religious, and moral convictions, property rights, patriotism, national honor, the state, and indeed all the assumed foundations of society—are, as I have already suggested, rarely the result of reasoned consideration, but of unthinking absorption from the social environment in which we live. Consequently, they have about them a quality of "elemental certitude," and we especially resent doubt or criticism cast upon them. So long, however, as we revere the whisperings of the herd, we are obviously unable to examine them dispassionately and to consider to what extent they are suited to the novel conditions and social exigencies in which we find ourselves to-day.

[42] The "real" reasons for our beliefs, by making clear their origins and history, can do much to dissipate this emotional blockade and rid us of our prejudices and preconceptions. Once this is done and we come critically to examine our traditional beliefs, we may well find some of them sustained by experience and honest reasoning, while others must be revised to meet new conditions and our more extended knowledge. But only after we have undertaken such a critical examination in the light of experience and modern knowledge, freed from any feeling of "primary certitude," can we claim that the "good" are also the "real" reasons for our opinions.

[43] I do not flatter myself that this general show-up of man's thought through the ages will cure myself or others of carelessness in adopting ideas, or of unseemly heat in defending them just because we have adopted them. But if the considerations which I propose to recall are really incorporated into our thinking and are permitted to establish our general outlook on human affairs, they will do much to relieve the imaginary obligations we feel in regard to traditional sentiments and ideals. Few of us are capable of engaging in creative thought, but some of us can at least come to distinguish it from other and inferior kinds of thought and accord to it the esteem that it merits as the greatest treasure of the past and the only hope of the future.

Questions on Meaning

1. In your own words, explain the author's point about the limitations of the contributions of philosophers to our understanding of the way people think. Find some sentences in which Robinson expresses especially strong criticism of philosophers. Do you think the evidence he gives justifies the strength of his language?

2. Convert your marginal notations of Robinson's classification of kinds of thinking into an outline of the essay, using Roman numerals for each cate-

gory and adding a section labeled "Introduction" and another labeled "Conclusion." Include under each major heading subheadings that indicate what Robinson thinks is especially important for us to know about each of the categories of thinking. Then compare your outline with the author's three-part organization. How do you account for the differences?

3 Consider the way this essay has been classified in this text. Do you think it is appropriately described as a "chiefly persuasive" piece? One could argue this point, since writers use classification for the purpose of organizing the *information* they provide. And there is certainly much information in this selection. However, before you defend the position that the Robinson essay should be placed in the "informative" category (the editors did consider placing it there), give thought to the following questions: (1) Does the essay have a thesis? If so, where is it expressed specifically? (2) Does the writer regard the categories as equally important? Does he regard each as "important" in the same sense? (3) Is he urging the reader to adopt a particular kind of action, making use of the information provided here, or is he providing the information for its own sake—that is, for the reader's enlightenment and pleasure?

Questions on Style and Structure

1 Of the techniques for introducing a paper that are discussed in the Introduction to Paragraph and Sentence Structure, which does Robinson employ?

2 An essay on a topic such as thinking is in danger of being too abstract, too diffuse. Does the author supply you with sufficient details and illustrations to clarify what he means? Examine, for example, his discussion of rationalizing.

3 Note how, in paragraph 11, coherence is achieved partly through the frequent use of the pronoun *we*. Can you find other paragraphs that are similarly made coherent through the use of pronouns?

4 What basic technique does Robinson use to make paragraph 23 coherent?

5 In paragraph 35, the author compares the behavior of human beings with the behavior of various animals. Is the analogy convincing and effective?

6 Which of the techniques for concluding an essay does Robinson employ?

Exploring Words

1 *ignoble.* Which of the meanings your dictionary lists for *ignoble* applies to Robinson's use of the word?

2 *omnipotent.* What does Robinson mean when he says that reverie is an "omnipotent rival" to all other kinds of thinking?

3 *imputation.* Which of the definitions for *imputation* fits Robinson's use?

4 *illicit.* Write a sentence using *illicit* appropriately.

5 *onus.* Which of the synonyms your dictionary lists could best be substituted for *onus* in Robinson's sentence?

6 *abstruse.* What studies that you have taken up in high school or college have you found to be very *abstruse*?

7 *gratuitous.* What relationships in meaning do you find between the words *gratis, gratuity,* and *gratuitous*? How do the connotations of the word *gratuitous* (in the sense that Robinson uses the word) differ from those of *gratis* and *gratuity*?

8 *pristine.* Your dictionary gives two quite different meanings for *pristine.* Only one of these fits Robinson's use. Which is it? How do you account for the development of two such different meanings?

9 *lethargic.* Consult your dictionary, and then decide under what conditions this word might apply to you.

Suggestions for Writing

1 As Robinson does with the topic of thinking, classify some things that you know well (for example, books you enjoy reading, behavior at weddings, people in your domitory).

2 Robinson writes, *"It will become apparent as we proceed that the fact that an idea is ancient and that it has been widely received is no argument in its favor, but should immediately suggest the necessity of carefully testing it as a probably instance of rationalization."* Select an "ancient" idea and subject it to this kind of rigorous "test." You might like to write about the "truth" embodied in maxims like the following:

   a A bird in the hand is worth two in the bush.
   b Love conquers all.
   c A penny saved is a penny earned.
   d Crime does not pay.
   e A good beginning makes a good ending.
   f A woman's place is in the home.
   g Big boys don't cry.
   h America—love it or leave it.

3 Think of a classification of human beings that easily lends itself to subclassifications: this might be an occupational group, such as doctors, ministers, salespeople, or teachers, or it might be a looser category, like students who work mainly for grades or teenagers who go on blind dates. Write a paper on this group of people, using the organizational principle of classification. You will probably develop a thesis that will make your essay more than a straight information piece, since most of us, when we write or talk about people, get quickly into opinions and attitudes.

The Energy Crisis—All of a Piece
BARRY COMMONER

Getting Started

With Ideas

As you begin reading this work, it will be a good idea to think of some of the possible implications of the title. What are some of the problems that are usually associated with the phrase "energy crisis"? What might the author mean by saying that this "crisis" is "all of a piece"? You will find as you read the introductory paragraphs that he provides general answers to these questions and that he makes clear that his basic purpose is to offer one solution to a group of related problems. What that solution is and how Commoner supports it you will discover as you complete this complex but carefully, logically, and classically developed essay.

With Words

1. intractable (1)—from the Latin prefix *in-*, meaning "not," and the Latin word meaning "to handle" or "to treat."
2. perversely (6)—the noun *pervert*, the verb *pervert*, the adjective *perverse*, and the adverb *perversely* are all related. The context will also help you with *perversely*.
3. surfeit (8)—remember that you discovered in "The Consolations of Illiteracy" (p. 75) that the source of this word meant "to overdo."
4. proliferation (33)—the context will be helpful here.
5. panacea (34)—what recent *panaceas* for the ills of the world have you heard about?

---

[1] We live in a time of unending crises. A series of grave, seemingly intractable problems clamor for attention: degradation of the environment; the rapid growth of world population; the food crisis; the energy crisis—rapidly mounting calamities that may merge into a worldwide economic collapse. And, overshadowing all, war and the threat of war.

[2] As each crisis rises to the top of the public agenda, we try to respond: the environmental crisis is met by pollution controls; population growth by attempts to control fertility; the energy crisis by efforts to con-

Reprinted by permission of the author.

trol demand and to develop new supplies; the economic crisis by proposals to control consumption, wages, and prices; the threat of war is met by a patchwork of negotiations.

[3] But each effort to solve one crisis seems to founder on conflict with another: pollution controls are blamed for the shortage of energy; population control conflicts with the need for economic development; energy conservation leads to unemployment; proposals to feed the hungry of the world are condemned as inflationary; in the growing economic panic we hear cries against almost any effort to alleviate all the rest; and already there are those who seek to end all these problems by incinerating them in the flames of war.

[4] All this seems to be a dismal confirmation that the world is staggering toward catastrophe. But the very links that make up this web of crises are themselves a source of optimism, a clue to what needs to be done. The close connections among them suggest that all these problems are symptoms of some common fault that lies deep within the design of modern society. The energy crisis is so closely linked to this pivotal defect as to offer the hope that it can become a guiding thread which, once seized, can lead us out of the labyrinth. In this sense, the energy crisis signalizes a great watershed in the history of human society. What we do in response to it will determine, I believe, for the United States and for every nation in the world, whether our future continues the progress toward humanism and democracy, or ends in catastrophe and oppression.

[5] When engineers want to understand the strength of a new material they stress it to the breaking point and analyze how it responds. The energy crisis is a kind of "engineering test" of the United States economic system, and it has revealed a number of deep-seated faults.

[6] Although energy is useless until it produces goods or services, and although nearly all the energy that we use is derived from limited, nonrenewable sources which will eventually run out (all of which pollute the environment), we have perversely reduced the efficiency with which fuels are converted into goods and services. In the last thirty years, in agriculture, industry, and transportation, those productive processes that use energy least efficiently and stress the environment most heavily are growing most rapidly, driving their energetically efficient competitors off the market.

[7] In agriculture the older, energy-sparing methods of maintaining fertility by crop rotation and manuring have been displaced by the intensive use of nitrogen fertilizers synthesized from natural gas. In the same way, synthetic fibers, plastics, and detergents made from petroleum have captured most of the markets once held by wood, cotton, wool, and soap—all made from energy-sparing and renewable resources. In transportation, railroads—by far the most energetically efficient means of moving people and freight—are crumbling, their traffic increasingly taken over by passenger cars, trucks, and airplanes that use far more fuel per passenger- or ton-mile.

[8] Naturally, such energy-wasting enterprises are threatened when the price of energy increases—the only real outcome of the illusory 1973 fuel shortage. If they were not so serious, some of these economic consequences could only be regarded as absurd. When the multi-billion-dollar petrochemical industry cheerfully bid up the price of propane—an essential starting material in plastics production—farmers had trouble finding the propane they needed to dry their grain, and then had to pay triple its former price. In order to sustain the surfeit of plastic trivia that gluts the modern market, food production was threatened. When, in response to urgent appeals, householders reduced their demand for electricity, the power companies asked for rate increases to make up for the lost business. Automobile manufacturers, having scornfully rejected environmentalists' appeals to produce smaller, more fuel-efficient vehicles, have lost about half their sales, throwing one hundred thousand auto workers out of work.

[9] The deepest fault that is revealed by the impact of the energy crisis on the United States' economic system is not that we are running out of energy or of environmental quality—but of capital. As oil wells have gone deeper, petroleum refineries have become more complex; power plants have given up the reliability of coal- or oil-fired burners for the elaborate, shaky technology of the nuclear reactor, and the capital cost of producing a unit of energy has sharply increased. The projected production of total United States energy is expected to rise from about 57,000 trillion Btu in 1971 to about 92,000 trillion Btu in 1985 (an increase of about sixty per cent) and requiring that annual capital expenditures for energy rise from about $26.5 billion to $158 billion over that period—an increase of about 390 per cent. This trend, coupled with the growing inefficiency in the use of energy, means that, if we follow the present course, energy production will consume an increasing fraction of the total capital available for investment in new enterprises including factories, homes, schools, and hospitals.

[10] One projection, based on present maximum estimates of energy demand, indicates that energy production could consume as much as eighty per cent of all available capital in 1985. This is, of course, an absurdly unrealistic situation in which the energy industry would, in effect, be devouring its own customers. Thus, the compounded effects of a trend toward enterprises that inefficiently convert energy into goods and services and power plants that inefficiently convert capital into energy production threaten to overrun the economic system's capacity to produce its most essential factor—capital. This may well explain why, according to a recent New York Stock Exchange report, we are likely to be $650 billion short in needed capital in the next decade. The economic effects of the increasingly large proportion of available capital that would need to be tied up in this vast enterprise would be broadly felt by society. For example, according to the recent New York Stock Exchange report, in order to assure the availability of capital, the following changes are called for: ". . . corporate tax rates should be adjusted to permit increased accumulation of funds

... tax exemption for reasonable amounts of capital gains ... excessive regulation and restrictive controls (especially in the utilities industry) should be relaxed ... environmental standards should be modified, with target dates deferred."

[11] The report acknowledges that federal tax revenues will be reduced, but proposes to match this deficit with a reduction in federal expenditures.

[12] What has gone wrong? Why has the postwar transformation of agriculture, industry, and transportation set the United States on the suicidal course of consuming, ever more/wastefully, capital goods and nonrenewable sources of energy, and destroying the very environment in which we must live?

[13] The basic reason is one that every businessman well understands. It paid. Soap companies significantly increased their profit per pound of cleaner sold when they switched from soap to detergents; truck lines are more profitable than railroads; synthetic plastics and fabrics are more profitable than leather, cotton, wool, or wood; nitrogen fertilizer is the corn farmer's most profit-yielding input; power companies claim that capital-intensive nuclear plants improve their rate of return; and as Henry Ford II has said, "minicars make miniprofits."

[14] All this is the natural outcome of the terms that govern the entry of new enterprises in the United States' economic system. Regardless of the initial motivation for a new productive enterprise—the entry of nuclear plants into the power market, of synthetics into the fabric market, of detergents into the cleaner market, or of trucks into the freight market—it will succeed relative to the older competitor only if it is capable of yielding a greater return of the investment. At times, this advantage may be expressed as a lower price for the new goods, an advantage that is likely to drive the competing ones off the market. At other times, the advantage may be translated into higher profits, enabling the new enterprise to expand faster than the older one, with the same end result.

[15] Some economists believe that private enterprise can adapt to the rising price of energy by turning to energetically efficient productive technologies in order to save costs. Where this can be accomplished by reducing the waste of energy within a given enterprise it may well succeed. But in other cases—for example, the petrochemical industry—the intensive use of energy is built into the very design of the enterprise in order to eliminate human labor, thereby raising labor productivity and the resultant profits. In these cases improved energetic efficiency can be achieved only by rolling back the rapid growth of such inherently inefficient industries—but, for that very reason, these are precisely the industries that are most profitable. Any attempt to reduce their level of activity would necessarily encroach on the profit yielded by the economic system as a whole.

[16] Another possible adaptation is to pass the extra cost of measures that conserve energy and reduce environmental stress along to the

consumer. Thus the energy dependence of agriculture could be reduced by cutting back on the rate of application of nitrogen fertilizer, with the inevitable result that the price of food would rise. This would place an extra burden on the poor, which, in turn, might be rectified *if* the principles of private enterprise could accommodate measures that would remedy the growing gap between the rich and the poor. Once more, this is a challenge to the basic design of the economic system.

[17] In a sense there is nothing new here, only the recognition that in the United States' economic system, decisions about what to produce and how to produce it are governed most powerfully by the expectation of enhanced profit. What *is* new and profoundly unsettling is that the thousands of separate entrepreneurial decisions that have been made during the last thirty years in the United States regarding new productive enterprises have, with such alarming uniformity, favored those which are less efficient energetically and more damaging to the environment than their alternatives. This is a serious challenge to the fundamental precept of private enterprise—that decisions made on the basis of the producer's economic self-interest are also the best way to meet social needs. That is why the environmental crisis, the energy crisis, and the multitude of social problems to which they are linked suggest—certainly as an urgently-to-be-discussed hypothesis—that the operative fault, and therefore the locus of the remedy, lies in the design of our profit-oriented economic system.

[18] Comparable claims of service to the public welfare are, of course, made by the Soviet and other socialist economic systems, and insofar as such systems are based on social rather than private decisions regarding the design of the productive system, these claims may, at least in principle, be justified. However, when we look at the recent practice of the Soviet Union and certain other socialist countries we see a strange tendency to acquire from the United States and other industrialized capitalist countries, precisely the productive technology that has driven these countries down the path of wasteful consumption of energy and capital. After all, when Fiat automobiles are produced in Moscow they can be expected to use as much gasoline and emit as much pollution as they do in Rome. And when the petrochemical complexes that are so largely responsible for the wasteful, environmentally destructive use of energy in the United States are imported by Russia, Poland, and even China, they will certainly impose these same pernicious hazards in their new locations.

[19] We are all aware, of course, that neither capitalist nor socialist societies will lightly tolerate inquiries that question the basic roots of their economic systems. The environmental crisis, the energy crisis, and all the difficult, interwoven social issues to which they are linked is an urgent signal that it is time to give up this taboo. Surely, those who are convinced that private enterprise is in fact the most effective way to live in harmony with our resources and the natural world now have an unparalleled opportunity to make their case and to convince a troubled citizenry that there are ways, within the context of that system, to right its grave

faults. And for those who see in the present situation opportunities to support socially oriented ways to organize our productive and economic enterprise, there is an equally important challenge to prove their case.

[20] If we pay heed to the basic facts about the production and use of energy, we can begin to find a rational way out of this tragic and absurd state of affairs.

[21] To begin with, we now know that we can readily squeeze out of the productive process much of the wasted energy that has been devoted, not to the improvement of human welfare, but to the replacement of worthwhile and meaningful labor by the cheaper and more tractable alternative of energy. A number of studies have shown that in the United States the nation's energy budget could be reduced by about a third in this way with no significant reduction in the standard of living. Every unit of energy thus saved is reduced in its environmental impact to zero and relieves the pressure for hasty adventures into dubious and dangerous power technologies such as the breeder and fusion reactors.

[22] In their place we can turn to solar energy, which has none of the faults that promise to cripple the present energy system. Unlike oil, gas, coal, or uranium, solar energy is renewable and virtually free of untoward environmental effects. Unlike the nonrenewable sources, which become more difficult and costly to acquire as the rate of their use increases, the use of solar energy is readily extendable at no loss in efficiency. The capture of one sunbeam, after all, in no way hinders the capture of the next one. Only solar energy can avoid the capital crunch which promises to paralyze the further development of the present energy system. Finally, solar energy is uniquely adaptable to different scales of economic organization. A conventional power plant now typically requires an investment approaching one billion dollars. In contrast, many solar collectors can be constructed in a range of sizes suitable for everything from a single household to an entire city.

[23] The myth that solar energy is impractical, or too expensive, or in the realm of future technology is easily dispelled by a series of recent analyses done for the National Science Foundation. For example, a project, based on installing readily constructed solar-heat systems in the nation's housing, could readily reduce the United States' energy budget by twelve to fifteen per cent, at a cost that could be recovered in the form of fuel savings in ten to twelve years.

[24] Thus, we are at a crossroads. Along one path lies the continued consumption of fossil fuels by productive enterprises that waste energy for the sake of extracting maximum profits out of labor; the continued pollution of the environment; an escalating scramble for oil, which, as it diminishes in amount, will inevitably become an irresistible lure to military adventures. Along this path lies the increasing expansion of the size of power units, even beyond the present billion-dollar size, so that the chief prerequisite to power production will become a huge accumulation of wealth. In a country such as the United States, this will mean that our

energy system will fall increasingly under the domination of a few huge, wealthy corporations. In the world at large it will favor the rich and the powerful nations as against the small, poor nations that are struggling to develop.

[25] Finally, along this road as the fossil fuels are exhausted and nuclear reactors begin to dominate the energy system, creating a plutonium economy that ties power production directly to the violence of nuclear weapons, the threat of terroristic thefts—whether real, or not—can be used as a pretext to establish a system of military "protection." Already a recent report to the Atomic Energy Commission calls for elaborate military protection of power plants, together with domestic espionage and all the other trappings of fascism—all in the name of enabling the operation of a nuclear energy system.

[26] The other path relies on energy conservation and the sun. Full use of existing methods of capturing solar energy for heating and cooling could remove fifteen to twenty per cent of the need for fossil fuels. By this means, together with feasible measures to conserve energy at no expense to the resulting goods and services, within perhaps the next decade about one-half of the present demand for energy from conventional sources could be deleted from the national energy budget—a step that with sensible planning could readily permit us to phase out the operation of most of the existing nuclear reactors.

[27] Meanwhile, with a research and development effort that would be quite modest relative to the expenditures that have been devoted to the development of nuclear power, the technology for the economic production of solar cells for the production of electricity could be reduced to practicality. (According to a recent government report such a program could, by 1990, establish economical solar-powered electric stations for cities of one hundred thousand.) Given the wide flexibility of solar power units with respect to size, they could then be adapted to enterprises of any size and degree of centralization that seem socially desirable. Such changes could take place in small, graded steps, avoiding the huge accumulation of capital necessary to create conventional power stations. In this way a nation's power system could be made to serve its own particular needs, reversing a situation now frequently encountered in which the huge size and centralized location of power sources often dictates what can be produced. Energy can then more readily serve social needs, rather than create them.

[28] And finally, through the wide use of solar energy and other alternative sources such as geothermal energy, the energy system can be separated from nuclear weaponry and freed from the dead hand of military control.

[29] Consider, now, the implications of these alternatives for international relations. If the industrial countries follow the conventional path, they will have little to offer in the way of useful energy technology to the developing nations, which lack capital, are rich in natural materials and

labor, and are usually favored by intense sunlight. In contrast, if the industrialized countries were to develop new productive technologies that emphasized the use of natural materials—synthesized from solar energy through photosynthesis—rather than synthetic ones, and techniques for solar power, they could provide real help in the struggle of the poor countries to develop their economies. This is the kind of help that would enable developing countries to increase both agricultural and industrial production, and to raise living standards to the levels that encourage the motivation for self-limitation of fertility.

[30] If we take this path we can begin to find also new ways to harmonize the needs of industrialized and developing nations and to end the growing trend toward the creation of opposing camps of nations that produce and use natural resources. For example, if for the sake of environmental and energetic sanity, the industrialized countries were to cut back on the production of synthetic substitutes for natural materials such as cotton, their needs could be met, in part, by goods produced from such natural products in developing countries. Thus, Malaysia, for example, may wish to supply the industrialized nations not with natural rubber, but with tires; India may wish to supply not cotton, but finished fabrics and even clothes; West Africa may wish to supply the world not with palm oil, but with soap.

[31] Perhaps the most immediate threat that has been generated by the energy crisis is the growing menace of a catastrophic worldwide economic collapse. International trade and monetary relations have already felt its heavy force, and the impact of the sharply rising price of energy has begun to disrupt industrial and agricultural production in both the rich nations and the developing ones. Here, too, a rational approach to the production and use of energy is a key to restoring the stability of world economic relations, without which no nation can hope to serve the needs of its own people.

[32] If for the sake of the world's ecological survival we undertake the massive reconstruction of the economies of both the industrialized and developing nations, clearly we are faced, as well, with equally sweeping political changes. Thus, it is inconceivable that the United States could find the huge capital resources for the needed reconstruction of industry and agriculture along ecologically sound lines unless we give up not only capital-intensive forms of energy production but also our preoccupation with large-scale military activities.

[33] But such a course would not only erode the economic motivations for war, it would also give us good grounds for ridding the world—at last—of the most dangerous means of modern war, nuclear weapons. This new course could halt the spread of nuclear reactors and, with it, the proliferation of nuclear weapons; and it encourages the existing nuclear powers to eliminate their own stocks of these insanely suicidal weapons.

[34] All this is described neither as a blueprint of the future nor as a panacea for the ills of the world. I am aware that, stated in these simplis-

THE ENERGY CRISIS—ALL OF A PIECE

tic terms, this picture does not take into account the numerous difficult obstacles that lie along the path to environmental and energetic sanity and peace. Rather, these views are put forward as a kind of exercise that is designed only to demonstrate the crucial role—for good or evil—that energy plays in determining our future. It shows, I believe, that we cannot hope to develop, either in an industrialized country such as the United States, or in the world as a whole, a rational system of production or an economic and social organization that fosters democracy and peace unless we do understand that the irrational production and use of energy is a fatal obstacle to this goal.

[35] The energy crisis has become the world's most dangerous political issue as it wrenches back into open view the brutality of national competition for survival, the basic faults in existing economic systems, and the tragic absurdity of war. The crisis forces us to make long-avoided choices. If ecological sanity demands the production of synthetics and built-in obsolescence, where in society will the necessary controls be localized? If nations must on ecological grounds become more dependent on each other's indigenous goods, how can we avoid the ancient evils of international exploitation?

[36] The lesson of the energy crisis is this: to survive on the earth, which is our habitat, we must live in keeping with its ecological imperatives. And if we are to take this course of ecological wisdom we must accept, at last, the wisdom of placing our faith not in the exploitation of one people by another, but in the equality of all peoples; not in arms which devastate the land and the people and threaten world catastrophe, but in the desire which is shared everywhere in the world—for harmony with the environment, and for peace among the peoples who live in it.

Questions on Meaning

1 In addition to having an introduction (paragraphs 1 through 4) and a conclusion (paragraphs 34 through 36), this essay has four major divisions: the first section (paragraphs 5 through 11) establishes the problem; the second section (paragraphs 12 through 19) explains why, in the author's opinion, the problem exists; the third section (paragraphs 20 through 28) contains the author's solution to the problem; and the fourth section (paragraphs 29 through 33) shows what results he thinks this solution would have. Using this outline, take brief notes on each section, noting the major points the author makes in each division.

2 Where do you find the author's thesis specifically stated?

3 Is the title appropriate for this essay? Why or why not?

4 State in a few sentences of your own the author's explanation of how the "pieces" of the energy problem all fit together.

ESSAYS CHIEFLY PERSUASIVE

Questions on Style and Structure

1 In this very formally organized and developed piece, the introductory section is longer than that of almost any other essay in this volume. However, its structure is one that you have found in previous selections with shorter introductions. Which kind of introductory passage treated in the Introduction to Paragraph and Sentence Structure does Commoner use, adapting it to his own purposes?

2 In the introductory section Commoner makes use of a number of metaphorical expressions—for example, "top of the public *agenda*" (paragraph 2) and "*staggering* toward catastrophe" (paragraph 4). What are the other metaphors in the introduction? There are occasional uses of figurative language in the body of this essay, and one metaphor—"path"—is used extensively throughout; however, Commoner's introduction is far richer in figurative language than any other portion of the work. Why is this appropriate?

3 Commoner sometimes begins sentences with *and* and *but*. Students often ask about the appropriateness of starting sentences with conjunctions, and there is some justification for their confusion. Although there is no grammatical reason a writer should not begin a sentence with a conjunction, in earlier times it was often considered crude and improper to do so. But in this century the use of *but* and *and* at the beginnings of sentences has become quite a common practice, and through its use many writers have learned to give their sentences considerable force. Below are some sentences of Commoner's beginning with these words. What is the function of the conjunction in each sentence? How could the sentence be revised to eliminate the initial conjunction? Would the revision be as effective as the original?

   a "But each effort to solve one crisis seems to founder on conflict with another. . . ." (paragraph 3)
   b "But the very links that make up this web of crises are themselves a source of optimism, a clue to what needs to be done." (paragraph 4)
   c "But in other cases—for example, the petrochemical industry—the intensive use of energy is built into the very design of the enterprise in order to eliminate human labor. . . ." (paragraph 15)
   d "And for those who see in the present situation opportunities to support socially oriented ways to organize our productive and economic enterprise, there is an equally important challenge to prove their case." (paragraph 19)
   e "And finally, through the wide use of solar energy and other alternative sources such as geothermal energy, the energy system can be separated from nuclear weaponry and freed from the dead hand of military control." (paragraph 28)

4 An outstanding characteristic of Commoner's writing is the way he supports generalizations with numerous highly appropriate details. His typical paragraph structure is topic sentence first followed by supporting examples. Sometimes, paragraphs operate on three levels of specificity, as does paragraph 30. In that paragraph, the first "for example" refers to developing na-

THE ENERGY CRISIS—ALL OF A PIECE

tions as a group, and the second "for example" refers to one particular nation, Malaysia. More often, all of the examples are on the same level, as are those in paragraph 13. There, the first two sentences state the topic (note the references to soap companies, truck lines, plastic plants, and so on). Are there other paragraphs that exemplify each of these methods of development?

5 Review the definition of *antithesis* provided in the first question on Style and Structure on page 308. Are there any examples of such a structure in this essay?

Exploring Words

1 *intractable.* Which of the meanings in the dictionary for *intractable* applies to Commoner's use of the word?

2 *perversely.* Write a sentence using *perversely* appropriately. Be as specific as possible.

3 *surfeit.* Which of the several definitions in your dictionary corresponds to Commoner's use of this word?

4 *proliferation.* Commoner speaks of the danger of the "*proliferation* of nuclear weapons." What other kinds of *proliferation* do you think are current threats to our society?

5 *panacea.* "*Panacea* for the ills of the world" is almost a cliché. Why do you suppose the word is often used in this phrase?

Suggestions for Writing

1 Write a problem-solution paper, following Commoner's basic pattern; that is, first establish the problem, then explain the reasons for its existence, and then, finally, state your solution. The problem could be one of national or international consequence if you have already done considerable reading or thinking on such a topic. However, you are more likely to write a successful argument if you take a subject with which you have had first-hand experience—a problem in your community, school, or an organization to which you belong, for example.

2 What measures do you recommend that individual citizens take to help ease the energy crisis?

History as Mirror
BARBARA W. TUCHMAN

Getting Started

With Ideas

To get the most out of this many-faceted essay, it will be a good idea to think first about several possible meanings of the title. In what sense can history be considered a mirror? What could a period in history mirror or reflect? When you read the first paragraph, you will find that Tuchman answers these questions in a general way there and that she also indicates the particular historical period with which she is concerned. When you know this much, and when you have become accustomed—as you probably will in that paragraph—to her serious, but lively style, you will be ready to read the rest of the essay, looking for the specific answers Tuchman provides to the questions she has raised.

With Words

1. poignantly (6)—related to *pungent,* but applied to feelings rather than to odors.
2. pogroms (15)—from the Yiddish word meaning "devastation."
3. schism (16)—from the Greek word meaning "to split" (you probably know the word *schizophrenic*).
4. partisans (16)—from the Latin root from which we get the word *party* (as in "political *party*").
5. heresies (18)—relate it to *heretic* and note carefully the context.
6. malignant (24)—relate it to *malevolent.* See "Peaceful Coexistence with Rattlesnakes" (p. 41).
7. anachronism (29)—Have you ever driven a car that was so old people considered it an *anachronism?*
8. demagogues (33)—from the Greek words meaning "leader" and "people." However, note that the context suggests a more specific sense than "leader of the people."
9. virulence (34)—related to *virus.*

[1] At a time when everyone's mind is on the explosions of the moment, it might seem obtuse of me to discuss the fourteenth century. But I think a backward look at that disordered, violent, bewildered, disin-

"History as Mirror" appeared in *The Atlantic Monthly,* September 1973. Copyright 1973 by Barbara Tuchman. Reprinted by permission of Russell and Volkening, Inc., as agents for the author.

tegrating, and calamity-prone age can be consoling and possibly instructive in a time of similar disarray. Reflected in a six-hundred-year-old mirror, a more revealing image of ourselves and our species might be seen than is visible in the clutter of circumstances under our noses. The value of historical comparison was made keenly apparent to the French medievalist, Edouard Perroy, when he was writing his book on the Hundred Years' War while dodging the Gestapo in World War II. "Certain ways of behavior," he wrote, "certain reactions against fate, throw mutual light upon each other."

[2] Besides, if one suspects that the twentieth century's record of inhumanity and folly represents a phase of mankind at its worst, and that our last decade of collapsing assumptions has been one of unprecedented discomfort, it is reassuring to discover that the human race has been in this box before—and emerged. The historian has the comfort of knowing that man (meaning, here and hereafter, the species, not the sex) is always capable of his worst; has indulged in it, painfully struggled up from it, slid back, and gone on again.

[3] In what follows, the parallels are not always in physical events but rather in the effect on society, and sometimes in both.

[4] The afflictions of the fourteenth century were the classic riders of the Apocalypse—famine, plague, war, and death, this time on a black horse. These combined to produce an epidemic of violence, depopulation, bad government, oppressive taxes, an accelerated breakdown of feudal bonds, working class insurrection, monetary crisis, decline of morals and rise in crime, decay of chivalry, the governing idea of the governing class, and above all, corruption of society's central institution, the Church, whose loss of authority and prestige deprived man of his accustomed guide in a darkening world.

[5] Yet amidst the disintegration were sprouting, invisible to contemporaries, the green shoots of the Renaissance to come. In human affairs as in nature, decay is compost for new growth.

[6] Some medievalists reject the title of decline for the fourteenth century, asserting instead that it was the dawn of a new age. Since the processes obviously overlap, I am not sure that the question is worth arguing, but it becomes poignantly interesting when applied to ourselves. Do *we* walk amidst trends of a new world without knowing it? How far ahead is the dividing line? Or are we on it? What designation will our age earn from historians six hundred years hence? One wishes one could make a pact with the devil like Enoch Soames, the neglected poet in Max Beerbohm's story, allowing us to return and look ourselves up in the library catalogue. In that future history book, shall we find the chapter title for the twentieth century reading Decline and Fall, or Eve of Revival?

[7] The fourteenth century opened with a series of famines brought on when population growth outstripped the techniques of food production. The precarious balance was tipped by a series of heavy rains

and floods and by a chilling of the climate in what has been called the Little Ice Age. Upon a people thus weakened fell the century's central disaster, the Black Death, an eruption of bubonic plague which swept the known world in the years 1347–1349 and carried off an estimated one-third of the population in two and a half years. This makes it the most lethal episode known to history, which is of some interest to an age equipped with the tools of overkill.

[8] The plague raged at terrifying speed, increasing the impression of horror. In a given locality it accomplished its kill within four to six months, except in the larger cities, where it struck again in spring after lying dormant in winter. The death rate in Avignon was said to have claimed half the population, of whom ten thousand were buried in the first six weeks in a single mass grave. The mortality was in fact erratic. Some communities whose last survivors fled in despair were simply wiped out and disappeared from the map forever, leaving only a grassed-over hump as their mortal trace.

[9] Whole families died, leaving empty houses and property a prey to looters. Wolves came down from the mountains to attack plague-stricken villages, crops went unharvested, dikes crumbled, salt water reinvaded and soured the lowlands, the forest crept back, and second growth, with the awful energy of nature unchecked, reconverted cleared land to waste. For lack of hands to cultivate, it was thought impossible that the world could ever regain its former prosperity.

[10] Once the dark bubonic swellings appeared in armpit and groin, death followed rapidly within one to three days, often overnight. For lack of gravediggers, corpses piled up in the streets or were buried so hastily that dogs dug them up and ate them. Doctors were helpless, and priests lacking to administer the final sacrament so that people died believing they must go to hell. No bells tolled, the dead were buried without prayers or funeral rites or tears; families did not weep for the loss of loved ones, for everyone expected death. Matteo Villani, taking up the chronicle of Florence from the hand of his dead brother, believed he was recording the "extermination of mankind."

[11] People reacted variously, as they always do: some prayed, some robbed, some tried to help, most fled if they could, others abandoned themselves to debauchery on the theory that there would be no tomorrow. On balance, the dominant reaction was fear and a desire to save one's own skin regardless of the closest ties. "A father did not visit his son, nor the son his father; charity was dead," wrote one physician, and that was not an isolated observation. Boccaccio in his famous account reports that "kinsfolk held aloof, brother was forsaken by brother . . . often times husband by wife; nay what is more, and scarcely to be believed, fathers and mothers were found to abandon their own children to their fate, untended, unvisited as if they had been strangers."

[12] "Men grew bold," wrote another chronicler, "in their indulgence in pleasure. . . . No fear of God or law of man deterred a crimi-

nal. Seeing that all perished alike, they reflected that offenses against human or Divine law would bring no punishment for no one would live long enough to be held to account." This is an accurate summary, but it was written by Thucydides about the Plague of Athens in the fifth century B.C.—which indicates a certain permanence of human behavior.

[13] The nightmare of the plague was compounded for the fourteenth century by the awful mystery of its cause. The idea of disease carried by insect bite was undreamed of. Fleas and rats, which were in fact the carriers, are not mentioned in the plague writings. Contagion could be observed but not explained and thus seemed doubly sinister. The medical faculty of the University of Paris favored a theory of poisonous air spread by a conjunction of the planets, but the general and fundamental belief, made official by a papal bull, was that the pestilence was divine punishment for man's sins. Such horror could only be caused by the wrath of God. "In the year of our Lord, 1348," sadly wrote a professor of law at the University of Pisa, "the hostility of God was greater than the hostility of men."

[14] That belief enhanced the sense of guilt, or rather the consciousness of sin (guilt, I suspect, is modern; sin is medieval), which was always so close to the surface throughout the Middle Ages. Out of the effort to appease divine wrath came the flagellants, a morbid frenzy of self-punishment that almost at once found a better object in the Jews.

[15] A storm of pogroms followed in the track of the Black Death, widely stimulated by the flagellants, who often rushed straight for the Jewish quarter, even in towns which had not yet suffered the plague. As outsiders within the unity of Christendom the Jews were natural persons to suspect of evil design on the Christian world. They were accused of poisoning the wells. Although the Pope condemned the attacks as inspired by "that liar the devil," pointing out that Jews died of plague like everyone else, the populace wanted victims, and fell upon them in three hundred communities throughout Europe. Slaughtered and burned alive, the entire colonies of Frankfurt, Cologne, Mainz, and other towns of Germany and the Lowlands were exterminated, despite the restraining efforts of town authorities. Elsewhere the Jews were expelled by judicial process after confession of well-poisoning was extracted by torture. In every case their goods and property, whether looted or confiscated, ended in the hands of the persecutors. The process was lucrative, as it was to be again in our time under the Nazis, although the fourteenth century had no gold teeth to rob from the corpses. Where survivors slowly returned and the communities revived, it was on worse terms than before and in walled isolation. This was the beginning of the ghetto.

[16] Men of the fourteenth century were particularly vulnerable because of the loss of credibility by the Church, which alone could absolve sin and offer salvation from hell. When the papal schism dating from 1378 divided the Church under two popes, it brought the highest authority in society into disrepute, a situation with which we are familiar. The schism

was the second great calamity of the time, displaying before all the world the unedifying spectacle of twin vicars of God, each trying to bump the other off the chair of St. Peter, each appointing his own college of cardinals, each collecting tithes and revenues and excommunicating the partisans of his rival. No conflict of ideology was involved; the split arose from a simple squabble for the office of the papacy and remained no more than that for the fifty years the schism lasted. Plunged in this scandal, the Church lost moral authority, the more so as its two halves scrambled in the political arena for support. Kingdoms, principalities, even towns, took sides, finding new cause for the endless wars that scourged the times.

[17] The Church's corruption by worldliness long antedated the schism. By the fourteenth century the papal court at Avignon was called Babylon and rivaled temporal courts in luxury and magnificence. Its bureaucracy was enormous and its upkeep mired in a commercial traffic in spiritual things. Pardons, indulgences, prayers, every benefice and bishopric, everything the Church had or was, from cardinal's hat to pilgrim's relic, everything that represented man's relation to God, was for sale. Today it is the processes of government that are for sale, especially the electoral process, which is as vital to our political security as salvation was to the emotional security of the fourteenth century.

[18] Men still craved God and spun off from the Church in sects and heresies, seeking to purify the realm of the spirit. They too yearned for a greening of the system. The yearning, and disgust with the Establishment, produced freak orders of mystics who lived in coeducational communes, rejected marriage, and glorifed sexual indulgence. Passionate reformers ranged from St. Catherine of Siena, who scolded everyone in the hierarchy from the popes down, to John Wycliffe, who plowed the soil of Protestant revolt. Both strove to renew the Church, which for so long had been the only institution to give order and meaning to the untidy business of living on earth. When in the last quarter of the century the schism brought the Church into scorn and ridicule and fratricidal war, serious men took alarm. The University of Paris made strenuous and ceaseless efforts to find a remedy, finally demanding submission of the conflict to a supreme Council of the Church whose object should be not only reunification but reform.

[19] Without reform, said the University's theologians in their letter to the popes, the damaging effect of the current scandal could be irreversible. In words that could have been addressed to our own secular potentate although he is—happily—not double, they wrote, "The Church will suffer for your overconfidence if you repent too late of having neglected reform. If you postpone it longer the harm will be incurable. Do you think people will suffer forever from your bad government? Who do you think can endure, amid so many other abuses . . . your elevation of men without literacy or virtue to the most eminent positions?" The echo sounds over the gulf of six hundred years with a timeliness almost supernatural.

[20] When the twin popes failed to respond, pressure at last brought about a series of Church councils which endeavored to limit and constitutionalize the powers of the papacy. After a thirty-year struggle, the councils succeeded in ending the schism but the papacy resisted reform. The decades of debate only served to prove that the institution could not be reformed from within. Eighty years of mounting protest were to pass before pressure produced Luther and the great crack.

[21] Despite the parallel with the present struggle between Congress and the presidency, there is no historical law that says the outcome must necessarily be the same. The American presidency at age two hundred is not a massive rock of ages embedded in a thousand years of acceptance as was the medieval Church, and should be easier to reform. One can wish for Congress a better result than the councils had in the effort to curb the executive—or at least one can hope.

[22] The more important parallel lies in the decay of public confidence in our governing institutions, as the fourteenth-century public lost confidence in the Church. Who believes today in the integrity of government?—or of business, or of law or justice or labor unions or the military or the police? Even physicians, the last of the admired, are now in disfavor. I have a theory that the credibility vacuum owes something to our nurture in that conspiracy of fables called advertising, which we daily absorb without believing. Since public affairs and ideas and candidates are now presented to us as a form of advertising, we automatically suspend belief or suspect fraud as soon as we recognize the familiar slickness. I realize, of course, that the roots of disbelief go down to deeper ground. Meanwhile the effect is a loss of trust in all authority which leaves us guideless and dismayed and cynical—even as in the fourteenth century.

[23] Over that whole century hung the smoke of war—dominated by the Anglo-French conflict known to us, though fortunately not to them, as the Hundred Years' War. (With the clock still ticking in Indochina, one wonders how many years there are still to go in that conflict.) Fought on French soil and extending into Flanders and Spain, the Hundred Years' War actually lasted for more than a century, from 1337 to 1453. In addition, the English fought the Scots; the French fought incessant civil wars against Gascons, Bretons, Normans, and Navarrese; the Italian republics fought each other—Florence against Pisa, Venice against Genoa, Milan against everybody; the kingdom of Naples and Sicily was fought over by claimants from Hungary to Aragon; the papacy fought a war that included unbridled massacre to reconquer the Papal States; the Savoyards fought the Lombards; the Swiss fought the Austrians; the tangled wars of Bohemia, Poland, and the German Empire defy listing; crusades were launched against the Saracens, and to fill up any pauses the Teutonic Knights conducted annual campaigns against pagan Lithuania which other knights could join for extra practice. Fighting was the function of the Second Estate, that is, of the landed nobles and knights. A knight without a war or

tournament to go to felt as restless as a man who cannot go to the office.

[24] Every one of these conflicts threw off Free Companies of mercenaries, organized for brigandage under a professional captain, which became an evil of the period as malignant as the plague. In the money economy of the fourteenth century, armed forces were no longer feudal levies serving under a vassal's obligation who went home after forty days, but were recruited bodies who served for pay. Since this was at great cost to the sovereign, he cut off the payroll as soon as he safely could during halts of truce or negotiation. Thrown on their own resources and having acquired a taste for plunder, the men-at-arms banded together in the Free Companies, whose savage success swelled their ranks with landless knights and squires and roving adventurers.

[25] The companies contracted their services to whatever ruler was in need of troops, and between contracts held up towns for huge ransom, ravaged the countryside, and burned, pillaged, raped, and slaughtered their way back and forth across Europe. No one was safe, no town or village knew when it might be attacked. The leaders, prototypes of the *condottieri* in Italy, became powers and made fortunes and even became respectable like Sir John Hawkwood, commander of the famous White Company. Smaller bands, called in France the *tards-venus* (latecomers), scavenged like jackals, living off the land, plundering, killing, carrying off women, torturing peasants for their small horde of grain or townsmen for their hidden goods, and burning, always burning. They set fire to whatever they left behind, farmhouses, vineyards, abbeys, in a kind of madness to destroy the very sources off which they lived, or would live tomorrow. Destruction and cruelty became self-engendering, not merely for loot but almost one might say for sport. The phenomenon is not peculiar to any one time or people, as we know from the experience of our own century, but in the fourteenth century it seems to have reached a degree and extent beyond explanation.

[26] It must be added that in practice and often personnel the Free Companies were hardly distinguishable from the troops of organized official wars. About 80 percent of the activity of a declared war consisted of raids of plunder and burning through enemy territory. That paragon of chivalry, the Black Prince, could well have earned his name from the blackened ruins he left across France. His baggage train and men-at-arms were often so heavily laden with loot that they moved as slowly as a woman's litter.

[27] The saddest aspect of the Hundred Years' War was the persistent but vain efforts of the belligerents themselves to stop it. As in our case, it spread political damage at home, and the cost was appalling. Moreover it harmed the relations of all the powers at a time when they were anxious to unite to repel the infidel at the gates. For Christendom was now on the defensive against the encroaching Turks. For that reason the Church, too, tried to end the war that was keeping Europe at odds. On the very morning of the fatal battle of Poitiers, two cardinals hurried with

offers and counter-offers between the two armed camps, trying in vain to prevent the clash. During periods of truce the parties held long parleys lasting months and sometimes years in the effort to negotiate a definitive peace. It always eluded them, failing over questions of prestige or put off by the feeling of whichever side held a slight advantage that one more push would bring the desired gains.

[28] All this took place under a code of chivalry whose creed was honor, loyalty, and courtesy and whose purpose, like that of every social code evolved by man in his long search for order, was to civilize and supply a pattern of rules. A knight's task under the code was to uphold the Church, defend his land and vassals, maintain the peace of his province, protect the weak and guard the poor from injustice, shed his blood for his comrade, and lay down his life if needs must. For the land-owning warrior class, chivalry was their ideology, their politics, their system—what democracy is to us or Marxism to the Communists.

[29] Originating out of feudal needs, it was already slipping into anachronism by the fourteenth century because the development of monarchy and a royal bureaucracy was taking away the knight's functions, economic facts were forcing him to commute labor dues for money, and a rival element was appearing in the urban magnates. Even his military prowess was being nullified by trained bodies of English longbowmen and Swiss pikemen, nonmembers of the warrior class who in feudal theory had no business in battle at all.

[30] Yet in decadence chivalry threw its brightest light; never were its ceremonies more brilliant, its jousts and tournaments so brave, its apparel so splendid, its manners so gay and amorous, its entertainments so festive, its self-glorification more eloquent. The gentry elaborated the forms of chivalry just *because* institutions around them were crumbling. They clung to what gave their status meaning in a desperate embrace of the past. This is the time when the Order of the Garter was founded by the King of England, the Order of the Star by the King of France, the Golden Fleece by the Duke of Burgundy—in deliberate imitation of King Arthur's Knights of the Round Table.

[31] The rules still worked well enough among themselves, with occasional notorious exceptions such as Charles of Navarre, a bad man appropriately known as Charles the Bad. Whenever necessity required him to swear loyal reconciliation and fealty to the King of France, his mortal enemy, he promptly engaged in treacherous intrigues with the King of England, leaving his knightly oaths to become, in the White House word, inoperative. On the whole, however, the nobility laid great stress on high standards of honor. It was vis-à-vis the Third Estate that chivalry fell so far short of the theory. Yet it remained an ideal of human relations, as Christianity remained an ideal of faith, that kept men reaching for the unattainable. The effort of society is always toward order, away from anarchy. Sometimes it moves forward, sometimes it slips back. Which is the direction of one's own time may be obscure.

[32] The fourteenth century was further afflicted by a series of convulsions and upheavals in the working class, both urban and rural. Causes were various: the cost of constant war was thrown upon the people in hearth taxes, salt taxes, sales taxes, and debasement of coinage. In France the failure of the knights to protect the populace from incessant ravaging was a factor. It exasperated the peasants' misery, giving it the energy of anger which erupted in the ferocious mid-century rising called the *Jacquerie*. Shortage of labor caused by the plague had temporarily brought higher wages and rising expectations. When these were met, especially in England, by statutes clamping wages at pre-plague levels, the result was the historic Peasants' Revolt of 1381. In the towns, capitalism was widening the gap between masters and artisans, producing the sustained weavers' revolts in the cloth towns of Flanders and major outbreaks in Florence and Paris. In Paris, too, the merchant class rose against the royal councillors, whom they despised as both corrupt and incompetent. To frighten the regent into submission, they murdered his two chief councillors in his presence.

[33] All these struggles had one thing in common: they were doomed. United against a common threat, the ruling class could summon greater strength than its antagonists and acted to suppress insurrection with savagery equal to the fury from below. Yet discontent had found its voice; dissent and rejection of authority for the first time in the Middle Ages became a social force. Demagogues and determined leaders, reformers and agitators came to the surface. Though all were killed, several by mobs of their own followers, the uprisings they led were the beginning of modern, conscious, class war.

[34] Meanwhile, over the second half-century, the plague returned with lesser virulence at intervals of every twelve to fifteen years. It is hardly to be wondered that people of the time saw man's fate as an endless succession of evils. He must indeed be wicked and his enemy Satan finally triumphant. According to a popular belief at the end of the century, no one since the beginning of the schism had entered Paradise.

[35] Pessimism was a mark of the age and the *Danse Macabre* or Dance of Death its most vivid expression. Performed at occasions of popular drama and public sermons, it was an actual dance or pantomime in which a figure from every walk of life—king, clerk, lawyer, friar, goldsmith, bailiff, and so on—confronts the loathsome corpse he must become. In the accompanying verses and illustrations which have survived, the theme repeats itself over and over: the end of all life is putrefaction and the grave; no one escapes; no matter what beauty or kingly power or poor man's misery has been the lot in life, all end alike as food for worms. Death is not treated poetically as the soul's flight to reunion with God; it is a skeleton grinning at the vanity of life.

[36] Life as well as death was viewed with disgust. The vices and corruptions of the age, a low opinion of one's fellowmen, and nostalgia for the well-ordered past were the favorite themes of literary men. Even Boc-

caccio in his later works became ill-tempered. "All good customs fail," laments Christine de Pisan of France, "and virtues are held at little worth." Eustache Deschamps complains that "the child of today has become a ruffian. . . . People are gluttons and drunkards, haughty of heart, caring for nought, not honor nor goodness nor kindness . . ." and he ends each verse with the refrain, "Time past had virtue and righteousness but today reigns only vice." In England John Gower denounces Rome for simony, Lollards for heresy, clergy and monks for idleness and lust, kings, nobles, and knights for self-indulgence and rapine, the law for bribery, merchants for usury and fraud, the commons for ignorance, and in general the sins of perjury, lechery, avarice, and pride as displayed in extravagant fashions.

[37] These last did indeed, as in all distracted times, reflect a reaching for the absurd, especially in the long pointed shoes which kept getting longer until the points had to be tied up around the knee, and the young men's doublets which kept getting shorter until they revealed the buttocks, to the censure of moralists and snickers of the crowd. Leaving miniskirts to the males, the ladies inexplicably adopted a fashion of gowns and posture designed to make them look pregnant.

[38] Self-disgust, it seems to me, has reappeared in our time, not without cause. The succession of events since 1914 has disqualified belief in moral progress, and pollution of the physical world is our bubonic plague. Like the fourteenth century, we have lost confidence in man's capacity to control his fate and even in his capacity to be good. So we have a literature of the anti-hero aimlessly wandering among the perverse, absurd, and depraved; we have porn and pop and blank canvases and antimusic designed to deafen. I am not sure whether in all this the artists are expressing contempt for their fellowman or the loud laugh that bespeaks emptiness of feeling, but whatever the message, it has a faint ring of the *Danse Macabre*.

[39] Historians until recently have hurried over the fourteenth century because like most people they prefer not to deal with failure. But it would be a mistake to imply that it was solid gloom. Seen from inside, especially from a position of privilege, it had beauties and wonders, and the ferment itself was exciting. "In these fifty years," said the renowned Comte de Foix to the chronicler Froissart in the year 1389, "there have been more feats of arms and more marvels in the world than in the three hundred years before." The Count himself, a famous huntsman, was known as Phoebus for his personal beauty and splendid court.

[40] The streets of cities were bright with colored clothes; crimson fur-lined gowns of merchants, parti-colored velvets and silks of a nobleman's retinue, in sky blue and fawn or two shades of scarlet or it might be the all-emerald liveries of the Green Count of Savoy. Street sounds were those of human voices: criers of news and official announcements, shopkeepers in their doorways and itinerant vendors crying fresh eggs, charcoal at a penny a sack, candlewicks "brighter than the stars," cakes and waffles, mushrooms, hot baths. Mountebanks entertained the public in the

town square or village green with tricks and magic and trained animals. Jongleurs sang ballads of adventure in Saracen lands. After church on Sundays, laborers gathered in cookshops and taverns; burghers promenaded in their gardens or visited their vineyards outside the city walls. Church bells marked the eight times of day from Matins through Vespers, when shops closed, work ceased, silence succeeded bustle, and the darkness of unlit night descended.

[41] The gaudy extravagance of noble life was awesome. Now and then its patronage brought forth works of eternal beauty like the exquisite illuminated Books of Hours commissioned by the Duc de Berry. More often it was pure ostentation and conspicuous consumption. Charles V of France owned forty-seven jeweled and golden crowns and sixty-three complete sets of chapel furnishings, including vestments, gold crucifixes, altarpieces, reliquaries, and prayer books. Jewels and cloth of gold marked every occasion and every occasion was pretext for a spectacle—a grand procession, or ceremonial welcome to a visiting prince, a tournament or entertainment with music, and dancing by the light of great torches. When Gian Galeazzo Visconti, ruler of Milan, gave a wedding banquet for his daughter, eighteen double courses were served, each of fish and meat, including trout, quail, herons, eels, sturgeon, and suckling pig spouting fire. The gifts presented after *each* course to several hundred guests included greyhounds in gem-studded velvet collars, hawks in tinkling silver bells, suits of armor, rolls of silk and brocade, garments trimmed with pearls and ermine, fully caparisoned warhorses, and twelve fat oxen. For the entry into Paris of the new Queen, Isabel of Bavaria, the entire length of the Rue St. Denis was hung with a canopy representing the firmament twinkling with stars from which sweetly singing angels descended bearing a crown, and fountains ran with wine, distributed to the people in golden cups by lovely maidens wearing caps of solid gold.

[42] One wonders where all the money came from for such luxury and festivity in a time of devastation. What taxes could burned-out and destitute people pay? This is a puzzle until one remembers that the Aga Khan got to be the richest man in the world on the backs of the poorest people, and that disaster is never as pervasive as it seems from recorded accounts. It is one of the pitfalls for historians that the very fact of being on the record makes a happening appear to have been continuous and all-inclusive, whereas in reality it is more likely to have been sporadic both in time and place. Besides, persistence of the normal is usually greater than the effect of disturbance, as we know from our own times. After absorbing the daily paper and weekly magazine, one expects to face a world consisting entirely of strikes, crimes, power shortages, broken water mains, stalled trains, school shutdowns, Black Panthers, addicts, transvestites, rapists, and militant lesbians. The fact is that one can come home in the evening—on a lucky day—without having encountered more than two or three of these phenomena. This has led me to formulate Tuchman's Law, as follows: "The fact of being reported increases the *apparent* extent of a

deplorable development by a factor of ten." (I snatch the figure from the air and will leave it to the quantifiers to justify.)

[43] The astonishing fact is that except for Boccaccio, to whom we owe the most vivid account, the Black Death was virtually ignored by the great writers of the time. Petrarch, who was forty-four when it happened, mentions it only as the occasion for the death of Laura; Chaucer, from what I have read, passes it over in silence; Jean Froissart, the Herodotus of his time, gives it no more than one casual paragraph, and even that second Isaiah, the author of *Piers Plowman,* who might have been expected to make it central to his theme of woe, uses it only incidentally. One could argue that in 1348 Chaucer was only eight or nine years old and Froissart ten or eleven and the unknown Langland probably of the same vintage, but that is old enough to absorb and remember a great catastrophe, especially when they lived through several returns of the plague as grown men.

[44] Perhaps this tells us that disaster, once survived, leaves less track than one supposed, or that man's instinct for living pushes it down below the surface, or simply that his recuperative powers are remarkable. Or was it just an accident of personality? Is it significant or just chance that Chaucer, the greatest writer of his age, was so uncharacteristic of it in sanguine temperament and good-humored view of his fellow creatures?

[45] As for Froissart, never was a man more in love with his age. To him it appeared as a marvelous pageant of glittering armor and the beauty of emblazoned banners fluttering in the breeze and the clear shrill call of the trumpet. Still believing, still enraptured by the chivalric ideal, he reports savagery, treachery, limitless greed, and the pitiless slaughter of the poor when driven to revolt as minor stumbles in the grand adventure of valor and honor. Yet near the end, even Froissart could not hide from himself the decay made plain by a dissolute court, venality in high places, and a knighthood that kept losing battles. In 1397, the year he turned sixty, the defeat and massacre of the flower of chivalry at the hands of the Turks in the battle of Nicopolis set the seal on the incompetence of his heroes. Lastly, the murder of a King in England shocked him deeply, not for any love of Richard II but because the act was subversive of the whole order that sustained his world. As in Watergate, the underside had rolled to the surface all too visibly. Froissart had not the heart to continue and brought his chronicle to an end.

[46] The sad century closed with a meeting between King Charles VI of France and the Emperor Wenceslaus, the one intermittently mad and the other regularly drunk. They met at Reims in 1397 to consult on means of ending the papal schism, but whenever Charles had a lucid interval, Wenceslaus was in a stupor and so the conference, proving fruitless, was called off.

[47] It makes an artistic ending. Yet in that same year Johann Gutenberg, who was to change the world, was born. In the next century appeared Joan of Arc, embodying the new spirit of nationalism, still pure like mountain water before it runs downhill; and Columbus, who opened a

new hemisphere; and Copernicus, who revolutionized the concept of the earth's relation to the universe; and Michelangelo, whose sculptured visions gave man a new status; in those proud, superb, unconquered figures, the human being, not God, was captain.

[48] As our century enters its final quarter, I am not persuaded, despite the signs, that the end is necessarily doom. The doomsayers work by extrapolation; they take a trend and extend it, forgetting that the doom factor sooner or later generates a coping mechanism. I have a rule for this situation too, which is absolute: you cannot extrapolate any series in which the human element intrudes; history, that is, the human narrative, never follows, and will always fool, the scientific curve. I cannot tell you what twists it will take, but I expect, that like our ancestors, we, too, will muddle through.

Questions on Meaning

1 What specific parallels does Tuchman draw between life in fourteenth-century Europe and life in our society today? Consider points she makes about the deterioration of important institutions, the attitudes of the people toward these changes, the relationship of social classes toward each other, respect for human life, and attachment to ideologies.

2 Why does the author blame advertising for what she calls the current "credibility vacuum" in America (paragraph 22)? Do you agree with her assessment of the role advertising has played in shaping our society's attitudes toward the integrity of public figures and others in influential positions?

3 In what way does "Tuchman's Law" (paragraph 42) apply to both the fourteenth and the twentieth centuries? Is her argument in support of this "law" a convincing one?

4 Express in your own words the important idea that Tuchman develops in the last paragraph of the essay. Be sure you look up the meaning of the word *extrapolate*, but try to express her idea without using this word. Would you consider this paragraph or any part of it a statement of her thesis? Explain.

Questions on Style and Structure

1 Where does the introduction of the paper end and the body begin?

2 Tuchman's paragraphs are worthy of close attention. They are generally tightly unified and concretely developed (examine, for example, paragraphs 8 and 41). Which other paragraphs do you find especially well unified and developed?

3 In paragraph 16, Tuchman describes the second great calamity of the time and in so doing uses the following phrases: "each trying to bump the other off the chair of St. Peter," "squabble for the office of the papacy," and

"scramble in the political arena." These words, on first reading, might strike the reader as too informal and thus inappropriate. Why is their use justified here?

4 In paragraph 30, we find a device that is commonly used for emphasis—the repetition of important words: "Yet in decadence chivalry threw its brightest light; never were its ceremonies *more* brilliant, its jousts and tournaments *so* brave, its apparel *so* splendid, its manner *so* gay and amorous, its entertainments *so* festive, its self-glorification *more* eloquent." Can you find other examples of such repetition?

5 Many of the sentences in this essay are carefully structured for emphasis. Compare the following versions (the first in each pair is Tuchman's). For each pair of sentences, explain why one version is more effective than the other.

a "In the year of our Lord, 1348," sadly wrote a professor of law at the University of Pisa, "the hostility of God was greater than the hostility of men." (paragraph 13)

"In the year of our Lord, 1348, the hostility of God was greater than the hostility of men," sadly wrote a professor of law at the University of Pisa.

b A knight's task under the code was to uphold the Church, defend his land and vassals, maintain the peace of his province, protect the weak and guard the poor from injustice, shed his blood for his comrade, and lay down his life if needs must. (paragraph 28)

A knight's task under the code was to uphold the Church, defend his land and vassals, shed his blood for his comrade, lay down his life if needs must, protect the weak and guard the poor from injustice, and maintain the peace of his province.

c Whenever necessity required him to swear loyal reconciliation and fealty to the King of France, his mortal enemy, he promptly engaged in treacherous intrigues with the King of England, leaving his knightly oaths to become, in the White House word, inoperative. (paragraph 31)

Whenever necessity required him to swear loyal reconciliation and fealty to the King of France, his mortal enemy, he promptly engaged in treacherous intrigues with the King of England, leaving his knightly oaths to become inoperative, in the White House word.

d "All good customs fail," laments Christine de Pisan of France, "and virtues are held at little worth." (paragraph 36)

"All good customs fail and virtues are held at little worth," laments Christine de Pisan of France.

e As our century enters its final quarter, I am not persuaded, despite the signs, that the end is necessarily doom. (paragraph 48)

As our century enters its final quarter, I am not persuaded that the end is necessarily doom, despite the signs.

6 Comments about modern problems are found in different sections of this essay. Would the essay be more effective if the author had discussed these problems in one section?

ESSAYS CHIEFLY PERSUASIVE

7 Like other writers you have studied before, Tuchman incorporates figurative language in her writing. How effective are the following examples?

   a Yet amidst the disintegration were sprouting, invisible to contemporaries, the green shoots of the Renaissance to come. In human affairs as in nature, decay is compost for new growth. (paragraph 5)

   b They too yearned for a greening of the system. (paragraph 18)

   c Death is not treated poetically as the soul's flight to reunion with God; it is a skeleton grinning at the vanity of life. (paragraph 35)

   d . . . and pollution of the physical world is our bubonic plague. (paragraph 38)

   e In the next century appeared Joan of Arc, embodying the new spirit of nationalism, still pure like mountain water before it runs downhill. . . . (paragraph 47)

8 What technique does Tuchman use to conclude her essay?

Exploring Words

1 *poignantly*. Check your dictionary's several listed meanings for *poignantly*. Which one fits Tuchman's use of the word?

2 *pogroms*. To what period in recent European history can the term *pogrom* be applied?

3 *schism*. What pronunciation does your dictionary indicate is preferred for the word *schism*? After checking the definition of the word, write a sentence using it appropriately—if possible in reference to a *schism* you have experienced.

4 *partisans*. You will note that your dictionary lists more than one noun meaning and at least one adjective meaning for *partisan*. Which of these meanings applies to Tuchman's use of the word? Write a sentence using the word in one of the other senses.

5 *heresies*. Although Tuchman uses this word in its earliest meaning (that is, in a religious sense), you should understand that it is also used in a more general sense. After checking your dictionary's treatment of the word, use it in its general sense in a sentence.

6 *malignant*. The word *malignant*, in one of its senses, is often applied to human behavior. What is the most *malignant* action you have read about or experienced recently?

7 *anachronism*. State in your own words what Tuchman means when she says that in the fourteenth-century feudalism was "slipping into *anachronism*."

8 *demagogues*. Think of three political leaders you would describe as *demagogues*, and give your reasons.

9 *virulence*. How many definitions does your dictionary cite? Which one comes closest to Tuchman's use?

HISTORY AS MIRROR

Suggestions for Writing

1 If a historian six hundred years from now had to use a single issue of a newspaper as a "mirror" for our times, what would he or she be apt to conclude about life in America in the 1970s? Be sure to anchor your essay in a specific issue of the newspaper you regularly read.

2 In paragraph 37, Tuchman describes the "absurd" fashions of medieval Europe. Write an essay in which you discuss the fashions of Americans in the 1970s. Do some of these fashions strike you as "absurd"? How might they be viewed in illustrated history books six centuries from now?

Politics and the American Language
ARTHUR SCHLESINGER, JR.

Getting Started

With Ideas

The title and the quoted passage that precedes the first paragraph are taken from George Orwell's "Politics and the English Language." But Schlesinger makes clear that he uses Orwell's comments on the corruption of political language in England in the 1940s only as a springboard for presenting his own ideas on the current (1975) state of political speech and writing in America. Therefore, you should not feel that you need to understand fully all of the specific allusions to Orwell in the opening of this essay (for example, the reference to Lancelot Hogben and Harold Laski) to let it serve its intended purpose: to prepare the groundwork for the essay's thesis. Which sentence in the first paragraph states the central idea most specifically?

With Words

1 exorcising (4)—this word is usually used in reference to devils. But be sure you understand the unusual, figurative sense in which it is used here.
2 chastening (4)—relate this word to *chaste* and *chastity*.
3 demagoguery (11)—Hitler is perhaps the most noted practitioner of *demagoguery* in the twentieth century. See also "History as Mirror" (p. 382).
4 patois (13)—ordinarily a local dialect, but note the special sense in which Schlesinger uses the term here.
5 verbicide (15)—think of other *cide* words you know (*suicide, fratricide,* and so on).
6 perspicuity (16)—the context will be helpful here. Think about the way it is used before looking it up.
7 oracularity (18)—from *oracle*.
8 quixotic (20)—pronounced kwik-sot'-ik. Remember Don Quixote and his battle with the windmills.
9 neologisms (20)—from *neos*—"new"—and *logos*—"word," "speech," or "thought."

Copyright © 1974 by *Today's Education*. This article, a shorter version of which originally appeared in the September–October 1974 issue of *Today's Education*, was reprinted in the Autumn 1974 issue of *The American Scholar*. Reprinted by permission of *Today's Education*

POLITICS AND THE AMERICAN LANGUAGE

> In our time, political speech and writing are largely the defense of the indefensible.
> —George Orwell

[1] It takes a certain fortitude to pretend to amend Orwell on this subject. But "Politics and the English Language"—which I herewith incorporate by reference—was written more than a generation ago. In the years since, the process of semantic collapse has gathered speed, verified all of Orwell's expectations and added new apprehensions for a new age. Americans in particular have found this a painful period of self-recognition. In 1946 we comfortably supposed that Orwell was talking about other people—Nazis and Stalinists, bureaucrats and sociologists, Professor Lancelot Hogben and Professor Harold Laski. Now recent history has obliged us to extend his dispiriting analysis to ourselves.

[2] Vietnam and Watergate: these horrors will trouble the rest of our lives. But they are not, I suppose, unmitigated horrors. "Every act rewards itself," said Emerson. As Vietnam instructed us, at terrible cost, in the limit of our wisdom and power in foreign affairs, so Watergate instructed us, at considerably less cost, in the limits of wisdom and power in the presidency. It reminded us of the urgent need to restore the original balance of the Constitution—the balance between presidential power and presidential accountability. In doing this, it has, among other things, brought back into public consciousness the great documents under which the American government was organized.

[3] The Constitution, the debates of the Constitutional Convention, *The Federalist Papers*—how many of us read them with sustained attention in earlier years? A few eccentrics like Justice Black and Senator Ervin pored over them with devotion. The rest of us regarded them, beyond an occasional invocation of the Bill of Rights or the Fourteenth Amendment, as documents of essentially historical interest and left them undisturbed on the shelf. Then, under the goad first of Vietnam and then of Watergate, legislators, editors, columnists, even political scientists and historians—everyone, it would seem, except for presidential lawyers—began turning the dusty pages in order to find out what Madison said in the convention about the war-making power or how Hamilton defined the grounds for impeachment in the sixty-fifth Federalist. Vietnam and Watergate are hardly to be compared. One is high tragedy, the other low, if black, comedy. But between them they have given the American people a spectacular reeducation in the fundamentals of our constitutional order.

[4] One cannot doubt that this experience will have abiding political significance. The effect of Vietnam in exorcising our illusions and chastening our ambitions in foreign affairs has long been manifest. Now we begin to see the effect of Watergate in raising the standards of our politics. But I am less concerned initially with the political than with the liter-

ary consequences of this return to our constitutional womb. For, in addition to their exceptional qualities of insight and judgment, the historic documents must impress us by the extraordinary distinction of their language.

[5] This was the age of the Enlightenment in America. The cooling breeze of reason tempered the hot work of composition and argument. The result was the language of the Founding Fathers—lucid, measured and felicitous prose, marked by Augustan virtues of harmony, balance and elegance. People not only wrote this noble language. They also read it. The essays in defense of the Constitution signed Publius appeared week after week in the New York press during the winter of 1787–88; and the demand was so great that the first thirty-six Federalist papers were published in book form while the rest were still coming out in the papers. One can only marvel at the sophistication of an audience that consumed and relished pieces so closely reasoned, so thoughtful and analytical. To compare *The Federalist Papers* with their equivalents in the press of our own day—say, with the contributions to the Op Ed page of the *New York Times*—is to annotate the decay of political discourse in America.

[6] No doubt the birth of a nation is a stimulus to lofty utterance. The Founding Fathers had a profound conviction of historical responsibility. "The people of this country, by their conduct and example," Madison wrote in *The Federalist*, "will decide the important question, whether societies of men are really capable or not of establishing good government from reflection and choice, or whether they are forever destined to depend for their political constitutions on accident and force." The substitution of reflection and choice for accident and force proposed a revolution in the history of government; and the authors of *The Federalist* were passionate exemplars of the politics of reason.

[7] The Founding Fathers lived, moreover, in an age when politicians could say in public more or less what they believed in private. If their view of human nature was realistic rather than sentimental, they were not obliged to pretend otherwise. *The Federalist*, for example, is a work notably free of false notes. It must not be supposed, however, that even this great generation was immune to temptation. When the Founding Fathers turned to speak of and to the largest interest in a primarily agricultural nation, they changed their tone and relaxed their standards. Those who lived on the soil, Jefferson could inanely write, were "the chosen people of God . . . whose breasts He has made His peculiar deposit for substantial and genuine virtue." Such lapses from realism defined one of the problems of American political discourse. For, as society grew more diversified, new interests claimed their place in the sun; and each in time had to be courted and flattered as the Jeffersonians had courted and flattered the agriculturists. The desire for success at the polls thus sentimentalized and cheapened the language of politics.

[8] And politics was only an aspect of a deeper problem. Society as a whole was taking forms that warred against clarity of thought and integ-

rity of language. "A man's power to conduct his thought with its proper symbol, and so to utter it," said Emerson, "depends on the simplicity of his character, that is, upon his love of truth, and his desire to communicate it without loss. The corruption of man is followed by the corruption of language. When simplicity of character and the sovereignty of ideas is broken up by the prevalence of secondary desires, the desire of riches, of pleasure, of power, and of praise . . . words are perverted to stand for things which are not."

[9] "The prevalence of secondary desires," the desire of riches, pleasure, power and praise—this growing social complexity began to divert the function of words from expression to gratification. No one observed the impact of a mobile and egalitarian society on language more acutely than Tocqueville. Democracy, he argued, inculcated a positive preference for ambiguity and a dangerous addiction to the inflated style. "An abstract term," Tocqueville wrote, "is like a box with a false bottom; you may put in what you please, and take them out again without being observed." So words, divorced from objects, became instruments less of communication than of deception. Unscrupulous orators stood abstractions on their head and transmuted them into their opposites, aiming to please one faction by the sound and the contending faction by the meaning. They did not always succeed. "The word *liberty* in the mouth of Webster," Emerson wrote with contempt after the Compromise of 1850, "sounds like the word *love* in the mouth of a courtezan." Watching Henry Kissinger babbling about his honor at his famous Salzburg press conference, one was irresistibly reminded of another of Emerson's nonchalant observations: "The louder he talked of his honor, the faster we counted our spoons."

[10] Other developments hastened the spreading dissociation of words from meaning, of language from reality. The rise of mass communications, the growth of large organizations and novel technologies, the invention of advertising and public relations, the professionalization of education—all contributed to linguistic pollution, upsetting the ecological balance between words and their environment. In our own time the purity of language is under unrelenting attack from every side—from professors as well as from politicians, from newspapermen as well as from advertising men, from men of the cloth as well as from men of the sword, and not least from those indulgent compilers of modern dictionaries who propound the suicidal thesis that all usages are equal and all correct.

[11] A living language can never be stabilized, but a serious language can never cut words altogether adrift from meanings. The alchemy that changes words into their opposites has never had more adept practitioners than it has today. We used to object when the Communists described dictatorships as "people's democracies" or North Korean aggression as the act of a "peace-loving" nation. But we are no slouches ourselves in the art of verbal metamorphosis. There was often not much that was "free" about many of the states that made up what we used to call, sometimes with capital letters, the Free World; as there is, alas, very often

little that is gay about many of those who seek these days to kidnap that sparkling word for specialized use. Social fluidity, moral pretension, political and literary demagoguery, corporate and academic bureaucratization and a false conception of democracy are leading us into semantic chaos. We owe to Vietnam and Watergate a belated recognition of the fact that we are in linguistic as well as political crisis and that the two may be organically connected. As Emerson said, "We infer the spirit of the nation in great measure from the language."

[12] For words are not neutral instruments, pulled indifferently out of a jumbled tool kit. "Language," wrote Coleridge, "is the armoury of the human mind; and at once contains the trophies of its past, and the weapons of its future conquests." Language colors and penetrates the depths of our consciousness. It is the medium that dominates perceptions, organizes categories of thought, shapes the development of ideas and incorporates a philosophy of existence. Every political movement generates its own language-field; every language-field legitimizes one set of motives, values and ideals and banishes the rest. The language-field of the Founding Fathers directed the American consciousness toward one constellation of standards and purposes. The language-field of Vietnam and Watergate has tried to direct the national consciousness toward very different goals. Politics in basic aspects is a symbolic and therefore a linguistic phenomenon.

[13] We began to realize this in the days of the Indochina War. In the middle 1960s Americans found themselves systematically staving off reality by allowing a horrid military-bureaucratic patois to protect our sensibilities from the ghastly things we were doing in Indochina. The official patter about "attrition," "pacification," "defoliation," "body counts," "progressive squeeze-and-talk," sterilized the frightful reality of napalm and My Lai. This was the period when television began to provide a sharper access to reality, and Marshall McLuhan had his day in court.

[14] But the military-bureaucratic jargon could be blamed on generals, who, as General Eisenhower reminded us at every press conference, habitually speak in a dialect of their own. What we had not perhaps fully realized before Watergate was the utter debasement of language in the mouths of our recent civilian leaders. How our leaders really talk is not, of course, easy to discover, since their public appearances are often veiled behind speeches written by others. I know that President Kennedy spoke lucidly, wittily and economically in private. President Johnson spoke with force and often in pungent and inventive frontier idiom. President Nixon's fascinating contribution to oral history suggests, however, a recent and marked decline in the quality of presidential table talk. "A man cannot speak," said Emerson, "but he judges himself."

[15] Groping to describe that degenerate mélange of military, public relations and locker-room jargon spoken in the Nixon White House, Richard N. Goodwin aptly wrote of "the bureaucratization of the criminal class." It was as if the Godfather spoke in the phrases of the secretary of

health, education and welfare. When one read of "stroking sessions," of "running out of the bottom line," of "toughing it out," of going down "the hang-out road," or "how do you handle that PR-wise," one felt that there should be one more impeachable offense; and that is verbicide. But what was worse than the massacre of language, which after all displayed a certain low ingenuity, was the manipulation of meaning. The presidential speech preceding the release of the expurgated transcripts was syntactically correct enough. But it proclaimed in tones of ringing sincerity that the transcripts showed exactly the opposite of what in fact the transcripts did show. "He unveils a swamp," as the *New Yorker* well put it, "and instructs us to see a garden of flowers." In the Nixon White House, language not only fled the reality principle but became the servant of nightmare.

[16] "The use of words," wrote Madison in the thirty-seventh *Federalist*, "is to express ideas. Perspicuity, therefore, requires not only that the ideas should be distinctly formed, but that they should be expressed by words distinctly and exclusively appropriate to them." Madison was under no illusion that this condition of semantic beatitude was easy to attain. "No language is so copious," he continued, "as to supply words and phrases for every complex idea, or so correct as not to include many equivocally denoting different ideas. . . . When the Almighty himself condescends to address mankind in their own language, his meaning, luminous as it must be, is rendered dim and doubtful by the cloudy medium through which it is communicated." Nevertheless, Madison and his generation thought the quest for precision worth the effort. It is an entertaining but morbid speculation to wonder what the Founding Fathers, returning to inspect the Republic on the eve of the two-hundredth anniversary of the independence they fought so hard to achieve, would make of the White House tapes.

[17] The degradation of political discourse in America is bound to raise a disturbing question. May it be, as Tocqueville seemed to think, that such deterioration is inherent in democracy? Does the compulsion to win riches, pleasure, power and praise in a fluid and competitive society make the perversion of meaning and the debasement of language inevitable? One can certainly see specific American and democratic traits that have promoted linguistic decay. But a moment's reflection suggests that the process is by no means confined to the United States nor to democracies. Language degenerates a good deal more rapidly and thoroughly in communist and fascist states. For the control of language is a necessary step toward the control of minds, as Orwell made so brilliantly clear in *1984*. Nowhere is meaning more ruthlessly manipulated, nowhere is language more stereotyped, mechanical, implacably banal and systematically false, nowhere is it more purged of personal nuance and human inflection, than in Russia and China. In democracies the assault on language is piecemeal, sporadic and unorganized. And democracy has above all the decisive advantage that the preservation of intellectual freedom creates the opportu-

nity for counterattack. Democracy always has the chance to redeem its language. This may be an essential step toward the redemption of its politics.

[18] One must add that it is idle to expect perfection in political discourse. The problem of politics in a democracy is to win broad consent for measures of national policy. The winning of consent often requires the bringing together of disparate groups with diverging interests. This inescapably involves a certain oracularity of expression. One remembers de Gaulle before the crowd in Algeria, when the *pieds-noirs* chanted that Algeria belonged to France, replying solemnly, "Je vous comprends, mes camarades"—hardly a forthright expression of his determination to set Algeria free. Besides, oracularity may often be justified since no one can be all that sure about the future. The Founding Fathers understood this, which is why the Constitution is in many respects a document of calculated omission and masterful ambiguity whose "real" meaning—that is, what it would mean in practice—only practice could disclose. Moreover, as Lord Keynes, who wrote even economics in English, once put it, "Words ought to be a little wild, for they are an assault of thought upon the unthinking."

[19] Keynes immediately added, however: "But when the seats of power and authority have been attained, there should be no more poetic license." Madison described the American experiment as the replacement of accident and force by reflection and choice in the processes of government. The responsibility of presidents is to define real choices and explain soberly why one course is to be preferred to another—and, in doing so, to make language a means not of deception but of communication, not an enemy but a friend of the reality principle.

[20] Yet presidents cannot easily rise above the society they serve and lead. If we are to restore the relationship between words and meaning, we must begin to clean up the whole linguistic environment. This does not mean a crusade for standard English or a campaign to resurrect the stately rhythms of *The Federalist Papers*. Little could be more quixotic than an attempt to hold a rich and flexible language like American English to the forms and definitions of a specific time, class, or race. But some neologisms are better than others, and here one can demand, particularly in influential places, a modicum of discrimination. More important is that words, whether new or old, regain a relationship to reality. Vietnam and Watergate have given a good many Americans, I believe, a real hatred of double-talk and a hunger for bluntness and candor. Why else the success of the posthumous publication of President Truman's gaudy exercise in plain speaking?

[21] The time is ripe to sweep the language-field of American politics. In this season of semantic malnutrition, who is not grateful for a public voice that appears to blurt out what the speaker honestly believes? A George Wallace begins to win support even among blacks (though ambition is already making Wallace bland, and blandness will do him in too).

Here those who live by the word—I mean by the true word, like writers and teachers; not by the phony word, like public relations men, writers and teachers—have their peculiar obligation. Every citizen is free under the First Amendment to use and abuse the words that bob around in the swamp of his mind. But writers and teachers have, if anyone has, the custodianship of the language. Their charge is to protect the words by which they live. Their duty is to expel the cant of the age.

[22] At the same time, they must not forget that in the recent past they have been among the worst offenders. They must take scrupulous care that indignation does not lead them to the same falsity and hyperbole they righteously condemn in others. A compilation of political pronouncements by eminent writers and learned savants over the last generation would make a dismal volume. One has only to recall the renowned, if addled, scholars who signed the full page advertisement in the *New York Times* of October 15, 1972, which read, as the *New Yorker* would say, in its entirety: "Of the two major candidates for the Presidency of the United States, we believe that Richard Nixon has demonstrated the superior capacity for prudent and responsible leadership. Consequently, we intend to vote for President Nixon on November 7th and we urge our fellow citizens to do the same."

[23] The time has come for writers and teachers to meet the standards they would enforce on others and rally to the defense of the word. They must expose the attack on meaning and discrimination in language as an attack on reason in discourse. It is this rejection of reason itself that underlies the indulgence of imprecision, the apotheosis of usage and the infatuation with rhetoric. For once words lose a stable connection with things, we can no longer know what we think or communicate what we believe.

[24] One does not suggest that the restoration of language is all that easy in an age when new issues, complexities and ambiguities stretch old forms to the breaking point.

> . . . Words strain
> Crack and sometimes break, under the burden,
> Under the tension, slip, slide, perish,
> Decay with imprecision, will not stay in place,
> Will not stay still.

Each venture is therefore the new beginning, the raid on the inarticulate with shabby equipment always deteriorating in the general mess of imprecision of feeling. Yet, as Eliot went on to say, "For us, there is only the trying. The rest is not our business." As we struggle to recover what has been lost ("and found and lost again and again"), as we try our own sense of words against the decay of language, writers and teachers make the best contribution they can to the redemption of politics. Let intellectuals never forget that all they that take the word shall perish with the word. "Wise men pierce this rotten diction," said Emerson, "and fasten words again to visible things; so that picturesque language is at once a commanding certificate that he who employs it, is a man in alliance with truth and God."

Questions on Meaning

1 What is Schlesinger's thesis? As you answer this question, consider how the writer brings together information on the following topics and makes a judgment about the relationship of that information: (a) the political ideas of the Founding Fathers; (b) the political language of the Founding Fathers; (c) the political language in America that developed between the Revolution and the present time (and the reasons for that development); (d) the language of Watergate and Vietnam.

2 Do you think Schlesinger's own political bias (he was one of President Kennedy's principal advisers) affects his analysis of this essay? If so, in what ways?

3 In his conclusion, Schlesinger suggests some solutions to problems that are implied or discussed earlier. What are these solutions?

4 Do you think the question "How would the Founding Fathers respond to the White House tapes if they were to return to life today?" is a fair question? Why? What do you think the answer is?

5 In paragraph 13, Scheslinger mentions several political expressions that could be called *euphemisms*—that is, words or phrases used to disguise unpleasant reality. Can you think of other euphemisms used by politicians, by other groups, by yourself?

Questions on Style and Structure

1 This essay contains numerous quotations. Do they strengthen the argument, or do you find them distracting?

2 Incorporating quotations gracefully within a paper requires considerable skill. Note the manner in which Schlesinger handles quotations. He always identifies the author in the text, usually in a phrase that interrupts the quotation. Study the examples below:

  a "The people of this country, by their conduct and example," Madison wrote in *The Federalist*, "will decide the important question, whether societies of men are really capable or not of establishing good government from reflection and choice, or whether they are forever destined to depend for their political constitutions on accident and force." (paragraph 6)

  b "A man's power to connect his thought with its proper symbol, and so to utter it," said Emerson, "depends on the simplicity of his character, that is, upon his love of truth and his desire to communicate it without loss. . . ." (paragraph 8)

c "An abstract term," Tocqueville wrote, "is like a box with a false bottom; you may put in what you please, and take them out again without being observed." (paragraph 9)

d "Language," wrote Coleridge, "is the armoury of the human mind; and at once contains the trophies of its past, and the weapons of its future conquests." (paragraph 12)

What would be lost if Schlesinger had begun the sentences in the following manner?

e Madison wrote in *The Federalist,* "The people of this country. . ."
f Emerson said, "A man's power. . ."
g Tocqueville wrote "An abstract term. . ."
h Coleridge wrote that "Language is the armoury. . ."

3 Schlesinger's sentences are worthy of close study. Observe how he, like other writers you have studied, structures sentences so that they begin and end with important words. Compare the following versions (the first of each pair is Schlesinger's):

a But they are not, I suppose, unmitigated horrors. (paragraph 2)

But they are not unmitigated horrors, I suppose.

b Democracy, he argued, inculcated a positive preference for ambiguity and a dangerous addiction to the inflated style. (paragraph 9)

He argued that democracy inculcated a positive preference for ambiguity and a dangerous addiction to the inflated style.

Can you find other sentences that are similarly structured for emphasis?

4 Identify examples of figurative language in the essay, and discuss their appropriateness and effectiveness.

5 This essay appeared in *The American Scholar,* a journal published by Phi Beta Kappa, a collegiate honor society. In what ways would the writing probably be different had the essay appeared in *Reader's Digest* or a similar mass-circulation magazine?

6 Concluding an essay with a quotation can be very effective. How effective is Schlesinger's conclusion?

Exploring Words

1 *exorcising.* Check your dictionary to verify your understanding of the literal meaning of *exorcise.* Then explain what Schlesinger means when he speaks of *"exorcising* our illusions."

2 *chastening.* Do the same with this word.

3 *demagoguery.* Which of the meanings your dictionary gives for *demagogue* applies, in a figurative sense, to Schlesinger's phrase "political and literary *demagoguery*"? Explain the relationship between the dictionary meaning and Schlesinger's.

4 *patois.* Write a sentence of your own in which you use the word in the literal, dictionary sense rather than in a figurative sense, as Schlesinger uses it.

5 *verbicide.* You will probably not find this word in a dictionary. How, then, can you be sure you know what it means?

6 *perspicuity.* Which of the meanings given for *perspicuity* applies to Schlesinger's use of the word? The words *perspicuity* and *perspicacity* are often confused. How does your dictionary treat the meanings of these two words?

7 *oracularity.* Your dictionary probably gives several separately numbered meanings for *oracular,* the adjective form of *oracle.* Which of the meanings given for *oracular* do you think comes closest to Schlesinger's meaning? What relationship do you find between these several meanings and the root word *oracle*?

8 *quixotic.* After noting the explanation the Getting Started section gives for the development of this word, and after checking your dictionary for further information on its meaning, try stating in your own words what you think Schlesinger means when he says that any attempt to prevent changes in American English from occurring would be *"quixotic."* Does your dictionary mention any synonymous word or phrase that you think could satisfactorily be substituted for Schlesinger's word here? Why or why not? Can you think of other adjectives that have been derived from the names of men or women?

9 *neologisms.* Which of the meanings of this word applies to Schlesinger's use here? Which of the political *neologisms* he mentions do you find particularly distasteful? Can you think of other *neologisms* you especially like or dislike?

Suggestions for Writing

1 Write two different versions of a hypothetical political speech. The first version should be written as if by one of the Founding Fathers. The second should be written as if by a modern politician of the sort that Schlesinger criticizes. Both speeches should be on the same topic. Then, in a separate essay, compare and contrast the two versions, using the criteria that Schlesinger uses to judge political language.

2 Locate a reprint of a political address (for example, an inaugural address). You will find many examples in *The Congressional Record* and *Vital Speeches.* Then, using Schlesinger's comments as a guideline, analyze the quality of the language you find in it. For example, does the writer use euphemisms, jargon, and so on? Does the language strike you as honest?

3 Schlesinger quotes Emerson, who said, "A man cannot speak but he judges himself." How would a person judge you if he or she had to do so solely on the basis of your speech, your language? Write an essay in which you analyze your own language habits. In what ways do your language habits change to fit different situations?